THE WORLD WAR II BOOK

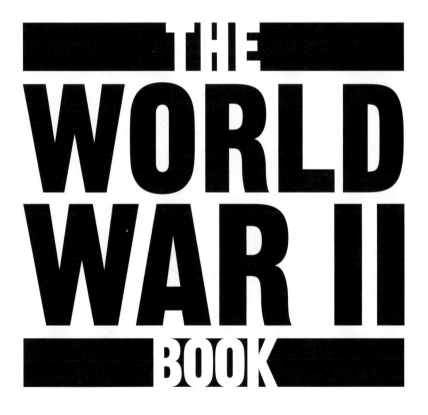

BIG IDEAS

THE ART BOOK
THE ASTRONOMY BOOK
THE BIBLE BOOK
THE BIOLOGY BOOK
THE BLACK HISTORY BOOK
THE BUSINESS BOOK
THE CLASSICAL MUSIC BOOK
THE CRIME BOOK
THE ECOLOGY BOOK
THE ECONOMICS BOOK
THE FEMINISM BOOK
THE HISTORY BOOK
THE ISLAM BOOK
THE LAW BOOK
THE LITERATURE BOOK
THE MATH BOOK
THE MOVIE BOOK
THE MYTHOLOGY BOOK
THE PHILOSOPHY BOOK
THE PHYSICS BOOK
THE POLITICS BOOK
THE PSYCHOLOGY BOOK
THE RELIGIONS BOOK
THE SCIENCE BOOK
THE SHAKESPEARE BOOK
THE SHERLOCK HOLMES BOOK
THE SOCIOLOGY BOOK
THE WORLD WAR II BOOK

SIMPLY EXPLAINED

THE WORLD WAR II BOOK

DK

DK | Penguin Random House

DK LONDON

SENIOR ART EDITOR
Nicola Rodway

SENIOR EDITORS
Stephanie Farrow, Julie Ferris, Victoria Heyworth-Dunne, Laura Sandford

SENIOR US EDITOR
Megan Douglass

EDITORS
John Andrews, Richard Gilbert, Tim Harris, Dorothy Stannard, Rachel Warren Chadd, Ed Wilson

ILLUSTRATOR
James Graham

ADDITIONAL TEXT
Leia D, Kingshuk Ghoshal, Mireille Harper, Bianca Hezekiah, Yuka Maeno, Rupa Rao

JACKET DESIGNER
Stephanie Cheng Hui Tan

JACKET DESIGN DEVELOPMENT MANAGER
Sophia MTT

PRODUCTION EDITOR
Jacqueline Street-Elkayam

SENIOR PRODUCTION CONTROLLER
Rachel Ng

SENIOR MANAGING ART EDITOR
Lee Griffiths

MANAGING EDITOR
Gareth Jones

ASSOCIATE PUBLISHING DIRECTOR
Liz Wheeler

ART DIRECTOR
Karen Self

DESIGN DIRECTOR
Philip Ormerod

PUBLISHING DIRECTOR
Jonathan Metcalf

DK DELHI

SENIOR ART EDITOR
Chhaya Sajwan

PROJECT ART EDITOR
Sourabh Challariya

ART EDITOR
Shipra Jain

ASSISTANT ART EDITOR
Ankita Das

SENIOR EDITOR
Janashree Singha

EDITOR
Aashirwad Jain

MANAGING EDITOR
Soma B. Chowdhury

SENIOR MANAGING ART EDITOR
Arunesh Talapatra

PROJECT PICTURE RESEARCHER
Deepak Negi

PICTURE RESEARCH MANAGER
Taiyaba Khatoon

SENIOR JACKETS EDITORIAL COORDINATOR
Priyanka Sharma-Saddi

SENIOR JACKETS DESIGNER
Suhita Dharamjit

DTP DESIGNERS
Ashok Kumar, Rakesh Kumar, Mrinmoy Mazumdar, Anurag Trivedi

PRE-PRODUCTION MANAGER
Balwant Singh

PRODUCTION MANAGER
Pankaj Sharma

EDITORIAL HEAD
Glenda Fernandes

DESIGN HEAD
Malavika Talukder

original styling by
STUDIO 8

First American Edition, 2022
Published in the United States by DK Publishing
1745 Broadway, 20th Floor, New York, NY 10019

22 23 24 25 26 10 9 8 7 6 5 4 3 2
003–310794–Jun/2022

Published in Great Britain by Dorling Kindersley Limited.

A catalog record for this book is available from the Library of Congress.
ISBN: 978-0-7440-4839-1

DK books are available at special discounts when purchased in bulk for sales promotions, premiums, fund-raising, or educational use. For details, contact: DK Publishing Special Markets, 1745 Broadway, 20th Floor, New York, NY 10019
SpecialSales@dk.com

Printed and bound in Malaysia

For the curious
www.dk.com

FSC
www.fsc.org
MIX
Paper | Supporting responsible forestry
FSC® C018179

This book was made with Forest Stewardship Council™ certified paper – one small step in DK's commitment to a sustainable future. For more information go to www.dk.com/our-green-pledge

CONTRIBUTORS

ADRIAN GILBERT

Adrian Gilbert is a military author and consultant, who has written extensively on World War II. Among his publications are the best-selling *Sniper One-on-One*; *Germany's Lightning War: From Poland to El Alamein; POW: Allied Prisoners in Europe 1939–1945;* and *The Imperial War Museum Book of the Desert War*, the latter volume a cowinner of the Duke of Westminster's Medal for Military Literature.

SIMON ADAMS

Simon Adams has written or contributed to numerous DK titles for both adults and children, notably in the best-selling *Eyewitness* series. He specializes in modern history, warfare, and politics, and recently wrote sections of *World War II Map by Map* (DK, 2019).

JOHN FARNDON

John Farndon is the author of many books on political history and the history of ideas, including *Modern History: 365; China Rises; India Booms;* and *Iran*. He has also been short-listed five times for the Royal Society's Young People's Book Prize. As a translator, he was joint winner of the 2019 European Bank literary prize, and finalist for the 2020 US PEN translation prize.

JACOB F. FIELD

Jacob F. Field is a writer and historian based in London. He has written books on a range of subjects related to military history, including on the D-Day landings and the life of Winston Churchill. His PhD is on the impact of the Great Fire of London, and he has worked as a research associate in economic history at the University of Cambridge.

R. G. GRANT

R. G. Grant has written extensively on military history. He has published some 40 books, including *Battle* (2005), *Soldier* (2007), and *World War I: The Definitive Visual Guide* (2013). He acted as consultant editor on DK's *The History Book* (2016).

JOEL LEVY

Joel Levy is a writer specializing in history and the history of science, and is the author of many books including *History's Worst Battles*; *50 Weapons that Changed the World*; *Meltdown: Stories of Nuclear Disaster and the Human Cost of Going Critical*; and *Gothic Science: The Era of Ingenuity & the Making of Frankenstein*.

OLIVIA SMITH

Olivia Smith is a public historian, who works in television across documentary and reality series. Olivia holds an MA in history and has worked on World War II documentaries for Sky History, Channel 5, Yesterday, and the Smithsonian Channel.

CHRISTOPHER WESTHORP

Christopher Westhorp is an editor, project manager, and writer. His recent projects include *A History of the Second World War in 100 Maps* and *Sailor Song: The Shanties and Ballads of the High Seas* (both British Library, 2020).

CONTENTS

THE WIDENING WAR
1941–1942

TURNING THE TIDE
1943–1944

ENDGAME
1945

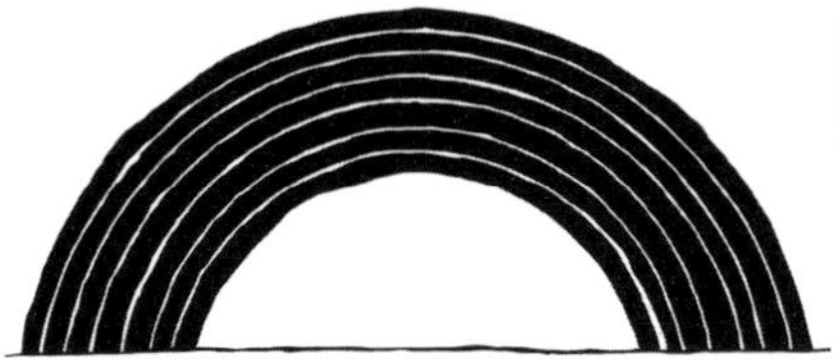

INTRODU

TION

World War II was the largest and most terrible conflict in history, an ideological contest that saw the two opposing sides—Axis and Allied—locked in a battle that could only end in the destruction of the other. The bitterness of the fighting was reflected in the casualty lists: more than 50 million people killed and millions more wounded in body and mind. The war culminated in the dropping on Japan of the atom bomb—a horrifying new weapon that could wipe out humankind itself.

Shared ambitions

The origins of the war lay in two, seemingly separate conflicts on opposite sides of the world. In the Far East, it began with Japan's invasion of the Chinese province of Manchuria in 1931, which led to a full-scale offensive against China six years later. In Europe, the war that began with Germany's invasion of Poland in 1939 was in many respects a resumption of World War I's contest for European domination. What linked the two was the shared ambition of Germany and Japan to amass territory on a vast scale and create a "new order" to rival and supplant the old empires of the European powers.

Italy, the third member of the Axis coalition, also set about creating an empire, first in east Africa and then in the Mediterranean. For all three Axis states, war was not considered an aberration from the diplomatic norm but rather an essential tool of foreign policy.

The pressure created by these separate military ventures would eventually explode into world war. Germany's invasion of Russia in June 1941 brought the USSR into the conflict, which encouraged Japan's attack in the Pacific and then Hitler's declaration of war against the US. By the end of 1941, the conflict had become global. The Axis nations were the aggressors throughout. They gambled on the idea that their "superior martial spirit" would somehow be sufficient to overcome the "decadent," if materially more powerful, Allied nations.

> Every healthy, vigorous people sees nothing sinful in territorial acquisition, but something quite in keeping with nature.
> **Adolf Hitler, 1928**

Relative strengths

While Italy's imperial pretensions were dashed from the outset, Germany and Japan scored a series of stunning military victories in the war's opening stages that seemed to indicate that they would achieve their aims. But they underestimated their opponents, who, after initial setbacks, reorganized their forces with enough skill and attack to make an Allied victory inevitable.

The armed forces of Germany and Japan were well-equipped and well-led on the battlefield. In addition, their determination was a remarkable factor that significantly prolonged the conflict.

At the highest level, Allied leadership was superior to that displayed by the Axis powers. Winston Churchill, Franklin D. Roosevelt, and Josef Stalin shared a global outlook, and were prepared to work together to achieve previously agreed objectives. By contrast, the Japanese military

government was undermined by chronic factionalism and had little vision beyond simple territorial aggrandizement. Hitler could not see beyond his obsession with gaining *Lebensraum* ("living space") in eastern Europe. Mussolini was merely a vain fantasist. None of the Axis governments made any serious attempt to cooperate with their ostensible partners.

The Allied nations had access to greater material resources, and used them more effectively than the Axis. The US and the USSR were masters of mass production, and Britain also made a useful contribution to the economic and military muscle that was needed. While the Allies produced well over 4 million tanks and other fighting vehicles, the Axis produced just 670,000. Good oil supplies were also vital, and by the end of 1944, the Axis could barely operate what mechanized weapons they still possessed because of fuel shortages.

The Allies also proved more capable than the Axis in the field of military intelligence—including breaking both the main German and Japanese secret codes—and in utilizing civilians to develop new technology. Germany, once a scientific powerhouse, found itself surpassed by the western Allies. It led in the fields of jet aircraft and rocket propulsion, but the advances made came too late to change the war's outcome.

Changing societies

World War II was more than just a military contest. Apart from the suffering experienced by many tens of millions of people, it offered new experiences and opportunities, which opened up political and social expectations. Women, for example, were conscripted into the world of work on a mass scale. Although many left the workforce again in the post-war period, the scale of their contribution to the war effort could not be ignored. In the US, millions of Black workers in the rural South were lured to the great industrial centers in California and the North, a profound demographic change that transformed America's racial landscape.

> Hitler is striking with all the force at his command. His is a desperate gamble, and the stakes are nothing less than the domination of the whole human race.
>
> **Winston Churchill, 1940**

In Asia and some parts of Africa, people saw their European colonizers humiliated by the Japanese and the Germans, opening up the possibility that they might rule themselves, a first step to the "end of empire." The war underlined the decline of Europe as a major world player and accelerated the emergence of the US and the USSR as the world's two great superpowers.

This book

The aim of *The World War II Book* is to consider how the war started, to look at how the Allies defeated the Axis, and to examine the results and consequences of this great conflagration. There can be no doubt that the conflict had lasting consequences, many of which continue into our own time. We also hope to give the reader an idea of what it was like to live through this most extraordinary six years in the history of humankind. ■

THE SEE
OF WAR
1914–1939

DS

1919
The Treaty of Versailles is concluded in June, marking the **end of World War I**. Germany **loses territory** and its armed forces are drastically reduced.

1922
In Italy, **Mussolini's fascist party** stages its "March on Rome" as part of **a coup** that **overthrows** the legitimate **Italian government**.

1923
Political unrest in Germany encourages **Hitler to mount a putsch** to **seize power** in Bavaria. It fails and Hitler is briefly imprisoned.

1924
The **Dawes Plan** reorganizes German **reparation payments** and helps stabilize the **German financial system**.

1925
Field Marshal **Paul von Hindenburg** becomes **president of Germany**. He is considered to be a steadying political influence.

1928
The US, Britain, France, Italy, Germany, and Japan sign the **Kellogg-Briand Pact renouncing aggressive war**.

1929
The New York Stock Exchange **collapses**, triggering a worldwide **economic depression**.

1931
Japanese troops **occupy** much of **Manchuria** in northeast China.

World War II had its origins in the terms of the Treaty of Versailles, signed in June 1919 to mark the end of World War I. The treaty represented an attempt by the victors—Britain, France, Italy, and the US—to prevent a repetition of the recent conflict, but it created more problems than it solved. Combined with the economic crises that wracked post-war Europe, it sowed the seeds for a new world war—one even more deadly than its predecessor.

New borders

The Treaty of Versailles reshaped the structure of central Europe. The Austro-Hungarian Empire was dismantled, with Austria becoming a small, weak state and Hungary ceding territory to Romania. New nations—Czechoslovakia and Yugoslavia—were created. Germany lost land to Czechoslovakia and the reborn state of Poland.

Although the concept of national self-determination had been one of the guiding principles of Versailles, it failed to resolve the competing national ambitions of central Europe. Latent antagonisms between the nations remained a potential cause of conflict, but more problematic was the creation of substantial German-speaking minorities in Czechoslovakia and Poland—a situation that German nationalists later exploited.

The terms of the Versailles treaty also weakened Germany politically, economically, and militarily. France regained Alsace-Lorraine and occupied the Saar industrial region; substantial reparations for war damage were exacted by the victors; Germany's overseas empire was dismembered and its armed forces cut to 100,000 men. The treaty humiliated the German people, causing resentment and a desire for retribution.

To avoid future wars, the League of Nations was created to resolve disputes through discussion or collective action. However, the League had no military backing, and the most powerful countries, the US and the USSR, did not become members, which limited its power. The League failed to stop a militarist Japan invading Manchuria in 1931 and Italy's conquest of Ethiopia four years later.

The rise of Hitler

Post-war economic problems led to the growth of right-wing political parties in many nations. These

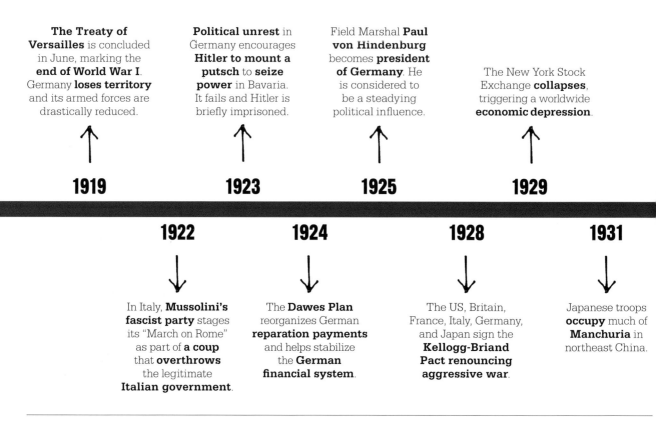

1932
The **Nazis become the largest party** in the German parliament but do not have an overall majority.

1933
Adolf Hitler outmaneuvers his **conservative rivals** and becomes **Chancellor of Germany**.

1934
Hitler kills many of his enemies and rivals in the "**Night of the Long Knives**" (June 30–July 2).

1935
Hitler **reintroduces conscription** and announces the start of **mass rearmament**. The **Nuremberg decrees** increase the **persecution of Jews**.

1936
Italy formally **annexes Abyssinia** (Ethiopia) following the **occupation of Addis Ababa**.

1937
Japan launches full-scale **war against China**, capturing Shanghai and advancing on Nanking.

1938
Britain brokers an agreement between **Germany** and **Czechoslovakia** that forces the Czechs to **cede border territories** to the Nazis.

1938
Nazis across Germany and Austria **attack Jewish people and property** on the night of November 9–10, an episode known as Kristallnacht.

achieved national power in Japan, Italy, and Germany. The success of Adolf Hitler's Nazi Party in German elections in 1933 was the single most important factor in pushing Europe toward war. Once Hitler had been appointed chancellor, he immediately set about destroying the democratic institutions through which he had achieved power. He then introduced new laws to suppress trade unions, opposition parties, Jewish people, and other "non-Aryans." Germany was soon a totalitarian dictatorship.

Hitler also sought to recover the territories Germany had lost after World War I and reassert its role in world politics. Although an attempt to seize power in Austria in 1934 was thwarted, Hitler's long-term intentions were clear. In contravention of the terms of the Versailles treaty, he began to rearm, concentrating on aggressive instruments of war, such as tanks, bomber aircraft, and submarines.

Unchecked aggression

Hitler was now ready to expand Germany's borders and reclaim its former territory. In March 1936, German troops reoccupied the Rhineland without facing any opposition from Britain or France. Emboldened, Hitler then supported General Franco's nationalists in the Spanish Civil War (1936–1939), using the conflict as a testing ground for the newly developed weapons and military tactics of Germany's armed forces. As the Luftwaffe demonstrated its capabilities by bombing Spanish towns, other European countries began to fear for the safety of their own populations. Unready for war, they adopted a policy of appeasement toward Germany.

Britain and France did nothing to prevent a Nazi takeover of Austria in March 1938. They even sanctioned the dismemberment of Czechoslovakia at the Munich conference six months later, when Hitler called for the incorporation of the German-speaking Sudetenland into Germany.

It was only when Germany invaded the rest of Czechoslovakia in March 1939 that the Allies prepared for the inevitability of war. When Hitler then demanded the return of the Polish corridor (a thin strip of land that gave Poland access to the Baltic Sea), appeasement gave way to firmer action. ■

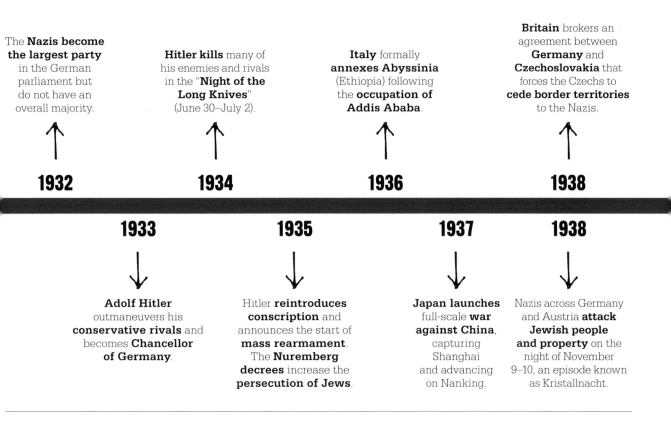

THIS IS A WAR TO END ALL WARS

THE GREAT WAR (1914–1918)

IN CONTEXT

FOCUS
A tense peace

BEFORE
1881 Germany forms the Triple Alliance with Austria–Hungary and Italy.

1897 Germany begins to build a high seas fleet, triggering a naval arms race with Britain.

1907 Britain, France, and Russia form the Triple Entente.

1912–1913 After two Balkan Wars, Serbia emerges as a strong, ambitious state.

AFTER
December 1, 1918 Yugoslavia is proclaimed an independent sovereign nation.

February 14, 1919 At the Paris Peace Conference, the Allied nations propose a League of Nations to promote international cooperation.

1923 Germany's struggling economy experiences debilitating hyperinflation.

Just weeks after World War I broke out, the writer H. G. Wells wrote an article entitled "The war to end all wars." This proved to be the most iconic and the most ironic saying of the conflict. By 1918, the saying had spread across Europe, becoming synonymous with hope for a better future. But were the grounds for hope justified? Between 1914 and 1918, more than 30 nations declared war. The majority joined on the side of the Allies, including Serbia, Russia, France, Britain, Italy, and the United States. They were opposed by Germany, Austria–Hungary, Bulgaria, and the Ottoman Empire. What began as a relatively small conflict in southeast Europe

Many politicians are **determined to ensure that the devastation** caused by **World War I never happens again**.

↓

The **Allied leaders** attempt to achieve this through the **negotiation of peace treaties** and **arms limitation agreements**.

↓

Nationalistic leaders in the defeated nations **vow to avenge** these treaties and **exploit political and economic instability**.

↓

World War I is not the war to end all wars.

See also: A flawed peace 20–21 ▪ Rise of the Nazis 24–29 ▪ Dictators and fragile democracies in Europe 34–39 ▪ German expansion 46–47 ▪ Failure of the League of Nations 50 ▪ Appeasing Hitler 51

French troops in a trench during the Second Battle of the Aisne, an immensely costly Franco-British attempt to drive the German army out of France in 1917.

became a war between European empires. Fighting occurred not only on the Western Front, but also in eastern and southeast Europe, Africa, and the Middle East. The war impacted life on the home front in fields and factories.

A profound impact

This was a "total war" and it was hugely destructive, leaving 17 million dead and 20 million wounded. There were other ramifications, however. It was indirectly responsible for new developments in medicine, such as artificial limbs, blood transfusions, antiseptics, and plastic surgery. Politics and social attitudes changed with the extension of voting rights, trade unions became mass organizations, and millions of women entered the workforce. There were also new developments in warfare technology, with planes, submarines, and tanks all playing key roles for the first time. These changes ensured there would be no return to the pre-war status quo.

It was the war that collapsed four empires: the German, Ottoman, and Austro-Hungarian empires fell, and in 1917 the Bolsheviks overthrew Czar Nicholas II, head of Russia's centuries-old Romanov dynasty. Germany thought Vladimir Lenin's return to Russia to foment civil unrest would take Russia out of the war and work in its favor. While the Bolshevik Revolution did take Russia out of the war, it also created a state whose radical political ideas would challenge governments throughout the world.

Shifting territories

Empire was at the heart of the war. Tens of millions of non-Europeans fought for their European colonizers and sacrificed their lives. The result for the Allies was that their empires were secured or enhanced. Japan, once a small empire, obtained German colonial possessions in Asia and sea lanes in the Pacific, which ignited its own imperial ambitions in Asia. The demise of old empires left a vacuum for new states like Poland, Yugoslavia, and Czechoslovakia to form, but the borders of those new states were soon contested.

The Treaty of Versailles saw Germany reduced in size, stripped of its colonies, and forced to pay substantial reparations. The kaiser went into exile, and Germany plunged into economic and political chaos—paving the way for Adolf Hitler. The mood in Germany was foreshadowed by the newspaper *Deutsche Zeitung*, which vowed: "We will never stop until we win back what we deserve."

At the end of the war in 1918, territorial disputes, competitive colonial ambitions, and national tensions remained and were now exacerbated by political, social, and economic instability. The hope that came with the idea of a "war to end all wars" was premature. ■

> This is not a peace. It is an armistice for 20 years.
>
> **Ferdinand Foch**
> **French general**

Adolf Hitler (right) serves in the 16th Bavarian Reserve Regiment during World War I. As a dispatch runner, he was injured twice, and awarded the Iron Cross First Class in 1918.

A PEACE BUILT ON QUICKSAND

A FLAWED PEACE (1919)

IN CONTEXT

FOCUS
Peace treaties

BEFORE
1648 The Peace of Westphalia ends Europe's Thirty Years' War and establishes the inviolability of sovereign states.

1814–1815 Agreements made at the Congress of Vienna end the Napoleonic wars and redraw the boundaries of Europe to maintain peace through the balance of power.

AFTER
1945 The Potsdam Agreement implements the military occupation of Germany and the division of European territory.

1945 Fifty countries sign the founding charter of the United Nations, a new forum for international peacekeeping.

1947 The Paris Peace Treaties include war reparations, minority rights, and major territorial changes.

Delegates discuss peace terms at the Palace of Versailles. Around 30 countries were represented at the talks, but the leaders of the US, Britain, France, and Italy dominated.

When the fighting of World War I finally ceased in November 1918, the terms of peace had to be worked out before the armies could be sent home. On January 18, 1919, leaders of the victorious countries convened for the Paris Peace Conference at the Palace of Versailles. More than five months later, they had thrashed out the Treaty of Versailles, subsequently described by most historians as "a flawed peace" because it contained the seeds of conflict that would lead to World War II.

Delegates from many countries attended the conference, but the details were determined by the leaders of the main Allied powers,

See also: The Great War 18–19 ▪ Failure of the League of Nations 50 ▪ Appeasing Hitler 51 ▪ Allied summits 225 ▪ Victory in Europe 298–303 ▪ Aftermath 320–327

> We shall have to fight another war again in 25 years' time.
> **David Lloyd George**

known as the Big Four—US president Woodrow Wilson, British prime minister David Lloyd George, French prime minister Georges Clemenceau, and Italian prime minister Vittorio Orlando. Russia, preoccupied by civil war, did not attend, and the defeated nations were excluded.

A victors' peace

The Big Four's dominance was both the strength of the treaty and its weakness. It gave these powerful nations a strong interest in keeping to its terms, but it also left excluded countries burning with resentment.

Wilson came to the conference armed with a 14-point plan to achieve lasting peace, including an end to secret treaties, a guarantee of free trade, fairness to colonial peoples, and proposals on settling borders and creating new nations according to the principle of self-determination—allowing people with a common ethnic identity to form their own state. The final, and for Wilson crucial, point was to establish a League of Nations, an international body that would protect large and small nations alike from outside aggression. The British and especially the French, whose country had been partially overrun by German forces during the war, wanted to make Germany pay for the catastrophe of war and strip it of its ability to make war in the future.

In exchange for British and French agreement to the League of Nations, Wilson accepted a "war guilt" clause blaming Germany for the war. Germany was punished with large financial reparations, and France took control of a key industrial region in Saarland. The German army was reduced and Rhineland was demilitarized.

Effects of the treaty

Germany's new leaders, elected after the abdication of the Kaiser, had no option but to accept the treaty, but many Germans blamed them for the economic disaster that subsequently overtook the country. The resulting hardships helped pave the way for the rise of Adolf Hitler.

Ticking time bomb though it was, the Treaty of Versailles had some positive aspects, allowing people to resume their lives in peace. Some new European states, including Czechoslovakia, were created in an attempt to reflect national self-determination, but the Middle East and Africa were later carved up between the great powers with no regard for what their people wanted, leaving a legacy of conflict still raging today.

The League of Nations created a framework for dealing with international tensions, but it lacked any military backing. An effective body for conflict resolution did not emerge until the United Nations was set up after World War II. ▪

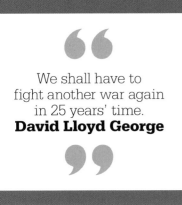

The **victors of World War I** meet to agree the terms of a peace treaty with Germany, but they **have different demands**.
The US president wants a **fair peace** and to establish a **League of Nations** to maintain **world peace**.
Britain and France want to impose **punishing terms** on Germany.
A **compromise is reached**. The US agrees to punishing terms in exchange for the establishment of the League of Nations.
Germany resents the terms of the treaty, and the new League of Nations is flawed.

DEMOCRACY IS BEAUTIFUL IN THEORY

ITALY AND THE RISE OF FASCISM (1922–1939)

IN CONTEXT

FOCUS
Totalitarianism

BEFORE
1914 Mussolini abandons the Italian Socialist Party for radical nationalism, adopting a militarist and racist ideology.

1915 The terms of the Treaty of London offer Italy future territorial gains in return for entry into World War I.

1919 Italian nationalists seize the Italian-speaking port of Fiume in Croatia.

AFTER
1943 After the Allies invade Italy, Mussolini is deposed and arrested, then rescued by German commandos.

1945 Mussolini is caught trying to escape to Switzerland and shot by partisans.

1948 In the first free elections since 1921, the neo-fascist Movimento Sociale Italiano wins just 2 percent of the vote.

Italy's move to fascism after World War I was brutal and surprisingly swift. In 1925, before Hitler had even finished *Mein Kampf*, Benito Mussolini declared himself the nation's dictator, demanding that he be called *Il Duce* ("the Leader"). In many ways, he was Hitler's inspiration.

Although Italy had been one of the victors in World War I, it had been costly in both lives and money, and the hoped-for territorial gains had not materialized. Wartime prime minister Vittorio Orlando was blamed. When the economy took a downturn, people began to look for alternatives to liberal democracy.

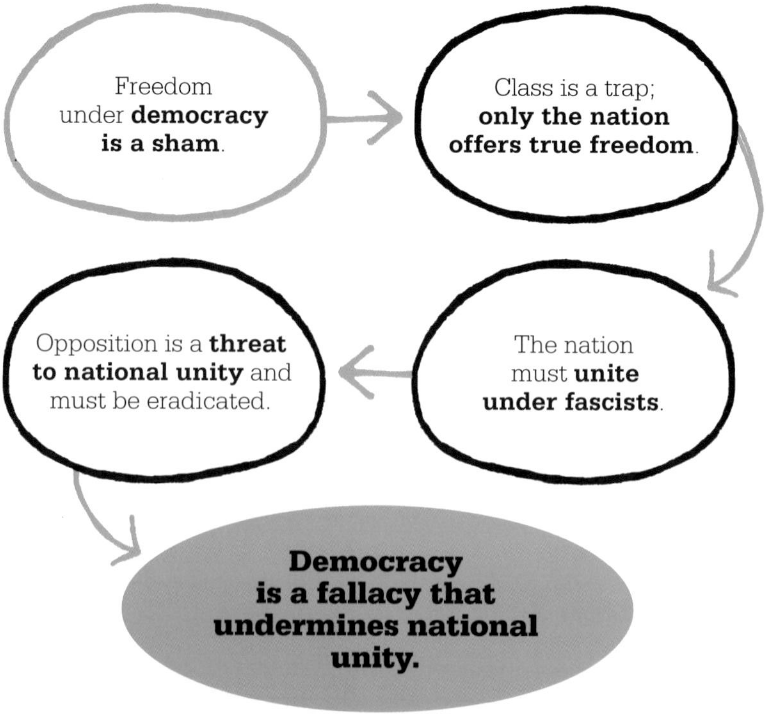

Freedom under **democracy is a sham**.
Class is a trap; **only the nation offers true freedom**.
The nation must **unite under fascists**.
Opposition is a **threat to national unity** and must be eradicated.
Democracy is a fallacy that undermines national unity.

See also: A flawed peace 20–21 ▪ Rise of the Nazis 24–29 ▪ Dictators and fragile democracies in Europe 34–39 ▪ The Spanish Civil War 40–41 ▪ Italy enters the war 88–89

The fascist Blackshirts' March on Rome was the inspiration for Hitler's failed November 1923 uprising, the Munich Beer Hall Putsch.

Millions of workers and peasants turned to socialism, calling for the collectivization of factories and farms. But scared landowners and the middle class looked instead to the *Fasci di combattimento*, led by ex-army officer Mussolini, who insisted that the army had been betrayed. The fascists, as they soon became known, took their name from the ancient Roman *fasces*, bundles of birch rods used as an emblem of unity and strength.

Dismantling democracy

Mussolini believed democracy was a failed system. He proclaimed liberty to be a sham and that state power was the only way to make people truly free, elevating the nation above class consciousness. According to him, anything that opposed national unity was a danger to be eradicated, violently if necessary. "Let us have a dagger between our teeth, a bomb in our hands, and an infinite scorn in our hearts," Mussolini declaimed.

> All within the state, nothing outside the state, nothing against the state.
> **Benito Mussolini**

Soon, fascist bands known as *Camicie Nere* (Blackshirts) were launching brutal attacks on their opponents, especially socialists. In October 1922, an army of 50,000 Blackshirts marched into Rome and took over the government. Mussolini was appointed prime minister.

Supreme leader

The socialists tried to resist but were ruthlessly suppressed, and the murder of their leader Giacomo Matteotti in 1924 silenced serious opposition. Mussolini declared a one-party state and took the reins as Italy's supreme leader, a position he held until his downfall in 1943.

He consciously built a leadership cult, giving powerful, emotional speeches, at which crowds were urged to shout "Believe, obey, fight!" and "Il Duce is always right." Everything was geared to the idea that the nation was supreme, and that Mussolini would lead it to military victory. In an attempt to achieve this, he restructured the economy, organizing agriculture, industry, and employers into state-controlled "corporations." Anyone who opposed him was in grave danger, although it wasn't until the 1930s that the Italian fascists adopted Hitler's policy of explicit aggression toward Jews.

To divert attention from continued problems at home, Mussolini began a drive to acquire colonies and foreign territories, invading Abyssinia (Ethiopia) in 1935. The following year, he backed Franco's fascists in Spain and, fatefully, he signed the Rome–Berlin Axis pact with Hitler, promising to divide Europe into spheres of influence that Germany and Italy would control equally. In May 1939, Hitler and Mussolini made the Pact of Steel, a military and political alliance that was a crucial part of their preparation for war. ■

CRUELTY COMMANDS RESPECT

RISE OF THE NAZIS (1923–1933)

IN CONTEXT

FOCUS
German politics

BEFORE
1919 The Spartacist uprising, a general strike in Berlin led by communists, is put down by members of the paramilitary Freikorps.

1920 German nationalist and monarchist factions stage a coup in Berlin. Wolfgang Kapp, one of its leaders, who had declared himself chancellor, flees after the coup's collapse.

1922 Under the Rapallo Treaty, Germany and the USSR waive reparation claims, expand Soviet-German trade, and later conclude secret agreements for German forces to train with the Red Army.

AFTER
1933 The Reichstag fire provides the pretext for Hitler to take total control over German democracy.

1934 Hitler eliminates rivals and Nazi Party opponents in the Night of the Long Knives.

1935 Nazi territorial ambitions become apparent as Hitler reclaims the western territory of Saarland, governed by France since 1920.

1936 At the outbreak of the Spanish Civil War, Hitler sends air and armored units to support General Franco.

1940 Under the Tripartite Pact signed in Berlin, Italy, Germany, and Japan become allies, soon joined by Hungary.

Hitler believed the Treaty of Versailles **betrayed the German people**, forcing them to accept total blame for World War I and the loss of their German homeland.

↓

He considered the root of Germany's problems to be the **Jews and Marxists, and the disloyal Democrats** who had signed the treaty.

↓

The Nazis would, he said, **bring a great leader to power** to reverse the treaty, expel Jews and Marxists, and end the tyranny of the masses.

↓

The Nazis would **rearm and regenerate Germany**, expanding it to give the Aryan race the room they needed to live, bringing a new, golden future.

In 1923, Germany's Weimar Republic was plunged into an economic and political crisis that over the next ten years would lead to its domination by Hitler and the Nazis. Relations with the victorious Allies had broken down over the issue of World War I reparations, while violent clashes between extremists on the left and right were causing domestic unrest.

Feeding resentment

The Allies had fixed reparations at 132 billion gold marks, specifying the gold-standard-based currency Germany had abandoned in 1914 to prevent repayment in the fluctuating post-war *Papiermark* (paper mark). The Allies ignored pleas for leniency from the German president, Social Democrat Friedrich Ebert, and more and more paper marks were printed to buy foreign currency to meet the payments, triggering hyperinflation as the paper mark depreciated. By 1922, the country could no longer pay its dues.

In January 1923, French and Belgian troops occupied Germany's Ruhr Valley industrial heartland in a bid to seize goods in lieu of reparations. The Weimar government responded by encouraging workers to engage in passive resistance. In subsequent strikes and protests 130 German civilians were killed, engendering further bitterness.

As hyperinflation soared higher, businesses failed and poorer people starved. Within 11 months, the price of a loaf of bread rose from

See also: The Great War 18–19 ▪ A flawed peace 20–21 ▪ Italy and the rise of fascism 22–23 ▪ Establishing the Nazi state 30–33 ▪ Dictators and fragile democracies in Europe 34–39 ▪ German expansion 46–47

Hitler's beginnings

Born in April 1889 in Braunau, Austria, Adolf Hitler was not a gifted student and, as a young man, failed in his bid to establish himself as an artist in Vienna. Although initially declared unfit for military service, a successful petition to Bavaria's king, Louis III, secured him a place in the Bavarian army in World War I. Finding the discipline and sense of mission his life required, he distinguished himself and twice won the Iron Cross for bravery.

In 1919, Hitler joined the German Workers' Party (later to become the Nazi Party) and was put in charge of propaganda. His gift for powerful oration and ability to exploit emotive issues propelled his party's rise, gaining it support across the classes, from communist-hating industrialists to the many who sought scapegoats for the nation's ills. Hitler's charisma also attracted devotees, such as Goebbels and Rudolf Hess.

Hitler's unwavering belief in himself as the savior of the German race and the ruthless pursuit of his aims ended in the horrors of World War II and his suicide in Berlin in 1945.

250 marks to 200,000 million marks. By November 1923, a US dollar was worth 4.2 trillion marks.

Rise of National Socialists

Support for the Weimar Republic plummeted to the benefit of far left and far right parties. Among the right-wing groups was the fledgling National Socialist German Workers' Party (Nazi Party), founded in 1919 as the German Workers' Party in Munich, Bavaria's largest city and a hotbed of extremism. In the fall of 1919, Adolf Hitler, a political agent for the Reichswehr (the army of the Weimar Republic), tasked with encouraging anticommunism and nationalism, was sent to infiltrate the party. Agreeing with its principles, he instead joined it and in 1920 announced its 25-point base plan. It included canceling the Treaty of Versailles and supporting German self-determination, and also stated ominously that only Germans could be citizens, specifically excluding those of Jewish extraction.

Anti-Semitism, street violence, and intimidation were early and enduring features of the Nazi Party. In 1920, Hitler founded the *Sturmabteilung* (SA), soon dubbed Brownshirts for their uniforms. Recruited from renegade ex-soldiers and unemployed young men, they would guard Nazi meetings and rallies and periodically beat up left-wing and other political opponents.

The Beer Hall Putsch

By 1923, Hitler—then leader of the Nazi Party—was delivering barnstorming speeches across »

Nazi Party members were a militant presence, already bearing swastika armbands and swastika flags when they gathered in Nuremberg in 1923 for a German Day rally addressed by Hitler.

Rival political factions frequently brawled in the 1920s. Here, members of the Red Front Fighters Alliance—often targeted by the Brownshirts—clash with Berlin police in 1927.

Bavaria, blaming the Berlin government and its alleged allies—Jewish bankers and communist subversives—for the nation's woes. Amid the misery of bankrupt Germany, they attracted audiences in their thousands.

Misjudging the strength of his support, however, on November 8, Hitler attempted a coup. With hundreds of his Brownshirts, he stormed a large Munich beer hall where Bavarian state commissioner Gustav von Kahr was due to address a large crowd. Hitler's aim was to persuade von Kahr to support a march on Berlin to overthrow the Weimar Republic. Hitler initially won over the gathering, but the city's military police foiled the Brownshirts' attempts to take over government buildings, and the next day state police officers blocked a Nazi march, killing 16 party members. Hitler fled but was later arrested.

Shaping the Nazi Party

Charged with high treason, Hitler responded with rousing speeches in his own defense, which were widely publicized and won him further support. Despite an initial five-year prison sentence, he was released after 10 months, during which he composed *Mein Kampf*, which became the Nazi "bible."

On his release, Hitler ensured that the 16 Nazi members killed in the putsch were honored as martyrs. A flag stained with their blood became the *Blütfahne* ("blood flag")—a sacred relic displayed at all major Nazi events.

The putsch attracted national attention, but its failure had also persuaded Hitler that overt violent rebellion was not the way forward. Instead, he resolved to pursue his quest for power via Germany's democratic political system.

Building support

Banned from public speaking until 1927, Hitler devoted his energies to strengthening and expanding the Nazis into a national political party, with him firmly at the helm. To attract support among young people, he created the National Socialist German Students League and the German Women's Order (fused into the National Socialist Women's League in 1931). He appointed *Gauleiter* ("regional leaders") across the republic, with lower-level officials below them, in a bid to gain broader political representation. In Berlin, his *Gauleiter* was the gifted Josef Goebbels, a skillful publicist, who used every possible opportunity to get the party noticed. The Nazi salute—right arm raised—became compulsory for all party members.

Hitler also reformed his security forces, tightening discipline among the Brownshirts and creating the

> There are only two possibilities: either the victory of the Aryan, or the annihilation of the Aryan and the victory of the Jew.
> **Adolf Hitler, 1921**

DAS VOLK
WÄHLT LISTE
1
NATIONALSOZIALISTEN

A Nazi Party election poster in 1932 depicted the masses (*Das Volk*) swarming toward the Nazi swastika, with the number one denoting the position the party sought in Germany.

Schutzstaffel (SS) as a small, personal bodyguard, which by 1930 was 3,000 strong and led by violent anti-Semite Heinrich Himmler.

The turning point

Between 1925 and 1929, Nazi membership expanded from 25,000 to around 180,000, but would soon rise into the millions. In 1927, Hitler returned to public speaking and went on the campaign trail. The following year, the Nazi Party gained its first 12 seats in the Reichstag (parliament), although the moderate Social Democrats won 153 seats, increasing their lead by 22.

The momentous events of 1929 changed the political landscape. In October, share prices on the Wall Street stock exchange crashed with disastrous effects for Germany. Without American loans, industries collapsed. Unemployment reached two million within a year and would soar to six million by 1934.

Against the will of the Reichstag, in July 1930, German president Paul von Hindenburg used an emergency decree to push through cuts in government expenditure, including wages and unemployment pay, recommended by Heinrich Brüning, his new chancellor. Infuriated, Reichstag members rejected the decree, triggering new elections.

With diminishing faith in the Weimar government, the German public again turned to extremist parties. Hitler seized the chance to portray himself as the potential savior of the German race, while also spinning virulent anti-Jewish and anticommunist propaganda.

In the September 1930 elections, the democratic parties suffered huge losses, and the Nazi Party gained 107 seats, only 36 fewer than the Social Democrats and 30 seats ahead of the German Communist Party, now in third place. Powerful industrialists began to back Hitler, fearing that further communist gains could cost them their wealth.

Believing erroneously that he could manipulate Hitler, Alfred Hugenberg, a media mogul and leader of the National People's Party, joined forces with the Nazi Party, forming the Harzburg Front in 1931 in a bid to topple Chancellor Brüning's government. Hitler and Goebbels exploited their access to wider publicity in Hugenberg's newspapers, but the two political parties never formed a unified front.

Hitler on the threshold

In February 1932, Austrian-born Hitler took German citizenship to compete in the March presidential elections and came second to Hindenburg, winning 37 percent of the vote. With the government in chaos, Hindenburg sacked Brüning, and the new chancellor, Franz von Papen, lifted a temporary ban on the paramilitary Brownshirts in a bid to gain Nazi support.

In July elections, the Nazi Party, capitalizing on Brownshirt intimidation of voters, a crumbling political establishment, and widespread unrest, became the largest party in the Reichstag, winning 230 of 608 seats. Hitler turned down the post of vice-chancellor, becoming chancellor in January 1933. The scene was set for his assumption of absolute power. ■

Mein Kampf

Published in two volumes in 1925 and 1927, Hitler's *Mein Kampf* ("My Struggle") was a powerful and sinister political manifesto. The first volume, composed during Hitler's 1924 prison sentence, tells of his youth; World War I; and the "betrayal" of Germany at Versailles, which he blamed on the Weimar government, "parasite" Jews, and Marxists—his long-term political targets. It also extols the Aryans as the master race who should seek the living space (*Lebensraum*) they deserved by expanding into Slavic and Soviet territories. The second volume set out how the Nazi Party should gain and hold power, using terror if necessary.

Though poorly written, the nationalist, anticommunist, and racist demagoguery of *Mein Kampf* found a ready audience among both the German elite and general public. By 1939, translated into 11 languages, its sales topped five million copies.

HEIL HITLER

ESTABLISHING THE NAZI STATE (1933–1934)

IN CONTEXT

FOCUS
Totalitarian rule

BEFORE
1923 Hitler stages the Munich Beer Hall Putsch, a failed coup that wins him public attention.

1928 Nazi politicians are elected to the Reichstag for the first time.

1931 Banks collapse in Austria and Germany as a result of the Depression and withdrawal of American loans.

AFTER
1938 Hitler annexes Austria and rigs a referendum to indicate Austrian approval.

1939 Germany invades Poland, igniting World War II.

During 1932, with the Weimar Republic's government in disarray, and Germany in a deep economic depression, Hitler's Nazi Party had attracted increasing public support and was now the largest in the Reichstag (parliament). Despite the Nazi Party's dominance, when Chancellor Franz von Papen, who had little Reichstag support, was forced to resign, President Paul von Hindenburg did not offer Hitler the post, as he despised and mistrusted him. Instead, he chose his close ally General Kurt von Schleicher.

Schleicher sought to secure the backing of the Nazi Party, but failed and resigned at the end of January 1933. During his brief term, his key achievement was the instigation of a huge program of building roads, canals, and railroads—later often wrongly attributed to Hitler.

See also: A flawed peace 20–21 ▪ Rise of the Nazis 24–29 ▪ German expansion 46–47 ▪ Nazi Europe 168–171 ▪ Germany and the reality of war 188–191 ▪ Germany's war industry 224

Hitler believed **democracy was moribund** and only a strong leader could give Germany the future it deserved.

→ He used the tools of democracy to seize power but **refused to compromise with democrats**, even in the short term.

→ Once he held power, Hitler **ruled without parliament**, making himself both chancellor and president.

→ To **maintain his total power**, Hitler eliminated all possible opposition, either by assassination or through confinement in concentration camps.

On January 30, 1933, Hindenburg was finally persuaded to offer Hitler the post of chancellor. Nazi Party supporters marched in triumph through the streets of Berlin.

Orchestrated crackdown

On February 27, a fire broke out in the Reichstag. Dutch communist Marinus van der Lubbe was arrested as the instigator of what Hitler claimed was a communist plot. Although a court later ruled that van der Lubbe acted alone, by that time the Nazis had used the incident as a pretext for a complete takeover of the government.

A few weeks earlier, Hitler's cabinet had enacted a temporary decree restricting press freedom and banning the right to assemble. The day after the fire, the cabinet extended its provisions in a Decree for the Protection of the People and the State (also called the Reichstag Fire Decree) and declared a state of emergency. The Communist Party was barred from the Reichstag, and the *Schutzstaffel* (SS) rounded up thousands of Nazi Party opponents and despatched them to the early concentration camps, including Dachau, near Munich.

> This man [Hitler] for a chancellor? I'll make him a postmaster and he can lick the stamps with my head on them.
> **Paul von Hindenburg, 1932**

Seizing power

On March 23, 1933, a fortnight after a further general election in which the Nazi Party still failed to gain a ruling majority, Hitler successfully steered the Enabling Act through the parliamentary process. The Act "enabled" the German cabinet and Hitler, as chancellor, to make and enforce laws without consulting the Reichstag or the president. Two months earlier, the *Frankfurter Zeitung* had declared that the diversity of German democracy was too strong for a dictatorship to prevail. The German Jewish *Jüdische Rundschau* newspaper was also convinced that the nation would always resist "a barbarian »

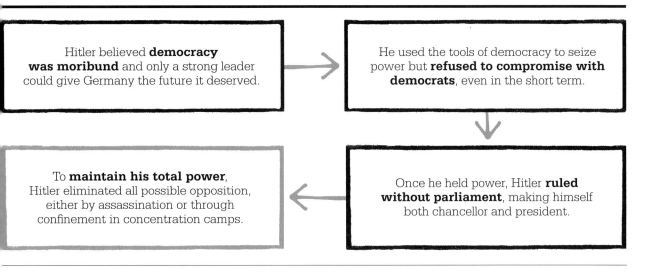

The Reichstag fire broke out around 9pm and destroyed the building's fine steel and glass cupola and a main hall. Bystanders reported hearing the sound of breaking glass before the blaze. Van der Lubbe was later arrested nearby.

Thousands of books burn in Berlin on May 10, 1933, in a student-led purge of "un-German" works judged inconsistent with Nazi ideology. Such events marked the start of strict censorship of the arts.

anti-Jewish policy." Both were wrong, and the Weimar democracy was effectively at an end.

On April 1, 1933, the Nazi Party orchestrated a national boycott of Jewish businesses in a fresh attempt to demonize Jewish people, long made scapegoats for Germany's economic ills. Uniformed guards harassed customers outside Jewish stores, dissuading them from buying goods. The Jewish businesses that did not collapse as a result of the harassment were often bought up by Nazis for far less than their true value.

On April 7, the new Nazi regime passed a law that revised the composition of the German civil service, compelling civil servants of non-Aryan descent to retire. This included all Jewish and non-Aryan teachers, lecturers, and members of the judiciary, with a few exceptions for those with extensive service or relatives killed in World War I. The aim of the purge was to swiftly organize German society so that it aligned with the political beliefs of the Nazi Party, including its passionate anti-Semitic ideology.

Total control

With a Concordat agreed in 1933, Hitler sought the Catholic Church's approval of his regime. He promised not to encroach on its influence in return for acquiescence to his policies (although priests would later be martyred for their protests). Nazi slogans such as *Kinder, Küche, Kirche* ("children, kitchen, church"), designed to encourage married women not to work but to stay at home and produce large families, neatly aligned with the Catholic Church's emphasis on motherhood.

In July 1933, Hitler banned all political parties but his own. With opposition extinguished, in November elections, 92 percent of the electorate voted for the Nazi Party or its "guests." In just over seven months, a democracy had become a totalitarian state.

Political purge

Early in 1934, Ernst Röhm, head of some two million Brownshirts—the *Sturmabteilung* (SA) paramilitary arm of the Nazi Party—suggested that his forces should become part of the new Wehrmacht that Hitler was covertly developing as a replacement for the Reichswehr (the German army), which was severely restricted by the terms of the 1919 Treaty of Versailles. Suspecting Röhm's ambition and not wishing to antagonize the Reichswehr generals, whose support he needed and who were resolutely opposed to Brownshirt involvement, Hitler decided to eliminate Röhm. On the pretext that Röhm was plotting against him, Hitler had him arrested and shot on June 30, 1934. The same night, he sent the SS and the *Geheime Staatspolizei* (Gestapo) to kill dozens more

> "National discipline governs our life!"
> **Nazi slogan, February 1933**

The Nazi propaganda machine

Manipulation of information was key to the Nazi Party's political success. It was masterminded by Josef Goebbels, a gifted orator and director of the party's propaganda from 1928.

Goebbels created evocative slogans and helped build the cult of Hitler as a redeemer of Germany's fortunes. The swastika, formerly a symbol of good fortune, was hijacked to foster a sense of ancient Aryan lineage. Goebbels knew how to use the media, pamphlets, mass rallies, and social gatherings effectively to spread the Nazi message and garner blind loyalty at a time when most German people had no access to other sources of information.

Hitler's close ally Albert Speer once noted cynically that a key distinction of the Third Reich was its ability to use communication to sustain itself and "deprive its objects of the power of independent thought."

SA members and other figures he perceived as a threat, including Schleicher, the former chancellor. The purge, later known as the "Night of the Long Knives," was publicly justified as an essential antirevolutionary measure.

Hunting down and detaining anyone deemed a threat to the Nazis would become a key role of the Gestapo. Formed a year earlier from sections of the Prussian police by Nazi leader Hermann Göring, it evolved into a secret police force that operated across Nazi Germany. Fueled by tips from informers and spies, it initially tracked down political opponents but later Jews, Roma, and homosexuals—mostly despatching them to forced labor and concentration camps.

Reshaping Germany

In August 1934, the natural death of President Hindenburg removed a final obstacle to Hitler's absolute power. Uniting the roles of president and chancellor, he dubbed himself Führer ("leader") and began to plot Germany's resurrection on the world stage. He delegated the running of domestic affairs to trusted subordinates, but—in a bid to keep their ambitions in check—judiciously ensured that roles overlapped. Local government was run by Nazi officials, trade unions were banned, and special courts featured in a legal system that eliminated any opposition.

Hjalmar Schacht, president of the Reichsbank in 1933 and appointed minister of economics in 1934, increased government spending to finance a vast infrastructure program of homes, highways, and waterways. This work slashed official unemployment figures. These took no account of Jews in public service who had been forced out of jobs and, in 1935, under the Nuremberg Race Laws, would lose all citizenship rights.

Patriotism and power

Patriotic propaganda—most visible at political rallies—served to brainwash the general public. Jewish and other "un-German" influences were excised from the arts, which were reshaped to highlight patriotism, military power, and Germany's physical prowess.

With a recovering economy, now boosted by munitions factories, the Führer could begin to devise his strategies for territorial expansion. ■

A Nazi salute in the Reichstag marks unanimous support for Hitler (fourth left, front row of desks) following his speech justifying the deaths of "state enemies" in the Night of the Long Knives.

THE CULMINATION OF ALIENATION

DICTATORS AND FRAGILE DEMOCRACIES IN EUROPE (1922–1939)

IN CONTEXT

FOCUS
Democracy under siege

BEFORE
1799 Napoleon Bonaparte seizes power in France.

1871 Otto von Bismarck becomes the self-appointed chancellor of Germany.

1919 The Treaty of Versailles dismantles the Imperial German Empire.

1922 Fascist politician Benito Mussolini becomes the leader of Italy.

AFTER
1974 Colonel Georgios Papadopoulos's military junta, which led Greece for seven years, collapses after Turkey's invasion of Cyprus.

1980 Josip Tito dies, freeing Yugoslavia from dictatorship.

1989 Nicolae Ceaușescu's dictatorship of Romania ends before a firing squad.

The breakup of empires after World War I—and the failure of democracy to prevent it—leaves people lost; fascism and nationalism **promise to restore people's identity**.

Why does fascism become popular?

Appeals to **those who lost much** in the depression, and **those with much to lose** to communism.

Offers **simple explanations to complex issues**. Scapegoating is a common practice.

Promises quick-fix solutions through **strong leadership and military force**.

World War I **left fertile ground for fascist and nationalist ideologies** to take root, and a huge pool of military men **ready to make fascism happen**.

Although the surge to power of Hitler in Germany and Mussolini in Italy stand out starkly, fascism grew strongly in many other places in Europe in the 1920s and 1930s. There were few places entirely untouched by ideas very similar to those expressed by Hitler, and many European countries fell into the hands of fascist dictators.

The tide of fascism was strongest in eastern and central Europe, a region squeezed between the threat of Stalin's communist Russia and the capitalist West. But there was considerable support for fascism in France, Britain, and the US. More so, among the soldiers of all nations who had a recent taste of command in World War I, there were many candidates ready to seize the reins of power.

Fascist appeal

Part of the appeal of fascism was its bold riposte to the threat of communism, especially among those with something to lose. Communist groups existed in every country, and the export of communism around the world was central to Russian communism, so it was not hard to imagine their ideology as a threat.

Another draw of fascism was disillusion with democracy, which, it was said, had failed to stop the horror of World War I, a conflict fought between democratic nations. Democracy was failing, too, to stop the economic disaster that was sweeping the post-war world, bringing the Great Depression and huge hardship to many people, especially those at the lower end of the economic scale. Democracy might mean well, fascists said, but it was fatally slow to act—and more crucially, it had failed to stop the rich exploiting the poor. It is hardly surprising that many people turned to an ideology that offered decisive action and a quick fix.

With national identities fractured and uncertain after the breakup of the German and Austro-Hungarian empires, people felt vulnerable—nationalism and racism offered potent rallying cries,

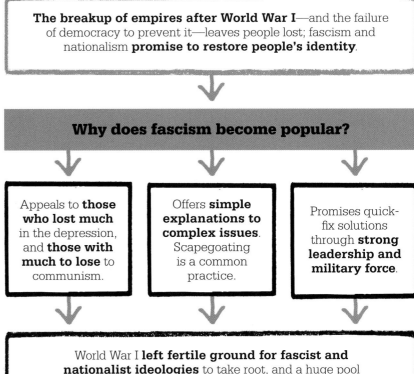

See also: A flawed peace 20–21 ▪ Italy and the rise of fascism 22–23 ▪ Rise of the Nazis 24–29 ▪ The Spanish Civil War 40–41 ▪ German expansion 46–47 ▪ The cost of war 314–317 ▪ Aftermath 320–327

The Great Depression hit the European populace hard during the 1930s, leaving hungry minds vulnerable to the nationalistic, racist quick fixes offered by fascism.

and an affirmation of identity. Historians have also identified more subtle aspects to the appeal of fascism. Fascists stressed the exciting thrill of individualism, passion, and instinct—not the dull, blanket hand of science and reason. They promised a comforting return to traditional values for those who felt alienated by the fast and callous modern world. And they offered meaning to the millions of soldiers who had found camaraderie and a sense of purpose on the battlefields of World War I, and who were now lost and without identity in the world of peace.

Democracies overthrown

Fascists in most countries were in the minority, but they were ruthless and determined, and often faced opposition parties that were invariably divided. Country after country fell into the hands of dictatorial rulers. Mussolini led the way in Italy, followed soon by Miguel Primo de Rivera in Spain, who made himself dictator in September 1923. An authoritarian nationalist who saw it as his mission to save Spain from the old politicians and to personally pave the way for a government takeover by "clean" patriots, he dispensed with the *Cortes* (the Spanish parliament), despatched dissidents to the Canary Islands, and took a very heavy hand to Catalonians campaigning for autonomy.

In neighboring Portugal, António de Oliveira Salazar assumed control in 1926 after a military coup, and became prime minister of a one-party state after elections in 1932. Historians are divided over whether Salazar was fascist or simply authoritarian, but his grip on power reflected the prevailing pattern of right-wing military takeovers.

António de Oliveira Salazar's leadership of Portugal typified the marriage of authoritarian rule and martial force that was common in Europe during the 1920s and 1930s.

Military might

The same year Salazar came to power, another army officer decided to take matters into his own hands. In Poland, Marshal Jósef Piłsudski marched into Warsaw at the head of an army, demanding more decisive government. An election gave him an overwhelming mandate, but he refused to become president because he deemed the role to have insufficient power. Five months later, he made himself prime minister and ruled as a dictator for the next nine years. In Lithuania, meanwhile, a military coup toppled the elected government and put the right-wing Lithuanian Nationalist Union party—led by Antanas Smetona—into power. The pretext was a Bolshevik plot, and Smetona immediately had 350 communists arrested. Evidence »

of a plot was never found, but Smetona stayed in power, banning all other political parties for 14 years. The USSR then invaded on the pretext that it was saving Lithuania from fascists, although Smetona's rule was more authoritarian than totalitarian. In Latvia, democracy barely survived a similar crisis to that of its Baltic neighbor.

Two years later, the earthquakes of fascism and nationalism began to strike at the heart of the continent, in central Europe. In the Kingdom of the Serbs, Croats, and Slovenes—a nation set up in 1918, with Serbian prince Alexander as king since 1921—an attempt was made to overcome national and ethnic rivalries. Bitter divisions between the Serbs and Croats came to a head in 1928, when Croat opposition leader Stjepan Radić was shot and killed in parliament in Belgrade during a heated debate. With the country descending into chaos, Alexander made himself sole ruler on January 6, 1929. In what came to be called the "January 6 Dictatorship," Alexander declared nationalities irrelevant, divided the country into nine regions, and changed its name to Yugoslavia—as it remained until the country's collapse in the 1990s.

Further to the south, democratic Greece swung uneasily between dictatorship, republicanism, and monarchy, finally succumbing to the totalitarian leadership of General Ioannis Metaxas in 1936.

Nazism and anti-Semitism

To aid his country's failing economy, Austrian chancellor Johannes Schober successfully sought a cut in the reparations owed to Czechoslovakia and Yugoslavia for their exploitation by the Hapsburg Empire. Shortly after, in September 1930 the Heimwehr—a right-wing militia that echoed the Brownshirts in Germany—took over the government and began to clamp down on all opposition. At the November elections of that year, although Austrian voters decisively rejected the Heimwehr and voted the Socialists to power, it proved to be only a temporary reprieve for democrats. As Hitler came to power in Germany, Nazis enjoyed growing influence in Austria. By summer 1933, the once-banned swastika was flown freely in Vienna, and Nazi sympathizers marched through the streets. By 1938, Austria had become part of Nazi Germany.

Meanwhile—egged on, no doubt, by Nazism and the general tide of racism—anti-Semitic views grew in popularity in countries such as Hungary and Romania, where the Iron Guard was created by charismatic fascist politician Corneliu Codreanu. Although still a minority party in 1930, the Iron Guard's violence against Jews was extreme. By the mid-1930s, it joined with other ultra-right parties to demand the elimination of Jews

> Fascism, Nazism, and Stalinism are the culmination of alienation.
>
> **Erich Fromm**
>
> **German-born philosopher (1900–1980)**

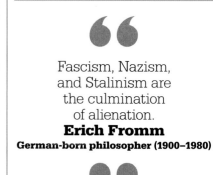

The fascist salute—based on a supposedly Roman custom—was adopted by far-right parties across Europe, including those in totalitarian Romania, pictured here in 1938.

The Red Army parades on May Day 1938 at Red Square in Moscow, displaying the might of communism so feared by European politicians.

and Hungarians from Romanian public life. Similarly, those with communist views were imprisoned.

In Britain, Sir Oswald Mosley—supported by press baron Lord Rothermere—formed the British Union of Fascists and its uniformed force, the Blackshirts. But despite some establishment sympathy for fascism and admiration for Hitler, there was serious public opposition. In October 1936, anti-fascist demonstrators—trade unionists, communists, anarchists, British Jews, Irish dockers, and socialists—clashed with police at a fascist march in London. The Battle of Cable Street is seen as the defeat of British fascism; wearing political uniforms in public was soon banned.

Communist repression

Fascism proved to be only one side of the extremist politics taking hold in the interwar years. In Russia, Josef Stalin cemented his grip on power to create a communist system that was as brutal and totalitarian as Hitler's. Using the *Cheka*—the Bolshevik security agency—and the NKVD (secret police), Stalin not only ruthlessly eliminated his opponents—with many sent to the gulags, executed, or simply murdered—but conducted one of the most horrific campaigns of repression in history.

In 1929, Stalin launched *dekulakization*, a program that involved removing the prosperous *kulaks* ("peasants") from the land to make way for collective farms. The *kulaks* were shot or imprisoned by the local secret political police; sent to Siberia, the north, the Urals, or Kazakhstan after confiscation of their property; or evicted from their houses and used in labor colonies within their own districts. This brutal repression is now regarded as genocide; more than five million Soviet citizens are thought to have died as a result.

As war loomed in the late 1930s, democracy was hanging by a thread across the world, assailed by fascism, communism, and other forms of extremist politics. ■

Charles Lindbergh

Handsome all-American hero Charles Lindbergh (1902–1974) became famous in 1927 when he made the first nonstop solo flight across the Atlantic between New York and Paris. His fame increased, tragically, when his two-year-old son was kidnapped and murdered five years later.

In 1938, Lindbergh was asked by the US government to tour Germany to inspect its growing air fleet. While there, he fell under Nazism's spell. Just a few weeks before Kristallnacht he was awarded a special medal by Hermann Göring. Thereafter, he became an apologist for Hitler, claiming that he "accomplished results (good in addition to bad) which could hardly have been accomplished without some fanaticism."

Lindbergh became deeply anti-Semitic and argued fervently against US Lend-Lease funding for the Allies in 1941. He claimed that the war was the Jews' fault, and the "greatest danger to [the US] lies in their large ownership and influence in our motion pictures, our press, our radio, and our government."

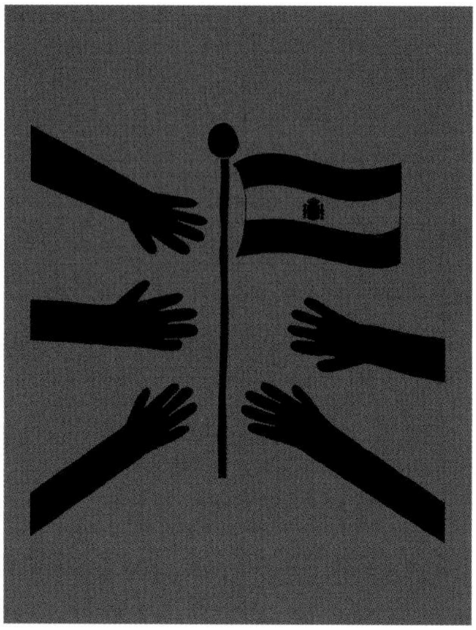

THERE WILL BE NO COMMUNISM

THE SPANISH CIVIL WAR (1936–1939)

IN CONTEXT

FOCUS
Totalitarianism

BEFORE
1922 Mussolini gains power in Italy. He describes his fascist state as *totalitario*—where individual freedoms are subordinate to the state.

1923–1930 General Miguel Primo de Rivera becomes Spain's first dictator, supported by the military and the king.

1928 In the USSR, Stalin implements state control of agriculture and industry in the first of his five-year plans.

AFTER
1975 Franco dies. He is succeeded by King Juan Carlos I, who leads Spain's transition to democracy.

1989 The Berlin Wall separating East and West Berlin falls, triggering the collapse of totalitarianism in eastern Europe.

The Spanish Civil War began on July 18, 1936, when right-wing military officers rose up to overthrow Spain's republican government, a left-leaning coalition called the Frente Popular (Popular Front). One of the officers, General Francisco Franco, broadcasting from the Canary Islands, called all army officers to join this "nationalist" rebellion. Beginning in Morocco with the "Army of Africa," the nationalists quickly took over much of northern Spain and some southern cities, including Seville. Franco claimed the coup was a fight against communism.

In Spain's 1931 general election, a large majority of the population had voted in favor of abolishing the monarchy and establishing a

Volunteer fighters march to defend the Spanish Republic in 1936. More than 1,000 women fought in militias; thousands more served in support roles.

See also: Italy and the rise of fascism 22–23 ▪ Rise of the Nazis 24–29 ▪ Dictators and fragile democracies in Europe 34–39 ▪ Failure of the League of Nations 50 ▪ The Blitz 98–99

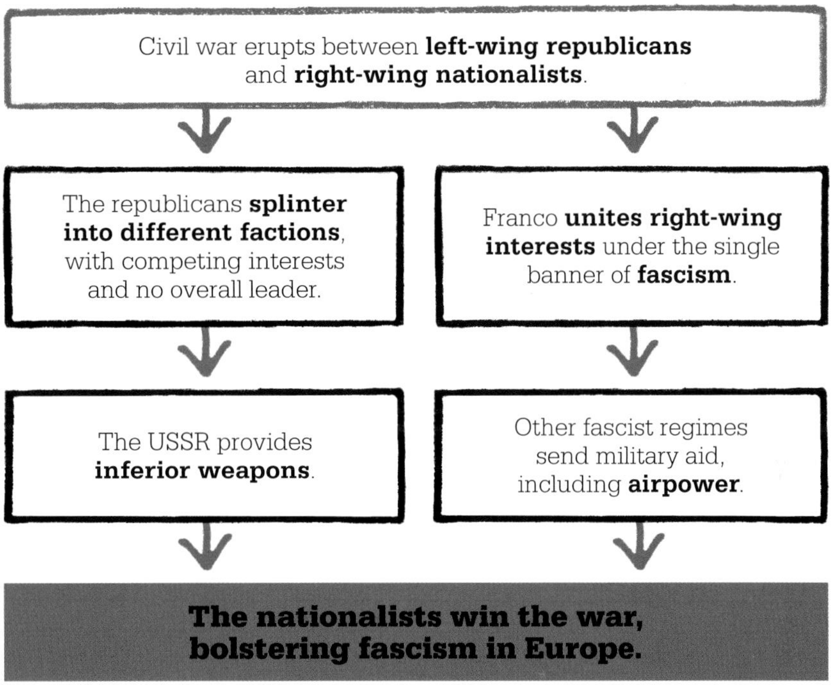

liberal republic, but the new leftist government had soon run into trouble. Its ambitious program of reform upset not only the traditional elite, who feared communism, but also people in the conservative heartlands, many of whom rejected the government's attacks on the Catholic Church. The impact of the Great Depression also made the proposed reforms unaffordable.

Civil war erupts between **left-wing republicans** and **right-wing nationalists**.
The republicans **splinter into different factions**, with competing interests and no overall leader.
Franco **unites right-wing interests** under the single banner of **fascism**.
The USSR provides **inferior weapons**.
Other fascist regimes send military aid, including **airpower**.
The nationalists win the war, bolstering fascism in Europe.

New elections in 1933 returned a right-wing government to power. Two years later, after crushing a socialist rebellion in northern Spain, Franco was appointed head of the army. Further elections in 1936 reinstated the republican Popular Front coalition, leading to the army's military coup five months later.

An international civil war

Franco unified the right under the Falange, Spain's fascist party, and received military support from Mussolini and Hitler, who offered the services of the Condor Legion, a unit of the Luftwaffe (German airforce). While the nationalists unified and advanced through Spain, the republicans began to split into different factions, ranging from moderate liberals to communists and anarchists, with armed conflict breaking out between them. In Barcelona, anarchist workers even launched their own revolution, converting the Ritz Hotel into a workers' canteen.

The republicans were aided by the USSR, which sent weapons, and thousands of idealistic foreigners from many countries joined the International Brigade on the republican side, including British writer George Orwell. Others, such as American writer Ernest Hemingway, provided powerful eyewitness accounts as foreign correspondents.

Hundreds of thousands of civilians died in the civil war, mainly through executions and bomb attacks, including carpet bombing, a new technique trialed by Hitler's Condor Legion. When Picasso was commissioned to create an artwork for the 1937 World's Fair in Paris, he painted *Guernica*, depicting the Basque town destroyed in 1937 in the first aerial bombing campaign against civilians in Europe.

The fall of Madrid

Madrid withstood early attacks by the nationalists, helped by the International Brigade. However, a 28-month siege from October 1936 left it freezing, starving, and virtually defenseless. On March 28, 1939, some 200,000 nationalist troops marched into the city. The republican government had already fled to France, but thousands of republican supporters who had stayed in the capital were executed. Franco triumphed and became Spain's absolute ruler for the next 36 years. ▪

> We strive to form a single national front … against Moscow and the Marxist societies.
> **Francisco Franco**

TO MAKE THE NATION FREE, WE MUST SACRIFICE FREEDOM

CHINA IN TURMOIL (1919–1937)

IN CONTEXT

FOCUS
China's warring factions

BEFORE
1899 The two-year Boxer Rebellion seeks to rid China of foreign influence.

1912 An uprising forces China's last emperor, six-year-old Pu-Yi, to abdicate. Sun Yat-sen becomes the first Chinese president but is compelled to give way to General Yuan.

AFTER
1949 Chiang Kai-shek is forced into exile in Taiwan, and Mao Zedong takes over as leader of the communist People's Republic of China.

1966–1976 Mao's Cultural Revolution roots out counter-revolutionary elements, forcing capitalists and intellectuals to become manual workers.

1976 Mao Zedong dies.

After the abdication of China's last emperor Pu-Yi in 1912, the country was bitterly divided between republicans led by Sun Yat-sen and his Kuomintang (KMT or "Nationalist Party") and the military faction led by General Yuan Shikai. These internal divisions were exploited by the Japanese, who took advantage of Western preoccupation with World War I to dominate China, virtually making it a protectorate.

Hopes dashed

When General Yuan died in 1919, many young Chinese hoped the West, redrawing the world at the Paris Peace Conference after World War I, would put pressure on Japan to forego control of China. Instead, France and the US withdrew their support for China, having already signed pacts with Japan. Motivated by feelings of betrayal, on May 4, 1919, 3,000 students from Beijing University took to the streets in protest. The Beijing authorities cracked down on the demonstrators, setting off a wave of further protests around the country.

Spurred on by the revolutionary events in Russia, some young protesters—including Mao Zedong and Zhou Enlai—united to create the Chinese Communist Party (CCP) in 1921. But before a revolution of the masses could be achieved, the CCP first had to defeat the northern army warlords who had followed General Yuan, so it joined forces with Sun Yat-sen and the KMT. When Sun Yat-sen died in 1925, he was succeeded by his brother-in-law, the young military chief Chiang Kai-shek.

> “If imperialism is not banished from the country, China will perish as a nation.”
> **Chiang Kai-shek**

Communism on the march

By 1928, the warlords had been defeated and Chiang was installed as leader of the republic, a position he held until 1975—first in China,

See also: A flawed peace 20–21 ▪ Japan on the march 44–45 ▪ Failure of the League of Nations 50 ▪ Japan's dilemma 137 ▪ China and Japan at war 250–253

The Chinese Republic is **controlled** by General Yuan Shikai, with support from **warlords**.

Following Yuan's death, the **KMT and the CCP join together** to defeat the warlords.

After their joint victory, the KMT and CCP **fight with each other**.

The KMT's strong attack forces the CCP to make the **Long March** in 1934–1935.

Imperial Japan is a **constant foe** of China.

Japan launches a **fresh offensive** on China in 1937.

The CCP escapes to safety, then joins with the KMT once again to combat Japan in an unsuccessful **"United Front."**

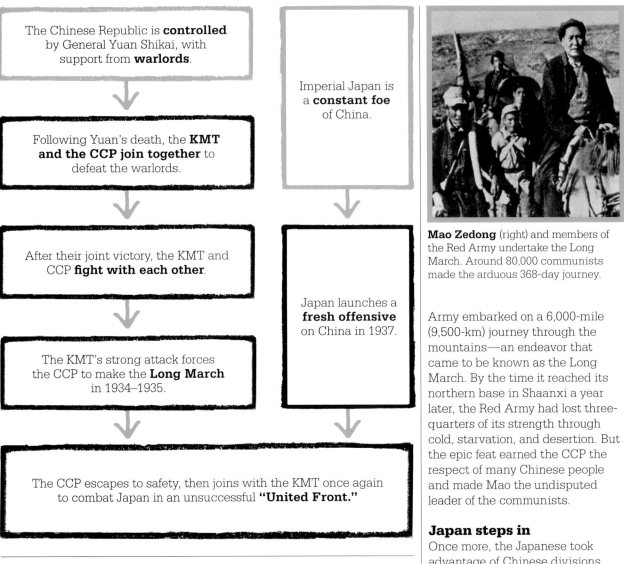

Mao Zedong (right) and members of the Red Army undertake the Long March. Around 80,000 communists made the arduous 368-day journey.

then in Taiwan, where he lived in exile from 1949. From the outset Chiang clashed with the CCP, who saw the KMT as elitists. Even before he became president, a CCP-organized factory strike in Shanghai in 1927 was crushed so violently by Chiang's troops that 5,000 workers and communists died. This became known as the Shanghai Massacre. Mao retreated to the countryside to mobilize the peasants, whom he felt were key to the revolution. He created the peasant Red Army in Jiangxi province, eastern China, making guerrilla strikes from the stronghold of the mountains.

In 1934, Chiang's KMT army encircled the ill-equipped Red Army in the Jinggang Shan mountains. Breaking through a weak point in KMT lines, the Red Army embarked on a 6,000-mile (9,500-km) journey through the mountains—an endeavor that came to be known as the Long March. By the time it reached its northern base in Shaanxi a year later, the Red Army had lost three-quarters of its strength through cold, starvation, and desertion. But the epic feat earned the CCP the respect of many Chinese people and made Mao the undisputed leader of the communists.

Japan steps in

Once more, the Japanese took advantage of Chinese divisions and launched an attack on Beijing in July 1937. Chiang insisted that his first priority was to defeat the communists, but his subordinates disagreed and forced him to join with the CCP in a "United Front" against Japan. Yet even the United Front was no match for the Japanese armed forces, who quickly took over eastern China, leaving the United Front in tatters. ■

EXPANSION IS THE DESTINY OF THE JAPANESE PEOPLE

JAPAN ON THE MARCH (1931–1941)

IN CONTEXT

FOCUS
Japanese expansion

BEFORE
1895 Japan defeats China in the First Sino-Japanese War.

1904–1905 Japan defeats Russia on land and at sea—first Asian victory over a European power in modern times.

1919 At the Paris Peace Conference, the US vetoes a Japanese proposal for international recognition of the principle of racial equality.

1933 Japan leaves the League of Nations after it is condemned as an aggressor for occupying Manchuria.

AFTER
July 1941 Vichy France allows Japanese troops to occupy southern Indochina.

December 7–8, 1941 Japanese forces attack the US base at Pearl Harbor and invade southeast Asia.

In the 19th century, Japan adopted Western technology and military organization while preserving or reinventing Japanese traditions such as emperor worship and the samurai warrior ethic. By World War I, it was a dominant regional power, ruling Korea and Formosa (Taiwan) as colonial possessions. But militant Japanese nationalists were not content with a subsidiary place in a white-dominated world. They aspired to build an Asian empire that would be recognized as an equal by the West. The chaotic conditions in China gave nationalists in the Japanese army the chance to act. In 1931, an explosion, allegedly detonated by Chinese nationalists, destroyed part of a railroad owned by the Japanese in the Manchurian city of Mukden, in northeast China. In response to the "Mukden Incident," Japanese troops occupied Manchuria.

This occupation was ordered not by Japan's civilian government but by extreme nationalist army officers, who throughout the 1930s staged a series of assassinations

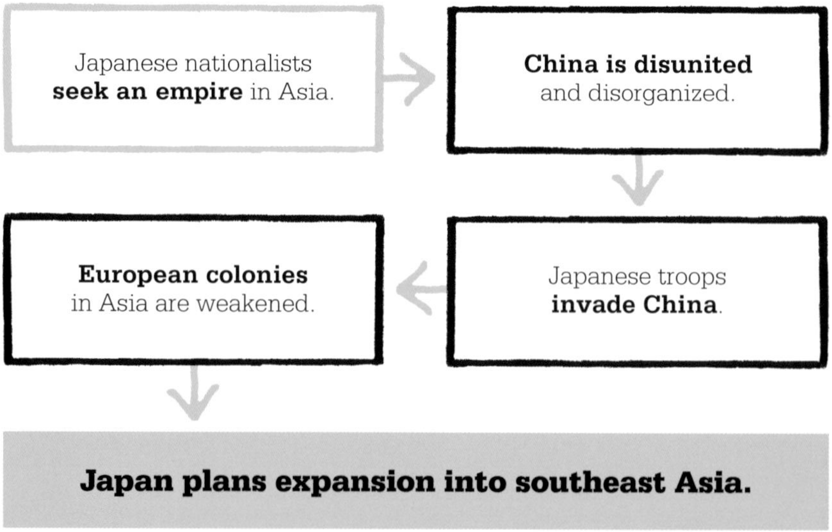
Japanese nationalists **seek an empire** in Asia.
China is disunited and disorganized.
Japanese troops **invade China**.
European colonies in Asia are weakened.
Japan plans expansion into southeast Asia.

See also: Japan's dilemma 137 ▪ The Japanese attack Pearl Harbor 138–145 ▪ Japanese advances 154–157 ▪ China and Japan at war 250–253

> The body of a little boy … had four bayonet wounds … A man cannot be silent about this kind of cruelty!
> **John Rabe**
> **Eyewitness to the Nanjing massacre**

and attempted coups in Tokyo that deterred civilian resistance to their expansionist ambitions.

Increasing ambition

Japan's army continued to encroach upon Chinese territory until a military clash near Beijing in July 1937 provided a pretext for a full-scale invasion and the Second Sino-Japanese War. After fierce fighting at Shanghai, Chinese government and communist forces, which had put aside their own civil war to form a United Front, were driven back. The fall of Nanjing, China's capital, in December was followed by weeks of massacre and rape in which thousands of Chinese civilians died. Reports by American missionaries set US opinion against Japan.

Japanese forces seized control of much of eastern China, and Chinese forces withdrew to the southwest. Japanese military leaders such as General Tojo Hideki planned further expansion. Incursions into northern Asia were blocked when Soviet forces defeated the Japanese in Mongolia in summer 1939, but British, French, and Dutch colonies in southeast Asia were vulnerable to attack. Rich in resources, they could supply the raw industrial materials, food, and fuel Japan needed for self-sufficiency.

In June 1940, Japan announced its goal to create a Greater Asian Co-Prosperity Sphere that would unite Asian nations, freed from Western imperialism, under its leadership. In September that year, Japanese troops invaded the northern part of French Indochina, and Japan signed a pact with Nazi Germany and fascist Italy, further alienating the US, which was already openly supporting China.

The US responded to Japanese pressure on southeast Asia with trade restrictions. By spring 1941, however, the two countries were engaged in unofficial negotiations to avert a growing risk of war. ■

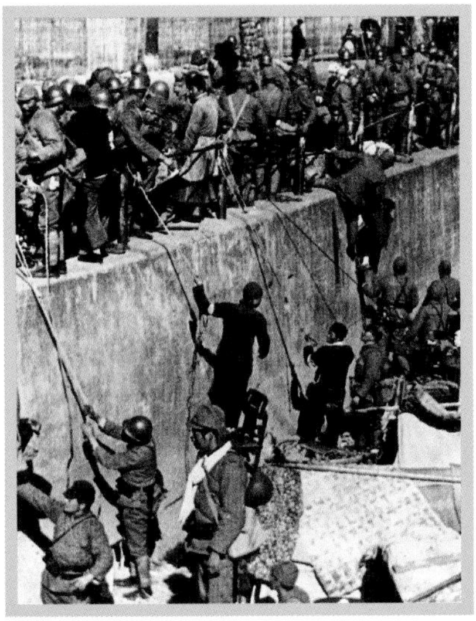

Japanese troops scale a harbor wall in the district of Hongkou during the 1937 Battle of Shanghai. The battle was one of the fiercest in the war with China.

General Tojo Hideki

Tojo Hideki was born into a low-ranking samurai family in 1884. Hardworking and efficient, he forged a career in Japan's army bureaucracy, rising to the rank of general by 1934. Tojo was not aligned with extreme nationalists who opposed the civilian government, and he helped suppress an uprising by disaffected officers in Tokyo in 1936. He did, however, believe fervently in founding a Japanese empire in Asia.

Appointed minister for war in July 1940, Tojo supported the decision to form an alliance with Nazi Germany, and as prime minister, from October 1941, he led Japan into war with the US.

By 1942, Tojo exercised near-dictatorial power as head of the government and the army, before a succession of Japanese defeats discredited him. In July 1944, he was dismissed from office.

At the war's end, Tojo was arrested by the Americans and tried for war crimes by the International Military Tribunal for the Far East. Having botched an attempt to shoot himself after Japan's surrender in 1945, he was hanged as a war criminal in 1948.

WE DEMAND LAND AND TERRITORY

GERMAN EXPANSION (1935–1939)

IN CONTEXT

FOCUS
Greater Germany

BEFORE
1742 King Frederick the Great of Prussia annexes much of Poland, moving German families in and abolishing the use of Polish.

1919 Under the Treaty of Versailles, Germany is forced to cede Alsace-Lorraine, the Saarland, and other territories to its neighbors.

1925 In his political manifesto *Mein Kampf*, Hitler outlines his doctrine of *Lebensraum* and plans for German expansion.

AFTER
1939 Germany invades Poland; Britain and France declare war on Germany.

1945 At the Potsdam conference, Germany is reduced to its modern borders and split into two parts: West and East Germany.

When Hitler came to power in 1933, he was determined to recover all the territory Germany had lost under the Treaty of Versailles. He aimed to unite all German-speaking peoples into one German nation-state called *Grossdeutschland* ("Greater German Reich") and to expand Germany eastward to give its people *Lebensraum* ("living space"). Hitler's doctrine of *Lebensraum* was based on his belief that "inferior" races—such as the Slavs of eastern Europe, whom he dismissed as lazy—should make way for "superior" races.

Once installed as German leader, Hitler embarked on the expansion of Germany with breathtaking speed. Having rearmed and reintroduced conscription, in contravention of the Treaty of Versailles, Hitler occupied the demilitarized Rhineland in 1936, then staged a rigged referendum to legitimize this move. A referendum a few months earlier had also reunited Germany with the French-

German soldiers cross the Rhine River into the city of Mainz in the demilitarized Rhineland. In direct contravention of the Treaty of Versailles, 22,000 troops entered the region.

See also: A flawed peace 20–21 ▪ Failure of the League of Nations 50 ▪ Appeasing Hitler 51 ▪ Europe on the brink 56–57 ▪ The destruction of Poland 58–63 ▪ Nazi Europe 168–171 ▪ Germany and the reality of war 188–191

> Those of the same blood belong in the same reich.
>
> **Adolf Hitler**
>
> **A banner on the Loos Haus, a public building in Vienna**

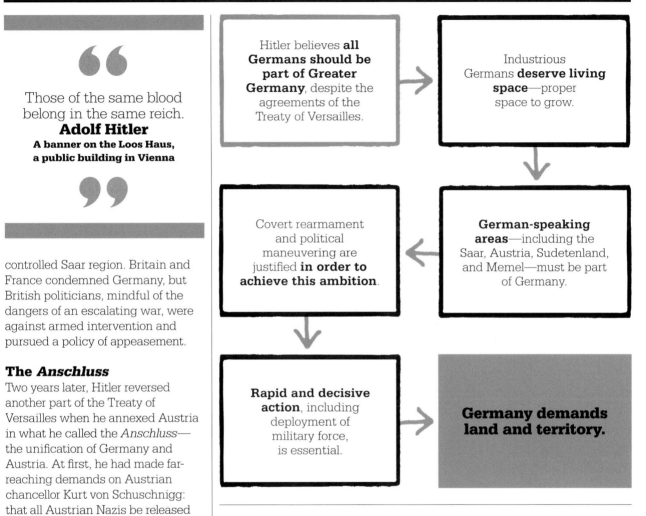

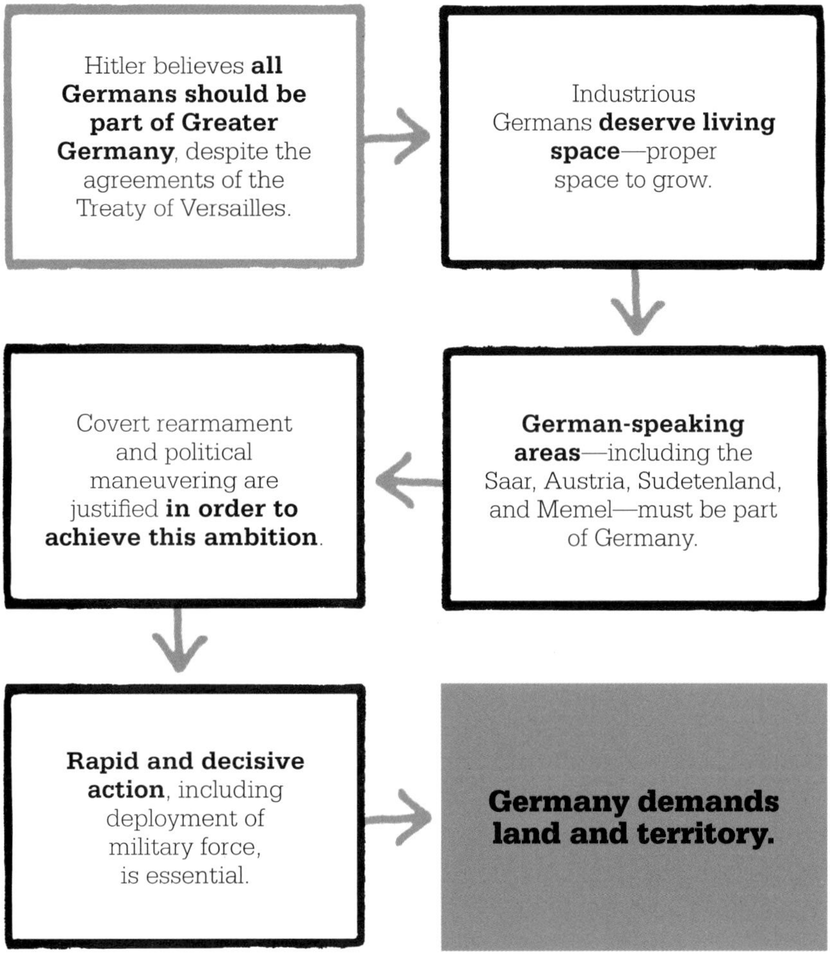

controlled Saar region. Britain and France condemned Germany, but British politicians, mindful of the dangers of an escalating war, were against armed intervention and pursued a policy of appeasement.

Hitler believes **all Germans should be part of Greater Germany**, despite the agreements of the Treaty of Versailles.
Industrious Germans **deserve living space**—proper space to grow.
German-speaking areas—including the Saar, Austria, Sudetenland, and Memel—must be part of Germany.
Covert rearmament and political maneuvering are justified **in order to achieve this ambition**.
Rapid and decisive action, including deployment of military force, is essential.
Germany demands land and territory.

The *Anschluss*

Two years later, Hitler reversed another part of the Treaty of Versailles when he annexed Austria in what he called the *Anschluss*—the unification of Germany and Austria. At first, he had made far-reaching demands on Austrian chancellor Kurt von Schuschnigg: that all Austrian Nazis be released from jail; that two leading Austrian Nazis be made interior minister and defense minister; and that Germany should absorb Austria's economy.

When Schuschnigg called a referendum on union with Germany, German troops marched into Austria and took over the country. A subsequent referendum was rigged by the Nazis to show that more than 99 percent of Austrians were in favor of the *Anschluss*. Without the backing of an effective League of Nations, the organization that had been set up after World War I to maintain global peace, France and Britain could do little but weakly protest.

Forced occupation

Emboldened, Hitler moved on to Czechoslovakia. Taking advantage of the fact that Czechoslovakia's Sudetenland had a sizable German population, Hitler bullied the Western Allies into accepting Germany's takeover of the Sudetenland under the Munich Agreement of September 1938, without participation from the Czechs. Six months later, German troops occupied the whole of Czechoslovakia, establishing the "Protectorate of Bohemia and Moravia" and making Slovakia a German satellite. They also moved into Memel in Lithuania, which Germany had lost at Versailles. Again, the Lithuanians had no choice but to accept.

By this time, it was finally clear that appeasement would not work, and the British agreed to protect Poland from German aggression. The die was cast for World War II. ■

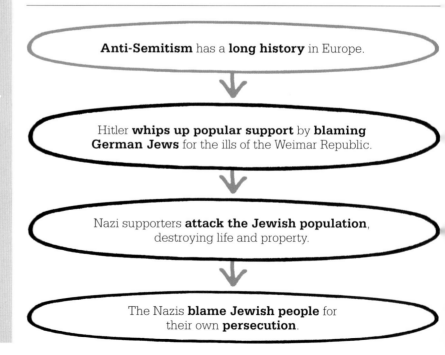

SAVAGERY TRIUMPHANT

KRISTALLNACHT (1938)

IN CONTEXT

FOCUS
Anti-Semitism

BEFORE
1348–1351 European Jews are falsely accused of causing the Black Death by poisoning wells; thousands are murdered.

1881–1884 Pogroms compel 2 million Jews to migrate from their home in southern Russia.

1935–1936 German Jews are stripped of their citizenship, businesses, and assets.

AFTER
1939 Over half of Germany's Jews flee the country before the outbreak of World War II.

1950 The Law of Return allows Jews from any country to settle in the newly created state of Israel.

1952 Thirteen Jewish writers, poets, actors, and other intellectuals are killed on the "Night of the Murdered Poets" in Moscow's Lubyanka prison.

On the night of November 9–10, 1938, Nazi supporters attacked Jewish people and their property across Germany and Austria in a wave of wanton destruction. It became known as Kristallnacht ("Crystal Night") for the piles of glass that lay strewn across the streets—the shattered windows of thousands of Jewish businesses and synagogues.

Attacks on Jewish people had been escalating ever since Hitler came to power in 1933, and their rights were gradually eroded. Jewish people were stripped of citizenship, they could not serve in the civil service, and could no longer marry or have sexual intercourse with Germans who were deemed Aryan. But Kristallnacht was the first organized Nazi attack.

Anti-Semitism has a **long history** in Europe.

↓

Hitler **whips up popular support** by **blaming German Jews** for the ills of the Weimar Republic.

↓

Nazi supporters **attack the Jewish population**, destroying life and property.

↓

The Nazis **blame Jewish people** for their own **persecution**.

See also: Rise of the Nazis 24–29 ▪ Nazi massacres 136 ▪ The Holocaust 172–177 ▪ Resistance movements 226–231 ▪ The Warsaw Ghetto Uprising 242–243 ▪ The Nuremberg Trials and denazification 318–319

The pretext for the attack was the shooting of German diplomat Ernst vom Rath by 17-year-old Polish Jewish student Herschel Grynszpan in Paris on November 7. The student was taking revenge for his parents' expulsion from Hanover to Poland. Seizing on the chance to fire up Nazi supporters, Joseph Goebbels, Hitler's minister for public enlightenment and propaganda, urged people to take reprisals against Jewish people. The order was issued from Munich, where he and Hitler were celebrating the anniversary of the Munich Beer Hall Putsch of 1923, Hitler's failed coup against the Weimar Republic.

Violence unleashed

The orchestrated violence was presented as spontaneous acts of outrage, but the head of the Gestapo had told the police not to intervene and fire brigades had been warned not to respond unless Aryan properties were threatened. Over nearly two days and nights, in cities all over Germany, more than 1,000 synagogues were torched, over 7,000 Jewish businesses smashed, and many hundreds of homes and schools were ransacked. Almost 100 Jews were murdered.

There were no punishments or reprisals for the perpetrators. Instead, the Gestapo arrested 30,000 Jewish men and boys, and had to expand the concentration camps to accommodate them. Placing the blame for the damage on Jews themselves, the authorities fined the Jewish community one billion Reichsmarks (more than $7 billion today), payable by all Jewish taxpayers in quarterly installments.

> We never thought that Germans would stand by, and not do something about it.
>
> **Margot Friedlander (née Bendheim)**
> **Jewish eyewitness**

Flames engulf a synagogue in Munich on Kristallnacht. After this night, it became almost impossible for Jewish people to hold religious services in public.

Persistent persecution

A few days after Kristallnacht, Jews were banned from schools, and within a month, from all public places. Numerous other anti-Jewish laws and decrees came into force. Although hundreds died, most of those incarcerated in concentration camps were quickly released—on condition that they leave Germany immediately. Most Jews who possessed passports were already leaving Germany, realizing they had little future there.

Kristallnacht provoked outrage across the world, yet President Roosevelt was alone in recalling his ambassador from Germany. Some countries began to take Jewish refugees. In Britain, the Kindertransport policy rescued thousands of unaccompanied Jewish children from Germany and German-annexed territory between 1938 and 1940. Although the unfolding horror in Germany was plain to see, most of the nation's Jews were left to their fate—the appalling "Final Solution" that Hitler was devising. ■

IT IS US TODAY. IT WILL BE YOU TOMORROW

FAILURE OF THE LEAGUE OF NATIONS (1930s)

IN CONTEXT

FOCUS
International cooperation

BEFORE
1899 The Permanent Court of Arbitration is set up in The Hague, the first multilateral body to address international disputes and agree the conduct of warfare.

1919 At the Paris Peace Conference, the victorious World War I powers set up the League of Nations.

1920 The League of Nations sets up the Permanent Court of International Justice (PCIJ).

AFTER
1944 At the Bretton Woods Conference in the US, the Allies propose establishing the International Monetary Fund (IMF) and the World Bank.

1945 The Allies establish the United Nations, which replaces the League of Nations in 1946.

A priority of the Treaty of Versailles of 1919 was to prevent a global war from ever happening again. The League of Nations was set up "to promote international cooperation and to achieve peace and security." It would solve disputes between countries before they erupted into open warfare.

Toothless gestures

Although demand for the League of Nations was led by US president Woodrow Wilson, the US Congress, wedded to a 19th-century isolationist ideal, refused to vote for US membership. Without the US, the league's resolutions seemed to be only token gestures. Moreover, the league had no armed forces to lend strength to its will.

Initially, the league had some success, such as intervening in disputes between Poland and Lithuania in the 1920s, but when empire-building dictatorships arose across the world in the 1930s, its weakness was exposed. Hitler withdrew Germany from the league in 1932, and Japan exited the following year, after the league opposed its invasion of Manchuria, in China. The league also objected to Mussolini's invasion of Ethiopia in 1935, but the French and British had already secretly agreed to it.

When Hitler threatened to invade Sudetenland in 1938, an ethnic German region of Czechoslovakia, the league was powerless to intervene due to the British and French policy of appeasement. ■

Emperor Haile Selassie of Ethiopia (man with beard, second left) attends a meeting of the League of Nations in 1936 to protest its failure to protect his country from invasion by Italy.

See also: A flawed peace 20–21 ▪ Italy and the rise of fascism 22–23 ▪ Dictators and fragile democracies in Europe 34–39 ▪ German expansion 46–47

PEACE FOR OUR TIME

APPEASING HITLER (1938–1939)

IN CONTEXT

FOCUS
Prelude to war

BEFORE
1620 After the Battle of the White Mountain, western Bohemia, later known as Sudetenland, is subsumed into the Austrian Empire and is settled by German-speakers.

1919 The Treaty of St-Germain places Sudetenland under Czechoslovakian rule.

1936 Hitler's troops enter the Rhineland, contravening the Treaty of Versailles.

AFTER
1945 Czechoslovakia becomes part of the Eastern Bloc—a group of communist states under the control of the USSR.

1989 The Velvet Revolution in Prague ends communist rule.

1993 Czechoslovakia splits into the independent states of Czech Republic and Slovakia.

In 1938, British prime minister Neville Chamberlain made three trips to meet Hitler in an attempt to settle the fate of Sudetenland, in Czechoslovakia. Hitler wanted to bring Sudetenland, which contained 3 million ethnic Germans, into the Reich and threatened to invade Czechoslovakia if his demands were not met. Czech prime minister Edvard Benes sought protection for his country from Britain and France, but their policy was to appease Hitler in order to avoid war. Chamberlain and French premier Edouard Daladier acceded to Hitler's demands and promised to put pressure on the Czechs to agree.

On September 30, Chamberlain disembarked from his third flight from Munich to waiting crowds. Waving a piece of paper, he declared: "This morning I had another talk with the German chancellor, Herr Hitler, and here is the paper which bears his name upon it." The agreement, he said, would bring "peace for our time." The following day, Nazi troops occupied Sudetenland.

> If you have sacrificed my nation to preserve the peace of the world, I will be the first to applaud you. But if not, gentlemen, God help your souls.
>
> **Jan Masaryk**
> **Czech foreign minister**

It soon became clear that sacrificing Sudetenland had not contained German expansion, yet some people still advocated appeasement. In May 1939, Joseph P. Kennedy, the US ambassador to London, tried to broker a deal with German officials, offering gold loans in exchange for nonaggression pacts. Washington quickly vetoed the plan, and no one knows if Hitler ever knew about it. ■

See also: A flawed peace 20–21 ▪ Rise of the Nazis 24–29 ▪ Establishing the Nazi state 30–33 ▪ German expansion 46–47 ▪ Europe on the brink 56–57

EUROPE TO WAR

1939–1940

GOES

AUG 23, 1939

Germany and the USSR sign a secret **nonaggression pact**. They agree to **partition Poland** between themselves.

SEP 1, 1939

Germany invades Poland. Two days later, **Britain and France**, who have a defense pact with Poland, **declare war on Germany**.

OCT 14, 1939

The **British battleship HMS *Royal Oak* is sunk** by a German U-boat inside its base **at Scapa Flow**, Scotland—a blow to British naval prestige.

NOV 30, 1939

The USSR's **Red Army invades Finland** but makes slow progress against Finnish defensive positions. Helsinki is bombed by the Red Air Force.

DEC 17, 1939

German Captain Hans Langsdorff, commander of the ***Graf Spee*, scuttles** his ship rather than **fight a battle** against what he believes to be **superior British forces**.

FEB 16, 1940

In breach of international law, the **British destroyer HMS *Cossack*** enters Norwegian waters and **releases 299 British prisoners** on the German transport ship ***Altmark***.

APR 13, 1940

Royal Navy warships sink eight **German destroyers** in the Narvik fjord, Norway—one of the few Allied successes in the Norwegian campaign.

MAY 10, 1940

The **German armed forces** launch their great **offensive in the west**, spearheaded by 10 mechanized divisions of the German army.

During its first two years, World War II was not a global conflict. To many historians, it was a continuation of World War I, the culmination of the 19th-century "struggle for mastery of Europe." In this phase of the war, Germany was in the ascendant, with the Allies, led by Britain and France, suffering repeated political and military setbacks.

Early days

On September 1, 1939, Hitler invaded Poland, and Britain and France declared war on Germany. The speed of Hitler's conquest of Poland caught the world by surprise. In less than a month, the Polish army had been destroyed and, under the terms of the Nazi-Soviet pact signed in August, Poland was divided between Germany and the USSR. After the fall of Poland there was an extended lull in military activity, popularly known as the Phony War. France and Britain took up positions along the Franco-German border but remained on the defensive.

During this period, the opposing armies were stationed in their trenches in a manner reminiscent of the 1914–1918 conflict. In the air, activity was restricted to occasional bombing forays and the mass dropping of propaganda leaflets. Only at sea was the war conducted in earnest. The British Royal Navy rounded up and destroyed German naval and merchant vessels while the German Kriegsmarine launched a U-boat campaign against British shipping.

Under the terms of its secret agreements with Nazi Germany, the USSR not only gained dominion over eastern Poland but also over the Baltic states of Estonia, Latvia, and Lithuania. Stalin also wanted Finland to cede territory close to Leningrad (St. Petersburg). When this was refused, the USSR invaded Finland. In the war that followed, the USSR achieved victory before the Allies could deploy help for Finland.

In April 1940, German forces seized Denmark and then invaded Norway. Although the British and French sent troops to support the Norwegians, they were unable to prevent the German conquest.

Continental Europe falls

While the fighting in Norway was still ongoing, Hitler launched his great offensive in the west. On May 10, 1940, German troops swept into Holland and Belgium. Unprepared for mobile warfare, the

JUN 4, 1940

Allied forces **complete the evacuation** of more than 300,000 troops **from Dunkirk**.

JUN 10, 1940

Mussolini declares war on France and Britain. Ten days later, his forces are repelled by French troops on the Franco-Italian border.

JUN 22, 1940

The **French surrender**. North and west France come under direct German rule; the remainder is ruled by a **puppet government** set up in the town of **Vichy**.

JUL 19, 1940

In a **speech to the Reichstag**, Hitler issues his "final appeal to common sense," **urging Britain to make peace**. The appeal is rejected three days later.

SEP 15, 1940

The **Luftwaffe** makes a final large-scale **effort** to **defeat the RAF** in the **Battle of Britain**.

NOV 14, 1940

The British city of **Coventry** suffers a devastating **bombing attack by the Luftwaffe**. Factories and historic buildings are destroyed.

DEC 3, 1940

Britain announces that it has placed a **first order with US shipyards** for the construction of 60 merchant vessels.

JAN 1941

In one month alone, the **Allies lose 76 ships** totaling 320,000 tons, mainly as a result of **U-boat action**.

Dutch were soon overwhelmed and forced to accept surrender terms. Meanwhile, Germany's armored (Panzer) divisions threaded their way through the Ardennes in Belgium to smash the French defenses on the Meuse River. From there, they headed to the English Channel, where they established a corridor that cut the Allied armies in two.

Outflanked and facing disaster, the British fell back toward the port of Dunkirk to prepare for evacuation, leaving the French in an increasingly desperate position, exacerbated by the surrender of the Belgians on May 28.

The Germans now turned south to deal with the remainder of the French army, which was attempting to establish a new line to protect Paris and the French interior. On June 5, the Germans sliced through the French defenses: Paris fell on the 14th, and on the 22nd, Marshal Philippe Pétain, the newly installed French prime minister, signed an armistice with the Germans. Within the space of six weeks, Hitler had defeated France and forced the British Army to retreat to England.

Attacks on Britain

Hitler assumed Britain would reach terms with Germany. When his offers of peace were rebuffed, he told his generals to prepare to invade Britain. Their first priority was to gain air supremacy over southern England.

Between July and September 1940, Britain's Royal Air Force engaged and defeated the Luftwaffe in a series of aerial engagements called the Battle of Britain. Without air supremacy, Hitler's invasion plan was abandoned, and the Luftwaffe redirected its aircraft to the wholesale bombing of London and other British cities. The ensuing campaign—dubbed the "Blitz"—lasted until April 1941. Although it caused heavy casualties to Britain's civilian population, it did not change the overall strategic situation: Britain remained safe from the threat of German invasion.

The failure to knock Britain out of the war would come back to haunt Hitler, but at the time he could take consolation in a series of stunning victories that made him master of continental Europe. The extent of his power stretched from the English Channel to the Soviet border. And it was the USSR that would become his next target. ■

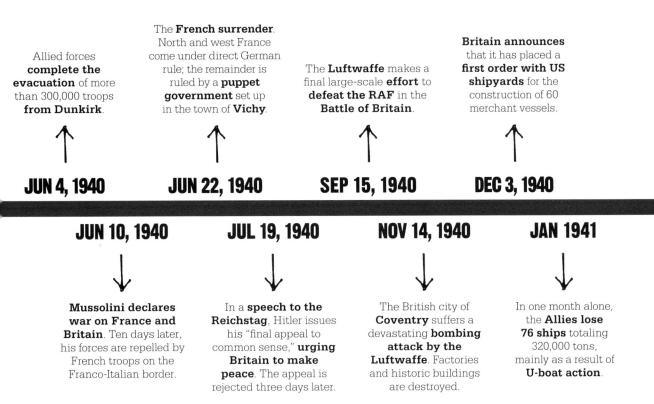

A TURNING POINT IN THE HISTORY OF EUROPE

EUROPE ON THE BRINK (1939)

IN CONTEXT

FOCUS
Diplomatic alliances

BEFORE
1935 Germany and Britain sign the Anglo-German Naval Agreement, determining the relative size of their navies. It allows Germany to exceed the tonnage specified in the Treaty of Versailles.

1936 After China and the USSR sign a nonaggression pact, Germany and Japan negotiate the Anti-Comintern Pact—an agreement to work against communism.

1937 Italy joins the Anti-Comintern Pact.

AFTER
1940 Germany, Italy, and Japan sign the Tripartite Pact, pledging mutual support.

1941 Hitler launches Operation Barbarossa, the invasion of Soviet territories, marking the end of the Nazi-Soviet nonaggression pact.

Hitler wants to **invade Poland**, but knows that the **USSR will intervene**.

Germany and the USSR sign a **nonaggression pact**, which agrees to their **mutual division of Poland**.

After Hitler invades Czechoslovakia, Britain and France **abandon their policy of appeasing** Germany.

Britain and France pledge that the **western powers will defend Poland** if it is attacked.

Germany is now free to attack Poland, while Britain and France are compelled to defend it.

Mirroring the buildup to war in 1914, the European states of 1939 scrambled to form alliances. Riven by rivalries and mutual fear, they needed to know who would intervene in any dispute and whose support could be relied upon in the event of an attack.

The Munich Agreement of September 1938, a settlement reached by Britain, France, and Italy to appease Germany, accepting its annexation of the Sudetenland in Czechoslovakia, unleashed paranoia in the USSR, which had been left out of the agreement and believed that Britain and France were encouraging Nazi Germany to head east. Yet on March 15, 1939, within six months of the settlement, Nazi Germany had invaded the rest of Czechoslovakia, breaking the

See also: German expansion 46–47 ▪ Appeasing Hitler 51 ▪ The destruction of Poland 58–63 ▪ The invasion of Denmark and Norway 69 ▪ The fall of France 80–87 ▪ The end of US neutrality 108 ▪ Operation Barbarossa 124–131

Joachim von Ribbentrop

Born to a military family in Prussia in 1893, Joachim von Ribbentrop served on both the Eastern and Western Fronts during World War I. After the war, he became a wine trader and married a wealthy heiress.

A meeting with Hitler in 1932 led him to join the National Socialist Party. Within a year, he had become an SS colonel and a member of the Reichstag.

By 1934, Ribbentrop was Hitler's chief agent abroad, negotiating with Britain, France, Italy, China, and Japan, and became Germany's foreign minister in 1938. He led the negotiations that produced the Munich Agreement that year and the Nazi-Soviet nonaggression pact of 1939, which paved the way for the invasion of Poland. Ribbentrop remained as foreign minister throughout World War II, but his influence had declined by late 1944, by which time Hitler relied more on his Nazi allies than his cabinet.

After the war, Ribbentrop was tried for war crimes, crimes against peace, crimes against humanity, and conspiracy. Found guilty, he was hanged in 1946.

Munich Agreement. In an attempt to block Hitler from then making aggressive moves on Poland, Britain and France pledged at the end of March to guarantee Poland's security and independence. By the end of May, Germany had signed the Pact of Steel with Italy, pledging mutual military support.

A secret pact

Hitler did not wish to have a war on two fronts, as had happened in World War I. He realized that to avoid this, while still gaining land to the east, he needed to swallow his hatred of communism and make an alliance with Stalin. He knew the USSR would act if he tried to occupy Poland—a step that would make Germany and the USSR neighbors. He also knew that he had to outfox British and French attempts to align the USSR against Germany.

In August 1939, German foreign minister Joachim von Ribbentrop flew to Moscow to meet Stalin and Soviet foreign minister Vyacheslav Molotov to form an alliance, known as the Molotov-Ribbentrop Pact. Hitler proposed that the pact should last 100 years; Stalin agreed to 10. It stipulated that neither country would aid any third party that attacked either signatory, thus neutralizing an existing USSR defense pact with France. It also contained a secret protocol that specified the signatories' respective spheres of influence in eastern Europe after Hitler had conquered Poland. The USSR would acquire the eastern half of Poland, along with Lithuania, Estonia, and Latvia. The pact gave Hitler the green light to attack Poland. Britain and France, knowing the Nazi-Soviet agreement was pending, reacted by formalizing their pledge to Poland, declaring each would fight in Poland's defense if it were attacked. ■

Joseph Stalin (right) toasts the signing of the Nazi-Soviet nonaggression pact with Soviet foreign minister Vyacheslav Molotov (on Stalin's immediate right) and German photographer Heinrich Hoffmann (left) in August 1939.

THEY WILL NEVER EMERGE FROM THE GERMAN EMBRACE

THE DESTRUCTION OF POLAND (SEPTEMBER 1939)

IN CONTEXT

FOCUS
Invasion of Poland

BEFORE
1918 Republic of Poland is established, with the Polish Corridor—providing access to the Baltic Sea—separating East Prussia from Germany.

March 31, 1939 Britain pledges its full support for Polish independence.

August 23, 1939 Nazi–Soviet (Ribbentrop–Molotov) Pact is concluded in Moscow.

AFTER
Fall 1939 Nazis and Soviets partition Poland, and systematically abuse, exploit, deport, and murder Poles, killing more than 5 million.

April–May 1943 Jews rise up against Nazi oppression in the Warsaw Ghetto.

August–October 1944 The Warsaw Uprising takes place.

1945 Communist puppet regime established in a reconstituted Polish state.

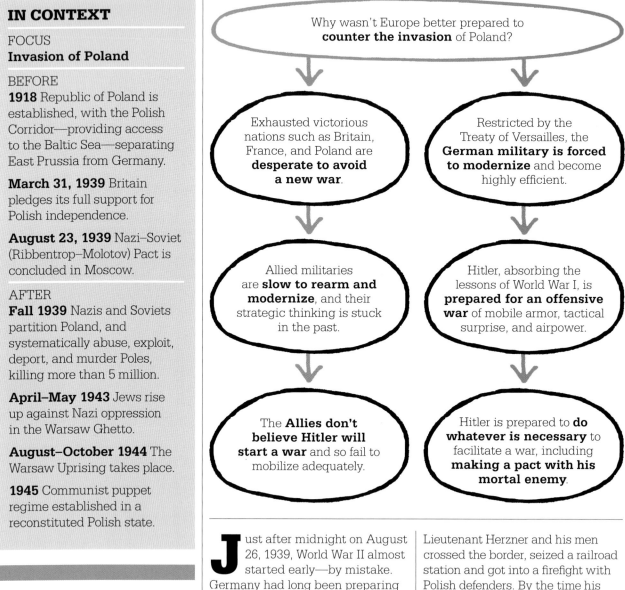

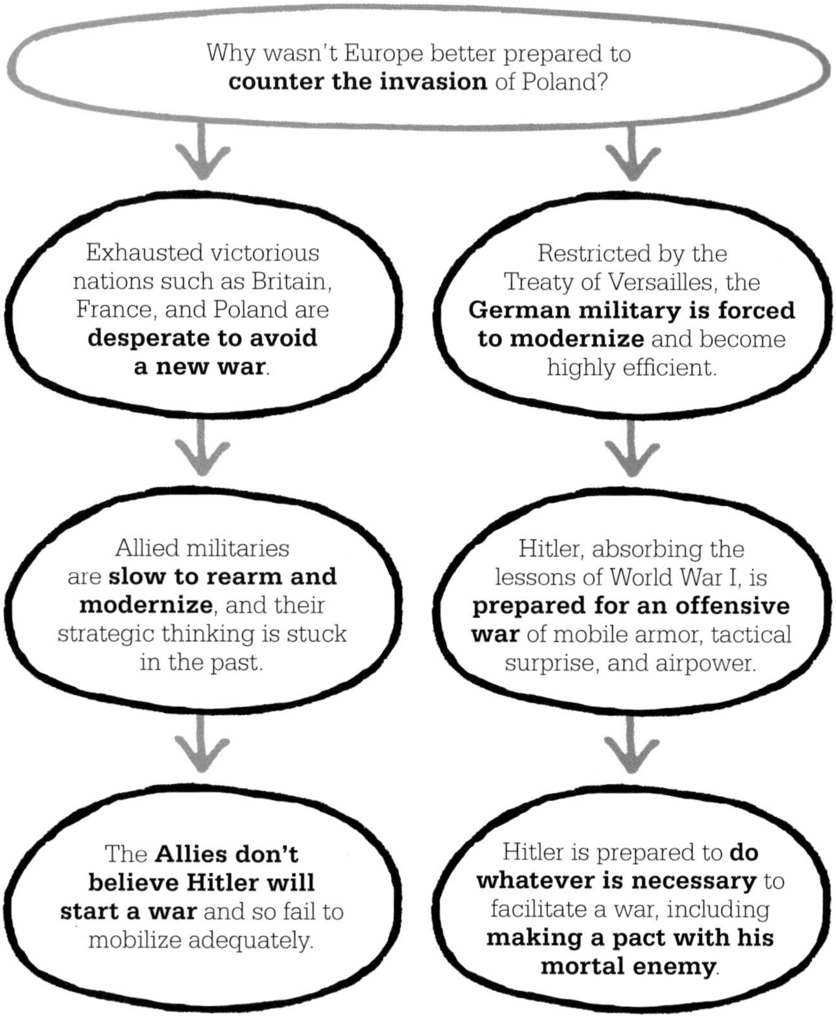

Why wasn't Europe better prepared to counter the invasion of Poland?
Exhausted victorious nations such as Britain, France, and Poland are desperate to avoid a new war.
Allied militaries are slow to rearm and modernize, and their strategic thinking is stuck in the past.
The Allies don't believe Hitler will start a war and so fail to mobilize adequately.
Restricted by the Treaty of Versailles, the German military is forced to modernize and become highly efficient.
Hitler, absorbing the lessons of World War I, is prepared for an offensive war of mobile armor, tactical surprise, and airpower.
Hitler is prepared to do whatever is necessary to facilitate a war, including making a pact with his mortal enemy.

> The victor will not be asked whether he told the truth.
> **Adolf Hitler**

Just after midnight on August 26, 1939, World War II almost started early—by mistake. Germany had long been preparing to invade Poland, and *Fall Weiss* (Plan White) called for small groups of Abwehr (German army intelligence) commandos to infiltrate the border and seize key strategic points. Hitler had set the invasion date for August 26, but called off the attack just hours beforehand when he learned that Mussolini's support was wavering. One Abwehr unit, however, was not informed, and at 12:30 am, Lieutenant Herzner and his men crossed the border, seized a railroad station and got into a firefight with Polish defenders. By the time his superiors contacted Herzner to order him to withdraw, one man on either side had been killed. Returning to German territory, Herzner put in a claim for overnight expenses, on the basis that it was technically still peacetime.

After this false start, which should have given the Poles ample warning of what was about to happen, Hitler received assurances from Mussolini and reset the launch

See also: A flawed peace 20–21 ▪ Dictators and fragile democracies in Europe 34–39 ▪ Europe on the brink 56–57 ▪ The Phony War 64–65 ▪ The Warsaw Ghetto Uprising 242–243 ▪ The Warsaw Uprising 271 ▪ Aftermath 320–327

date for the invasion of Poland, to September 1. The Nazis needed a *casus belli*, and so they thought up Operation Himmler, a ludicrous but cynical propaganda ploy. This involved the Gestapo bringing a prisoner from a German concentration camp to a radio station near the Polish–German border, just outside Gleiwitz, the night before the invasion was scheduled to begin. The prisoner was dressed in a Polish army uniform and shot, with the Nazis promptly claiming that they had thwarted a Polish attack, and would thus be justified in invading Poland in self-defense. The unnamed man was thus arguably the first official casualty of World War II; there would be more than 50 million other deaths in the years that followed.

A quick land grab

At the border, German forces massed to unleash a devastating campaign that would demonstrate to its befuddled enemies that, while they had been preparing to refight the previous war, Hitler and his generals were ready to fight a more modern kind of war. His personal experience of World War I informed Hitler's support for the principles of modern warfare embraced by the German military, under his personal leadership. In particular, these emphasized the importance of tactical surprise and mobile armor. More broadly, Hitler had absorbed another hard-won lesson of World War I: Germany would do well not to go to war on both its Eastern and Western fronts at the same time.

Although he had secured a nonaggression pact with the Soviets—a colossal betrayal of both parties' purported core ideological principles—Hitler knew that he was taking a gamble by invading Poland while France and Britain were supposedly mobilizing on his Western Front. But he trusted that the Wehrmacht's new doctrine of Blitzkrieg ("lightning war") would deliver such a rapid victory that the French and British would simply capitulate as they had done so many times in the previous four years of appeasement. Hitler would have achieved his strategic aim of grabbing large portions of Poland and reuniting Germany with East Prussia. And the Nazis would also have acquired vast new realms—what they called *Lebensraum* ("living space")—across which to pursue their fantasies of racial superiority and Aryan destiny.

> The Polish Army will never emerge from the German embrace.
> **Hermann Göring**
> **Commander-in-chief of the German Luftwaffe**

The Germans had amassed 60 divisions in total, including five Panzer divisions with 1,500 tanks, in addition to other motorized divisions, along with 3,600 aircraft and much of the Kriegsmarine (German Navy). Their invasion strategy was supposedly modeled on the tactics of Hannibal at the ancient Battle of Cannae, with a relatively weak center and strong »

Preparing for attack, civilians dig air-raid trenches to provide shelter from Nazi aircraft. The Polish defenses were hopelessly inadequate, and more than 100,000 civilians died in the invasion.

> Warsaw will be defended to the last breath.
> **Wacław Lipiński**
> **Lieutenant colonel in the Polish army**

wings that would fight hard and move fast, punching through Polish lines of defense, cutting Polish lines of support, and encircling a great mass of defenders. Army Group North, under Colonel-General Fedor von Bock, leading 630,000 men, was tasked with driving through the so-called Polish Corridor (the strip of land separating Germany from East Prussia) to link up with the German Third Army in East Prussia, before turning south to fall on Warsaw. Army Group South, under Colonel-General Gerd von Rundstedt, leading 886,000 men, would strike east all the way to Lviv, and also link up with Bock's forces to take Warsaw.

A bleak choice

Opposing this immense force, the Poles faced a number of challenges. Despite having nearly a million men under arms, they were outnumbered, and on almost every front they were outclassed. They had only light and medium tanks, and only 300 of them. Their navy comprised only four modern destroyers and five submarines. And of their 400 combat-ready aircraft only 36 were modern models capable of matching the Luftwaffe (German Air Force). The Poles had begun to mobilize their reservists, but too late. The Polish commander-in-chief, Marshal Edward Śmigły-Rydz, faced a bleak choice between overextending his forces in an attempt to cover the entire front, or withdrawing behind natural barriers. The latter would mean abandoning key territory, cities, and citizens, so he bravely chose the former—but in so doing, he doomed his army.

Trapping the Poles

At dawn on September 1, Hitler unleashed his Blitzkrieg on Poland. Light and heavy bombers hit Polish airfields, destroying most of the Polish air force and securing air superiority. Stuka dive-bombers with special "screaming" sirens helped drive large numbers of civilians onto the roads, even as railroads, roads, and other strategic targets were hit. The Polish Corridor was cut off within days, and by September 6 the two German army groups had linked up at Łódź in the center of Poland, cutting the country in two and trapping most of the Polish army against the western frontier. Panzer divisions herded the Polish forces into isolated pockets, and shelled and bombed them into submission. By September 8, German tanks had reached the outskirts of Warsaw, and two days later all remaining Polish forces were ordered to fall back to the east, and await relief from a major Franco–British offensive on Germany's Western Front—an offensive that never came.

A popular myth about the Poles, spread by German and Italian propaganda, was that Polish cavalry engaged in futile charges with lances and sabres against tanks. While it is true that the Poles had cavalry regiments, these were only used (with some success) against infantry, and they never charged tanks. Yet there was great truth to the observation by Major-General Friedrich von Mellenthin, a German intelligence chief during the Polish campaign, that "All the dash and bravery which the Poles frequently displayed could not compensate for a lack of modern arms and serious tactical training."

German Stuka dive-bombers in action. Among the explosives they dropped on Poland were fragmentation bombs, which caused appalling injuries to troops and civilians.

A Polish antiaircraft unit takes aim at German bombers during the Siege of Warsaw. On September 10 (Bloody Sunday), there were 17 consecutive raids over the city.

The German war machine was too modern, too efficient, too powerful, and too well managed for the Poles, just as it would later prove too much for more powerful foes.

A policy of terror

By September 15, Warsaw was surrounded by German forces, and on September 17 the Soviets invaded from the east. Besieged on all sides, and with no hope of relief, Warsaw was hammered continuously for 18 days with shells and bombs, and eventually capitulated on September 27. In four weeks, 8,082 Germans were killed and 27,278 wounded, against Polish losses of 70,000 soldiers and 25,000 civilians killed, and 130,000 soldiers wounded. On October 5, Hitler entered Warsaw in triumph.

The Germans took 693,000 Polish troops prisoner, while the Soviets captured 217,000 (their security forces rounded up a further 100,000 targets and shipped them off to concentration camps, where almost none survived). German and Soviet leaders quickly agreed on partition of the captured territory, and the Soviets began to round up and massacre thousands of Poles. Even worse horrors were being perpetrated in areas the Germans had captured, because their plan was to cleanse the westernmost parts of Poland of ethnic Slavs and, especially, Jews to clear the way for ethnic German colonization. The eastern part of their captured territory was used as a labor colony and repository for deported populations. The Germans, led by *SS Totenkopf* ("Death's Head") regiments, instituted a policy of *Schrecklichkeit* ("frightfulness"), that would eventually help achieve the annihilation of more than 17 percent of the Polish population. Jews across the territory were herded into ghettos, the largest of which would be in Warsaw, where half a million people were concentrated, mainly so that they could later be murdered.

Around 95,000 Polish soldiers and airmen managed to escape both the Germans and the Russians, passing into Lithuania, Hungary, and Romania. Many of the escaped soldiers eventually made their way west and joined the Free Polish forces in exile, under General Władysław Sikorski, who set up a government in exile, initially in Angers in France. ■

The Katyn massacre

Some 15,000 officers among the Polish prisoners of war taken by the Red Army were separated from their men and sent to special camps run by the Soviet secret police, the NKVD. In April and early May 1940, more than 4,000 of them were taken to the Katyn forest, near Smolensk, and shot in the back of the head.

The chief executioner of the NKVD, Vasily Blokhin, led the murder squad. Dressed in leather overalls, apron, and gloves to protect his uniform, he used a German-made pistol that would not jam through overheating. Nearly 22,000 Polish soldiers were murdered by the Soviets at Katyn and other sites, but when the Germans announced the discovery of the mass grave at Katyn in 1943, the Soviets claimed that the Nazis were responsible. Even after the war, the Allies colluded in maintaining this fiction, which was not finally exploded until the 1990s.

THERE IS A HUSH OVER ALL EUROPE

THE PHONY WAR (SEPTEMBER 3, 1939–APRIL 1940)

IN CONTEXT

FOCUS
Military tactics

BEFORE
1915 Overwhelming defensive firepower leads to stalemate in the trenches on the Western Front in World War I.

September 1938 At the Munich Peace Conference, France and Britain try to appease Hitler by agreeing to his claims on Sudetenland in Czechoslovakia.

AFTER
June 1944 In the Battle of Normandy, German troops flood fields and employ successive lines of defense to slow the Allied attack.

1947–1951 During the Cold War, the US and its Allies intervene to prevent the spread of communism but do not attack countries that are already communist.

The Phony War refers to the period between September 1939 and April 1940 when Britain and France were officially at war with Germany but there was little or no fighting on land or in the air. After the September invasion of Poland by Germany, the Polish government had pinned all its hopes on a relief operation by its Anglo-French allies, counting on Neville Chamberlain's April guarantee of "all support in the power" of the Allies in the event of an attack. Polish hopes—and Hitler's worst fears—of a powerful invasion across Germany's western borders were dashed, however.

Defense was the Allies' strategy; any action was limited. British planes bombed a German naval base on September 4, and on September 6,

A train carries soldiers of the British Expeditionary Force to the front in early 1940. The force began moving to France on September 4, 1939, joining the French on the northeastern front.

See also: The destruction of Poland 58–63 ▪ Preparations for war 66 ▪ Battle of the River Plate 67 ▪ The Winter War in Finland 68 ▪ The U-boat war intensifies 110–113

> It is ignominious to wage a confetti war against an utterly ruthless enemy.
>
> **General Edward Spears**
> **On the British leaflet campaign**

French troops advanced 5 miles (8km) into Germany's Saarland along a 15-mile (24-km) front. German forces reacted by retreating behind the Siegfried Line—a system of fortifications along their western border—and after five days, the French pulled back. On September 9, Britain's vanguard army, the British Expeditionary Force, crossed into France but did not venture beyond the fortifications and defenses of the French Maginot Line stretching along the country's eastern frontier.

Calm before the storm

For the next eight months the Western Front saw no action. Although French and British forces on the Western Front outnumbered the German divisions by two to one, the Allies spurned what was later recognized as their best chance to mount an effective war. Instead, governed by the assumptions and tactics of World War I, they put their faith in defense. There was a general belief and hope that once Hitler had achieved his strategic aims in Poland he would seek peace with the Allies, something Hitler's own generals pressed him to do. In a speech on October 6, three days before issuing orders to attack northern Allied armies through Belgium, Hitler alluded to seeking peace while also insisting on recognition of German conquests. The Allies rejected these vague overtures.

At the same time, the Allies, who needed time to build up their forces, thought it prudent to avoid antagonizing the Germans. In places on the German border, French troops put up polite signs saying,"Don't shoot please, we won't shoot either!" The British refused to bomb German munitions factories on the basis that they were private property. Instead, they dropped millions of propaganda leaflets on German towns. In the end, however, further German aggression in 1939 was prevented by the onset of a severe winter.

War at sea

While calm prevailed on land and in the air, the war was far from phony at sea; just nine hours after Britain's declaration of war on September 3, a German U-boat submarine torpedoed the British cruise liner SS *Athenia* with the loss of more than 100 people. Over the next month, German U-boats claimed victories against British naval power, including the sinking of aircraft carrier HMS *Courageous* on September 17, and the loss of the battleship HMS *Royal Oak* in the supposedly impregnable harbor of Scapa Flow, in Scotland's Orkney Islands, with the loss of more than 800 crew. The German invasion of Denmark and Norway in April 1940 would finally signal the end of the Phony War on land. ■

The Maginot Line

Named for André Maginot, a French minister of war in the 1930s, the Maginot Line consisted of a series of fortifications along the Franco-German border. It ran from Pontarlier on the Swiss frontier to the borders of Luxembourg and Belgium, although there were also sections in southern France. The line was built in the wake of World War I, with the aim of creating an impenetrable wall.

The northern section of the line was 280 miles (450km) long, and manned by 400,000 troops. Its concrete and steel structure contained a network of passages and living quarters; an underground railroad took troops to their command posts. It was proposed that the line would run all the way to the English Channel, but lack of money—and Belgian objections—curtailed such plans. This made it easy for the Germans to outflank the line. It was later said that the defensive mindset engendered by the Maginot Line undermined French military morale.

The Maginot Line was topped by gun cloches and rotating armored turrets, some of which were retractable.

MEN... STAND FIRM

PREPARATIONS FOR WAR (1939)

IN CONTEXT

FOCUS
Impact on civilians

BEFORE

1935 Denouncing the military restrictions imposed by the Treaty of Versailles, Hitler introduces conscription in Germany.

1937–1938 Britain recruits an Air Raid Wardens Service to enforce a national blackout against bombing raids in the event of war.

AFTER

December 1941 In Britain, the National Service Act requires all unmarried women aged 20–30 and childless widows to register for war work.

January 1943 German women are conscripted for civil duties.

1950 Germany ends rationing.

1954 Britain ends rationing, 14 years after it began.

As Europe's armies awaited battle, civilians on the home front had to prepare for the fast-approaching war. Conscription was reintroduced in all combatant countries. Germany had been conscripting since 1935; Britain started to conscript single men aged 20–22 in May 1939, but widened this to all men aged 18–41 on the day war was declared. At the same time, a "home army" of messengers, ambulance drivers, heavy rescue teams, and firefighters was formed to face the enemy in the event of an attack.

Evacuation and rationing

Plans were also made to evacuate the most vulnerable citizens from urban areas likely to be targeted by bombing. In September 1939, the British government launched Operation Pied Piper to evacuate more than 1.5 million people, 800,000 of whom were children. In France, the government made parents responsible for getting their children to safety with relatives or religious organizations in the countryside.

All combatant nations introduced rationing. Germany rationed food from August 1939, with extra portions given to people considered important to the war effort. Britain, which launched a "Dig for Victory" campaign in October 1939, encouraging people with gardens to grow their own food, introduced rationing in January 1940. Every British family was issued with coupons that had to be surrendered before rationed food (everything other than bread or potatoes) and clothes could be purchased. ■

French conscripts report for duty in Paris in 1939. France extended national service to two years in 1935, in response to a resurgent Germany.

See also: German expansion 46–47 ▪ Appeasing Hitler 51 ▪ Europe on the brink 56–57 ▪ Blitzkrieg 70–75 ▪ Dunkirk 76–79 ▪ The fall of France 80–87

ATTACK AT ONCE, BY DAY OR NIGHT

BATTLE OF THE RIVER PLATE (DECEMBER 1939)

IN CONTEXT

FOCUS
Attacks at sea

BEFORE
June 1935 The Anglo-German Naval Agreement limits the size of the Kriegsmarine (German navy) to 35 percent of the British Royal Navy.

September 1939 German U-boats torpedo British liner SS *Athenia* and aircraft carrier HMS *Courageous*.

October 1939 A British battleship, HMS *Royal Oak*, is torpedoed by a U-boat at Scapa Flow in Orkney, Scotland.

AFTER
February 1940 Hitler orders U-boats to target any vessel, not allied with Germany, sailing toward enemy waters.

1941 U-boats start targeting US shipping on the east coast of the US. They later extend operations into the Caribbean and the Gulf of Mexico.

At the start of the war, Britain's Royal Navy was the strongest navy in the world. The Kriegsmarine (the German navy) was limited by treaty, but the German *Panzerschiff*—compact, heavily armored ships with massive guns, dubbed the "pocket battleship" by Britain—evaded restrictions. Germany's main aim at sea was to disable British merchant shipping and prevent a blockade that would starve the German war effort.

Under fire

The first major naval battle, near the mouth of the Plate River off Argentina in December 1939, involved the *Panzerschiff Admiral Graf Spee*, under Captain Hans Langsdorff. Having already sunk nine ships in the Indian Ocean and South Atlantic, Langsdorff steamed toward a convoy he expected to find off the Plate River, only to run into three British naval vessels that had foreseen his arrival.

On December 13, three British ships, HMS *Ajax*, HMS *Achilles*, and HMS *Exeter*, engaged the *Admiral Graf Spee*, but by focusing his firepower on each in turn, Langsdorff forced them to withdraw and was able to limp into the port of Montevideo in neutral Uruguay, where he was given 72 hours to remain. Ploys by the British, which included fake broadcasts on the BBC, fooled Langsdorff into scuttling his ship because he believed British ships would arrive imminently. The British claimed this outcome as a major, morale-boosting victory; Langsdorff shot himself a few days later, and his crew were interned in Argentina. ■

The *Admiral Graf Spee* sinks on the orders of Captain Hans Langsdorff, who decided to scuttle the vessel rather than let his crew fight a losing battle.

See also: A flawed peace 20–21 ▪ The sinking of the *Bismarck* 109 ▪ The U-boat war intensifies 110–113 ▪ A showdown in the Atlantic 214–219

THE WOLVES WILL EAT WELL THIS WINTER

THE WINTER WAR IN FINLAND (NOVEMBER 30, 1939–MARCH 13, 1940)

IN CONTEXT

FOCUS
Military tactics

BEFORE
December 6, 1917 Finland declares its independence from Russia.

August 23, 1939 The Molotov–Ribbentrop Pact between the Nazis and Soviets is concluded in Moscow, allocating Finland and the Baltic states to the USSR.

AFTER
June 26, 1941 Finland allies with Germany and starts the Continuation War, retaking lost territory and occupying parts of the USSR.

June 1944 A Soviet offensive drives back the Finns on the Karelian Isthmus.

September 19, 1944 Finland and the USSR sign an armistice, ending war between the two nations.

The Winter War of 1939–1940 pitted Finland against the USSR. The Molotov–Ribbentrop Pact had allotted the northern Baltic region to Stalin's sphere of influence, but his territorial demands on the Finns were rejected. On November 30, 1939, Soviet forces numbering 1.2 million men invaded Finland at four points. Very heavily outnumbered and with scant and mostly obsolete equipment, the Finns seemed doomed. However, smart tactics, Soviet incompetence, and harsh conditions enabled them to mount a ferocious resistance.

Poorly led Soviets

Stalin's purges, which had seen 43,000 officers killed or imprisoned, including the majority of the army's high command, meant that the Soviet military was poorly led. Initially, their tanks were not supported by infantry, allowing the tank-less Finns to successfully hunt them using just gasoline bombs. And Soviet soldiers, expecting rapid victory, were not equipped for the freezing conditions.

Finnish troops in white winter gear and equipped with skis relentlessly harassed the invaders, securing a string of successes. The Soviets were forced to change their tactics. After mastering combined air, armor, and infantry tactics, they pushed back the exhausted Finns. By March 1940, with international support slow to materialize, Finland was compelled to negotiate, giving away much territory. But its animosity toward the Soviets would lead it to join the Nazi invasion of the USSR the following year. ■

Finnish troops on skis used the harsh winter conditions to their advantage. They fought effectively in deep snow with temperatures sometimes below −40°F/C.

See also: Dictators and fragile democracies in Europe 34–39 ▪ Europe on the brink 56–57 ▪ The destruction of Poland 58–63 ▪ Operation Barbarossa 124–131

GERMAN PLANES BOMBED AND STRAFED US

THE INVASION OF DENMARK AND NORWAY (APRIL 9–JUNE 10, 1940)

IN CONTEXT

FOCUS
Strategic invasions

BEFORE
December 14, 1939 Grand Admiral Erich Raeder urges Hitler to invade Norway.

January 1940 Hitler orders high command to start planning invasion.

February 16, 1940 HMS *Cossack* rescues British prisoners from a German vessel in Norwegian waters, violating Norwegian neutrality.

April 8, 1940 British Navy launches Operation Wilfred, which involves laying mines to blockade Norwegian waters.

AFTER
June 10, 1940 Norway surrenders to Germany.

February 1942 Nazis appoint Vidkun Quisling minister-president of Norway.

Germany had been eyeing an invasion of Norway since the start of the war, hoping to safeguard the route for vital imports of Swedish iron ore and secure strategically important new bases for U-boat operations. For the same reasons, the Allies were planning their own invasion of Norway, and British troops were already embarked on transport ships when the Germans launched Operation Weserübung ("Weser Exercise") on April 9, 1940. Daring German paratroop and naval raids seized vital locations in Norway, while Denmark was swiftly forced to surrender when it became apparent the country was encircled.

Hard lessons

The Allied response was haphazard. A counterinvasion force aimed at taking Trondheim (Norway) was thwarted by German airpower, and Allied troops had to be evacuated. Another attempt, further north at Narvik, was hampered by interservice rivalry between the Royal Navy and British Army.

A Danish Army artillery crew before the German invasion of April 9. The rapid invasion was a prelude to Germany's attack on Norway, which was more valuable strategically.

The disastrous experience taught the Royal Navy hard lessons about the importance of airpower. But the Germans paid a high price for victory, losing many men and aircraft, as well as some of their best warships, which would seriously hamper their chances of invading Britain. They also had to garrison Norway with 350,000 men for the rest of the war, long after their successes elsewhere made obsolete their original strategic aims. ■

See also: The Phony War 64–65 ▪ Blitzkrieg 70–75 ▪ The Battle of Britain 94–97 ▪ Nazi Europe 168–171 ▪ Resistance movements 226–231

IF THE TANKS SUCCEED THEN VICTORY FOLLOWS

BLITZKRIEG (MAY 10–JUNE 4, 1940)

IN CONTEXT

FOCUS
German military ambitions

BEFORE
1905–1906 Field Marshal von Schlieffen develops a strategic plan to achieve German victory against France.

August 1914 The Schlieffen Plan fails, partly due to the limitations of mobile warfare at the time.

September 1939 The German military hones its execution of rapidly advancing armor with close air support in the invasion of Poland.

AFTER
May 26–June 4, 1940 Allied troops are evacuated from Dunkirk to England.

June 5, 1940 German forces begin their offensive from the Somme south into France.

June 22, 1940 France surrenders to Germany.

Long planned, often delayed, and widely expected, the German attack on the Western Front nonetheless managed to surprise the Allies with its speed and devastating effectiveness—a style of warfare that came to be known as Blitzkrieg ("lightning war"). Hitler's generals had prepared an updated version of the German World War I strategy known as the Schlieffen Plan, code-named *Fall Gelb* ("Plan Yellow"). This called for a strong right flank that would sweep through Belgium and northern France, while a weaker left flank engaged the enemy in the main French border zone, protected by the Maginot Line.

When a copy of these plans accidentally fell into Belgian hands in January 1940, German general Erich von Manstein developed a variation, Operation Sichelschnitt ("Sickle-Slice"). As before, Army Group B in the north would swing through the Low Countries, while Army Group C in the south was much weaker; the difference was that Army Group A in the center was strengthened.

A German motorized division advancing toward Rotterdam in May 1940 prepares to cross a river by raft. The Dutch destroyed many bridges to slow the Wehrmacht's advance.

Brilliant plan

According to the Sichelschnitt plan, Group B's strike, expected by the Allies, would see them respond by advancing their main forces northward to the defensive positions known as the Dyle Line. These forces included the French First Army and the British Expeditionary Force (BEF). At that point, Army Group A, under Gerd von Rundstedt, would burst out of the supposedly impassable Ardennes region to strike at what German strategists called the *Schwerpunkt* ("point of maximum effort"). This was the fulcrum in the Allied lines between their strong southern flank and the northern forces. Thus, the Germans would sidestep the Maginot Line and hope to cut off the Allied forces in the north. A follow-up plan, *Fall Rot* ("Plan Red"), would then be executed to reduce the rest of the French forces.

> You hit somebody with your fist and not with your fingers spread.
> **Heinz Guderian**
> **German army general**

See also: The destruction of Poland 58–63 ■ Dunkirk 76–79 ■ The fall of France 80–87 ■ War in the Balkans 114–117 ■ Operation Barbarossa 124–131 ■ The D-Day landings 256–263

It was a brilliant plan that depended on flawless execution of what would later be understood as a new doctrine of warfare (see box), and which would bring stunning success despite the Germans being outnumbered in terms of both men and tanks. Facing a total of 144 French, British, Belgian, and Dutch divisions, the Germans had 136 divisions. The French had 3,000 tanks, while the Panzer divisions had only 2,700, but unlike the French the Panzers were heavily concentrated to deliver devastating blows. The Germans had embraced the possibilities of tank warfare, while the French were mired in the defensive mindset of World War I. Marshal Philippe Pétain insisted as late as 1939 that "tanks do not change the tenets of war."

The Germans had at least parity in terms of airpower. Unlike the Allies, they had dive-bombers and knew how to use them in close support of ground forces. Also, their edge in fighter technology worried the Allies. Crucially, German Messerschmitts were faster than any Allied planes. A 1937 French senate defense committee report had warned: "The German air force is in a position to fly over France with complete impunity."

Formidable assault

Operation Sichelschnitt was launched early on the morning of May 10, 1940, and everything went according to plan for the Germans. Army Group B made what German Panzer general and later military historian Friedrich von Mellenthin described as a "formidable, noisy, and spectacular" assault on Belgium and the Netherlands, and the Allies responded as predicted, advancing to the Dyle Line. "The more they committed themselves to this sector," Mellenthin observed, "the more certain would be their ruin."

On May 13, with perfect timing, the spearpoint of Army Group A, the Panzer Group under Paul von Kleist, which included Heinz Guderian's XIX Panzer Corps, delivered the *Schwerpunkt* against French forces at Sedan, a massive fortress with tremendous historical significance but lacking effective modern defenses. The French were unable to cope with the combination of concentrated armor, close air support, and operational initiative displayed by the Germans. One Panzer commander said: "Time and »

No such thing as Blitzkrieg?

The Germans did not initially call their new attack doctrine Blitzkrieg. Paratroop general Kurt Student said, "there was never any such thing as a Blitzkrieg," and Hitler himself derided the term. In truth, it was not really a new doctrine but an evolution of existing German military traditions combined with the application of new technology.

Blitzkrieg owed much to the writings of 19th-century military strategists Carl von Clausewitz and Alfred von Schlieffen. Clausewitz proposed the concept of *Schwerpunkt* in *On War* (1832). Its core principle is that the major force of an attack should be concentrated at points of weakness in the enemy's defense, rather than being evenly spread. It also requires every active unit to have a clear set of objectives. Schlieffen developed this idea prior to World War I, but it only became workable with the development of fast aircraft and tanks.

Blitzkrieg tactics

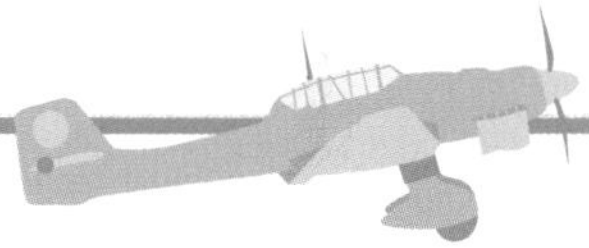

A surprise aerial assault with dive-bombers and supporting fighter planes takes out military and air bases, destroying enemy aircraft before they have any chance of getting airborne.

With air dominance achieved, tanks smash their way into enemy territory to seize rail lines and communication hubs; terrify the local civilian population; and establish control of key strategic centers.

Motorized infantry—transported in trucks—follow in the wake of the tank advance to drive out any remaining opposition and consolidate control of strategic points such as bridges, fortified buildings, and roads.

> This was no war of occupation, but a war of quick penetration and obliteration—Blitzkrieg, Lightning War.
> **Anonymous**
> ***Time* magazine, 1939**

again the rapid movements and flexible handling of our Panzers bewildered the enemy."

The Panzer divisions pierced the Allied lines and raced through. Guderian famously called out "*Fahrkarte bis zur Endstation!*" ("To the end of the line!") to his Panzer commanders as they passed by, heading toward the coast to cut off the Allied forces in Belgium. British military strategist and writer Liddell Hart called this "a deep strategic penetration by independent armored forces—a long-range tank-drive to cut the main arteries of the opposing army far back behind its front."

Forcing the advantage

Ignoring increasingly angry orders to hold back and wait for support, Guderian—known as "Hurry-Up Heinz" for his devotion to mobility—drove home his advantage, reaching Abbeville near the English Channel on May 20. His progress that day epitomized the Blitzkrieg in miniature. At 7 am, two of his tank divisions left Péronne, heading west. By 10 am, they had reached Albert, where a small troop of British soldiers vainly tried to stop them from behind a barricade of cardboard boxes. At 11 am, at Hédauville, the tanks encountered a British artillery battery, which was armed only with dummy shells. At noon, they entered Amiens, where Guderian paused briefly to view the cathedral, and by 4 pm they had taken Beauquesne, where they seized the map archive of the BEF. They reached Abbeville—the "end of the line"—at 9 pm. Nearby, on the shores of the English Channel, they pointed their guns at England.

Encirclement

By this time, the Dutch had already surrendered. Horrified by the destruction rained on Rotterdam by the Luftwaffe, they capitulated on May 15. Fear of air strikes drove between 6 and 10 million refugees out of their homes across northern France and Belgium, clogging roads and further impeding the Allied response.

On May 18, French prime minister Paul Reynaud reshuffled both his government and his military command, making World War I hero Marshal Philippe Pétain vice-premier. That same day, a tank division led by Charles de Gaulle, about to become the youngest general in the French army, attempted a spirited counterattack on German forces at Laon, and on May 21, British forces tried to break the German lines near Arras. Both attempts failed, the latter assault

Belgian refugees flee their homes, hoping to find safety in France. As many as 2 million fled, and while most later returned, others stayed in France and some reached the UK.

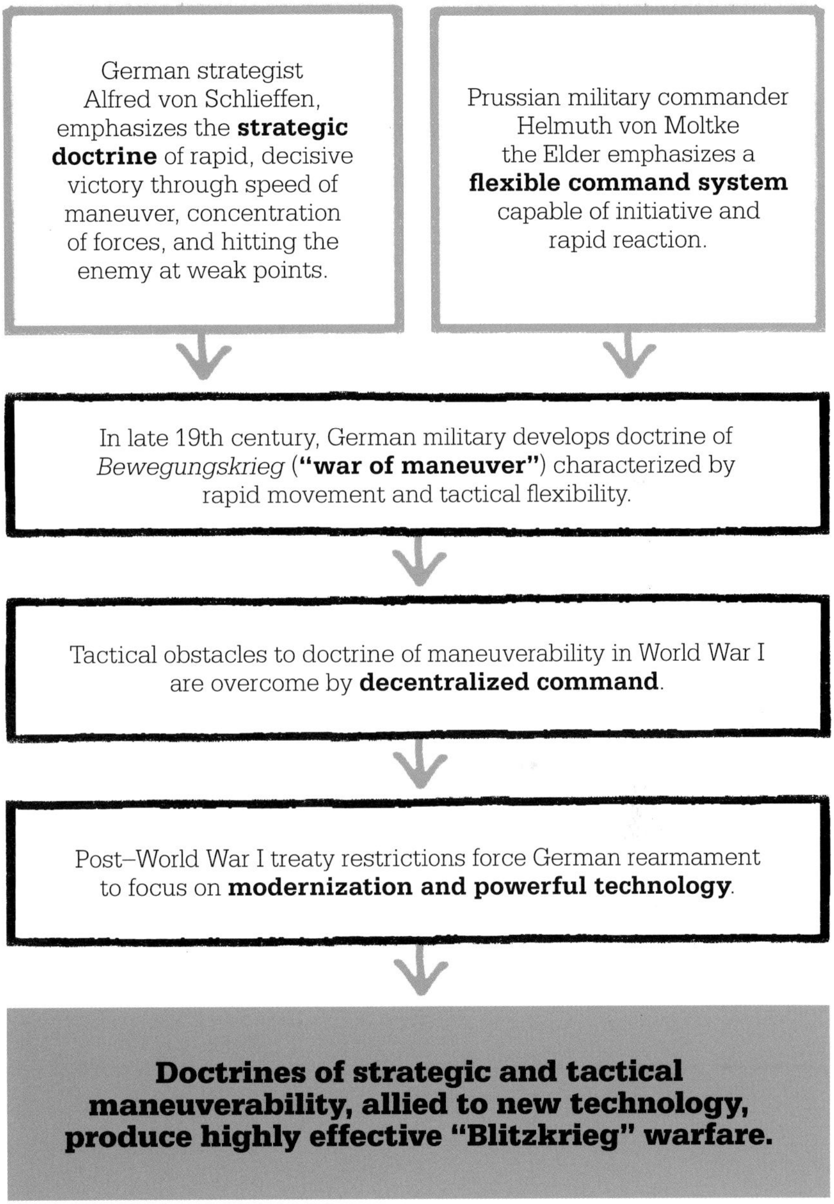

beaten back by troops under Erwin Rommel. German armor acted in concert to overpower Allied efforts, whereas Allied armor was too widely stretched to be effective.

German strategist Alfred von Schlieffen, emphasizes the **strategic doctrine** of rapid, decisive victory through speed of maneuver, concentration of forces, and hitting the enemy at weak points.
Prussian military commander Helmuth von Moltke the Elder emphasizes a **flexible command system** capable of initiative and rapid reaction.
In late 19th century, German military develops doctrine of *Bewegungskrieg* (**"war of maneuver"**) characterized by rapid movement and tactical flexibility.
Tactical obstacles to doctrine of maneuverability in World War I are overcome by **decentralized command**.
Post–World War I treaty restrictions force German rearmament to focus on **modernization and powerful technology**.
Doctrines of strategic and tactical maneuverability, allied to new technology, produce highly effective "Blitzkrieg" warfare.

Unable to break the encirclement and link up with French forces to the south, the BEF and French First Army fell back toward Dunkirk, as the Germans advanced relentlessly. On May 22, the RAF lost its last airfield in the region. From this time on, all its sorties would have to be launched from England, severely reducing the duration of missions and thus limiting its ability to contend with the Luftwaffe. On May 24, German Army Groups A and B joined forces to bottle up the Allies still further. Kleist's Panzers were then just 18 miles (29 km) from Dunkirk, and he later recollected his tanks cresting the heights overlooking Flanders, from where they could command the approaches to Dunkirk. Hundreds of thousands of Allied troops were trapped in a small pocket around the port, their situation desperate.

The Halt Order

Even as the Germans were poised to deliver the killing blow, an order came from the highest authority telling them to stop. Hitler's infamous Halt Order of May 24 would give the Allies a vital 48 hours' grace in which to organize a colossal evacuation. With the benefit of hindsight, German generals were unsparing in their assessment: "Hitler spoilt the chance of victory," Panzer general Wilhelm von Thoma said after the war, while Kleist later called it "the stupid order of Hitler."

Although history would suggest it was a terrible blunder, there was a rationale for Hitler's decision. Group A commander Rundstedt himself had already called for a halt. He and Hitler both feared that the tanks had far outrun their infantry support and would fall into an Allied trap in the boggy ground around Dunkirk. They also reasoned that strong French forces remained to be dealt with elsewhere. Meanwhile, Hermann Göring had promised that the Luftwaffe would wipe out the Dunkirk pocket. And Hitler and many others were convinced that the British would simply give up the war. They were more concerned with the French, and were intent upon defeating their old enemy. Consequently, their attention next turned to *Fall Rot*, the plan to conquer France. ■

A MIRACLE OF DELIVERANCE

DUNKIRK (MAY 26–JUNE 4, 1940)

IN CONTEXT

FOCUS
Troop evacuation

BEFORE
September 4, 1939 The British Expeditionary Force (BEF) begins to arrive in northern France.

May 10, 1940 The Battle of France begins as German troops invade France and the Low Countries.

May 20, 1940 German forces reach the Channel coast; the BEF is cut off in Flanders.

AFTER
June 5, 1940 German forces begin an offensive southward from the Somme.

June 22, 1940 France surrenders.

June 6, 1944 Allied forces return to continental Europe in the D-Day landings.

Between May 26 and June 4, 1940, more than 340,000 Allied troops were evacuated from the beaches of Dunkirk, France. This hugely successful operation had consequences both for Britain's ability to continue to prosecute the war and, perhaps more importantly, for British morale. Churchill would later describe Dunkirk as "a miracle of deliverance."

By May 24, the devastating success of the German invasion had bottled up over 400,000 men in a pocket around the port of Dunkirk, but the halt ordered by Hitler gave the Allies two vital days to strengthen defenses around the town and prepare an evacuation

See also: Blitzkrieg 70–75 ▪ The fall of France 80–87 ▪ The Battle of Britain 94–97 ▪ The D-Day landings 256–263

Soldiers line up on the beach at Dunkirk, awaiting evacuation. With no protective cover, they would have been easy targets had the Luftwaffe not been grounded by bad weather.

plan. Led by Vice-Admiral Bertrand Ramsay, Operation Dynamo expected to evacuate 45,000 men at best before the Germans crushed the pocket. Churchill was even less optimistic, later writing that, "I thought … that perhaps 20,000 or 30,000 men might be re-embarked. The whole root and core and brain of the British army … seemed about to perish upon the field, or to be led into ignominious and starving captivity."

Defending Dunkirk

A key element of the success at Dunkirk was the bravery of the forces defending the pocket. The French First Army, with some British forces, dug in and kept up a dogged rearguard action, which could end, at best, only with their capture. They were helped by the boggy nature of the ground around Dunkirk, which prevented the Germans from bringing their Panzers to bear—one of the factors that had convinced Hitler to proceed cautiously in the first place. By May 27, though, General Walther von Brauchitsch, the German commander-in-chief, had persuaded Hitler to allow the advance to proceed. However, Hitler decided that the tanks should be conserved for what he believed to be more important battles, and had them redirected to join the forces massing along the Somme–Aisne line for the imminent offensive against the French.

Now came the first of a series of lucky breaks that were widely interpreted in Britain as miracles. Hitler had assumed, not without reason, that his Luftwaffe would accomplish more easily than his Panzers the destruction of the pocket, but on May 28 a colossal storm broke over Flanders, grounding the German planes. Under cover of the poor visibility and rain, thousands more British »

> Dunkirk … should be regarded as a series of crises. Each crisis was solved, only to be replaced by another …
>
> **Walter Lord**
>
> ***The Miracle of Dunkirk*, 1982**

Winston Churchill

Remembered by some as Britain's greatest prime minister, Winston Spencer Churchill (1874–1965) was often a controversial figure. His youth had been spent in military adventures in Cuba and Africa, and during World War I—as First Lord of the Admiralty—he had overseen the disastrous Gallipoli campaign in southwest Turkey.

As a politician he had changed party more than once, and held most of the major offices of state. He had a high opinion of his own expertise and instincts in military matters, combining fascination with technological advances with genuine concern for the well-being of frontline troops. In the 1930s, he had been in the political wilderness, but his long support for rearmament and opposition to appeasement made him a natural choice when Chamberlain's government fell. On May 10, 1940, the very day that the Germans launched their offensive on Belgium, France, and the Netherlands, he took over as prime minister, recalling that, "I felt as if I were walking with destiny, and that all my past had been but a preparation for this hour and for this trial."

soldiers moved up to the coast without being strafed. On May 30, three days after boasting about how the British would soon be annihilated, General Halder, German chief of the general staff, recorded in his diary: "Bad weather has grounded the Luftwaffe, and now we must stand by and watch countless thousands of the enemy getting away to England …."

Chaotic scenes

A concurrent miracle was that, even as this storm was raging, an unnatural calm settled on the English Channel, facilitating the passage of British ships. Bombing by the Luftwaffe had destroyed the harbor at Dunkirk, so men had to be embarked from the beach, where the gently shelving bottom made it hard to approach. Later, a long jetty projecting from the east of the harbor was pressed into service, making it easier to embark. Initially, however, scenes were chaotic, with soldiers wading into deep water, sailors using oars to beat off men threatening to capsize launches, and officers threatening to shoot unruly, desperate men. At first, the British did not even tell the French they were planning to evacuate, and when the operation began, their policy was not to allow French soldiers to embark (expecting them, instead, to defend the pocket); on at least one occasion French soldiers were fired upon for trying to join the exodus.

The Little Ships

Ferrying away the evacuees was an armada of Royal Navy vessels, but the shallow draught at the beach meant that smaller vessels were needed to transfer men from the shore to the bigger ships. On May 29, boats drawn from the Small Vessels Pool—privately owned power craft less than 100 ft (30 m) long—arrived to help. Further appeals brought more of what would become known as the Little Ships, including fishing boats and pleasure cruisers, hopper barges from London County Council, and tug boats pulling Thames sailing barges, sent by the Port of London. Among the crew of the Little Ships was 66-year-old Charles Herbert Lightoller, who had been second officer on the *Titanic*.

Hitler's **halt order** of May 24 prevents tanks reaching Dunkirk.
The **Flanders storm** of May 28 grounds the Luftwaffe.
Calm weather over the English Channel **allows the passage** of the Little Ships.
Desperate defense of the Allied pocket delays the German advance until June 4.

A vital role was played by the RAF, flying sortie after sortie to try to keep the Luftwaffe at bay. Pilot

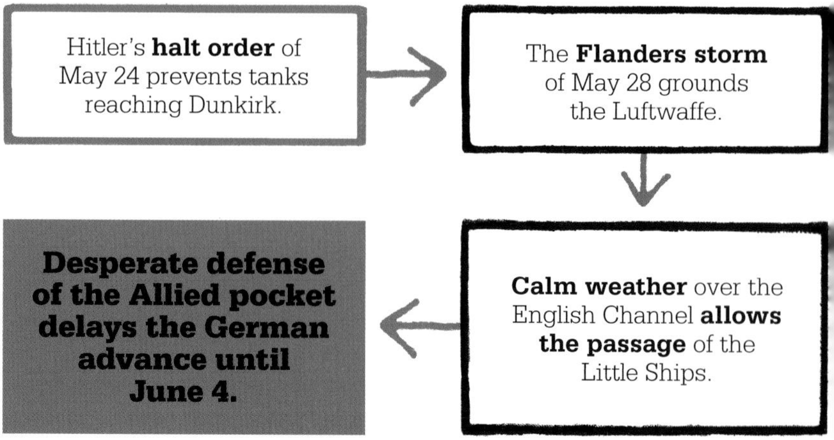

Douglas Bader described the scene from the air: "The sea from Dunkirk to Dover ... was solid with shipping. One felt one could walk across without getting one's feet wet." Bader also described how easy it was to locate Dunkirk "by the huge pall of black smoke rising ... from the oil tanks which were ablaze just inside the harbor". These tanks had been hit by German bombs, but this, too, proved to be a stroke of luck, since the smoke gave vital cover to the Allies. On May 31 alone, 68,000 men were evacuated.

Rising to the occasion

With few defenses of their own, however, the evacuation fleet was extremely vulnerable. A break in the weather on June 1 enabled the Luftwaffe to sink three destroyers and a passenger ship and badly damage four others. Vice-Admiral Ramsay banned daylight sailings, but evacuations continued by night. The last British warship was withdrawn at dawn on June 2, and the remaining troops of the BEF were evacuated by ferry. That night, ships returned to pick up French troops but were unable to complete their mission and were forced to try again the following night, when they managed to evacuate 27,000—even as the Germans closed in.

On June 4, Churchill told the House of Commons how "335,000 men had been carried out of the jaws of death." In fact, around 25,000 noncombatant British personnel had already been evacuated before Operation Dynamo, and the official count for Dynamo is usually given as 340,000 (220,000 British and 120,000 French), along with 34,000 vehicles and 170 dogs (regimental mascots). Another 220,000 Allied troops were rescued from other French ports, including Cherbourg, Saint-Malo, Brest, and Saint-Nazaire, bringing the total number evacuated to 558,000. In the UK, Sunday June 9, 1940, was made a Day of National Thanksgiving. The Dunkirk evacuation boosted national morale, as well as preserving much of the British Army. It has been seen as a turning point in the war. ■

> "The beach, black with men, illumined by the fires, seemed a perfect target."
>
> **Arthur Devine**
> **Little Ship crew member**

Scores of troops crowd on a rescue ship. Larger vessels picked up soldiers from the East Mole, a jetty that ran into deeper water. Only smaller boats could approach the gently shelving beach.

CRUSHED BY THE FORCES HURLED AGAINST US

THE FALL OF FRANCE (JUNE 5–22, 1940)

IN CONTEXT

FOCUS
Surrender of France

BEFORE
1923 French and Belgian troops occupy Germany's industrial Ruhr area to exact unpaid World War I reparations.

September 3, 1939 Two days after Germany's invasion of Poland, France and Britain declare war on Germany.

May 1940 German forces advance from Belgium into France and reach the English Channel, compelling British troops to evacuate at Dunkirk.

AFTER
July 19, 1940 Hitler promotes 12 generals to the rank of field marshal to reward them for their victory over France.

November 1942 Germany occupies Vichy France.

June 6, 1944 Allied troops land in Normandy on D-Day.

On May 9, the eve of the German offensive in western Europe, Hitler had promised his general staff, "Gentlemen, you are about to witness the most famous victory in history." By June 4, with the British chased off the Continent and the French in disarray, this prediction was well on the way to coming true. The Germans now turned their attention to *Fall Rot* ("Plan Red"), their scheme for taking over the rest of France, especially the French forces massed redundantly along the Maginot Line, France's fortified eastern border.

Antitank fortifications mark the Maginot Line, built by France in the 1930s along its eastern border and designed to be an impenetrable barrier against invasion by German forces.

French commander-in-chief Maxime Weygand had drawn up 49 divisions along the Somme and Aisne rivers in northeast France—the so-called Weygand Line—but his nation's situation was precarious. The British Expeditionary Force (BEF) had fled, leaving only a handful of British forces still in France. The French had lost 22 of their 71 field divisions, 6 of 7 motorized divisions, and 8 of 20 armored divisions. Some 17 divisions were pinned down along the Maginot Line. As Hitler had planned, the French army's reserves had all been committed to the Low Countries in the wake of Germany's sweep across the Netherlands, Belgium, and Luxembourg. The British Royal Air Force (RAF) refused to send more planes; the Advanced Air Striking Force they had sent earlier had lost Hurricanes at the rate of 25 a day, when the factories making them could only produce four or five daily. RAF chiefs knew that all available planes would be needed for the inevitable Battle of Britain. The French troops along the Weygand Line were outmatched, and it took forces under Rommel just two days to break through near Rouen. On June 9 the Germans crossed the Seine and the Aisne; France was now at their mercy.

The exodus

On June 10, the day that Italy declared war on France and Britain, the French government fled to Bordeaux, declaring Paris to be an open, non-militarized city, in an

> Morale was a question of faith … How could these people have faith in the leaders who had abandoned them?
>
> **Virginia Cowles**
> **American journalist describing the exodus**

See also: The Great War 18–19 ▪ Blitzkrieg 70–75 ▪ Dunkirk 76–79 ▪ Italy enters the war 88–89 ▪ Colonial ties 90–93 ▪ Nazi Europe 168–171 ▪ The D-Day landings 256–263

attempt to spare it from destruction. Of the roughly five million Parisians, three million fled, joining millions more crowding the roads in what became known as *l'exode* ("the exodus"), amid horrifying scenes. Nurses administered euthanizing injections to patients who could not be moved. Babies were abandoned. Looting, by refugees and soldiers, was widespread. On June 12, a Swiss journalist encountered a herd of cattle wandering through the empty streets of Paris. There were similar scenes elsewhere. The Nazi official Albert Speer, arriving in Rheims on June 26, described untouched meals on tables laid with glasses, plates, and cutlery—"as though the lives of the townspeople had, for one mad moment, stood still." In the Loire Valley, a French tank commander preparing to defend a river crossing was killed by locals desperate to prevent their town being caught up in a battle.

An unlikely union

On June 11, as German forces advanced at speed, French and British leaders had convened a meeting of the Supreme War Council. Churchill and his war minister, Anthony Eden, flew to Briare, south of Paris, to join French prime minister Paul Reynaud, his new vice premier, Marshal Philippe Pétain, and Weygand. British liaison officer, Major-General Edward Spears later recalled the ashen faces of the French ministers present and their evident defeatism. Only the young General Charles de Gaulle, recently made a junior war minister, showed any fighting spirit, backing Churchill who was working desperately to persuade France to stay in the war. A few days later, de Gaulle also endorsed a radical proposal for a Franco-British union. The policy institute Chatham House had earlier drafted an "Act of Perpetual Association between the United Kingdom and France," which the Foreign Office had given serious consideration from March 1940. French diplomat Jean Monnet, head of the Anglo-French Coordination Committee drew up the offer of "indissoluble union," which the British Cabinet approved on June 16. Although Churchill was skeptical, with his blessing, de Gaulle telephoned a delighted Reynaud that afternoon. The plan was short-lived, however. The French Council of Ministers rejected it, fearing a British plot to dominate France. Pétain, who now felt that only capitulation and an armistice with Germany could save France, declared that the union would be "fusion with a corpse." Churchill, later called the proposal's rejection "the narrowest escape »

French civilians flee Paris as the Germans advance toward the city. Vehicles often broke down or ran out of gas, clogging roads and forcing their occupants to escape on foot.

German troops on motorcycles study road maps of France as they pour into the country in the summer of 1940, frequently looting and commandeering homes that the French had fled.

we'd had," noting how much the union would have hamstrung Britain in the later years of the war.

Inevitable collapse

Churchill's hopes that France could somehow hold on until 1941, were fast evaporating. On June 14, the Germans had entered an almost deserted Paris. The next day, as they breached a large section of the Maginot Line, the historic fortress at Verdun fell, and German forces contained and trapped the French Third, Fifth and Eighth Armies at the Swiss border; 400,000 men surrendered en masse. On June 18, the evacuation of the Second BEF, which had arrived in France only about two weeks earlier, was completed. A day later, the Germans reached Nantes, having fanned out at high speed across France. Weygand advised Reynaud that defeat was inevitable, and counseled against schemes to continue the fight from French colonies overseas. On June 17, Reynaud resigned in favor of Pétain, and on June 20, when the XVI Panzer Corps reached Lyon, he conceded a cease-fire. The French will to fight had crumbled. They had suffered an estimated 90,000 dead and 200,000 wounded, while 1.9 million people were missing or had been taken prisoner. German army and air force deaths totalled 29,640, with 163,213 other casualties.

Humiliating surrender

Not all Frenchmen had accepted defeat. Charles de Gaulle escaped France on June 16, and two days later, on the BBC, he broadcast a stirring message of defiance, exhorting his countrymen to believe in France's resurrection and eventual victory—"the flame of French resistance must not and shall not die." Yet de Gaulle at this time was a relatively obscure figure, only weeks earlier promoted to brigadier general and having served only a fortnight in the French government. Weygand was scathing in his dismissal of de Gaulle's rallying cry, declaring that within three weeks England would "have her neck wrung like a chicken." A Vichy court later found de Gaulle guilty of treason and sentenced him to death in absentia; one condition of the surrender the Germans dictated to France was that anyone supporting what de Gaulle and the British were calling the "Free French" would be subject to the death penalty.

On the evening of June 22 at Compiègne, 44 miles (70 km) northeast of Paris, French general Charles Huntziger signed the formal surrender. Hitler insisted that the signing take place in the

> France has lost a battle. But France has not lost the war! I ask you to believe me when I say the cause of France is not lost.
> **Charles de Gaulle**

> The most terrible collapse in French history.
> **Marcel Bloch, 1940**
> **French industrialist**

same railroad carriage in which, 22 years earlier, the French had accepted the German surrender. After viewing the nearby granite memorial to the 1918 Armistice, Hitler ordered it to be destroyed; "the greatest German humiliation of all time," wrote Field Marshal Wilhelm Keitel, had to be "blotted out once and for all."

Under the terms of the surrender, three-fifths of French territory, including most of the north and west and the entire Atlantic seaboard, had to submit to German occupation at a cost of 400 million francs ($8 million) a day, to be borne by the French themselves. Pétain was installed as the president of a new *État français*, ruling over the remainder, known as Vichy France after the spa town in the Auvergne where the Assemblée Nationale voted on July 10 to dissolve France's 70 year-old Third Republic.

Dividing France

Having slaughtered their prey, the Germans now butchered it. Italy was permitted to annex the southeast corner of France around Nice, while parts of the north that bordered Belgium were placed under the aegis of the German military authorities in Brussels. Germany had annexed Alsace and Lorraine, and other areas of the northeast were reserved for future German colonization. The rest of the north was ruled by a German military governor.

Vichy France

Just 40 percent of French territory was left for Pétain, and his government was assigned to Vichy because the spa town in central France, with its 300 hotels, had the rooms to house the ministries and functionaries driven out of Paris (including some 100,000 civil servants). Pétain was enthusiastic as it had an international telephone exchange, good communications with Paris, and a pleasant climate.

Here Pétain would set up what was, after the war, characterized as a relatively harmless and passive regime that simply tried to keep its citizens safe, but was, in reality, an ambitious, reactionary dictatorship. Pétain's rule was authoritarian, profoundly Catholic, hierarchical, »

Adolf Hitler poses by the Eiffel Tower in Paris on June 23, 1940, the day after the signing of the French surrender at Compiègne. Five days later, he visited Strasbourg, also occupied in 1940.

Charles de Gaulle

Born in Lille in 1890, the son of a professor, de Gaulle had been a young infantry officer in World War I, wounded three times and taken prisoner. In the interwar years, he studied modern warfare and proposed that France's army should be more mobile and mechanized, but with little success. When World War II broke out, he was the commander of a tank regiment. With political patronage from Paul Reynaud, in early June 1940, he was promoted to the rank of brigadier general; joined the government; and traveled to London, meeting Churchill, whom he impressed.

When France fell and Pétain replaced Reynaud as France's leader, de Gaulle left for Britain. Over the next four years, he built the Free French into a government-in-waiting, and in August 1944 he made a triumphant entry to Paris.

De Gaulle's Free French had ensured that the French played a part in the war and in their own liberation. He himself went on to serve as his country's president until January 1946 and again from 1958 to 1969. He died at his home in Colombey-les-deux-Églises in 1970.

> Marshal, here we are! Savior of France, we, your men, swear to serve and follow in your footsteps.
>
> **André Montagard**
> **French lyricist, from the song "*Maréchal, nous voila!*"**

and anti-semitic. Most days, the Marshal would come out onto the balcony of the Hotel du Parc, his private residence and seat of the Vichy government, to hear supporters singing a popular song written in his honor: "*Maréchal, nous voilà!*" ("Marshal, here we are!"). The 84-year-old Pétain thought of himself as a latter day Joan of Arc, claiming that his new government would institute *la Révolution nationale,* a movement for national revival. In practice, he was an old man, whose periods of lucidity and energy were interspersed with sleepiness and forgetfulness. He also oversaw a crudely reactionary regime. For instance, for the crime of performing an abortion, Pétain sent Marie-Louise Giraud to the guillotine; she was the last woman in France to be executed in this way. While not full-blooded Nazis, the Vichy government comprised militant right-wing ideologues, such as the author Robert Brasillach, who confessed just before his execution for collaboration in 1945 that they were "bedfellows with the Germans" and admitted they were close to their Nazi occupiers.

Vichy anti-Semitism

The institution of anti-Semitic laws was among the first acts of the Vichy regime, which began to round up Jews. Although French Jews survived in relatively high numbers in Vichy France, they were relegated to the status of second-class citizens. Foreign Jews, who had flooded into France as refugees, were rounded up in what the Germans called *Razzien* (raids) and the French called *rafles.* In German-occupied France, too, thousands of French policemen collaborated with the SS to detain French and foreign Jews.

In Paris on July 16–17, during what was known as *la grande rafle* ("the great raid") or the *Vél d'hiv rafle* (as they were impounded in the Vélodrome d'Hiver cycling stadium), more than 12,000 Parisian Jews were arrested for deportation to concentration camps. Two weeks later, more than 10,000 policemen in Vichy France joined a massive search for fugitive Polish and German Jews. The Italian-occupied area around Nice became a safe haven for Jews, with Mussolini insisting they be protected. This brief respite lasted only until Italian forces withdrew in September 1943.

Forced labor

Pétain and his Vichy government remained popular with many of the French. When Pétain visited Notre Dame in Paris in April 1944, more people came out to cheer him than those who took to the streets to see de Gaulle when the city was liberated four months later. Initial enthusiasm for Vichy had been even greater, but two events had a highly adverse effect on Pétain's popularity. The first was Pétain's decision to stay in office when Germany occupied Vichy France in November 1942, which damaged his reputation as a

Child inmates of the Rivesaltes Internment Camp, near Perpignan in Vichy France. The camp, initially used to house Catalan refugees, later interned Jews sent on to Auschwitz.

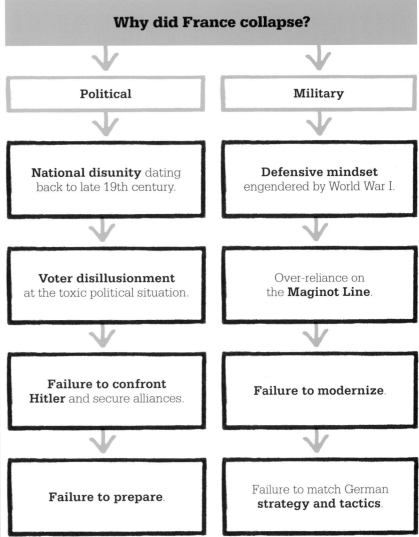

A Vichy poster declares "No more bad days! ... Dad makes money in Germany" in a bid to make forced labor seem attractive. The initial request became conscription under new Vichy laws.

Why did France collapse?

Political	Military
National disunity dating back to late 19th century.	**Defensive mindset** engendered by World War I.
Voter disillusionment at the toxic political situation.	Over-reliance on the **Maginot Line**.
Failure to confront Hitler and secure alliances.	**Failure to modernize**.
Failure to prepare.	Failure to match German **strategy and tactics**.

staunch French patriot. The second was the institution of the *Service de Travail Obligatoire,* the compulsory draft of 650,000 French workers into forced labor in German factories from 1942 to 1944. It caused widespread resentment and persuaded many join French Resistance movements.

Vichy collaborators

From its creation in January 1943, the primary force countering the Resistance was the Milice, a Vichy paramilitary organization that relentlessly pursued and persecuted members of the Resistance and Jewish refugees. Milice death squads carried out torture and massacres. In one atrocity, in the Loire Valley in July 1944, a Milice unit led by violent anti-Semite Joseph Lécussan pushed 36 Jews into three wells, and threw in sacks of cement and stones to crush them alive. Although Pétain made weak formal objections, he did nothing to stop such barbarity. By the end of the war, Vichy France had deported up to 80,000 Jews, interned 70,000 "enemies of the state," and put on trial 135,000 French citizens.

Germany's control of France was aided by the scale of collaboration among the French. Thousands spied for the Gestapo for small monthly stipends, and tens of thousands of anonymous denunciations were sent to the Gestapo. In the absence of some 1.5 million Frenchmen held prisoner of war, liaisons between German troops and French women, were numerous; with as many as 200,000 babies born as a result. Collaborators were also motivated by hunger. Half of all food produced in France between 1940 and 1944 was requisitioned by the Germans.

It took time for post-war France to come to terms with its Vichy past. It was not until 1995 that President Jacques Chirac first acknowledged France's role in the Jewish genocide. ■

I ONLY NEED A FEW THOUSAND DEAD

ITALY ENTERS THE WAR (JUNE 1940)

IN CONTEXT

FOCUS
Italian military action

BEFORE
1920–1930s Italy's military-industrial base erodes as a result of corruption in industry and government incompetence.

1936 Italy conquers Abyssinia, thereby expanding its colonial presence in East Africa.

May 22, 1939 Mussolini and Hitler sign the Pact of Steel.

AFTER
June 25, 1940 Armistice between France and Italy; France cedes territory to Italy.

February 1941 Italian forces in Egypt's Western Desert suffer shattering defeat at the Battle of Beda Fomm.

July 25, 1943 Mussolini is deposed and arrested after Allied landings in Sicily.

September 1943 Germans and Allies fight for control of Italy.

On June 10, 1940, Italy declared war on the Allies, a move that was to have fateful ramifications for the nation and its dictator, Benito Mussolini. In May 1939, Italy and Germany had forged what Mussolini called the Pact of Steel, a mutual defense treaty signed by the Italians on the verbal understanding that neither party would provoke a war until 1943. Mussolini blew hot and cold over Hitler's increasing belligerence through 1939, but by the summer of 1940 it was Germany that was keen for Italy to stay neutral, reasoning that she would provide a useful buffer, helping to keep the Mediterranean theater quiet.

Mussolini, however, driven by imperialist pretensions and cynical opportunism, had other ideas. By late May it was clear that France would fall and it seemed likely that the war would shortly be concluded in Hitler's favor. Mussolini wanted

Mussolini inspects troops of the Italian Eighth Army, which was formed in February 1940 and based in the north of the country. It was disbanded in October of the same year.

See also: Italy and the rise of fascism 22–23 ▪ North Africa and the Mediterranean 118–121 ▪ The invasion of Italy 210–211

A motorcycle division, part of the Italian Tenth Army, in action during the invasion of western Egypt in September 1940. The Italians reached Sidi Barrani before the advance stalled.

to get in on the action, and on May 26 he told his top generals that he intended to join the war in order to win a place at the peace table "when the world is to be apportioned." Ignoring their arguments that Italian forces were ill-prepared, on June 5 he told Marshal Pietro Badoglio, chief of the Supreme General Staff, "I only need a few thousand dead so that I can sit at the peace conference as a man who has fought." Accordingly, on June 10, Mussolini's foreign minister Galeazzo Ciano told the British and French ambassadors that Italy would declare war against the two nations at midnight. The French ambassador, André François-Poncet, called the move "a dagger blow to a man who has already fallen."

Ill-equipped

Italian forces included about 1 million men in Italy and another 600,000 overseas, but they were badly equipped and poorly prepared. Italian tanks, for example, were widely derided and did not even have radios. Nonetheless, Mussolini was eager to seize territory before the French could conclude an armistice with Germany, and on June 15 he ordered an offensive along France's southeastern border, which would become known as the Battle of the Alps. The Italian army assaulted the French Armée des Alpes, but came off badly, with the French mounting a stiff resistance. The Italians achieved just one of their objectives: the capture of the border town of Menton, which had already been evacuated by the French several days before.

Elsewhere, Italy faced other major problems. British naval strength in the Mediterranean now threatened Italian shipping, which suffered almost immediate heavy losses, and Italian forces soon faced reverses in North Africa. However, as Germany consolidated their grip on Vichy France, Italian dominance in the southeast of France also increased. By late 1942, Provence and Corsica, among other regions, were under Italian occupation. ■

The Battle of the Alps, 1940

At the French–Italian border in the Alps, the Italians sought to take advantage of the rapid advance of German troops south through France by striking through mountain passes. Mussolini hoped this would trigger the collapse of the French defenses. The Italian Fourth Army hoped to reach Albertville, but they struggled to get past fortifications at the border.

Poor weather and difficult terrain ruled out air support, and the Italians mostly failed to deploy their Alpine units to best effect, instead wasting them on frontal assaults. Only in a few places did these units break through. Even then, fortified French outposts held out behind them, while Italian motorized divisions struggled to get through the passes. In the four days before an armistice brought a halt to operations, the Italians had failed to pierce the full depth of the fortified border zone and nowhere advanced more than 11 miles (18 km).

Italian mountain troops from an Alpine regiment struggle up rugged terrain toward the French border near the Seign Pass in late June 1940.

DEFENSE OF THE MOTHER COUNTRY

COLONIAL TIES (1939–1945)

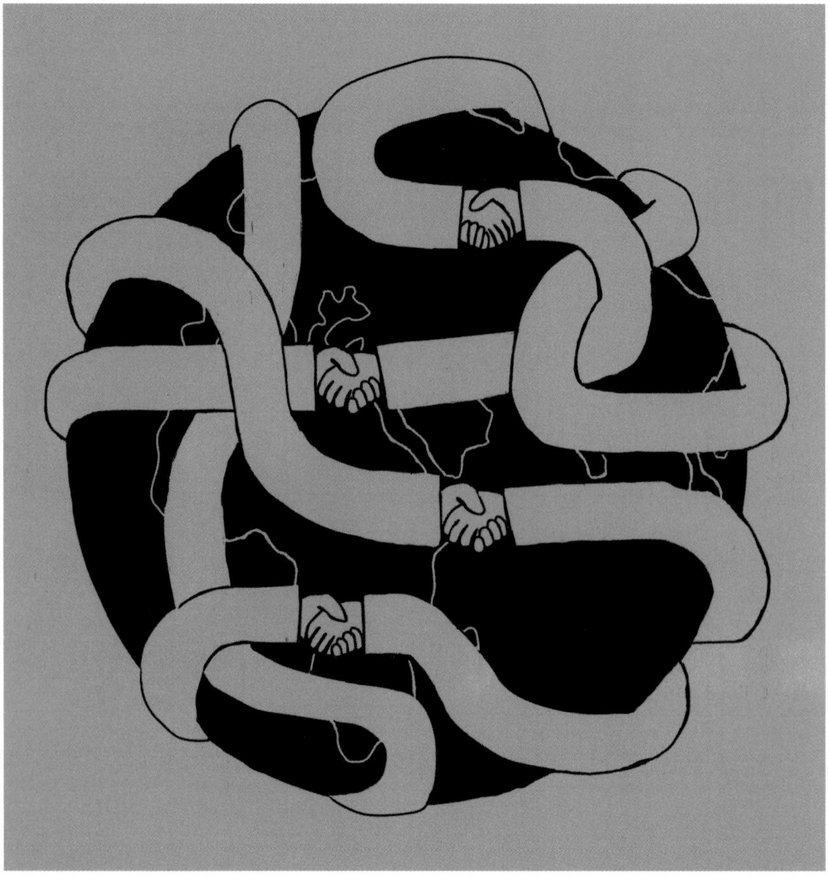

IN CONTEXT

FOCUS
Impact on colonies

BEFORE
1914–1918 Vast numbers of people in the colonies fight for the Allies in World War I.

AFTER
1947 India achieves independence from Britain.

1949 Some former British colonies agree to recognize the British monarch as head of the Commonwealth but not as their head of state.

1954 The Battle of Dien Bien Phu marks the defeat of French colonial forces in Indochina.

1962 Algeria wins its independence from France after a bitter eight-year war.

Germany possessed some overseas colonies at the start of the war, but its empire was small compared to the imperial domains of Britain, France, and Belgium, whose colonies provided resources and manpower for their war effort. The British assumed that their colonies would support them, and the Belgian Congo declared for the Allies in January 1941. However, after the creation of Vichy France following the German occupation of France, French colonies had to decide whether to recognize Vichy or the Free France government led by Charles de Gaulle in exile in London.

French colonies

Initially, most of the French Empire recognized Vichy authority. This included Indochina, where the French ruled a series of provinces

See also: The Great War 18–19 ▪ The fall of France 80–87 ▪ North Africa and the Mediterranean 118–121 ▪ Japan's dilemma 137 ▪ India in World War II 158 ▪ Defending Australia 159 ▪ Operation Torch 196–197 ▪ Aftermath 320–327

Félix Eboué

Adolphe-Félix-Sylvestre Eboué was born in French Guiana, a French colony on the coast of South America, in 1884. A brilliant student, he won a scholarship to study at the top schools in France and enjoyed a distinguished career in the French colonial bureaucracy. He became the first person of African ancestry to hold the post of colonial governor, first in Guadeloupe and then in Chad.

In World War II, Eboué recognized the invidious nature of Nazi doctrine and declared support for the Free French in July 1940, rallying Chad and then the rest of French Equatorial Africa to resist the Nazi puppet regime of Vichy France.

In November 1940, de Gaulle appointed Eboué General Governor of French Equatorial Africa. Settling in Brazzaville, the capital of Free French Africa, in the Congo, Eboué worked for the Free French and proposed reforms to French colonial policies in the post-war period.

Eboué died in Cairo in 1944. His ashes were interred in the Panthéon in Paris in 1949, making him the first Black person to be buried there.

consisting of modern-day Vietnam, Cambodia, and Laos. In July 1940, the Vichy regime installed a new governor-general, Vice-Admiral Jean Decoux, who quickly discovered that French authority there was a fiction. The real power in the region was Japan, which was demanding free access and garrison rights.

Japanese control

In September 1940, Japanese troops invaded French Indochina. Despite raising a local army, supplemented by 20,000 Foreign Legion troops, the French were completely outmatched by the Japanese military. For most of the rest of the war the Japanese had free rein to exploit the region for natural resources, food, and transportation links. They allowed nominal French governance, to control the provinces.

The only effective resistance to Japanese hegemony came from the Viet Minh, a communist guerrilla organization formed in May 1941 by Ho Chi Minh with support from the US Office of Strategic Services (OSS). By October 1944, the Viet Minh had pushed back the Japanese and established an administration in northern areas. Disruptions to rice supplies eventually led to a famine in Tongkin (northern Vietnam) in 1945, which claimed the lives of up to 2 million people.

When French Indochina came under the aegis of the Free French toward the end of the war, the Japanese suppressed the remaining French forces, massacring 1,700 troops. After the war, French colonial control was nominally reasserted, but Ho Chi Minh's independence movement could not be denied, and the French would eventually be driven out.

A few French colonies courageously held out against the Vichy regime, including territories in India and the Pacific, and French Equatorial Africa, where the bold decision of Félix Eboué, governor of Chad, to declare support for Free France gave de Gaulle a vital base from which to build an alternative French Empire.

Belgium's colonies

The Belgian Congo, including the mandate of Ruanda-Urundi, was a vast territory 80 times bigger than Belgium itself. In January 1941, after initial reluctance, the Belgian »

A detachment of Algerian *spahis*, a light cavalry regiment, ride through the desert in 1940. Algeria at the time was part of Vichy France but some *spahi* regiments supported Free France.

A British recruitment poster gives an impression of equality between colonial and dominion forces. In reality, few Black soldiers were allowed to fight on the frontline.

government in exile allowed the British to exploit the immense natural resources of the territory. The British eventually bought the Congo's entire wartime production of copper, along with other metals and radioactive ores. The initial supplies of uranium used in the development of the atomic bomb in the US also came from there.

Men from the Belgian Congo also fought in the war, serving in the Belgian Congo's Force Publique, which saw action in Africa and the Middle East. However, wartime Congo also saw miners' strikes, army mutinies, and rebellions against the colonial authorities, partly in reaction to Belgium's long history of brutal colonial rule.

Britain's Black combatants

Thousands of Africans were pressed into the British war effort, sometimes working as forced labor, supplying raw materials. Reduced traffic through the Suez Canal as a result of the war forced British ships traveling to South Asia and the East to travel around Africa via the Cape of Good Hope. More than 150,000 West African troops, and some East African brigades, were sent to Burma, where they served under white officers.

African soldiers were not used as combatants in the European theater because it was felt to be unacceptable for Black Africans to kill white people. Although there was no official color bar to Black people joining the British military services, Churchill stipulated that "administrative means" should be found to prevent their acceptance.

This informal bar was overcome by West Indians, who protested at being denied the opportunity to serve. Eventually, around 300 West Indians served in the Royal Air Force as aircrew, winning 90 decorations, including seven Distinguished Service Orders. In 1944, a Caribbean Regiment was recruited and posted to Egypt to guard prisoners of war, only to be drawn into conflict with white South African troops who objected to Black men being allowed to bear arms.

India joins the conflict

British India was not permitted the luxury of choice when it came to joining the war. In 1939, without consulting the Indian Congress, British viceroy Lord Linlithgow declared that India was at war with Germany. This failure to consult sparked bitter debate among Indian politicians, especially those who were already seeking independence from Britain, such as Mahatma Gandhi and Jawaharlal Nehru. Over 2.5 million Indians would serve during the war. The Fourth Indian Division, for instance, fought in North Africa, Syria, Palestine, Cyprus, Italy (where it participated in the bloody assault on Monte Cassino), and Greece, winning four Victoria Crosses (VCs). The Fifth Indian Division fought in North Africa and guarded Iraqi oil fields, before being sent to Burma, Malaya, and Java, also winning four VCs.

Bravery and sacrifice

In all, the Indian armed forces, which included the Royal Indian Navy and the Indian Air Force (later Royal), lost more than 36,000 members, with another 64,000 injured, and won 4,000 awards for gallantry, including 31 VCs.

One of those to receive a Victoria Cross was Havildar Gaje Ghale of the Fifth Royal Gurkha Rifles, who was badly wounded during an attack on Japanese forces in Burma in May 1943. According to his citation, Gaje Ghale "dominated the fight … Hurling grenades and covered in blood from his own wounds, he led assault after assault."

India would pay a high price for its service to Britain. Along with millions of troops, including the

> "We resist British Imperialism no less than Nazism. If there is a difference, it is in degree."
>
> **Mahatma Gandhi**
> **Anticolonial Indian nationalist**

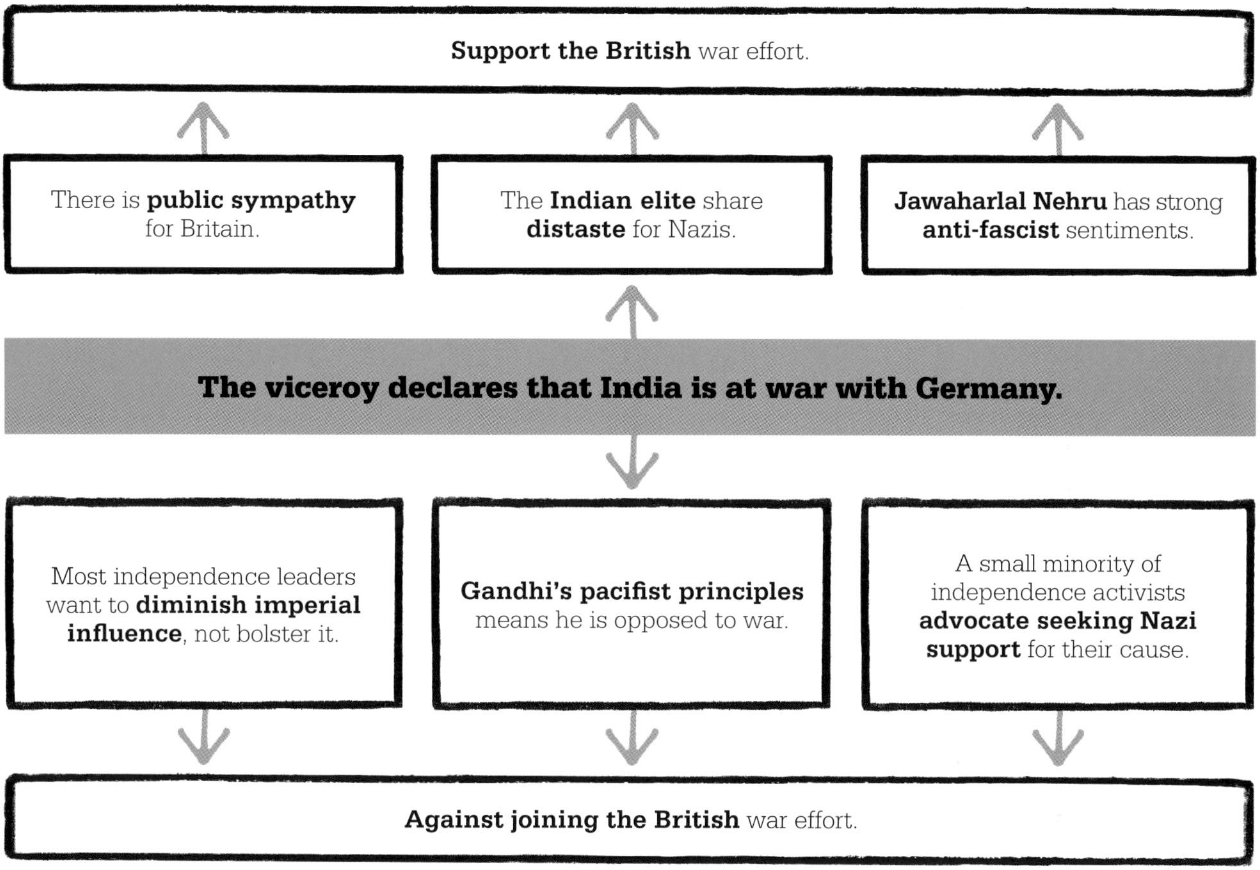

Support the British war effort.
There is public sympathy for Britain.
The Indian elite share distaste for Nazis.
Jawaharlal Nehru has strong anti-fascist sentiments.
The viceroy declares that India is at war with Germany.
Most independence leaders want to diminish imperial influence, not bolster it.
Gandhi's pacifist principles means he is opposed to war.
A small minority of independence activists advocate seeking Nazi support for their cause.
Against joining the British war effort.

largest volunteer army in history, it provided vast quantities of food and raw materials for Britain. The impact on domestic resources led to disastrous food shortages in 1942–1943, with the loss of 3 million lives in the Bengal Famine.

War in the dominions

While they were no longer British colonies, the dominions of Australia, New Zealand, and Canada all declared war alongside Britain, even though they still bore the scars of the losses they had sustained in World War I and public opinion was divided about the war in Europe. In Australia, for instance, there was widespread opposition, yet in April 1939, the country's new prime minister, Robert Menzies, declared "If Britain was at war, Australia was, too." Later on, after the 1941 Japanese bombing of the US naval base at Pearl Harbor and, especially, the fall of Singapore and Japan's raid on Darwin in 1942, Australian support for the war hardened.

In Canada, the political skill of premier Mackenzie King was vital in securing support for the war, partly by pledging that there would be no conscription for overseas service and partly by promising a war of "limited liability"—supplying only as many men as was necessary at any given time. New Zealand made the greatest contribution, proportionately, of any of Britain's existing or former colonies, losing a greater percentage of its population (0.67 percent) and spending a proportion of national income that was equal to the UK's. South Africans were more wary than other dominions, but narrowly voted to join Britain's declaration of war.

The participation of colonies and dominions created multiple fronts on which the war could be prosecuted. India, which occupied a strategic position between the African, Middle Eastern, and Pacific theaters, came under threat both in the west, with Nazi dreams of striking through the Middle East, and in the east, with Japan's successes bringing the war perilously close. North Africa, which was under the control of Vichy France, became the theater where the Allies tried to turn the tide of war in their favor. ■

NEVER WAS SO MUCH OWED BY SO MANY TO SO FEW

THE BATTLE OF BRITAIN (JULY 10–SEPTEMBER 17, 1940)

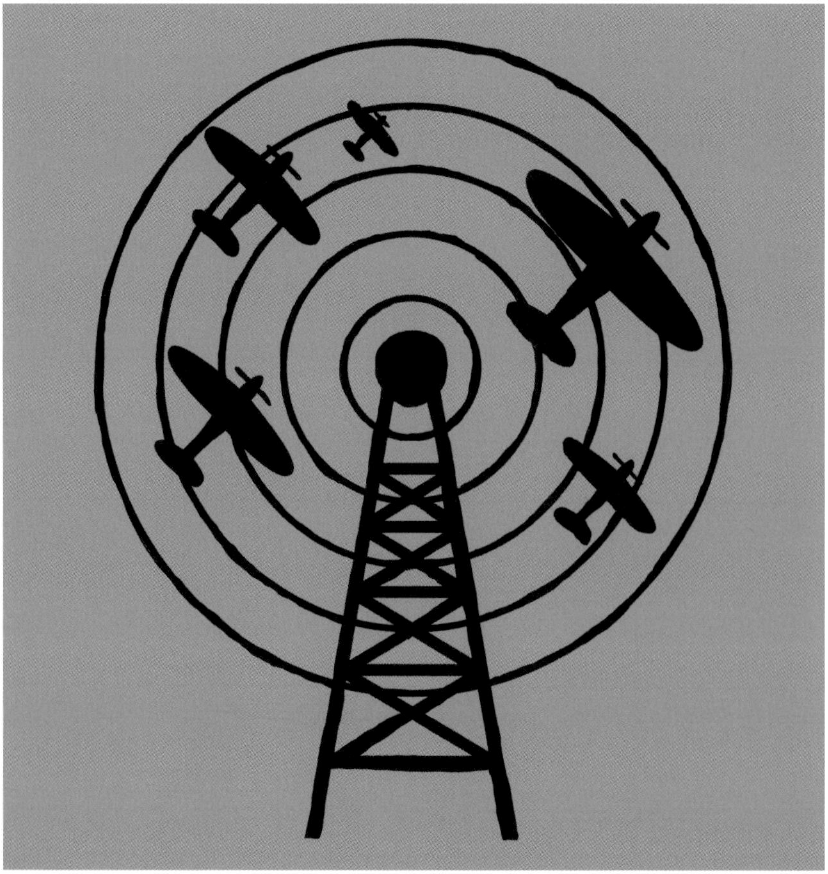

IN CONTEXT

FOCUS
War in the air

BEFORE
1933 Nazis start to build up the Luftwaffe, illegally.

1935 British invent a working form of radar.

1936 First flight of Spitfire prototype.

AFTER
May 1941 Blitz peters out as German airpower is redirected to the Eastern Front.

1942 Beginning of UK's strategic air offensive against Nazi Germany.

March 1944 American long-range fighters deplete the Luftwaffe.

April 1944 German Me-262 jet fighter enters service.

1954 Last operational sortie by an RAF Spitfire.

The Battle of Britain was a struggle for control of the skies above Britain and, crucially, the English Channel, fought in several phases between June and September 1940.

With the fall of France, Britain tensed for invasion by sea and air. On July 16, Hitler issued Directive No.16, "on preparations for a landing operation against England." His generals were instructed to put together an invasion plan, Operation Sealion. Its guiding assumption was that any chance of success for an amphibious landing depended on Luftwaffe bombers chasing away the British Royal Navy, as they had done with some success in Norway,

See also: The destruction of Poland 58–63 ▪ The invasion of Denmark and Norway 69 ▪ Blitzkrieg 70–75 ▪ The fall of France 80–87 ▪ The Blitz 98–99 ▪ Britain organizes for total war 100–103 ▪ Bombing of Germany 220–223

> Outwardly calm, inwardly anxious covers the general tone of today.
>
> **British Mass Observation survey recorded on May 19**

and this in turn depended on first securing air superiority. As Hitler commanded: "The British Air Force must be eliminated to such an extent that it will be incapable of putting up substantial opposition to the invading troops."

Luftwaffe versus RAF

Göring assured his leader that the Luftwaffe would smash the RAF, and he had some grounds for confidence. At the start of the battle, the Germans had around 1,300 bombers and dive-bombers, and about 900 single-engined and 300 twin-engined fighters. This force was set against about 650 planes at the disposal of RAF Fighter Command. However, several important factors now mitigated against the Luftwaffe. Previously, it had operated close to its own bases and—as an arm of Blitzkrieg—in support of ground and naval forces. During this campaign, Junkers 87 (Stuka) bombers had achieved great speed by diving from height. Now, operating without ground support and further from their home bases, they would have to fly on the level and thus much more slowly. The Messerschmitt Me-109, though superior in many respects to RAF fighters, had a small fuel tank that allowed it to spend just 30 minutes in British airspace. Meanwhile, British pilots who were shot down and survived might be back in the air later the same day.

The impact of radar

Perhaps most significantly, Fighter Command was able to marshal its scanty resources highly effectively because it had advanced warning of attacks thanks to intelligence and especially Radio Direction Finding (RDF, later known as radar), which had been developed just before the war began. The Chain Home network of radar stations, which had been established around the British coast, fed into a sophisticated command-and-control system that more than doubled the intercept rate of fighter squadrons.

The first phase of the battle started on July 10 as the Luftwaffe began bombing British shipping and ports. German planes from three *Luftflotten* (air fleets) operated from 50 bases in northern France and Holland. Opposing them were the 52 squadrons of RAF Fighter Command, led by Air Chief Marshal Hugh Dowding.

It took as little as six minutes for enemy aircraft to cross the English Channel; even with radar early warning, it took four minutes to deliver the "scramble" message to mobilize and another 13 minutes for Spitfires to reach intercept altitude. Fighter Command wanted to avoid falling victim to bluffs designed to lure planes away from defending airfields. As a result, it dispatched interceptors in small squadrons of 12 planes, whereas the smallest »

British fighter pilots scramble to their Spitfires during the Battle of Britain. At the end of August 1940, 372 Spitfires and 709 Hurricanes were engaged in the battle.

How the radar defense system worked

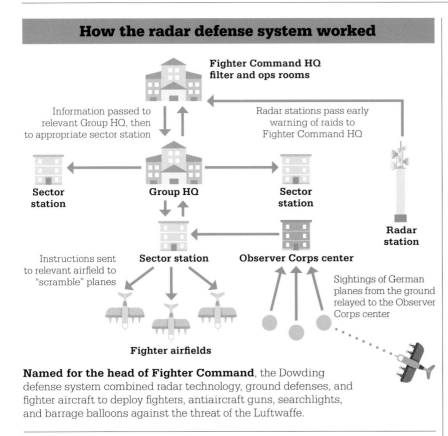

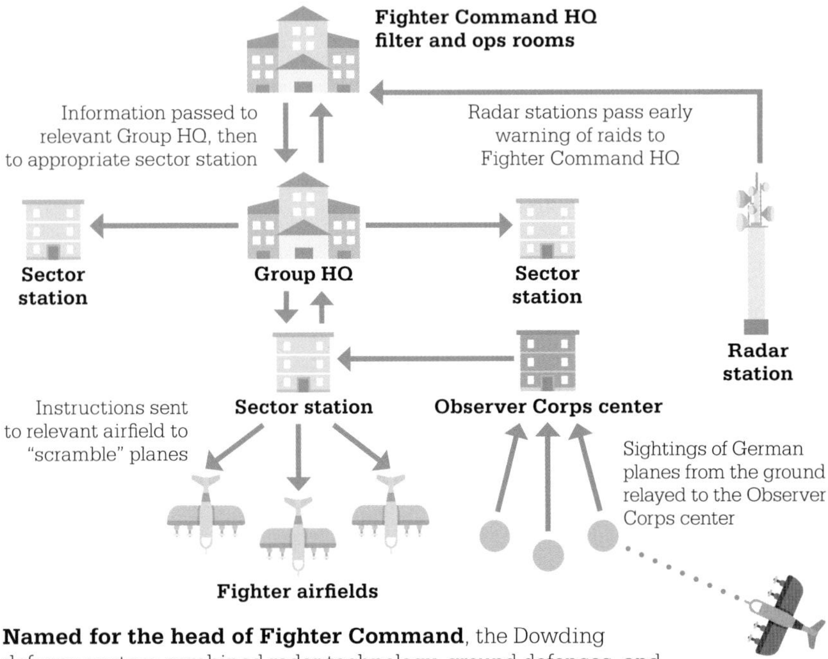
Fighter Command HQ filter and ops rooms
Information passed to relevant Group HQ, then to appropriate sector station
Radar stations pass early warning of raids to Fighter Command HQ
Sector station
Group HQ
Sector station
Radar station
Sector station
Observer Corps center
Instructions sent to relevant airfield to "scramble" planes
Sightings of German planes from the ground relayed to the Observer Corps center
Fighter airfields

Named for the head of Fighter Command, the Dowding defense system combined radar technology, ground defenses, and fighter aircraft to deploy fighters, antiaircraft guns, searchlights, and barrage balloons against the threat of the Luftwaffe.

Luftwaffe unit was the *Gruppe* of 30 aircraft. Only later in the battle, as the prediction of bomber attacks improved with time, did Fighter Command start to assemble the "Big Wing" based out of Duxford—five squadrons of Hurricanes and Spitfires working together.

Intensified attacks

Initially, the Luftwaffe targeted Channel shipping, hoping to draw the RAF into wasting its resources on escort missions. The Luftwaffe sank 33,000 tons (30,000 metric tons) of shipping, but this was only a tiny fraction of the tonnage passing through the Channel every week. By the end of July, it was clear that Sealion was not progressing and it was time for the Luftwaffe to increase the intensity. On August 1, Hitler signaled the imminence of *verschärfter Luftkrieg* ("intensive air war") with Directive No.17: "the Luftwaffe is to overcome the English air force with all means at its disposal and in the shortest possible time. The attacks are to be primarily directed against the planes themselves ...." This plan made sense, but in the end it did not materialize. The air war did indeed intensify as a second phase of the Battle of Britain began on August 8, but it was across a broad front with multiple and dispersed targets, as the Luftwaffe launched a mass of virtually continuous bombing attacks. There were 1,485 sorties on the first day, rising to 1,786 by August 15. The Germans called August 13 *Adlertag* ("Day of the Eagle"). They marked it as the true start of the Battle of Britain, for this was the day they intended to begin targeting airfields. Despite flying nearly 1,500 sorties that day, German pilots were hampered by poor weather and unclear orders. The Luftwaffe lost 46 planes to 13 losses for the RAF.

Radar was demonstrating its value. According to RAF Wing Commander Max Aitken, "radar really won the Battle of Britain ... We wasted no petrol, no energy, no time." In contrast, the German effort was hamstrung by poor intelligence, which wildly overestimated RAF losses and Luftwaffe successes.

Aerial dogfights

Range limitations on German fighter planes—such as the Dornier Do-17—meant that much of the dogfighting was concentrated over southeast England. The combat was brutal and desperate. Although the Me-109 was slightly faster, and better at diving and climbing, than the RAF fighters, its turning circle was not as tight, and German pilots complained that they could not pin down the British Hurricanes and Spitfires.

The third phase of the battle began on August 24, as the Luftwaffe finally concentrated its firepower on bombing air bases,

> "The British had an extraordinary advantage which we could never overcome throughout the entire war."
>
> **Colonel Adolf Galland**
> **German fighter ace, on radar**

Hermann Göring

Born in 1893, Göring was a highly decorated World War I flying ace, who became the second most powerful man in Nazi Germany. Wounded in the 1923 Beer Hall Putsch, his power grew as the Nazis' did. He established the Gestapo and the first concentration camps. In 1933, he took charge of the secret plan to reconstitute the air force, building the Luftwaffe and unleashing it to devastating effect in Poland, Norway, and France.

By July 1940, Göring was Hitler's designated successor, but defeat in the Battle of Britain began a string of failures, not least his incompetent running of the German economy. He degenerated into a drug-addicted megalomaniac. With Hitler surrounded in Berlin, Göring suggested that he assume control of the Reich, provoking a furious response that saw him arrested by the SS. He escaped into Allied custody but in 1946 was found guilty at the Nuremberg Trials for crimes against humanity, having signed up to the Final Solution plan in 1941. He escaped execution by dying by suicide.

as it should have done to begin with. Fleets of 80–100 German bombers, accompanied by up to 100 fighters, battered British bases such as Biggin Hill, Manston, and Lympne. On August 30, for instance, the Luftwaffe flew 1,345 sorties, and the RAF was stretched to breaking point; it lost 39 fighter planes the following day.

That month, 304 British pilots were killed or wounded; some pilots were sent up with only 20 hours of training. But another strategic error by Hitler offered them respite.

Bombing cities

On August 24, a Heinkel He-111 bomber, possibly lost, had dropped its bombs on the City of London, and the RAF responded with a series of raids on Berlin on August 25–29. Hitler, who had promised the German people that their capital would be protected, was goaded into a furious mistake, thundering on September 4 that, "When they declare that they will attack our cities ... then we will eradicate their cities." The Luftwaffe's objectives were abruptly altered from bombing airfields to bombing cities. The Blitz had begun, but although it was not clear at the time, the Germans had effectively lost the Battle of Britain. On September 15, a massive raid on London ended with the Luftwaffe losing twice as many planes as the RAF. Two days later, Hitler postponed Operation Sealion "until further notice." Although the Blitz continued, the Battle of Britain tailed off. The balance sheet of losses was appalling. Since May 1940, the Germans had lost 1,733 planes to the RAF's 915. Although these numbers would be dwarfed by the scale of air battles and losses later in the war, the RAF had inflicted the first defeat on Hitler's Germany, and saved Britain from the immediate threat of invasion. ■

Luftwaffe Dornier Do-17 bombers over London in 1940. Dubbed the "Flying Pencil" for its narrow fuselage, this plane suffered heavy losses to the more maneuverable RAF fighters.

STABBED WITH GREAT FIRES, SHAKEN BY EXPLOSIONS

THE BLITZ (SEPTEMBER 7, 1940–MAY 10, 1941)

IN CONTEXT

FOCUS
Impact on civilians

BEFORE
1937 Guernica in Spain is bombed by the Luftwaffe on April 26, the first major air raid on a civilian target and a harbinger of the new terror strategy of aerial bombing.

1940 By September, weeks of continuous bombing reduce much of Warsaw to rubble.

AFTER
1942 The British strategic air offensive begins, targeting German industrial sites and civilian locations.

1942 The "Baedeker raids" occur from April to June, so called because a German official said that the Luftwaffe would bomb every English building with three stars in the Baedeker guidebook.

1944 The second London Blitz takes place, with V-weapons fired at southeast England.

The Blitz was an intensive bombing campaign by the Luftwaffe against British cities. Although "air raids" on Birmingham and Liverpool occurred in August 1940, the Blitz began in earnest on September 7 with a massive daytime raid on London, followed by months of nightly raids.

At first the air raids were intended to support German objectives in the Battle of Britain. After losing this battle, the Germans changed their objective to instead inflict terror and degrade infrastructure. Hitler's redirection of the Luftwaffe's bombing efforts from Royal Air Force (RAF) airfields to urban targets has been seen as a strategic blunder that cost the Germans victory in the air war. So why did the Luftwaffe change tack?

It may have been because Hitler was goaded by RAF raids on Berlin. Alternatively, Göring might have

London's streets were devastated during the initial phase of the Blitz, but in winter of 1940 the Luftwaffe's scope widened to other British cities, such as Liverpool, Bristol, and Coventry.

See also: The destruction of Poland 58–63 ▪ Bombing of Germany 220–223 ▪ V-weapons 264–265 ▪ The destruction of German cities 287

Monthly civilian casualties

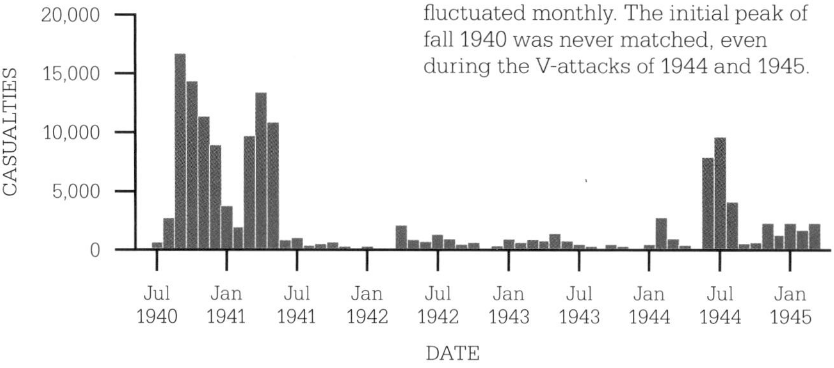

As the war continued, the number of civilian casualties in the London Blitz fluctuated monthly. The initial peak of fall 1940 was never matched, even during the V-attacks of 1944 and 1945.

been seeking to force the RAF to spend what he falsely believed to be its last strength on the raids, drawing out fighters that would be vulnerable to Luftwaffe fighters.

Another theory is that Hitler had already decided Operation Sealion would not proceed, or expected that imminent defeat of the RAF would render Britain open to be bombed into submission, while the German army and navy moved to the Eastern Front. Or perhaps the Germans believed they could break Britons' spirits through terror.

Surviving the air raids

Air defenses could do little to counter the raids; even when the number of antiaircraft guns defending London was doubled soon after the first attack, the only real effect was to boost civilian morale. Many Londoners fled the city or retreated to cellars, but the poorest—who could not afford to leave—also lived in the most heavily targeted areas, around the East End and the docks. The authorities were slow to react; the public took matters into their own hands, occupying Underground rail stations and other sheltered spaces.

There was considerable anger among those most affected, resulting in incidents such as the occupation of the Savoy Hotel by a crowd of 100 East Enders on September 15, 1940. The shelters provided by the government, such as the Morrison shelter (a reinforced table), were of dubious quality. Many who had them preferred not to use them.

In mid-November 1940, attacks shifted focus to other British cities, and from February 1941 ports were targeted even more heavily. In mid-May 1941, the Germans redeployed their bomber squadrons to Russia, but the last night of the Blitz, May 10, during which 3,000 Londoners were killed, was the worst. In total, 43,000 British civilians died and 139,000 were injured for the loss of 600 Luftwaffe bombers. However, the Blitz did not force Churchill to negotiate and British attitudes toward the war remained largely unchanged. ■

Mickey Davies

East End optician Mickey Davies (1910–1954) took on a new project when his business was bombed on September 13, 1940: improving conditions for the mass of people sheltering from the Blitz in the warren of tunnels beneath the London Fruit and Wool Exchange in Stepney.

The authorities' failure to protect the lives of the poorest resulted in them taking matters into their own hands, with around 5,000 people crammed into a space only intended for 2,000.

Confronted by official indifference, Davies led a self-organized committee of local people who transformed the unsanitary space into a model facility, popularly known as "Mickey's Shelter."

Described as "a giant in mind and spirit" by politician Joseph Westwood, Davies organized and fund raised for electricity, bedding, sanitation, health care, and other facilities. The shelter and its community-elected committee was lauded as a "showplace of British democracy." After the war, Davies became a local councillor and served as deputy mayor of Stepney.

WE SHALL NEVER SURRENDER

BRITAIN ORGANIZES FOR TOTAL WAR (JUNE–DECEMBER 1940)

IN CONTEXT

FOCUS
Britain at war

BEFORE
April 27, 1939 Conscription introduced in Britain for the first time in peacetime history.

August 24, 1939 Emergency Powers (Defence) Bill enacted.

September 3, 1939 Britain and France declare war on Germany in response to its invasion of Poland.

December 1939 Blackout measures cause a slew of traffic accidents.

AFTER
December 1944 Britain's Home Guard is stood down.

1954 Rationing of meat products is ended.

December 29, 2006 UK finally pays off its war debt to the US and Canada.

On June 4, 1940, Prime Minister Churchill gave a rousing speech in the British House of Commons, vowing that, although the British now stood alone against the Nazi tide, "We shall not flag or fail. We shall go on to the end. We shall fight ... we shall defend our island, whatever the cost may be." As the country plunged into total war, almost the entire economy, and the whole of society, would be enlisted in the war effort; a Herculean mobilization that would push the nation to the brink.

This mobilization had begun during the Phony War, when inaction at the battlefront starkly contrasted with rapid changes on

See also: Europe on the brink 56–57 ▪ The Phony War 64–65 ▪ The Blitz 98–99 ▪ US troops in Britain 255 ▪ The cost of war 314–317

Inspectors examine ammunition at a British armaments factory. Tens of thousands of workers—mostly women—were employed to fill shells and bombs with explosives.

the Home Front, as bureaucracies swung into action. Even before war was declared, the UK Parliament had passed the Emergency Powers (Defence) Act, which made provisions for such "regulations as appear necessary or expedient for securing the public safety, the defence of the realm … and the efficient prosecution of … war."

Blackouts and rationing

The slew of new rules and restrictions helped convert the initial public mood of determination into one of bewilderment and even resentment. More emergency laws were passed in the first two weeks of World War II than in the entire first year of World War I, and life was disrupted by restrictive blackout rules, rationing, the apparently needless evacuation of children, and censorship. Member of Parliament Harold Nicholson captured the absurdity of the time in his diary, noting that the Ministry of Information refused to make public the wording of the leaflets dropped on the Germans by the million because, "We are not allowed to disclose information that might be of value to the enemy."

Both Britain and France scrambled frantically to get their economies onto a war footing and speed up the rearmament they had so reluctantly and tardily begun in the preceding years. Britain, for instance, had mandated the reintroduction of conscription in April 1939, but at the outbreak of war the measure had only just been instituted, with just a single intake of 35,000 men called up on July 15.

Fear of invasion

In the aftermath of the fall of France and the evacuation from Dunkirk, British government considerations took on a more apocalyptic tone. In June 1940, the Ministry of Information printed over 1 million leaflets entitled "If the Invader Comes: What to do and how to do it," which pointed out that "Hitler's invasions of Poland, Holland, and Belgium [France was still at war] were greatly helped by the fact that the population … did not know what to do." Instructions included "Stay put"—the authorities did not want the roads clogged, as had occurred in France; "Do not believe rumours and spread them"; and "Do not give any German anything." Ministers discussed the possibility of relocating the government and the bulk of the armed forces to Canada if there was an invasion, and plans were drawn up to evacuate ministers, the royal family, and others to North America, although in the end it was only the nation's gold reserves that made the crossing.

American support

More important was what came the other way, as vital US support flooded into Britain. America helped rearm the British Army after Dunkirk. On June 11, 1940, the US transferred to the UK 500,000 »

> Britain is fighting two wars: Nazi aggression abroad and Nazi tendencies at home.
>
> **Dingle Foot, MP**
> **On restrictions of civil rights in the UK**

Enfield rifles with 129 million rounds of ammunition; 895 artillery pieces with 1 million rounds; over 80,000 machine guns; and many other weapons, including 143 bomber planes.

The driving force behind this assistance was President Roosevelt, who made clear that America would provide massive support to the anti-Axis allies. He pushed Congress until it approved the Lend-Lease Act in March 1941. This provided an instrument whereby the US could supply war materials to the Allies. Some $7 billion was appropriated for the Act in 1941 and $26 billion in 1942. By the end of the war, the US had loaned more than $31 billion to Britain alone.

In Britain the battle with fascism ironically meant taking drastic measures with domestic civil liberties. In May 1940, Churchill introduced a new subsection to the Emergency Powers (Defence) Act, which gave him the most dictatorial powers of any British leader since Cromwell, including the ability to intern fascists indefinitely, without trial—a suspension of civil liberties that he described as "in the highest degree odious." It was a time for desperate measures.

War work

The most immediate concern was food; with over 70 percent of British food imported via vulnerable shipping routes, it was vital to secure domestic food production. The Dig for Victory campaign increased by 43 percent Britain's amount of arable land, with 7 million acres (2.8 million hectares) of grassland put under the plow. Meanwhile, the number of cultivated allotments rose from 815,000 in 1939 to 1,400,000 in 1943. Together with rationing, Britain was able to become almost self-sufficient in food. It was able, for instance, to produce enough sugar to supply all domestic consumption by the end of the war. Rationing of butter, sugar, bacon, and ham were introduced in January 1940. During 1941, rationing was extended to all foodstuffs except bread and potatoes. Other rationed goods included clothes, gas, and soap.

Women in the workforce

After a slow start, the transformation of the economy and workforce picked up pace. One of the most notable aspects was the wholesale enrollment of women in the workforce, with 80,000 in the Women's Land Army taking over farming jobs, and 160,000 women keeping transportation going through the Blitz. "Results such as the [continued running that the] railways have achieved are only won by blood and sweat," Churchill said in December 1943.

By June 1944, 7.1 million out of 16 million British women aged 14–59 had been mobilized for war work. Partly, this was achieved by a kind of conscription: in December 1941, the government introduced compulsory enlistment for women in auxiliary services; any woman between 18–60 could be ordered into work, where they would likely be paid less than their male counterparts. Male employment was even higher: by late 1944, 93.6 percent of the 15.9 million men aged 14–54 were employed in various aspects of national service, along with 1.75 million serving in the Home Guard and another 1.75 million in Civil Defence.

Children were also caught up in the national mobilization, mainly through the evacuation program, which started with the outbreak of

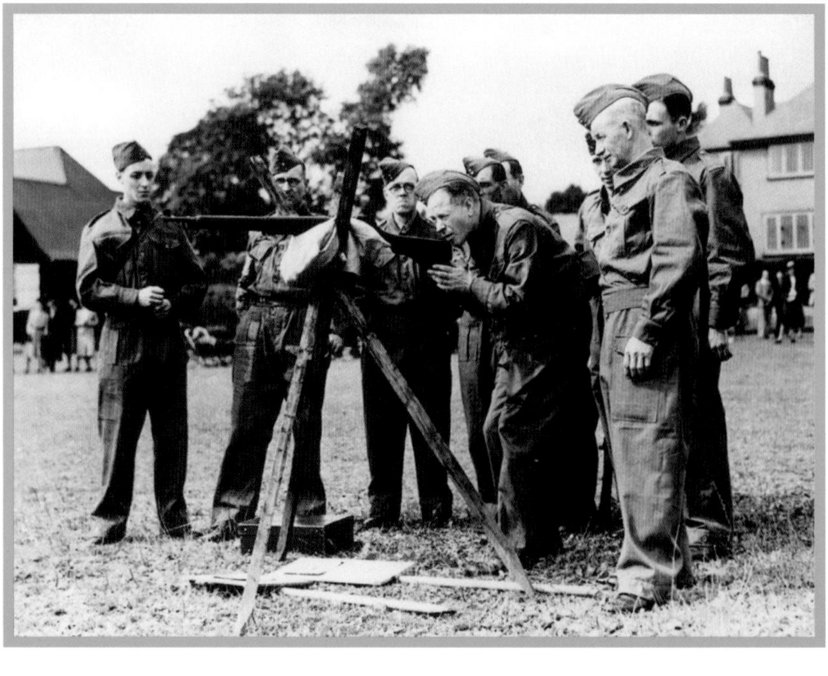

An instructor provides tuition for members of the Home Guard. This corps was trained in bomb disposal and antiaircraft gunnery, as well as raising civilian morale.

Military aircraft production

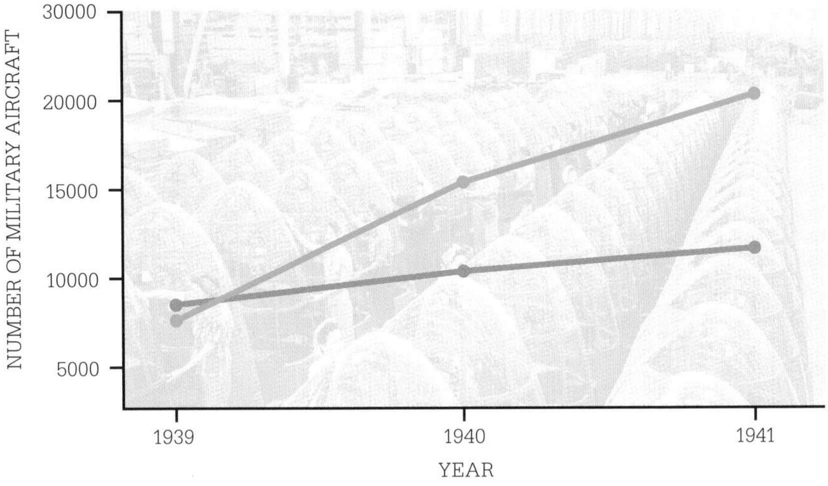

In the first two years of the war, military aircraft production increased more rapidly in the UK than in Germany—20,000 compared with 12,000 by 1941. Both countries' production was eventually dwarfed by the US and the USSR.

war and was repeated during the first and second stages of the Blitz. Between 1939 and 1944, more than 1 million children were evacuated from the cities to the countryside.

National debt

Paying for the mobilization drove the British state to the edge of bankruptcy. Income tax rates rose from 37.5 percent to 50 percent. With so much production devoted to war material, exports collapsed and Britain amassed a negative balance of trade of over £1 billion in 1945, almost three times more than before the war. Britain was compelled to liquidate most of her financial reserves and foreign assets. Even so, by the end of the war, the national debt had quintupled to £3.35 billion, the largest in the world. Only a loan of $3.75 billion from the US in December 1945, negotiated by British economist John Maynard Keynes, saved the country from what Keynes had warned would be "a financial Dunkirk."

Economic problems aside, Britain's mobilization had succeeded where it counted, however, with war production accelerating remarkably. Compared with 1939 levels, production of small arms doubled by 1940 and increased sevenfold by 1942; the manufacture of shells increased tenfold by 1942; and production of armored fighting vehicles was 17 times greater in 1942. Astonishingly, aircraft production tripled between January 1940 and January 1942 (compared with the Germans, who could only double production over the same period). Coal mining was the only industry in which production actually fell. A combination of archaic technology and working practices, inefficient corporate organization, and labor problems hampered the industry. ■

Women at work

One of the most significant cultural impacts of the war was the intensive mobilization of women for the war effort. This saw women entering many areas of employment previously reserved mostly for men. Women joined every industry except coal mining and were especially prominent in agriculture, where a World War I venture—the Women's Land Army (WLA)—was revived. More than 200,000 women eventually served as "Land Girls," with a peak of 80,000 in 1944, and they contributed to every aspect of agriculture, including hard labor. In one celebrated instance, a former hairdresser beat male competitors to win a horse-plowing competition in Yorkshire.

"The land army fights in the fields," declared the WLA director Lady Gertrude Denman. "It is in the fields of Britain that the most critical battle of the present war may well be fought and won." The WLA operated from June 1939 to November 1950.

These WLA members are taking in the harvest. They also milked cows, planted hedges, dug ditches, and cut timber. Without their efforts, the UK would have starved.

THE WID
WAR
1941–1942

ENING

MAR 24, 1941

Rommel's Afrika Korps opens an offensive in Libya, **capturing** the British-held town of **El Agheila**.

APR 1941

The Germans deploy 31 **U-boats** in the **Battle of the Atlantic**. In April alone, they **sink 195 Allied ships** totaling 687,000 tons.

APR 6, 1941

German forces invade Yugoslavia and Greece. Yugoslavia falls in a matter of days but mainland Greece holds on until the end of the month.

APR–MAY 1941

The **Allies advance into Vichy-held Syria** and **Lebanon**, while German sympathizers in Iraq are expelled by the British.

MAY 20, 1941

German airborne forces attack the British-held island of **Crete**. The Germans suffer heavy casualties but are in control of the island by the end of May.

MAY 24, 1941

The **German** battleship ***Bismarck* sinks** the **British battle cruiser HMS *Hood***. Only three of *Hood's* 1,416 men survive.

JUN 13, 1941

The **Vichy French** puppet government announces the **arrest** of more than **12,000 Jews**, held in internment camps prior to transportation to Germany.

JUN 22, 1941

German troops invade the USSR in the opening phase of **Operation Barbarossa**. The Germans swiftly overcome Soviet border defenses.

As master of continental Europe, Hitler spent the opening months of 1941 preparing his forces for the invasion of the USSR. In the diplomatic sphere, he tried to persuade the Balkan nations to agree to the free passage of German troops through their territories. Most of the Balkan states fell into line, with just Yugoslavia and Greece resisting.

Hitler's preparations were interrupted by the actions of Axis partner Benito Mussolini, whose declaration of war against Britain had turned the Mediterranean region into a conflict zone. Italy's invasion of Egypt brought a British counter response that forced the Italians back into Libya. Hitler felt obliged to send reinforcements: German commander Erwin Rommel's Afrika Korps stabilized the Italian retreat and began a long see-saw campaign that would only end at the Battle of El Alamein in November 1942.

From Greece to Russia

The Italian intervention in Greece also proved disastrous, and Hitler again came to Mussolini's aid. Britain and Greece were now allies and the establishment of British air bases in Greece put the Romanian oil fields—vital to Germany—at risk of aerial attack. In April 1941, German forces invaded Yugoslavia and Greece with remarkable success. However, it drained resources away from the main theater of operations: the USSR.

Carving out new lands in eastern Europe in order to provide German people with *Lebensraum* ("living space") had long been Hitler's great ambition. On June 22, 1941, he launched Operation Barbarossa, in which more than 3 million Axis troops crossed the Soviet borders. The war on the Eastern Front was the most ferocious in the history of warfare. Tens of millions of soldiers were involved in a conflict stretching from the Baltic to the Black Sea, and the fighting was pitiless.

Hitler believed the war on the Eastern Front to be one of extermination, and the German armed forces were instructed to behave accordingly: Jewish people and Soviet officials were killed on the spot; civilians were left to starve. Prisoners of war were treated so badly in the USSR that over half of the 6 million Axis prisoners of war died of starvation and disease.

AUG 9–12, 1941

Churchill and **Roosevelt meet** at Placentia Bay in Newfoundland, an **important step** in the US's gradual move to a war footing.

DEC 6, 1941

A mass **Soviet counteroffensive catches the Germans** off-guard. They are thrown back from the outskirts of Moscow in disarray.

DEC 7, 1941

The **Japanese launch a surprise attack** against the **US naval base at Pearl Harbor**, the opening move in Japan's war against the Western Allies.

JAN 20, 1942

Senior Nazis attend the **Wannsee Conference** in Berlin to discuss what they call the "**Final Solution**"—the systematic **extermination of Europe's Jews**.

FEB 15, 1942

British forces in Singapore surrender to the Japanese. More than 80,000 British and Allied soldiers march into captivity.

MAY 1942

In the **Battle of the Coral Sea**, the Japanese and Allied navies fight a series of engagements that results in a **tactical draw** but a strategic victory for the Allies.

MAY 26, 1942

Rommel opens his **attack on the British-held Gazala Line**, the first stage of an offensive that forces the British to fall back from Libya into Egypt.

AUG 23, 1942

In the USSR, German forces **penetrate the city of Stalingrad**. The Red Army mounts an **epic defense** of the city.

The battle on the Eastern Front was the central struggle of the war in Europe. Whoever won would be the winner overall.

In the initial phase of Operation Barbarossa, the Germans scored a remarkable series of victories against Stalin's poorly deployed and cumbersome Red Army. At one point it seemed that Moscow might fall to a German thrust late in 1941, but this represented the high-water mark of Hitler's invasion. In December 1941, the exhausted German armies began to falter, and the arrival of reinforcements from Siberia tipped the scales in favor of the Red Army.

The Soviet offensive came as a grave shock to the German armed forces, but they were eventually able to hold their positions and await the arrival of reinforcements for a spring offensive. Instead of renewing the assault on Moscow, however, Hitler decided to strike southward to secure the oil-rich region around the Caucasus mountains. At the same time, he ordered an attack on the city of Stalingrad, a diversion that proved to be one of his biggest mistakes.

Japan's objectives

While the Red Army was gaining the upper hand in the USSR, on the far side of the globe, Japan prepared for war. Unable to gain direct access to vital raw materials and faced by opposition from the West, the Japanese government believed war to be the only solution to its problems. Its military planners hoped that a swift naval campaign would destroy US might in the Pacific, and that conquests in the Dutch East Indies, Malaya, and the Philippines would form the basis for a "Greater East Asia Co-Prosperity Sphere" to provide Japan with economic self-sufficiency. This strategy was, however, reckless in the extreme—a desperate hope that superior Japanese martial spirit would overcome the greater economic and military might of the Western powers.

Japan's audacious attack on Pearl Harbor, a US naval base in Hawaii, in December 1941—and its assaults on the Dutch East Indies, the Philippines, and Malaya—were stunning military victories, but the US-led Western Allies soon recovered. At the Battle of Midway in June 1942—just six months after the attack on Pearl Harbor—the Japanese suffered their first military defeat. ■

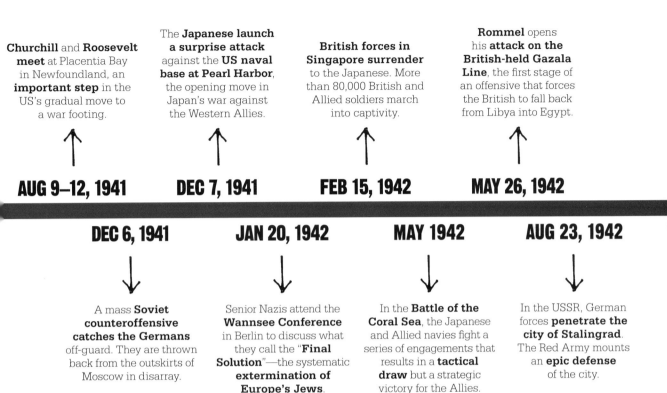

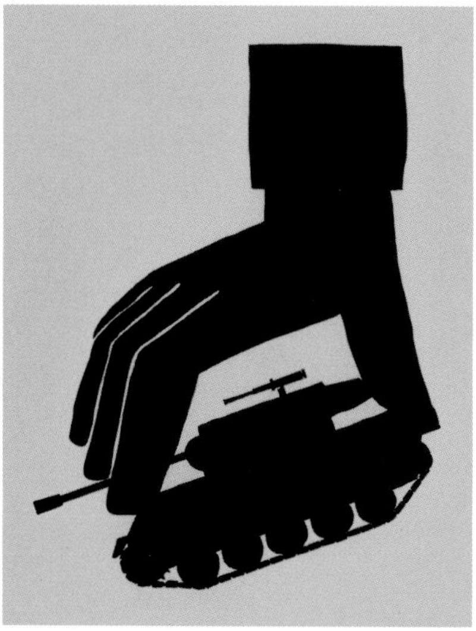

WE MUST BE THE GREAT ARSENAL OF DEMOCRACY

THE END OF US NEUTRALITY (MARCH 1941)

IN CONTEXT

FOCUS
Military aid

BEFORE
March 1920 The US Senate rejects the Treaty of Versailles.

August 27, 1928 The Kellogg–Briand Pact calls for the peaceful settlement of international disputes.

August 1935–November 1939 Congress passes a series of Neutrality Acts to prevent the US being dragged into another global conflict.

AFTER
August 14, 1941 The US and UK declare the Atlantic Charter, setting out their joint war aims.

December 7, 1941 Japan launches a surprise attack on Pearl Harbor naval base in Hawaii.

December 11, 1941 Nazi Germany declares war against the United States.

Although the United States had emerged from World War I as the world's most powerful nation, its voters preferred not to be obligated to other nations. In 1935, Congress passed the first Neutrality Act, making it illegal for the US to sell or transport arms to warring nations. Even after Germany attacked Poland in September 1939, only 16 percent of Americans wished to assist Britain and France. But in November 1939, in the final Neutrality Act, Congress agreed that a belligerent nation could acquire military supplies if paid for immediately and borne on non-US ships (the cash-and-carry policy).

Supporting Britain

In the fall of 1940, the CBS radio network broadcast the Blitz into American homes, telling listeners that the bombs they heard in London would eventually fall on their cities. Most (52 percent) now backed aid. When Winston Churchill confessed that Britain was broke and unable to fund "cash-and-carry," President Roosevelt exhorted Americans to become the "arsenal of democracy." In January 1941, he introduced a plan that allowed the president to supply, without immediate payment, military resources to any country considered to be the first line of defense for the US. On March 11, 1941, Lend–Lease became law. The outwardly neutral US was now tied closely to the Allied war effort. ■

President Roosevelt signs the Lend–Lease bill, pledging that the US will give military aid to Britain, China, and Greece.

See also: A flawed peace 20–21 ▪ Failure of the League of Nations 50 ▪ Appeasing Hitler 51 ▪ The Blitz 98–99 ▪ The Japanese attack Pearl Harbor 138–145

SHE WENT DOWN WITH HER COLORS FLYING

THE SINKING OF THE *BISMARCK* (MAY 18–27, 1941)

IN CONTEXT

FOCUS
Naval supremacy

BEFORE
1935 Contract for battleship *Bismarck* placed with Blohm & Voss shipyard in Hamburg.

February 14, 1939 *Bismarck* is launched.

May 5, 1941 Hitler visits the *Bismarck* with Field Marshal Wilhelm Keitel and Chief of Fleet Admiral Günther Lütjens.

AFTER
1943 German naval activity restricted to "wolf packs," rapidly assembled groups of U-boats to attack British convoys, but this tactic is largely abandoned by May due to heavy losses.

1944–1945 The surviving Kriegsmarine is heavily engaged in artillery support for retreating German land forces along the Baltic coast, and in ferrying civilian refugees in large rescue operations.

Armed with 70 guns and measuring 823 ft (251 m) in length, the 57,000-ton *Bismarck* was the first full-scale battleship built by Germany since World War I, and a symbol of the country's revived military might. On May 19, 1941, it made its maiden combat voyage, under orders to attack Allied convoys in the Atlantic. The next day, the British received reports of its location, and the hunt for the pride of Hitler's navy began.

Bismarck was joined by the heavy cruiser *Prinz Eugen* and both headed into the North Atlantic. British capital ships HMS *Prince of Wales* and HMS *Hood* dashed to Iceland in pursuit. On May 24, they opened fire. *Bismarck* responded, hitting *Hood* and sinking it. In return, *Bismarck* was struck twice, limiting its speed. Meanwhile, engine problems forced *Prinz Eugen* to return to base.

British aircraft carriers HMS *Ark Royal* and HMS *Victorious* then launched their Swordfish biplane torpedo bombers, striking *Bismarck* on May 25 and 26. The safety of Nazi-occupied France was 750 miles (1,200 km) away for the *Bismarck* and, when dawn broke on May 27, battleships HMS *King George V* and HMS *Rodney*, alongside heavy cruisers HMS *Norfolk* and HMS *Dorsetshire*, honed in on it. At 10:40 am *Bismarck* sank. Hitler responded by pursuing a more cautious strategy with his surface fleet, reducing the risk to which it was exposed but also diminishing its threat. ■

> We have for the first time in years a ship whose fighting qualities are at least a match for any enemy.
>
> **Captain Ernst Lindemann**
> ***Bismarck* commander, April 1941**

See also: Battle of the River Plate 67 ■ The invasion of Denmark and Norway 69 ■ The U-boat war intensifies 110–113 ■ Attacks on Arctic convoys 166

ONE TORPEDO, ONE SHIP

THE U-BOAT WAR INTENSIFIES (JUNE 1940–DECEMBER 1941)

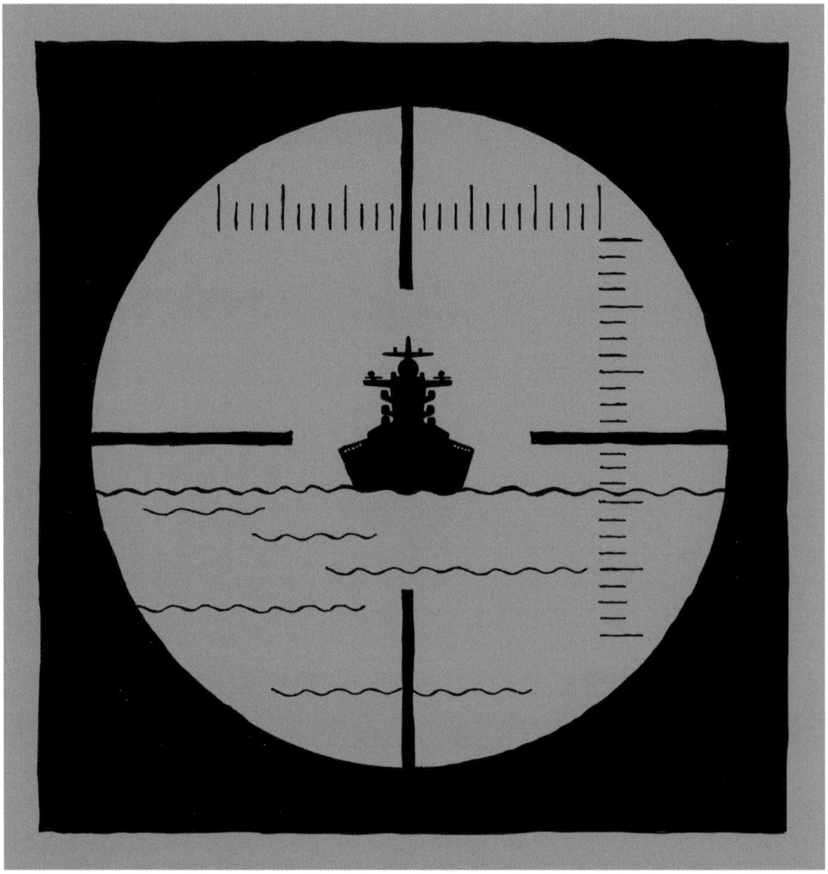

IN CONTEXT

FOCUS
War at sea

BEFORE
1917 During World War I, Germany's Atlantic U-boat campaign almost destroys Britain's economy.

1935 The Anglo-German Naval Agreement allows Germany to build submarines.

1939 In July, Polish cryptographers reveal to the British and French their methods for breaking the German Enigma codes.

AFTER
1942 U-boats dominate the eastern seaboard of the United States, sinking hundreds of cargo ships.

1943 In "Black May," U-boat losses become unsustainable and the submarines are withdrawn from the Atlantic.

The survival of Britain in World War II depended on the transport by sea of vital supplies from across the world. The struggle to secure shipping routes in the face of German attack, which became known as the Battle of the Atlantic, stretched across six years of war and went through multiple phases. In the opening period, from late 1939, German naval surface forces had some success but were outmatched by the size of the British Royal Navy. Also, Britain had learned from its heavy shipping losses in World War I and employed the convoy system, whereby ships sailed in groups protected by warships.

See also: Battle of the River Plate 67 ▪ The invasion of Denmark and Norway 69 ▪ The end of US neutrality 108 ▪ The sinking of the *Bismarck* 109 ▪ Attacks on Arctic convoys 166 ▪ The secret war 198–203 ▪ A showdown in the Atlantic 214–219

Sailors abandon HMS *Courageous* on September 17, 1939, after being torpedoed by U-boat U-29. The aircraft carrier was the first British warship sunk by German forces in World War II.

From summer 1940, however, the balance was tipped in Germany's favor by its fleet of *Unterseeboots* (U-boats). They would go on to inflict catastrophic losses on British shipping in what Churchill called "a war of groping and drowning."

The campaign begins

On August 19, 1939, all U-boat captains received a message about an officers' reunion. In reality, it was a coded message telling them to take up positions around the British Isles in anticipation of war. It did not take long for the submarines to claim their first kill, but it was a terrible mistake. Just nine hours after the declaration of war, on September 3, the captain of U-30, sailing west of Ireland, saw what he thought was the silhouette of an armed merchant cruiser. He launched a torpedo and turned his guns on the ship, a passenger liner, the SS *Athenia*, which sank with the loss of more than 100 lives.

In the early months of the war, German U-boats proved relatively ineffective. Their torpedoes often malfunctioned and they struggled to cope with the tactics employed by the British. On September 16, the first transatlantic convoy of the war left Halifax, Nova Scotia, in Canada. The merchant ships followed zigzag courses to confuse the enemy, while their naval escorts listened out for U-boats with the asdic—or sonar—echolocation system, developed during World War I. The convoy arrived safely in Liverpool fourteen days later.

While the convoy system was broadly successful at first, U-boats still managed to sink nearly 50 merchant ships by the end of 1939. Many craft were fatally damaged by magnetic mines distributed by U-boats around the shipping lanes of the British Isles. This threat, however, was reduced after the defusing of a mine in November 1939 allowed British scientists to devise a way of demagnetizing ship hulls to prevent them attracting the explosive weapon.

A turning point

Between September 1939 and February 1940, Britain lost around 140 merchant ships in the Atlantic. In terms of tonnage, this loss was almost twice that suffered by Germany, but Britain had begun the war with nearly 2,000 merchant ships—one-third of the world total—and proportionally the British losses were less than half those of the Germans.

As a result, Germany was not making enough of an impact on British shipping to affect the war effort. On February 15, 1940, Hitler attempted to apply more pressure by issuing a directive that any ship, hostile or neutral, heading for British-controlled waters, should be sunk without warning. The turning point came in April–June 1940, when the capture of Norway and Denmark, and the fall of France, gave the Germans a range of Atlantic bases from which to operate and also narrowed the strategic focus of »

> No warning shot was fired before the torpedo was launched. I myself observed much commotion aboard the torpedoed ship.
>
> **Adolf Schmidt**
> **Crew member of U-30, on the sinking of the SS *Athenia***

The wolf pack attack technique

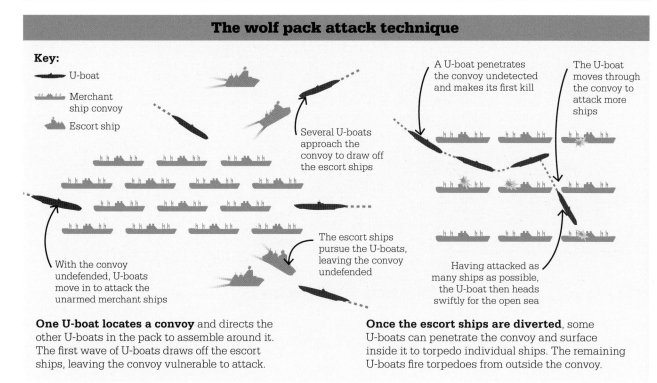

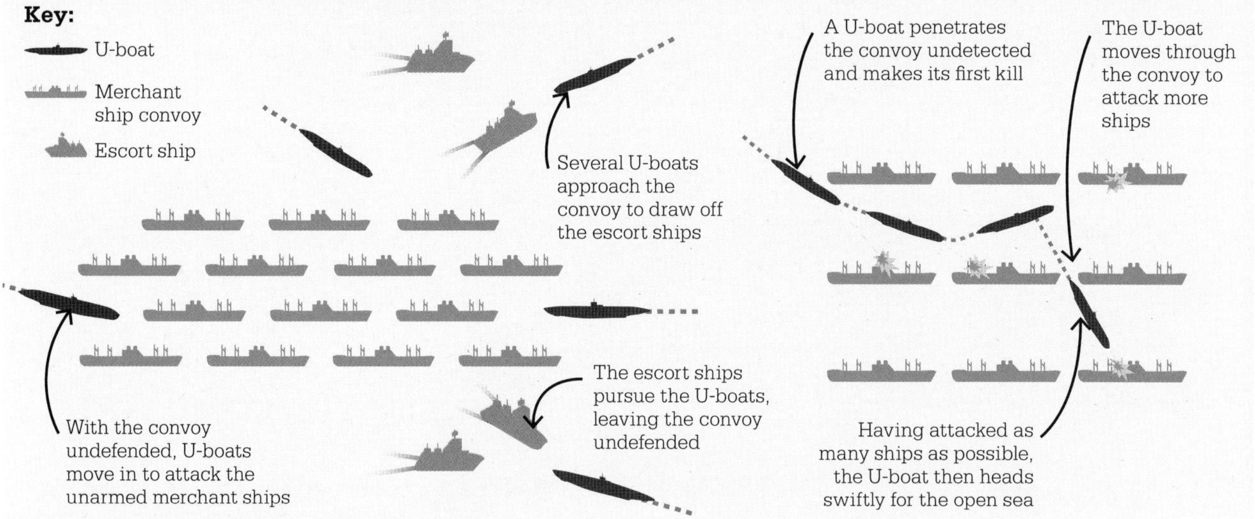

Key:
U-boat
Merchant ship convoy
Escort ship
Several U-boats approach the convoy to draw off the escort ships
The escort ships pursue the U-boats, leaving the convoy undefended
With the convoy undefended, U-boats move in to attack the unarmed merchant ships
A U-boat penetrates the convoy undetected and makes its first kill
The U-boat moves through the convoy to attack more ships
Having attacked as many ships as possible, the U-boat then heads swiftly for the open sea

One U-boat locates a convoy and directs the other U-boats in the pack to assemble around it. The first wave of U-boats draws off the escort ships, leaving the convoy vulnerable to attack.

Once the escort ships are diverted, some U-boats can penetrate the convoy and surface inside it to torpedo individual ships. The remaining U-boats fire torpedoes from outside the convoy.

German naval operations to British shipping, in an ocean siege that would bring the country to its knees.

Britain's "worst evil"

Before 1939, Hitler's champion of U-boat strategy, Karl Dönitz, had argued that "the decisive point in warfare against England lies in attacking her merchant shipping in the Atlantic." Churchill concurred with this assessment, writing after the war, "The U-boat attack was our worst evil. It would have been wise for the Germans to stake all on it."

Throughout the war, Britain was highly dependent on shipping for imports, relying on merchant vessels to bring in two-thirds of the nation's food, and an even higher proportion of goods such as petroleum products (95 percent) and rubber and chrome (100 percent). Hitler, however, was slow to realize the strategic vulnerability of Britain to maritime blockade, and even acknowledged his blind spot for naval considerations, admitting "On land I am a hero but at sea I am a coward." Accordingly, the Kriegsmarine (the German navy) was ill-equipped to exploit Britain's trading weakness. The head of the Kriegsmarine, Admiral Raeder, had, in 1939, formulated his "Z" plan to expand the German navy to the point where it could win the battle for the Atlantic, but it was predicated on waiting until 1944 before going to war. Dönitz himself argued that he needed at least 300 operational submarines to achieve a successful blockade of Britain, but had only around 45 at the outbreak of war and even fewer capable of playing a role in the Atlantic.

> "The only thing that ever really frightened me during the war was the U-boat peril."
>
> **Winston Churchill**
> **writing in his memoirs, 1949**

Over the winter of 1940–1941, Dönitz's U-boat forces declined still further. In August 1940, he had just 27 operational craft, declining to 21 by February 1941. Nonetheless, through bold new tactics and astute use of reconnaissance and intelligence, Dönitz managed to make dramatic improvements to the effectiveness of his small force.

Dönitz's first masterstroke was to turn on its head the accepted submarine doctrine of submerged daytime attacks. He introduced the "wolf pack" tactic, in which groups of U-boats attacked by night while surfaced, sidestepping Britain's asdic underwater detection system. The wolf packs, strung out in lines across convoy routes, located their prey through aerial reconnaissance, provided by long-range Kondor spotter aircraft—operating from bases in Norway and France—and advanced radio technology that enhanced communications across the fleet. A relatively small number of submarines could now cover a vast area but congregate quickly around identified targets. Between July and October 1940, nearly 300 Allied ships were sunk, and as the losses mounted into early 1941, German U-boat crews considered this the "happy time" of the war.

The impact of Enigma decryptions

The German military used a sophisticated encryption device resembling a small typewriter, called the Enigma machine, to encode many of its radio signals. The code was eventually broken by an Allied intelligence operation, Ultra, based at Bletchley Park, north of London.

From 1939, thanks to Polish intelligence, the Allies had replica Enigma machines, but the German naval version contained extra code wheels that added levels of complexity. In February 1940, the British recovered code wheels from a captured submarine, U-33, and in May 1941 seized an intact Enigma machine and its associated codebooks from U-110. Until the Germans altered their system in 1942, Bletchley Park code breakers could read German naval transmissions, leading to dramatically improved convoy evasion rates. In the second half of 1941, the Ultra decryption of Enigma probably saved hundreds of Allied ships.

Plugging the Atlantic gaps

The British attempted to adapt their tactics, deploying small warships (corvettes) to enhance thinly spread escort capacity, and making use of mid-Atlantic air and naval bases on Iceland, which Britain had first occupied in May 1940. Allies also came to Britain's assistance. The Royal Canadian Navy expanded rapidly from late 1940, taking on much of the convoy escorting and U-boat hunting work, as did the US Navy from May 1941. Air cover was a vital weapon against the U-boats. The threat of being bombed could drive a U-boat to submerge, while Allied airpower could chase off the Kondor spotter aircraft. Range limitations, though, left Britain with a "mid-Atlantic gap" in its air support for convoys. Striving to close the gap, the British resorted to desperate measures, including the fitting of catapults to merchant ships (known as Catapult Aircraft Merchant ships, or CAMs), which could launch fighter planes into the middle of the Atlantic. With nowhere to land, the aircraft had to ditch in the sea after only one sortie. By September 1941, light escort carriers—loaded with fighter aircraft—started to enter service. Their attacks on both U-boats and Kondor aircraft began to close the mid-Atlantic gap. But perhaps the most significant acts in the U-boat war were the attacks on U-33 and U-110, in February 1940 and May 1941 respectively, which delivered into British hands vital intelligence about German naval Enigma coding machines. This would allow Bletchley Park code breakers to read the majority of Kriegsmarine radio transmissions as they happened.

The entry of the United States into the war in December 1941 then heralded a new phase in the Battle of the Atlantic. Emboldened by encryption advances on their naval Enigma machines in February 1942, U-boat commanders turned their sights on rich pickings along the east coast of America—the second, and final "happy time" for German submariners. ■

An Allied soldier and naval gun overlook Reykjavik Bay in Iceland. By July 1941, more than 25,000 British and Empire troops occupied the island—vital to combatting the U-boat threat.

I HAVE NEVER SEEN SUCH DEFIANCE OF DEATH

WAR IN THE BALKANS (APRIL–MAY 1941)

IN CONTEXT

FOCUS
Military invasion

BEFORE
May 1913 Crete, nominally under Ottoman sovereignty, is ceded to Greece by the Treaty of London.

April 1939 Italy invades and occupies Albania.

August 1940 An Italian submarine provocatively torpedoes the Greek cruiser *Elli* off Tinos in the Aegean.

AFTER
June 22, 1941 Hitler launches Operation Barbarossa in a bid to conquer the USSR.

October 1944 German troops evacuate Athens and then quit the rest of the country.

October 20, 1944 Partisans and Soviet troops liberate Belgrade; German troops finally quit Yugoslavia in May 1945.

With the war in the west largely won by June 1940, Hitler could focus on his main ambition—to advance east and attack and destroy the USSR. Planning for this vast operation began in July 1940, but events in the Balkans intervened.

The invasion of Greece

Although Italy and Germany were now allies, neither fully confided in the other. Jealous of Germany's growing influence in the Balkans, Mussolini set his sights on neutral Greece but did not inform Hitler of his plans. On October 28, 1940, the Italian leader issued a three-hour ultimatum to the Greek government

See also: Italy and the rise of fascism 22–23 ▪ Dictators and fragile democracies in Europe 34–39 ▪ Italy enters the war 88–89 ▪ Operation Barbarossa 124–131 ▪ Resistance movements 226–231 ▪ The Soviets push into Germany 288–289

Greek women bearing guns and ammunition are shown heading into the mountains to fight off the Italians in a propaganda poster from the war that sparked the Balkan conflict.

demanding free passage for his troops to occupy strategic strongholds in the country. When prime minister Ioannis Metaxas refused, Italian troops invaded.

The Greeks quickly halted the invaders' initial three-pronged offensive from Italian-controlled Albania on the mountainous border in northwestern Greece, and pursued them into Albania. British RAF squadrons provided air cover for the Greek forces and inflicted considerable losses on the Italian air force. By January 11, 1941, the Greeks had captured the strategic Klisura Pass inside Albania. The Italians' final attempt to defeat the Greeks failed in March 1941, although Greek troops were fast running out of arms and equipment.

Hitler was angry that he had received no advance warning of the war Italy had blundered into, and alarmed that his main ally was faltering. He was also concerned that, in late 1940, British troops and aircraft had arrived on the island of Crete to help defend Greece. He feared that from there Britain could launch an air attack on Romania's oil fields, whose fuel he required for the planned Soviet offensive.

In spring 1941, German forces gathered on the Bulgarian border with northeastern Greece. Britain then sent in 62,000 Commonwealth troops—dubbed the "W" force after their leader, Lieutenant General Henry Maitland Wilson—but were reluctant to deplete their troops in North Africa by sending more.

The Yugoslav coup

Hitler faced further problems to the north of Greece in Yugoslavia, whose government had resisted an alliance with Germany. In a bid to consolidate support from his allies,

> There was no other course open to us but to make certain that we had spared no effort to help the Greeks who had shown themselves so worthy.
>
> **Winston Churchill**

Hitler had negotiated the Tripartite or Berlin Pact, signed with Italy and Japan on September 27, 1940, and later joined by Slovakia, Hungary, Romania, and Bulgaria. However, Prince Paul, the pro-British regent of Yugoslavia, related by marriage to the British royal family, was reluctant to sign. He was finally persuaded on March 25, but the reaction inside Yugoslavia was immediate. Two days later, »

Resistance to Hitler

Nations that resisted Germany were not all freedom-loving democracies. King Alexander I of Yugoslavia had abolished the constitution, banned political parties, and assumed executive power after an attack on the National Assembly in 1929 that killed two deputies. When Macedonian revolutionaries supported by Croatian fascists assassinated Alexander, Prince Paul, regent to his nephew, Peter, ruled that the kingdom should remain unchanged until Peter's accession to the throne, creating what was termed "a dictatorship without a dictator."

In Greece, George II returned from exile in 1935, when the Greek monarchy was restored, and in 1936 supported the rise to power of General Ioannis Metaxas, who established an authoritarian, nationalist, and anticommunist government.

The coup in Yugoslavia and the Italian attack on Greece forced both despotic regimes to take sides against Germany—as would Stalin's USSR, when Germany attacked in June 1941.

Hitler wants to **protect his southern flank** as he **prepares to invade** the USSR.

↓

Balkan states are forced to **sign a defensive pact** with Germany and its allies.

↓

After a coup that **overthrows its government**, Yugoslavia **refuses to sign** the pact.

↓

Hitler is alarmed when Italy **invades Greece without telling him**.

↓

Greece repels the Italian invasion, **weakening the German southern flank**.

↓

Hitler invades and conquers Yugoslavia and Greece; Germany now controls most of Europe.

pro-Western and Serb-nationalist Royal Yugoslav Army Air Force officers overthrew Prince Paul and replaced him with the 17-year-old king, Peter II, who assumed full royal powers. His new government promptly signed a nonaggression pact with the USSR and entered into talks with Britain about a Balkan coalition.

Hitler invades

The combination of initial Italian weakness, British intervention in Greece, and a hostile Yugoslavia forced Hitler's hand. On April 6, 1941, German forces simultaneously attacked Yugoslavia and Greece. Air attacks were launched against the Yugoslav capital Belgrade and Piraeus, the main port of Athens. These destroyed most of the Yugoslav air force and damaged the British supply line into Greece. German troops then flooded into Yugoslavia from *Grossdeutschland* ("Greater German Reich"), Bulgaria, and later from Romania, while the Hungarian Third Army attacked northeast Yugoslavia. In the south, German troops cut through southern Yugoslavia to attack Greece from the north and, on April 9, took Monastir and Salonika, cutting Greece off from Yugoslavia.

German troops took the northern city of Zagreb on April 10, with the local Croats declaring independence and support for Italy. As the Italians secured the coastline of Yugoslavia from north and south, meeting up in Dubrovnik, the Germans took Belgrade on April 13 before sweeping southwest to take Sarajevo. Faced with such losses, Yugoslavia surrendered on April 17.

As the Germans headed south into Greece, the British W Force had retreated from the defensive Aliakmon Line in northern Greece south to Mount Olympus. Over the next two weeks, the Germans pushed on, driving a wedge between the W Force in the east and the Greek First Army now isolated in Albania. Italian troops at last achieved some success in Albania and joined in the fight, forcing the Greek First Army to surrender on April 20. Facing the Germans alone, the British made plans to evacuate. W Force fell back further south to Thermopylae and on April 22 began to withdraw its troops to Crete. Three days later German paratroopers landed in Corinth. By the end of April, they had secured the far south of Greece, marking a decisive victory.

The last retreat

Anxious to pursue his advantage, Hitler ordered an immediate attack on Crete, about 100 miles (160km) south of mainland Greece. The first of a 22,000-strong German invasion force landed by parachute in two waves along the north coast of the island on May 20. They were met

> "The Yugoslav coup came suddenly out of the blue. When the news was brought to me on the morning of the 27th, I thought it was a joke."
>
> **Adolf Hitler**

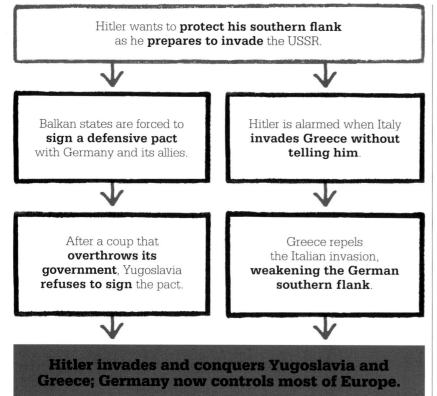

A German paratrooper shoots around a corner in Corinth, Greece, in April 1941 when German forces took the Corinth Canal, a critical access point to the Aegean Sea.

by around 30,000 British and Commonwealth troops, supported by around 11,000 Greek troops, and many Cretan civilians.

Outnumbered, the Germans lost many parachutists to fire from Greek troops at Chania on the island's northwest coast and to New Zealand troops defending Maleme Airfield in the west, but managed to secure the airfield on May 21. However, British Royal Navy forces resisted an initial German troop landing on May 21–22 and a second invasion force on May 22–23. In spite of these setbacks, German forces repelled repeated attacks on Maleme Airfield and advanced east along the island.

At sea, strikes by German dive-bombers cost Britain nine ships, with another 13 badly damaged, eventually reducing the Royal Navy's Eastern Mediterranean strength to only two battleships and three cruisers. Facing defeat, the Royal Navy began to evacuate large numbers of troops to Egypt on May 28. By the end of the month, the British had left the island. The fighters who remained joined the Cretan resistance.

The British had lost their last foothold in continental Europe. With the fall of Crete, the Germans had secured the Balkans and were ready to resume their march to the east and into the USSR.

Afterthoughts

The war in the Balkans was heavily weighted in favor of Germany, whose forces and equipment were far superior. Yugoslav resistance had quickly collapsed as its troops were defending a 1,000-mile (1,600-km) frontier with around 25 ill-equipped divisions—half the number of the better supplied Germans. Most of the Greek troops were still fighting in Albania, leaving only their Second Army and a relatively small consignment of British soldiers to defend against the invasion.

German troops parachute in to invade Crete in the largest German airborne attack of World War II, after the Luftwaffe had already bombed the British fighter planes based there.

Despite the victory in Crete, German paratroopers, making the first mainly airborne invasion in military history, suffered very high casualties. Hitler became reluctant to authorize further airborne operations, preferring to use paratroopers as ground troops. The Allies, in contrast, recognized the potential of paratroopers and started to form airborne-assault and airfield defense regiments. The Germans also faced their first—but far from last—experience of mass resistance from the civilian population of Crete; more than 6,000 died during the invasion.

Some historians have suggested that the war in the Balkans delayed and adversely affected Operation Barbarossa (Hitler's attack on the USSR in June 1941). Others contend that victory in Greece boosted German morale, and the delay it caused discredited Soviet intelligence, which had predicted the May date initially planned for the invasion of the USSR. ■

THE DESERT IS A GODFORSAKEN LAND

NORTH AFRICA AND THE MEDITERRANEAN (1940–1941)

IN CONTEXT

FOCUS
Military tactics

BEFORE
1912 Italy acquires Libya from the Ottoman Empire to add to its East African colonies in Somalia and Eritrea.

1936 Italy occupies Ethiopia, linking up its colonies in Eritrea to create a large East African empire.

AFTER
November 4, 1942 Rommel is defeated at El Alamein in Egypt and begins to retreat.

November 8, 1942 American and British troops land in Morocco and Algeria during Operation Torch.

May 6–13, 1943 Axis troops surrender in Tunisia, ending the war in Africa.

On June 10, 1940, the Italian leader Mussolini declared war on Britain and France, and immediately sought to expand his Mediterranean and East African empire. With their greater air and ground forces, the Italians imperilled Britain's influence in Egypt and its control of the Suez Canal, as well as British colonies to the south in Sudan, Somalia, and Kenya, and French colonies in North Africa.

Italian planes bombarded Port Sudan on the Red Sea coast and Kassala on the Sudanese border with Eritrea on June 11. On July 4, Italian ground forces left Ethiopia to take Kassala and also Moyale in Kenya. In August, their invasion of British Somaliland forced British troops to evacuate to Aden.

See also: Italy and the rise of fascism 22–23 ▪ Italy enters the war 88–89 ▪ The siege of Malta 167 ▪ From Gazala to El Alamein 192–195 ▪ Operation Torch 196–197 ▪ Victory in the desert 208–209 ▪ The invasion of Italy 210–211

Erwin Rommel

Born in Heidenheim, Germany, in 1891, Erwin Rommel was highly decorated during his service as an officer in World War I. In 1937, drawing on his war experiences, he wrote a definitive military textbook—*Infanterie greift an* (*Infantry Attacks*).

At the start of World War II, Rommel distinguished himself as commander of the Seventh Panzer Division during the 1940 invasion of France and was appointed commander of the new Afrika Korps in North Africa in February 1941. One of the ablest tank commanders of the war, he earned the nickname *der Wüstenfuchs*, "the Desert Fox." He described his North Africa campaigns as "war without hate."

Rommel accepted the Nazi regime but was not a Nazi Party member. By early 1944, he had become disillusioned with Hitler. Implicated in the July 20 plot to assassinate the Führer, he was arrested. Recognizing Rommel's status as a national hero, Hitler offered him the choice of suicide or a trial and disgrace. Rommel died by suicide near his home in Herrlingen and was given a state funeral.

On January 19, 1941, the British retaliated. They took back Kassala, advanced into Eritrea, and occupied its capital, Asmara, on April 1. Other British forces from Kenya had taken Mogadishu, the Somali capital, on February 26. A combined force then headed west from Somalia into Ethiopia, and on April 6 seized its capital, Addis Ababa; forces loyal to the deposed emperor, Haile Selassie, joined them on May 5. The Italian empire in East Africa was at an end.

The Libyan campaign

Four days after Italy's declaration of war in 1940, the British sent troops from Egypt into Libya to capture border forts, with patrols reaching the port of Tobruk 93 miles (150km) to the west. On September 13, the Italians sent their own troops 50 miles (80km) into Egypt, setting up fortified camps at Sidi Barrani. The British then withdrew to defensive positions further east along the Egyptian coast at Mersah Matruh, waiting until December 9, when the Allied Western Desert Force (WDF) launched Operation Compass. Within three days it retook Sidi Barrani and soon captured Tobruk. The force's Sixth Australian Division chased the Italians along the coast while its Seventh Armored Division headed inland to trap the retreating Italians on February 6–7, 1941, at Beda Fomm. More than 130,000 Italians were taken prisoner as the Italians were cleared out of the eastern Libyan province of Cyrenaica.

The arrival of Rommel

Hitler saw North Africa, and indeed the Mediterranean, as secondary to his main ambition to attack and defeat the USSR. However, »

Italian pilots plot their next move during Italy's invasion of Egypt from Libya in September 1940. In the first three months of the war in North Africa, Italy lost 84 aircraft and 143 aircrew.

Rommel observes enemy positions from his command post vehicle near Tobruk in 1941. Much-photographed, the German commander was a hero figure whom even Churchill admired.

he recognized that he had to send German troops to Libya to support Italy. On February 12, 1941, he dispatched his favorite general, Erwin Rommel, with the newly formed Afrika Korps, to rescue the situation. The general's orders were to hold his position in Libya and prevent further Italian defeats, but Rommel had only an instinct for attack and knew that diverting troops to defend Greece had weakened the British forces.

Early gains

After an initial air reconnoiter, Rommel judged his tanks to be superior and headed east from Tripoli, quickly seizing the coastal city of El Agheila in far western Cyrenaica on March 24. He met almost no resistance and carried on around the coast to take Benghazi on April 4. A second arm of his force crossed the desert and took Fort Mechili on April 8, capturing some 2,000 British troops. He then headed to Tobruk and surrounded it on April 10, besieging the Ninth Australian Division. Rommel had orders to capture Tobruk but decided instead to head further west toward Egypt. Tobruk would remain under siege for 231 days until November 27; its Australian and Polish defenders subject to heavy German artillery and aircraft bombardment but supplied by sea from the British Mediterranean fleet.

Rommel advanced rapidly to the Halfaya Pass, just inside the Egyptian border, which he captured on April 14, 1941. In May and June, the British twice failed to recover it. At this point, British prime minister Churchill appointed General Claude Auchinleck as commander in chief to replace General Archibald Wavell, and also authorized substantial reinforcements, notably tanks. The new commander's varied desert forces now included Australians, New Zealanders, Poles, South Africans, British Indians, and Free French forces, reorganized as the British Eighth Army.

Operation Crusader

After extensive preparations, Auchinleck launched Operation Crusader, thrusting west into the desert, and captured Rommel's HQ, at Gambut airfield southeast of Tobruk, on November 20. A few days later, Rommel's experienced tank commanders outfought the British in a confused tank battle at Sidi Rezegh airfield, southeast of Tobruk. Here, Rommel lost sight of the Eighth Army and advanced into empty desert, while New Zealand forces headed toward Tobruk. With dwindling supplies and fearful of being surrounded at Tobruk, Rommel retreated back west again, reaching El Agheila on January 6, 1942.

The naval war

For both sides fighting in the deserts of North Africa, control of the Mediterranean was vital. Each strove to destroy the other's vital supply lines while securing their own, and each aimed to inflict maximum damage in their bid to dominate the sea. Both sides also used their many local air bases to try to take command of the skies. The Italian fleet was numerous and included fast new cruisers with a good gun range, but in 1941, its ships lacked sonar and radar. Unlike the British Mediterranean fleet, the Italians also had no fleet air arm nor aircraft carriers.

> Gentlemen, you have fought like lions and been led by donkeys.
>
> **Erwin Rommel**
> **to captured British officers during the siege of Tobruk**

On June 11, 1940, a day after Italy declared war, its planes bombarded Malta, while on June 28, the British sank the Italian destroyer *Espero*. After an inconclusive outcome on July 9, when Italian and British fleets met off Calabria in southern Italy, action was halted. On November 11, the British staged a daring attack on the Italian fleet at Taranto, using outdated Fairey Swordfish biplanes. Two waves of assaults, launched from the HMS *Illustrious*, severely damaged half the Italian fleet. The rest retreated to Naples.

The British scored a second decisive victory on March 28–29, off Cape Matapan, at the southern tip of mainland Greece. First, the Royal Air Force (RAF) spotted a fleet the Italians had despatched to intercept British convoys ferrying troops to Greece. The British Mediterranean fleet from Alexandria closed in for the kill, sinking three Italian cruisers and two destroyers, and seriously damaging the battleship *Vittorio Veneto*. From that time, the Italians avoided major battles at sea.

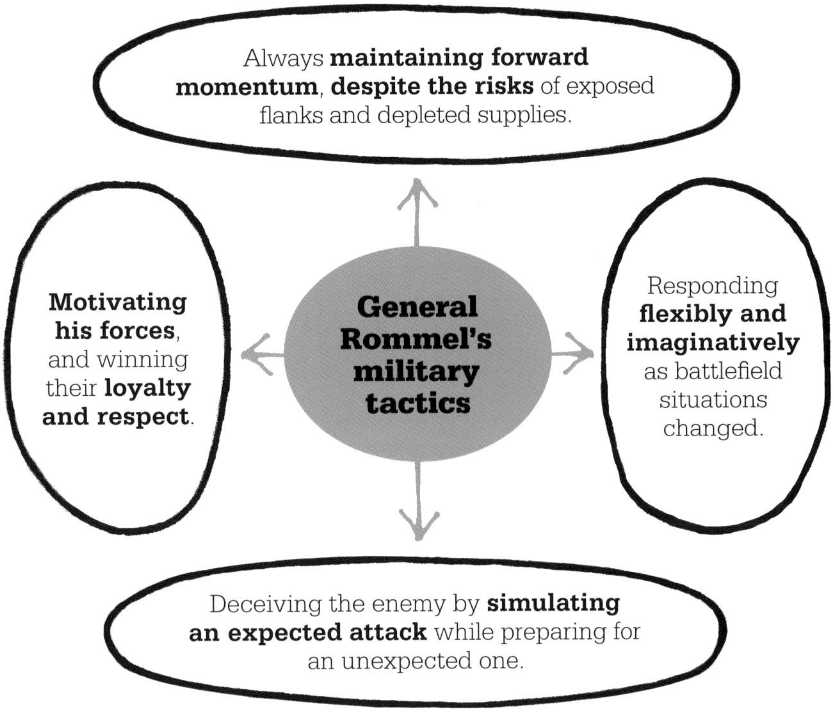

General Rommel's military tactics
Always **maintaining forward momentum**, **despite the risks** of exposed flanks and depleted supplies.
Responding **flexibly and imaginatively** as battlefield situations changed.
Deceiving the enemy by **simulating an expected attack** while preparing for an unexpected one.
Motivating his forces, and winning their **loyalty and respect**.

Vying for supremacy

Both Italy and Britain sent convoys through the Mediterranean—the Italians supplying troops in North Africa, and the British their forces in Malta. The Malta convoys from the east entered via the Suez Canal and those from the west through the Straits of Gibraltar, where German U-boats could attack. Both lines of supply were vulnerable to Italian naval action, and Malta itself was under bombardment from Sicily. While weakened at sea when Crete fell to the Germans in June 1941, the British fleet was still able to attack Axis convoys. In November, it sank a destroyer and all seven merchant ships in the Italian Duisburg convoy between Sicily and Greece and, on December 13, two Italian cruisers off Cape Bon in Tripoli, supplying the German Luftwaffe in North Africa.

On December 19, the British suffered a reverse when its ships ran into a minefield off Tripoli: two were sunk and two badly damaged. The same day, Italian mines damaged two battleships and a destroyer in Alexandria harbor. The Italian fleet had reasserted itself, but the battle for the Mediterranean was far from over, as the campaigns of Rommel and Montgomery would prove in 1942. ■

The Italian battleship *Roma* was one of three ships that was moved from Taranto in southeastern Italy to Naples in response to the Allied invasion of North Africa.

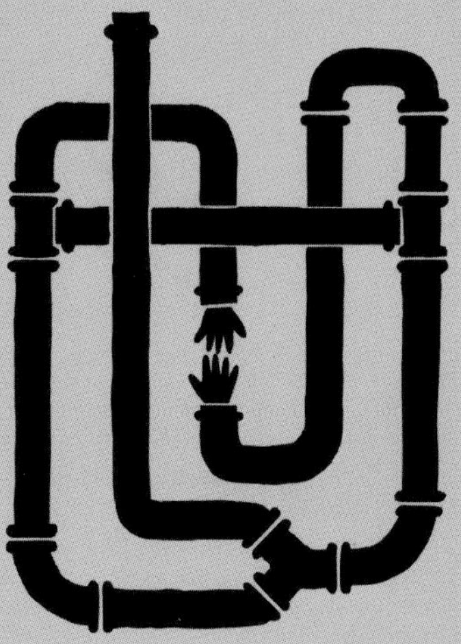

JOIN HANDS WITH RUSSIA THROUGH IRAN

CONTROL OF THE MIDDLE EAST (1941)

IN CONTEXT

FOCUS
Strategic territories

BEFORE
October 3, 1932 Britain grants independence to the Kingdom of Iraq.

September 9, 1936 France grants autonomy to Syria with the right to maintain forces in the territory.

June 1940 Syria and Lebanon both declare their support for Vichy France.

AFTER
November 8, 1943 Lebanon declares its independence from France.

April 17, 1946 Syria gains full independence from France.

March–May 1946 British, then Soviet, troops leave Iran.

October 26, 1947 British occupation of Iraq finally ends.

Away from the massive battles of the Western and Eastern Fronts, some often forgotten but important events occurred in several countries of the Middle East in 1941. The region's plentiful supply of oil meant it was strategically significant for both Allied and Axis nations.

An unstable region

With the fall of France in June 1940, the French-mandated territories of Lebanon and Syria came under the control of Vichy France. The pro-German sympathies of the latter presented a potential threat to British interests in the region, notably the Suez Canal. Iraq, which had gained its independence from Britain in 1932, was considered more secure as the British retained military bases as well as transit rights for its forces, but it proved to be politically unstable. Lebanon, Syria, and Iraq were immensely important strategically, because oil from Kirkuk in northern Iraq flowed through two pipelines to Tripoli in Lebanon and Haifa in Palestine. Britain desperately needed this oil to supply its forces in the Mediterranean and North Africa.

> Should the disembarkation be opposed … overcome the Iraqi forces by force and occupy suitable defensive positions ashore as quickly as possible.
>
> **General Archibald Wavell**
> **Commander-in-chief Middle East, July 1939–July 1941**

The Iraqi coup

This delicate political situation imploded on April 1, 1941, when the former prime minister of Iraq, Rashid Ali—a known supporter of Nazi Germany—along with a pro-fascist cohort of military officers known as Golden Square, overthrew the pro-British government of the regent, 'Abd al-Ilah. Once in power, Rashid Ali worked with German intelligence and accepted military support from Germany and Italy.

The situation then moved rapidly. Iraqi soldiers besieged the British air base at Habbaniyah near

See also: The fall of France 80–87 ▪ Colonial ties 90–93 ▪ War in the Balkans 114–117 ▪ North Africa and the Mediterranean 118–121 ▪ Operation Barbarossa 124–131 ▪ India in World War II 158

An aerial photo from an air attack on the Royal Dutch Shell Oil Depot near Beirut by British planes as part of Operation Exporter, the British invasion of Syria and Lebanon.

Baghdad, British and Indian troops landed at Basra in the south of the country, and a taskforce headed out of Palestine to relieve the base. German planes based in Mosul in the north supported the Iraqis. As the British forces neared Baghdad, Rashid Ali fled to Iran on May 27. Three days later, an armistice was signed and the pro-British government restored.

Free French invade

The Allies responded immediately to Vichy French support for Rashid Ali. On June 8, British and Free French forces invaded Lebanon and Syria. The Vichy French resisted on land and sea, but after the fall of Damascus, and with Beirut under threat, they sought an armistice. Fighting ended on July 12, as power was handed to the Free French.

Following Operation Barbarossa in June 1941, Britain and the USSR became allies. Bordering the latter, Iran was a major supplier of oil and presented the easiest route for supplies to reach the beleaguered Soviets. However, Iran's ruler Reza Shah Pahlavi had refused both to expel all German nationals and to declare for the Allies. Realizing the danger, the Allies struck on August 25, with British and Indian forces invading Iran from the Persian Gulf, and the Red Army attacking from the Caucasus and Central Asia. Outnumbered and outfought, Iran agreed to a cease-fire on August 30. Reza Shah Pahlavi abdicated and his young son Mohammad replaced him as shah. By early 1942, Soviet and British troops occupied the north and south of the country respectively, remaining there to the war's end. ■

> “The Arabian Freedom Movement in the Middle East is our natural ally against England.”
> **Adolf Hitler**

Indian troops enter an oil refinery in southern Iran to prepare to guard oil supplies for the Allies. Other Indian units invaded central Iran.

THE WORLD WILL HOLD ITS BREATH

OPERATION BARBAROSSA (JUNE–DECEMBER 1941)

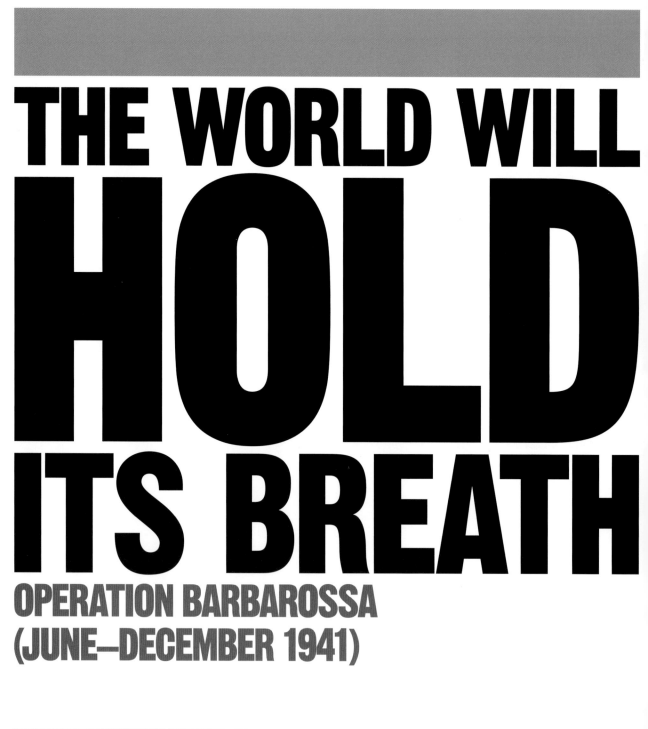

IN CONTEXT

FOCUS
Military invasion

BEFORE

1939 The USSR and Germany pledge nonaggression through the Molotov–Ribbentrop Pact.

1939 Germany and the USSR invade Poland in September, jointly occupying and dividing its territory.

June–July 1940 The USSR invades the Baltic states, then Romania's Bessarabia and Northern Bukovina.

AFTER

January–April 1942 A series of Red Army counterattacks fail to decisively force back the Axis, but secure the Soviet position.

June 1942 Axis forces launch Case Blue, a two-pronged attack on Baku and Stalingrad.

August 23, 1942 The Battle of Stalingrad begins.

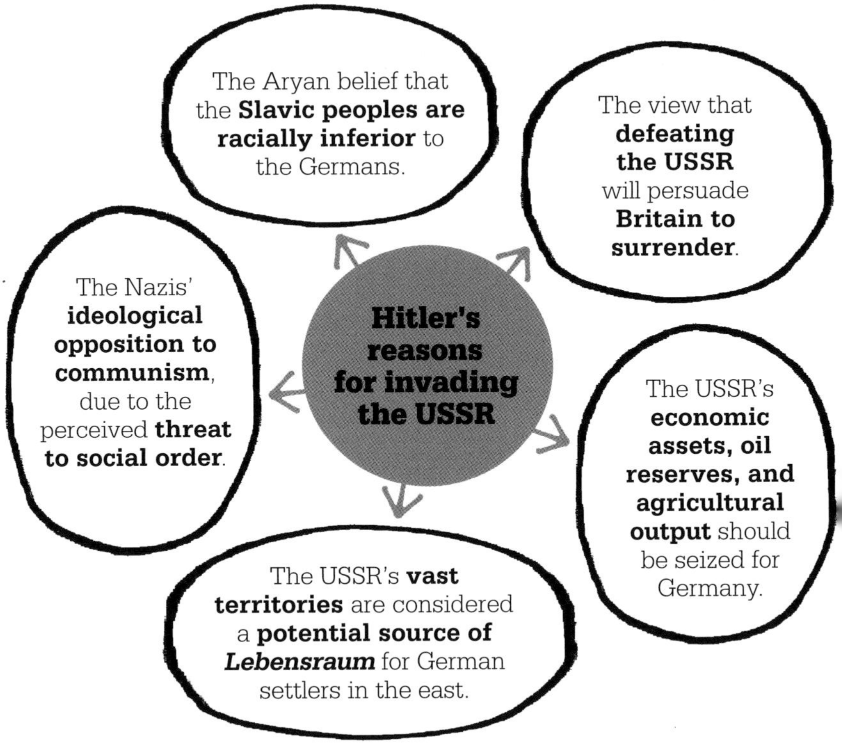

Hitler's reasons for invading the USSR
The Aryan belief that the Slavic peoples are racially inferior to the Germans.
The view that defeating the USSR will persuade Britain to surrender.
The Nazis' ideological opposition to communism, due to the perceived threat to social order.
The USSR's economic assets, oil reserves, and agricultural output should be seized for Germany.
The USSR's vast territories are considered a potential source of Lebensraum for German settlers in the east.

On December 18, 1940, Hitler issued Führer Directive No.21, calling for the crushing of the USSR in an invasion in the first half of 1941. Yet in 1939, the two countries had signed a nonaggression pact, which included a secret agreement to divide Polish territory between themselves and their allies following the German invasion of Poland in September of that year. A further sign of the easing of German–Soviet relations was a 1940 trade treaty, after which German manufactured goods were exchanged for Soviet raw materials. So Hitler's planned invasion of the USSR, code named Operation Barbarossa after Frederick Barbarossa ("Red Beard"), a powerful 12th-century emperor of German descent, had to be kept secret.

German ambitions

Despite the apparent friendliness between the USSR and Germany, fierce antipathy toward Bolshevism was one of the central tenets of Nazi ideology. Hitler and other leading Nazis had frequently predicted a final, armed showdown with the USSR. Also, in *Mein Kampf* and in his speeches, Hitler identified Soviet territory in eastern Europe as a source of *Lebensraum* ("living space") for the German people. The local population, most of whom the Nazis viewed as *Untermenschen* ("sub-humans"), were to be either enslaved, forced out, or eliminated. Unfolding events also persuaded Hitler that Stalin was not to be trusted, and that the time was right to invade the USSR, even though Germany had not yet defeated Britain and her allies. In June 1940, the Red Army struck west and occupied Latvia, Estonia, and Lithuania. Soon after, Soviet forces drove south into Bessarabia

> We are now directing our gaze at the lands in the east.
>
> **Adolf Hitler**
> ***Mein Kampf***

See also: German expansion 46–47 ▪ Europe on the brink 56–57 ▪ The destruction of Poland 58–63 ▪ War in the Balkans 114–117 ▪ The Great Patriotic War 132–135 ▪ Nazi massacres 136 ▪ The Battle of Stalingrad 178–183

and Northern Bukovina, which had been part of Romania. The latter annexation was more worrying for Germany, as it brought the USSR close to the Romanian oil fields that the German war machine heavily relied on. Following these gains, the USSR began to build the Molotov Line—a series of defenses on their new western frontier, from the Baltic Sea to the Carpathian Mountains.

Preparing to invade

Operation Barbarossa was initially slated for May 15, 1941. The German army high command believed this allowed sufficient time to defeat the USSR before winter set in. This view was based on Hitler's and his generals' opinion that the Red Army would not be able to hold out for long. Such confidence stemmed from recent military triumphs in France, as well as the Nazi ideology of innate superiority of the Aryan race over the largely Slavic Red Army. Also, German military planners believed that Stalin's "Great Purge" of 1936–1938, in which thousands of seasoned officers had been executed or dismissed, had undermined the Soviet forces. The difficulties faced by the Red Army in the 1939–1940 Winter War against Finland only solidified German disdain for Soviet military effectiveness.

The execution of Operation Barbarossa was delayed when, in April 1941, Germany joined Italy (and then Hungary) in the invasion of Yugoslavia and Greece. Although the Axis won in the Balkans by June 1, the date of the invasion of the USSR had to be pushed back by five weeks. Despite this, the objective remained the same: for Germany to reach the "A–A Line" (so-called because it stretched from Astrakhan in the south to Arkhangelsk in the north), thereby yielding control of the western USSR's resources. Because it was believed this could be done within five months, no plans were made for winter uniforms or to adapt equipment for cold weather.

By June 1941, over 3 million German soldiers (as well as 690,000 from Romania and Finland) were at the borders of the USSR. Despite being warned of an invasion by his generals and intelligence sources (as well as by the British and Americans), Stalin—who wanted to delay any potential conflict with Germany—refused to believe an attack was imminent. Even so, he had ordered an upgrading of the Soviet military early in 1941, raising manpower as well as production of tanks, aircraft, and artillery. By the middle of that year around 3 million Red Army soldiers were on guard at the USSR's western border.

> We need only kick in the door and the whole rotten structure will come crashing down.
> **Adolf Hitler**

The invasion begins

At around 3:15am on June 22, Operation Barbarossa commenced with an artillery and aerial bombardment of Soviet targets. Fighting on the Eastern Front had begun. The German attack aligned the USSR with the Allies—Stalin, »

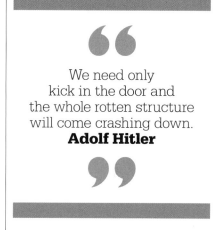

German infantry march past a bombed house as they cross into the USSR in 1941. Shelling of Soviet targets, combined with aerial attacks, heralded the beginning of the German invasion.

Axis invasion forces in Operation Barbarossa

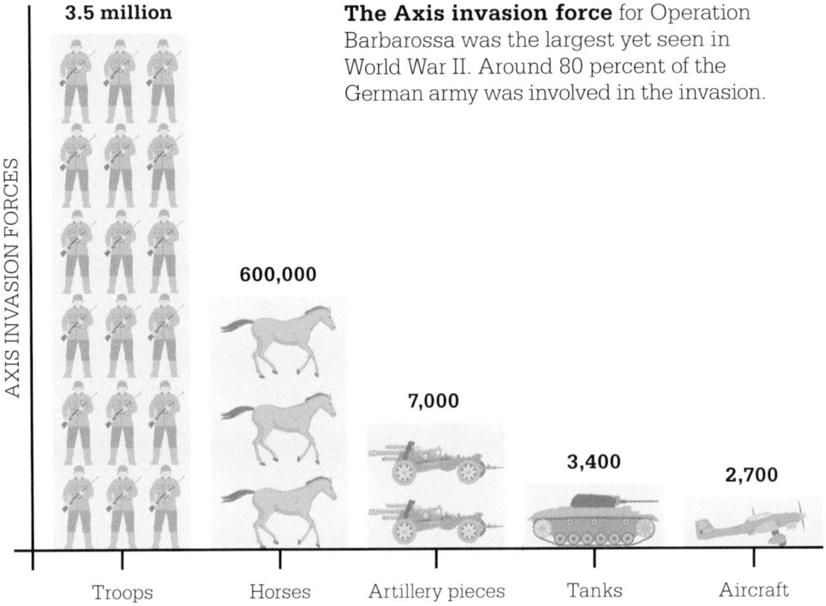

The Axis invasion force for Operation Barbarossa was the largest yet seen in World War II. Around 80 percent of the German army was involved in the invasion.

previously highly suspicious of the West, was forced into an alliance with first Britain, then the US.

The German invasion plan was relatively simple: a three-pronged advance into the USSR along a front 1,800 miles (2,900 km) long. Army Group North, commanded by Wilhelm Ritter von Leeb, would advance through the Baltic states and take Leningrad, while Army Group Center, under Fedor von Bock, would drive through Belorussia toward Smolensk. Army Group Center would then push on to take Moscow. Finally, Gerd von Rundstedt's Army Group South would capture Ukraine and Kiev, before advancing into the Caucasus. Pace and constant movement would be central to German success. Panzer units, supported by aircraft, aimed to advance rapidly, shattering enemy lines and destroying their cohesion. The infantry would then sweep up any pockets of resistance. Once Germany had consolidated control of Soviet territory, the "Hunger Plan" would be initiated—a plan to divert food supplies away from the USSR to feed both German armed forces and civilians. Under this plan, millions of Soviet citizens would die of starvation.

Germany gains ground

The early stages of the invasion went to plan for Germany and the Axis. The Soviets, not fully prepared, were thrown into total disarray. Coordination of defenses was difficult, and any resistance often lacked cohesion or organization. Although the Red Army had as many tanks as the enemy, their crews lacked training and experience. The Luftwaffe destroyed much of the Soviet Air Force while it was on the ground, and used its aerial dominance to destroy Soviet supply dumps, local headquarters, and transportation routes.

As a result, the German forces progressed rapidly, often more than 20 miles (30 km) in a single day. The greatest gains were made by Army Group Center, which had captured Minsk—along with 280,000 Soviet soldiers—by June 28. By July 17, the Germans had reached Smolensk, 300 miles (480 km) inside the USSR.

Germany's initial dominance on the Eastern Front masked major structural and strategic weaknesses. The Panzer units' rapid pace left

German troops cross the Bug River near Warsaw, entering Soviet territory—seized by the USSR from Poland in September 1939—on the morning of June 22, 1941.

Burning buildings in Smolensk after Germany's Army Group Center captures the city in mid-July. The Red Army suffered heavy losses, but constantly harried German forces.

gaps with the following infantry, meaning the tank units often had to wait and hold positions instead of advancing east. The Germans' quick gains stretched military supply lines to the breaking point. Soviet roads were clogged and congested, and to make matters worse, the railroad tracks used a different gauge to German trains, which had to be converted. Supply issues were particularly serious for the Panzer units. Within a month of the invasion, Germany's tank strength had dropped by half.

Civilian resistance

The citizens of the USSR began to create problems for the Germans. On July 3, Stalin exhorted them to fight to the last drop of blood, and to enact a scorched-earth policy to deny the invaders any succor. As the German army was expected to supply itself by foraging supplies from conquered territory, this order exacerbated their increasingly serious logistical issues. German forces' often brutal treatment of the local population, not to mention the mass executions of "undesirable elements" by the *Einsatzgruppen* (mobile killing units) , also stiffened the resolve of the Soviet people. In response to the frequent cruelty, massacres, and wanton destruction and plundering of property, units of partisans sprang up across the countryside. Initially, the partisans' effect was limited, but later in the war they were to create havoc behind enemy lines.

The Red Army fights back

After the initial shock of the invasion, Soviet forces regrouped and reconsolidated. Reinforcements were called up, increasing the number of divisions from 170 to 212 (albeit with only 90 at full strength), while reserve artillery regiments were created and moved to key points on the front. Soviet officers and generals gained experience and effectiveness at fighting the invaders. In particular, the Red Army mounted fierce resistance in Ukraine, where Germany's Army Group South fell behind schedule. However, the invasion force began to break through from the middle of July, and was joined by contingents from Romania and Italy.

On September 15, German forces trapped 650,000 Soviet soldiers around Kiev, the largest encirclement in military history. Five days later, the Soviet commander, General Mikhail Kirponos, was killed by a land mine. This led to a Soviet collapse in the area, allowing German forces to capture Kiev and more than 400,000 Red Army soldiers. The Germans advanced farther south and east into Ukraine, taking much of the industrial region of Donbas. On November 21, the port city of Rostov-on-Don was captured, leaving Germany poised to advance into the oil fields of the Caucasus. »

Soviet soldiers in German custody. Red Army troops captured by German forces were treated much more harshly than their Allied counterparts, and more than half did not survive.

However, six days later the Red Army counterattacked, forcing the Germans to abandon Rostov-on-Don on November 29—their first major withdrawal of Operation Barbarossa.

Meanwhile, Army Group North had secured the Baltic states, and reached the outskirts of Leningrad by September 8. Rather than storm the city, Hitler ordered his armies to bombard it and try to starve it out, beginning a siege that would last 872 days. Army Group Center had made little progress since capturing Smolensk, due to supply issues and diversion of its Panzers to assist the other battle groups, delaying the attack on Moscow.

Fighting for Moscow

On September 6, 1941, Hitler issued Führer Directive No.35 for an attack on Moscow. The assault, named Operation Typhoon, would concentrate the bulk of the Panzer forces on Army Group Center and use them to penetrate Moscow's defenses. However, fall rains brought the *rasputitsa* ("sea of mud") season, making the already poor Russian roads near-impassable in places. This gave Stalin and his

German forces maneuver to trap the Red Army during the Battle of Kiev. By mid-September, Panzers of Army Group South met those of Army Group Center, completing the encirclement.

leading general, Georgy Zhukov, time to organize the defenses of Moscow and call up reinforcements from Siberia and the Far East.

Operation Typhoon began on September 30. At first, German forces made steady advances, capturing 700,000 Soviet soldiers in three weeks. By October 19, Moscow was under threat and the Germans had closed to within 15 miles (25 km) of the city, glimpsing the famed cupolas of St. Basil's Cathedral. Germany believed the Red Army would collapse, but the Soviets fought on, launching counterattacks that prevented the fall of Moscow. By early November, it was clear to the German army high command that they would not be able to take Moscow, or indeed defeat the USSR, in 1941. The goal of Operation Barbarossa—to win a quick, decisive victory—had failed.

Counterattack

Stalin—who had remained in Moscow, even appearing in the annual October Revolution Day celebrations in Red Square—now had a chance to strike back. He had nine reserve armies that—unlike the Germans—were well-prepared for fighting in the cold. Freezing conditions also disrupted Luftwaffe operations, denying the Germans aerial superiority.

On December 6, 1941, the Soviet counterattack, led by Zhukov, was launched. Red Army soldiers, many clad in white to camouflage against the snow, struck hard. Hitler refused to countenance retreat, ordering his armies to stand fast and defend their positions at all costs. This went against the advice of his generals, who proposed a tactical retreat to consolidate their lines. Hitler's response was to

Civilians seek refuge in the ruins of the city of Leningrad. The inhabitants held out for more than two years against starvation and almost continual shelling.

The siege of Leningrad

Emblematic of the sacrifice of the Soviet people was the plight of the citizens of Leningrad. As German forces closed in on the city in September 1941, hundreds of thousands of its residents dug 340 miles (550 km) of antitank ditches and 1,600 miles (2,600 km) of trenches. This helped prevent the Germans from storming the city—instead they surrounded it and tried to starve its occupants.

When the siege began on September 8, Leningrad had a population of 2.6 million. There was only enough food to last for one month. Over time, people resorted to eating wallpaper paste, as well as horses, cats, and dogs. Leningrad faced near-constant bombardment; in total, German forces rained 150,000 artillery shells and 104,600 bombs on the city. On January 18, 1943, the blockade was broken, allowing supplies to be brought to the city. However, the siege was not fully lifted until the Red Army arrived on January 27, 1944. The official death toll was 632,000, but may have been up to 1 million.

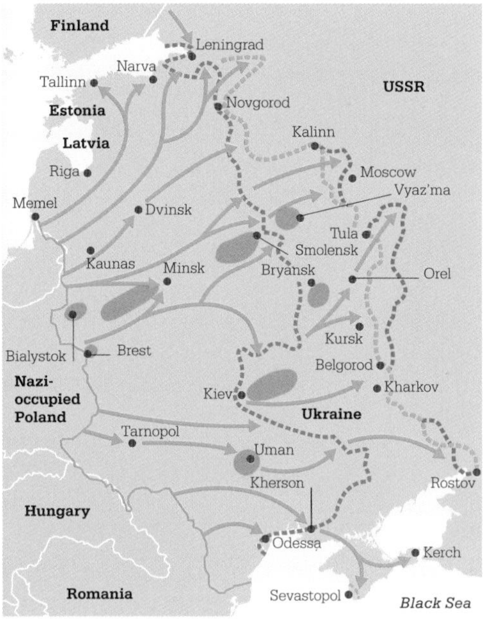

Despite its initial success in overwhelming Soviet defenses, Germany's progress was hindered by the vast distances involved, the harsh winter, and the USSR's huge reserves of men. Ultimately, the Red Army succeeded in preventing the Nazis from reaching Moscow.

Key:

- German advance
- German frontline, June 21, 1941
- German frontline, September 1
- German frontline, November 15
- German frontline, December 5
- Pocket of Soviet troops

dismiss Walther von Brauchitsch, commander-in-chief of the German army, and take the position himself. Any generals who went against Hitler, who was now in personal charge of the armed forces, faced dismissal and replacement.

The war drags on

By the end of December, German units had been forced between 50 and 150 miles (80 and 240 km) from Moscow, ending the immediate threat to the city. Hitler ordered his soldiers to dig in and construct "hedgehogs," defensive strongpoints that would be highly costly to capture. But due to the cold, his engineers had to use explosives to blast the frozen-solid earth.

As 1942 dawned, the rapid movement that had characterized the initial phase of Operation Barbarossa was a distant memory. Almost one million German soldiers had been killed or wounded, while the Red Army had suffered around 1 million deaths, 3 million wounded, and 3.3 million captured. It was clear that fighting on the Eastern Front would continue for months or even years, and take a heavy toll on the militaries of both sides, and on the civilian population of the USSR. ■

Nazi propaganda shows a German sled convoy advancing in Soviet territory during Operation Barbarossa. In reality, the harsh Russian winter severely disrupted Hitler's plans.

Joseph Stalin

Born in 1878 in modern-day Georgia—then ruled by Russia—Joseph Stalin became involved in revolutionary, communist politics in his early twenties. After the 1917 Russian Revolutions, Stalin became one of the leading figures in Lenin's communist government. After Lenin died in 1924, Stalin outmaneuvered his rivals, creating a totalitarian regime that consolidated power entirely on himself.

Under Stalin's leadership, the Soviet system was forced into centralizing economic reforms and industrialization, which caused the 1932–1933 famines in which millions died. In 1936–1938, his "Great Purge" involved the execution of around 700,000 internal "enemies of communism," and imprisonment of more than 1 million more. His regime's 1939 nonaggression pact with Germany kept the USSR out of World War II until the shock of Operation Barbarossa in 1941. Under Stalin's leadership, the USSR survived, and by the end of World War II was poised to establish hegemony over much of central and eastern Europe. By the time Stalin died in 1953, the USSR had become a nuclear superpower.

FIGHT FOR MOTHERLAND AND VICTORY!

THE GREAT PATRIOTIC WAR (1941–1945)

IN CONTEXT

FOCUS
The Soviet home front

BEFORE
1924 After Vladimir Lenin's death, Joseph Stalin becomes leader of the ruling Communist Party and the USSR.

1928 Stalin introduces the first Five-Year Plan to reform and modernize the Soviet economy through industrialization and collectivization of agriculture.

June 22, 1941 Breaking the nonaggression pact, Germany launches Operation Barbarossa, the invasion of the USSR.

AFTER
1945 The Red Army captures Berlin in May, and Germany surrenders to the Allies.

1946–1949 Following its military occupation of much of eastern and central Europe, the USSR establishes a series of communist satellite states.

During World War II, no nation's population suffered as much as the people of the USSR. The country lost around 26.6 million people as a result of the conflict—more than two-thirds of them civilians. After Hitler launched Operation Barbarossa in June 1941, the Axis armies wreaked havoc as they invaded and then occupied great swathes of Soviet territory. Millions were killed in the fighting, while countless others died as a result of summary executions, starvation, and disease. In total, the Axis forces destroyed completely or partially 1,710 towns and cities, 70,000 villages, and 6 million

See also: War in the Balkans 114–117 ▪ Operation Barbarossa 124–131 ▪ Nazi massacres 136 ▪ Nazi Europe 168–171 ▪ The Battle of Stalingrad 178–183 ▪ Prisoners of war 184–187 ▪ Germany's war industry 224

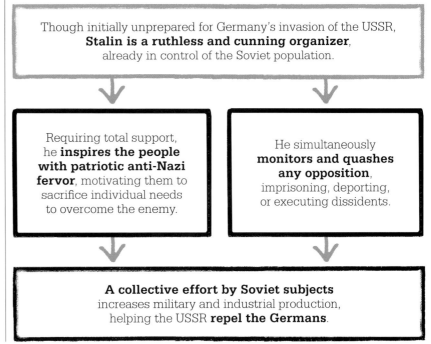

Propaganda, such as this 1941 poster depicting Lenin urging people to defend Leningrad, galvanized the Russian population. More than a million citizens helped to construct the city's defenses.

houses, making more than 25 million citizens homeless. However, helped by the winter weather, which slowed the German advance, the USSR survived to force back the invaders. There was no widespread collapse of social order or halt to economic production—the Soviet people mobilized en masse to defeat fascism in what was named by Russia's communist leadership as the "Great Patriotic War."

Moving the war effort east

Fighting Germany and the other Axis powers required a huge volume of munitions and vehicles, as well as supplies such as food and fuel. Manufacturing these became a major problem for the Soviet leadership: the nation's industrial and agricultural heartland was located in the European part of the USSR, which was either occupied by Germany or threatened with invasion. From June to December 1941, the USSR lost around two-thirds of its coal and iron output, over half of its steel production, and 40 percent of its farmland. As a result, the government had to find a way to relocate production of these vital materials east of the Ural Mountains, to Soviet Asia, where it would be out of reach of attack.

With the launch of the first Five-Year Plan in 1928, Soviet leader Joseph Stalin had begun the process of relocating factories and mining operations to Soviet Asia. By 1941, more than one-third of the country's coal, iron, and steel production had already been moved, but more than 90 percent of light industry—including most weapons and vehicle production—was still west of the Urals. As German forces approached during Operation Barbarossa, hundreds of factories were dismantled and moved east, safely distant from the threat of the fighting or aerial bombardment. Just one year after the German invasion, more than three-quarters of the USSR's military goods were produced in Soviet Asia.

Galvanizing public support

From the outset, the Soviet leadership recognized that the entire population would need to be motivated and unified behind the war effort. This was done by invoking the historical example of Russia's resistance to Napoleon's invasion in 1812—the first "Great Patriotic War"—when the Russian people had bravely fought back and repulsed a foreign invader despite facing overwhelming odds and privations. On June 23, the day after Operation Barbarossa was »

Though initially unprepared for Germany's invasion of the USSR, **Stalin is a ruthless and cunning organizer**, already in control of the Soviet population.

↓

Requiring total support, he **inspires the people with patriotic anti-Nazi fervor**, motivating them to sacrifice individual needs to overcome the enemy.

He simultaneously **monitors and quashes any opposition**, imprisoning, deporting, or executing dissidents.

↓

A collective effort by Soviet subjects increases military and industrial production, helping the USSR **repel the Germans**.

launched, *Pravda* (the official Soviet newspaper) named the conflict a second "Great Patriotic War." The phrase, which appeared on posters alongside great figures from Russian history, became a potent way of harnessing the efforts of the Soviet population, invoking feelings of patriotism and nationalism. Further appealing to Russian nationalism and history, the Soviet leadership introduced the Order of Glory medal for bravery, modeled on the czarist Cross of St. George.

Every Soviet citizen was expected to contribute to the war effort in some way—embodied in a propaganda slogan, "Everything for the front, everything for victory!" To keep up the supply of soldiers and labor, in February 1942 all able-bodied men aged 16 to 55 and women aged 16 to 45 (raised to 50 that September) were conscripted for the war effort, either serving in the military or drafted into the workforce. Although the majority of military personnel were male, women served in the armed forces in a range of roles, from sniper to pilot to military police.

From 1943, in a calculated bid to boost public support, Stalin relaxed his earlier suppression of the Russian Orthodox Church, allowing the reopening of theological colleges and officially permitted churches, something that had previously been antithetical to the avowedly secularist Soviet state. To appeal to non-Russian elements of the huge and diverse USSR, the strictly regulated government wartime radio service was broadcast in 65 different languages.

Boosting production

Groups of factory workers were encouraged to use their initiative to cut down production times, improve organization, and increase output—those that did were given the honorary title of "front brigades."

Lyudmila Pavlichenko—pictured here in her role as a Red Army sniper—was decorated in 1943 with the highest Soviet distinction, the Gold Star of the Hero of the Soviet Union.

> Educate the workers in a fiery hatred of the German-fascist scoundrels … Inspire our people to a great patriotic war of liberation …
> **Soviet government directive to regional newspaper editors, 1942**

Within six months of the USSR entering World War II, the "movement of the two-hundreds" began. This referred to workers who successfully completed at least 200 percent of their daily work quota, thereby making up for the absence of comrades who had been sent to the frontline. Komsomol (the main youth organization in the USSR) was also active in recruiting workers; by 1944, 400,000 young people had volunteered to join the workforce. The USSR provided a range of incentives for their best workers, including improved rations and public recognition through awards and prizes.

The increased productivity levels of Soviet workers reveals that the propaganda efforts (or fear of both the Germans and the Soviet state) soon bore fruit. By 1943, thanks to around-the-clock toil of workers, the output of the Soviet armaments industry was far in excess of pre-war levels. That year, the country produced 229 million rounds of ammunition, 3.4 million rifles, 2 million submachine guns, 458,000 machine guns, 24,100

Men and women worked long hours—sometimes deep underground, as in this secret munitions factory pictured in 1942—to produce the weapons required to arm the USSR's forces.

tanks, 29,900 combat aircraft, 69,400 mortars, and 122,400 artillery pieces.

To keep the workforce fed, the government introduced a strict rationing system, with industrial workers and military personnel prioritized. To help make up for the loss of farmland, gardens were converted into allotments (there were over 5 million by summer 1942). Even so, food was in short supply—largely as a result of the loss of Ukraine, the former "bread basket" of the USSR. Sowing wheat in the eastern regions, which were less fertile, made up some of the difference. However, even by 1943 most Soviet workers received rations of only about 1,500 calories per day—roughly half the recommended daily amount.

Aid from the West

The USSR supplemented its domestic production with vast quantities of aid from the Allied powers (as well as captured enemy equipment). Within a few weeks of the German invasion, British naval convoys of military aid to the USSR began. The first British convoys, which had undertaken the perilous voyage across the Arctic Ocean, arrived at the Russian port city of Murmansk in September 1941. Over the course of the war, Britain delivered thousands of aircraft, tanks, motorcycles, and antitank guns to the Soviets.

The vast majority of Allied shipments to the USSR came from the US. Under Roosevelt's Lend-Lease program, the Soviets benefited from shipments of American vehicles, weapons, and other goods. Food shipments from the US totalled more than 4 million tons, and were especially valued because they came in the form of ration packs that could be easily distributed to the armed forces. Another vital supply line was that of trucks and jeeps; of the 665,000 motor vehicles in service in the Red Army in 1945, two-thirds came from the Allies. The Americans provided the USSR with 250,000 telephones and 35,000 radio sets, as well as valuable raw materials including aluminum and copper. The US authorities even dismantled and transported a complete tire factory to the USSR.

> Our cause is just!
> The enemy will be beaten!
> Victory will be ours!
>
> **Vyacheslav Molotov**
> **Soviet foreign minister, 1941**

Enduring memory

The polemic of the "Great Patriotic War" retains a totemic importance in Russian self-identity and popular culture to this day. Even though very few veterans survive, the modern Russian state remains eager to preserve the memory and perpetuate the narrative of the sacrifice of Soviet citizens as being central to the defeat of fascism, and the salvation of Europe from Nazi tyranny. ■

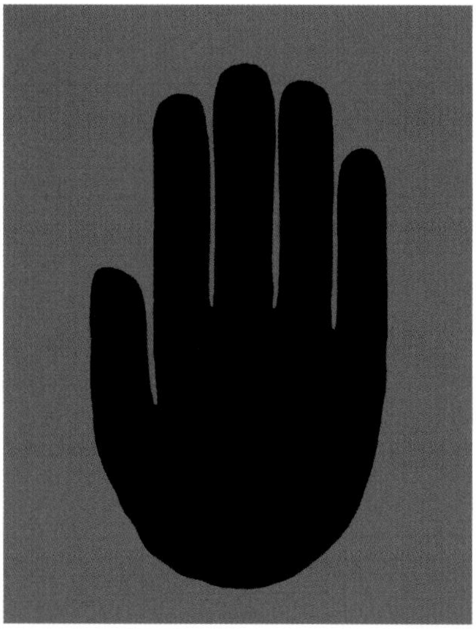

THE HOLOCAUST OF BULLETS

NAZI MASSACRES (JULY–DECEMBER 1941)

IN CONTEXT

FOCUS
Genocide

BEFORE
September 15, 1935 The Nuremberg Laws exclude Jews from German citizenship.

October 1939 The euthanasia program "T4" begins on patients in German institutions.

July 31, 1941 SS General Reinhard Heydrich begins plans for the *Endlösung* ("Final Solution") to the *Judenfrage* ("Jewish question").

AFTER
January 1942 Estonia is declared *Judenfrei* ("free of Jews").

January 20, 1942 Nazi officials meet in Wannsee to discuss the "Final Solution."

March 1942 The SS murders nearly 2 million Jews and other minorities at Bełżec, Sobibór, and Treblinka camps in occupied Poland.

Hitler's long-declared aim was to colonize the lands of eastern Europe, whom he viewed belonged to "sub-human" Slavic people. He also considered Jews to be instigators of the Soviet communist state. When Germany invaded the USSR on June 22, 1941, he launched a systematic campaign of murder against Slavs and Jews. He had decreed that Soviet leaders could be eliminated, and that his troops need not observe international laws on protecting civilians.

Following in the Wehrmacht's wake were four SS *Einsatzgruppen* ("Special action groups"—A, B, C, and D) of 3,000 men tasked with "cleansing." In effect, they were mobile squads licensed to murder and incite pogroms in plain view.

Mass murder

As Germany's land offensive stalled, the genocide escalated. By the year's end, the *Einsatzgruppen*, SS units, police organizations, and collaborators had shot as many as 1 million Jewish men, women, and children at selected killing sites—often ravines on the edges of towns, such as at Ratomskaya near Minsk and Drobitsky at Kharkov.

Although violence occurred in the Baltic states and Belarus, the bulk of atrocities were in Ukraine. On September 29–30, 33,771 Jews were massacred at Babi Yar. In early October, 35,782 Black Sea inhabitants were slaughtered. By late fall, gas vans were introduced as a mechanized weapon of mass murder. ■

> Hitler's troops occupied Kiev … and from the very first day started to rob and kill Jews. We were living in terror.
>
> **Dina Pronicheva**
> **Survivor of the Babi Yar massacre**

See also: Operation Barbarossa 124–131 ▪ The Holocaust 172–177 ▪ Liberating the death camps 294–295 ▪ The Nuremberg Trials and denazification 318–319

THIS MEANS WAR WITH AMERICA

JAPAN'S DILEMMA (JULY–NOVEMBER 1941)

IN CONTEXT

FOCUS
Japan's path to war

BEFORE
1931 Japan stages the Mukden Incident as a pretext to invade Manchuria, where it sets up a puppet state.

1937–1938 China is invaded by Japan, which occupies the eastern part of the country.

September 1940 The Vichy French colonial authorities allow Japanese troops to enter northern Indochina.

AFTER
November 26, 1941 The US secretary of state issues the "Hull note," calling for Japan to leave Indochina and China.

December 7–8, 1941 Japan attacks the US naval base at Pearl Harbor and invades southeast Asia.

May 1942 Japan controls Malaysia, Indonesia, Thailand, Burma, and the Philippines.

In summer 1941, Japan reached a decisive point in its colonial conquests. When Japanese troops moved into southern Indochina on July 25, unopposed by the Vichy French rulers, the US retaliated with an economic blockade. It was a clear statement that further expansion would not be tolerated. Japan's leaders were faced with a stark choice: humiliating abandonment of their dream of an Asian empire, or war with the US, which they feared they would lose.

Japanese soldiers—pictured here in Saigon—effectively occupied Indochina after Japan pressured Vichy France. Indochina's value lay in its proximity to Japan's foe, China.

Duplicitous diplomacy

Japan edged toward war in a confused and hesitant fashion, via a series of government conferences presided over by Emperor Hirohito in the fall of 1941. The emperor issued a statement counseling caution on September 6, so his ministers and generals pursued an ambivalent policy, negotiating with the US while secretly planning to invade southeast Asia. Even after the militarist General Hideki Tojo became prime minister on October 17, the Japanese continued to offer concessions to the Americans. However, US cryptographers had cracked Japan's secret codes, so the American negotiators were well aware of Japan's true intentions.

Ultimately Japan had to choose between fighting for an extensive empire that would bring economic self-sufficiency, or accepting a permanently subsidiary place in a world order dominated by the West. By the end of November, Japan had made the fateful decision to gamble on war with America. ■

See also: Japan on the march 44–45 ▪ The Japanese attack Pearl Harbor 138–145 ▪ Japanese advances 154–157 ▪ Japan surrenders 312–313

A DATE WHICH WILL LIVE IN INFAMY

THE JAPANESE ATTACK PEARL HARBOR (DECEMBER 7, 1941)

IN CONTEXT

FOCUS
War in the Pacific

BEFORE
1937 The United States expresses strong disapproval of Japan's invasion of China.

April 1940 President Franklin D. Roosevelt advances the US Pacific Fleet to Pearl Harbor to deter Japanese aggression.

August 1, 1941 The US imposes an embargo on oil exports to Japan following the Japanese occupation of southern Indochina.

November 26, 1941 Japan rejects American demands for the withdrawal of its forces from China and Indochina.

AFTER
December 11, 1941 Nazi Germany declares war on the US in support of Japan.

May 1942 Japanese forces complete the conquest of southeast Asia.

September 1945 World War II ends with Japan's surrender.

Japanese war planes prepare to take off for Pearl Harbor from one of six aircraft carriers in the staging area north of Oahu. The Japanese strike force included 353 aircraft.

On November 26, 1941, a Japanese naval task force, including six aircraft carriers, sailed from the Kuril Islands northeast of Japan bound for Hawaii. Its objective was to destroy the United States Pacific Fleet at its Pearl Harbor base on the island of Oahu, Hawaii, with a surprise air attack timed to coincide with Japan's declaration of war on the United States. The bold gamble was the brainchild of the commander-in-chief of the Japanese Imperial Combined Fleet, Admiral Isoroku Yamamoto.

Though essentially pessimistic about his country's chances of winning a war against America, Yamamoto reasoned that the only course to victory lay in seizing a massive advantage at the outset of hostilities, before the Americans could mobilize their superior forces of industry and population. A single bold stroke that put the US Navy temporarily out of action would give Japan time to establish a formidable defensive perimeter in mid-ocean, while its armies overran southeast Asia and seized control of the economic resources the nation required to keep its military machine functioning. Such a sequence of events could result in a Japanese position that might then prove too strong for the US to reverse, forcing its government to accept Japanese dominance in southeast Asia as a fait accompli.

Covert planning

Planning and preparation for the attack had continued through the summer and fall of 1941, even as the two countries' negotiators continued to debate a compromise that might avoid war. Japanese spies discreetly reconnoitred Pearl Harbor. As a target it posed substantial difficulties, especially because the water in the port was too shallow for conventional airborne torpedoes to function. Yamamoto was inspired, however, by the example of the British Fleet Air Arm's successful torpedo attack on the Italian fleet in harbor at Taranto in January 1941, which his commanders studied intensively. In conditions of absolute secrecy, Japanese naval pilots practiced endless attack runs with specially adapted torpedoes, as well as dive-bombing and level bombing. Thanks to Yamamoto's consistent support for naval aviation during

See also: Japan on the march 44–45 ▪ The end of US neutrality 108 ▪ Japan's dilemma 137 ▪ America at war 146–153 ▪ Japanese advances 154–157 ▪ The Battle of Midway 160–165

the 1930s, both the carrier-based aircraft and their pilots were of the highest quality, a precondition for any hope of success in what was undoubtedly a risky operation.

Yamamoto's plan to attack Pearl Harbor was officially sanctioned at a conference of Japanese government ministers and military chiefs in the presence of Emperor Hirohito on November 5. Yet the Japanese leadership continued to hope for some way of avoiding war with the US by offering a series of concessions. On November 26, however, a blunt statement by US Secretary of State Cordell Hull, demanding a complete Japanese withdrawal from China, ended all hesitation. Japan might possibly have accepted the abandonment of its aspiration to control southeast Asia, but could not relinquish all its gains in East Asia. The final go-ahead for the Pearl Harbor attack was given at an imperial conference five days later—by which time the secret naval task force was already on its way.

Undetected by the US

The fleet of 6 aircraft carriers and 14 escorting warships was commanded by Admiral Chuichi Nagumo. Refueled by oil tankers, it sailed for 10 days across hundreds of miles of ocean to within striking distance of Hawaii. That this advance remained completely unnoticed was a tribute to the discipline with which the Japanese maintained radio silence, avoiding detection by US naval intelligence, but it was also a consequence of American complacency.

To most Americans, the attack on Pearl Harbor may have come as a shattering surprise, but American military commanders should have anticipated such a move. It was obvious to any informed observer from July 1941 onward that hostilities between Japan and the US were likely to commence. By December, the US government knew war was imminent as negotiations had effectively broken down. Those with a knowledge of military history might also have recalled that Japan had launched its successful war against Russia in 1904 with a surprise attack against the Russian naval base at Port Arthur, made before a formal declaration of war. The commanders at Pearl Harbor had even been officially alerted to the imminence of war, but had not reacted with sufficient seriousness.

> The moment has arrived. The rise or fall of our empire is at stake …
>
> **Admiral Yamamoto**
> **Message to the fleet**
> **December 6, 1941**

Preparing to attack

The first wave of 183 Japanese aircraft, which included Nakajima "Kate" torpedo-bombers and Aicha "Val" dive-bombers, escorted by Mitsubishi "Zero" fighters, took off from their carriers at dawn on December 250 miles (7,400 km) »

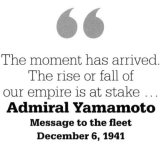

An aerial view shows Pearl Harbor just before the attack. The Japanese knew the locations of the American warships, as revealed by an annotated map found later on a captured midget submarine.

Three American battleships catch fire as the Japanese bombard Pearl Harbor. A total of 19 US naval ships were damaged or destroyed in the attacks and more than 2,400 Americans died.

north of Hawaii. It was a Sunday morning and a relaxed peacetime atmosphere reigned among the US forces in Hawaii. Commander Mitsuo Fuchida, the lead pilot on the raid, was able to listen in to entertainment programs being broadcast by a Honolulu radio station, which included useful updates on the local weather. The Americans had two clear warnings of something amiss. In support of the air attacks, the Japanese had decided to infiltrate a number of two-man midget submarines into the harbor, launched from full-size submarines offshore. One of these tiny vessels was spotted by American sailors, yet no general alert was triggered. More surprisingly, when American radar operators registered a large body of incoming aircraft, they blandly assumed they must be friendly planes.

Caught off guard

Reaching Pearl Harbor at 7:55 am, the Japanese first wave found a total of 90 American warships at anchor or in dry dock. These included eight battleships, but crucially not the US carrier fleet vessels, all four of which were, by chance, absent from the harbor. Surprise was total. As the bombs began to fall, a band was playing on the deck of the battleship USS *Nevada*. Some 300 American aircraft that might have intercepted the attackers were strafed and bombed by the Japanese as they stood on their airfields and were never able to get off the ground. Heroic efforts by US naval personnel to bring antiaircraft guns into action had only a limited effect. Within 20 minutes, hit by four bombs, the battleship USS *Arizona*, had exploded, killing 1,777 men, and the torpedoed battleship USS *Oklahoma* had capsized with the loss of 429 lives. A squadron of B-17 bombers, flying in from the US mainland, arrived in the middle of the attack and was decimated.

Calculated obfuscation

As Japanese planes wreaked havoc in Hawaii, confusion and delays in Washington, D.C., frustrated a timely response to a deliberately abstruse warning from Japan. Admiral Yamamoto had planned that the Japanese ambassador should

> The Japanese Government regrets … it is impossible to reach an agreement through further negotiations.
> **14-Point Message**

present a declaration of war to the US government half an hour before the first strike on Pearl Harbor, thus conforming with international conventions that outlawed attacks on another country's forces in peacetime. But, as the operation's success hinged entirely on surprise, the Japanese were nervous about any move that might alert American defenses. Up to the last minute, they needed to maintain the deception that diplomatic negotiations were being seriously pursued. The eve of the attack, a long, convoluted text, known as the 14-Point Message, was transmitted in code from Tokyo to the Japanese Embassy in Washington, for presentation to the Americans in the morning. Because of the time it took Japanese staff to decode and transcribe the text, and the difficulty of locating American officials on a Sunday morning, it was not delivered to US Secretary of State Hull until an hour after the attack had commenced.

Although it announced that Japan was breaking off peace negotiations, the complex and evasive text fell far short of a formal declaration of war. The message had, in fact, been intercepted by US intelligence and decoded before the attack on Pearl Harbor began, but intelligence officers failed to understand that it was meant to announce the immediate start of hostilities. Whether attacking before war was declared constituted a serious crime in the context of 20th century total war, or was merely a breach of etiquette, is hard to judge. However, it was much exploited in American propaganda that denounced the "sneak attack" and became a major element in war crimes trials of Japanese leaders after the war.

Another attack

A second wave of 170 Japanese naval aircraft struck Pearl Harbor an hour after the first attack, and faced a much fiercer response from fully alert American antiaircraft defenses. The battleship USS *Nevada* had succeeded in weighing anchor and was sailing for the open sea when it was struck by dive-bombers. Hit by six bombs and set afire, it was deliberately beached to avoid sinking in deep water. The USS *Pennsylvania*, the flagship of the Pacific fleet, suffered relatively minor damage in dry dock, but destroyers docked on both sides of it were wrecked.

Devastating losses

Overall the devastation was shocking. By the time the last Japanese aircraft had disappeared back to their carriers, all eight US battleships in the harbor had been sunk or damaged, along with seven other significant warships. The Americans had also lost 188 aircraft, most of them destroyed on the ground. Their military casualties totalled 2,335 killed and 1,143 wounded. In contrast, Japanese losses were light, with only 29 aircraft destroyed. The »

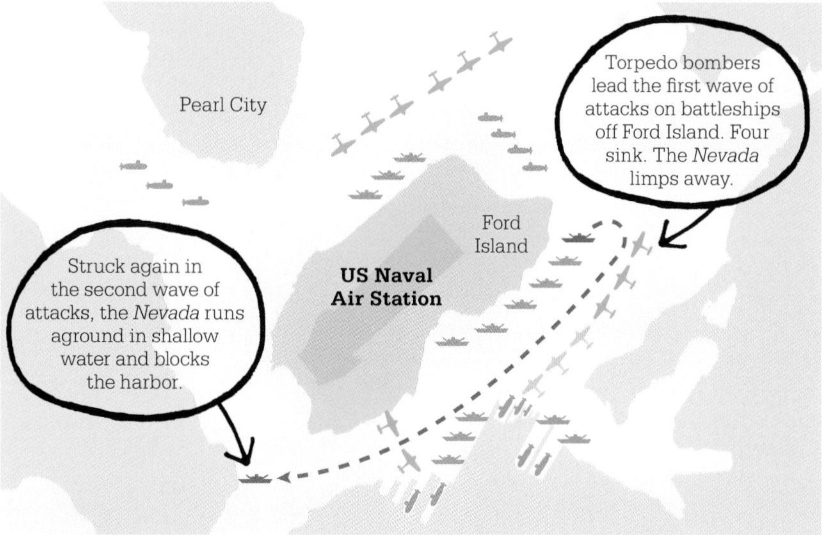

Pearl City
Torpedo bombers lead the first wave of attacks on battleships off Ford Island. Four sink. The *Nevada* limps away.
Ford Island
US Naval Air Station
Struck again in the second wave of attacks, the *Nevada* runs aground in shallow water and blocks the harbor.
Key:
First wave of Japanese bombers
Second wave of Japanese bombers
US battleship or cruiser
US destroyer or submarine
USS *Nevada*
Route of USS *Nevada*

The Japanese planes attacked the US naval base at Pearl Harbor from the north in a minutely planned attack, delivering torpedoes as well as armor-piercing and general bombs. Planes approached at different heights and from different directions, with US battleships their prime targets.

Isoroku Yamamoto

Born Takana Isoroku in 1884, the future admiral graduated from the Japanese Naval Academy in 1904 and, a year later, lost two fingers fighting as an ensign at the Battle of Tsushima. In 1916, his adoption by the Yamamoto samurai family, whose name he took, hastened his rise to high rank. He spent time in the US, first studying English at Harvard University (1919–1921) and, five years later, as a naval attaché in Washington, D.C.

In the 1930s, Yamamoto advocated that Japan should give priority to aircraft carriers over battleships. Acutely aware of Japan's weaknesses, he wished to avoid war with the US and opposed alignment with Nazi Germany. Though such views were unpopular with Japanese militarists, he was appointed commander-in-chief of the Japanese Combined Fleet in 1939. When war with America seemed inevitable, he pushed through his plan for the strike on Pearl Harbor as Japan's only chance of victory. In April 1943, he died when the plane in which he was traveling was shot down by US aircraft over the Solomon Islands in a targeted attack.

attack with midget submarines failed, as only one penetrated the harbor and was quickly sunk, but these losses were relatively minor in an otherwise complete victory.

Tactical error

When the Japanese pilots returned to their carriers, many expressed disappointment that the American aircraft carriers had been missed and much of the harbor left undamaged. They were eager to launch a third wave of attacks that targeted port facilities, such as oil storage tanks and repair yards, but Admiral Nagumo felt he had done enough and decided to withdraw his force before the Americans could mount a counterattack—a decision endorsed by Admiral Yamamoto.

Many military historians have since concluded that a third strike on base targets would have done more to disable the US Navy in the long term than the sinking of battleships. Aided by the fact that its aircraft carriers were absent at the time of the attack, the US Pacific Fleet was able to recover reasonably quickly. Salvage operations would eventually allow five of the American battleships to return to service. Critics of Japan's military tactics at Pearl Harbor have also pointed out that the Japanese neglected the future threat posed by US submarines, which were not targeted.

The major miscalculation of such an offensive, however, was a matter of psychology rather than of naval strategy or logistics. The shock of the attack and the heavy casualties it inflicted destroyed at a stroke the essentially isolationist and pacifist tendencies of American public opinion. President Roosevelt had held back from entering World War II because he felt he needed the American people united behind him. With Pearl Harbor shattered, he had his wish. On the day after the attack, the US Congress backed a formal declaration of war on Japan. Japan's war strategy had assumed, somewhat vaguely, that it could achieve a defensive position strong enough to deter a sustained US counteroffensive. Outraged American opinion, however, would from that moment support any and every measure to achieve total revenge against the Japanese.

A war on two fronts

Roosevelt did not want to be limited to a Pacific War. He believed Nazi Germany remained the principal threat to American interests and ideology, and Adolf Hitler's jubilant response to the news of the Pearl Harbor attack made war with Germany unavoidable. Hitler was

President Roosevelt signs the declaration of war against Japan the day after the attack. In his address to the nation, he declared December 7 "a date that will live in infamy."

> It is impossible for us to lose the war. We now have an ally which has never been vanquished in 3,000 years.
> **Adolf Hitler**

clearly delighted with Japan's triumph at Pearl Harbor and the possibility of associating himself with such an ally—especially, perhaps, as his Soviet invasion, launched in June 1941, had stalled. A defensive pact between Germany and Japan, signed in summer 1940, did not in fact oblige the Germans to support their ally in a war that Japan had started. Japan itself had legitimately maintained a neutrality deal with the USSR, despite Germany going to war with the Soviets. However, to the relief of the US administration, on December 11, Hitler and his Axis partner Mussolini declared war on the US in support of Japan. Despite the reservations of some American military commanders, Roosevelt was able to impose his own priorities and commit America first and foremost to the war in Europe. This decision gave the Japanese breathing space in the Pacific War until previously unimaginable American resources were brought to bear against them.

A provoked attack?

Conspiracy theorists have long been impressed by the degree to which the Japanese raid on Pearl Harbor served the aims of both Roosevelt and British prime minister Winston Churchill. The British wanted to draw America into World War II, and the president wanted to convince his people that joining the war was necessary. However, most historians who have studied the issue reject the idea that the attack on Pearl Harbor was deliberately provoked and allowed to succeed to achieve these goals. It is true that America cornered Japan into war, insisting on terms that the Japanese felt bound to reject, forcing them to choose between war and humiliation. Yet no country could have been expected to accept the punishment inflicted on America at Pearl Harbor or tolerated the losses that the Allies suffered from the initial Japanese advances in the Pacific and Asia.

> The American people in their righteous might will win through to absolute victory.
> **Franklin D. Roosevelt**
> **December 8, 1941**

Pearl Harbor was unquestionably a tactical triumph for Japan and a military disaster for the US. Yet the Japanese had found no answer to a basic problem that troubled their politicians and generals from the outset: how would Japan cope in the long term with America's overwhelming superiority in population and industrial power? Having provoked the US to violent anti-Japanese feeling, Japan would soon face a war to the death that it could not win. ■

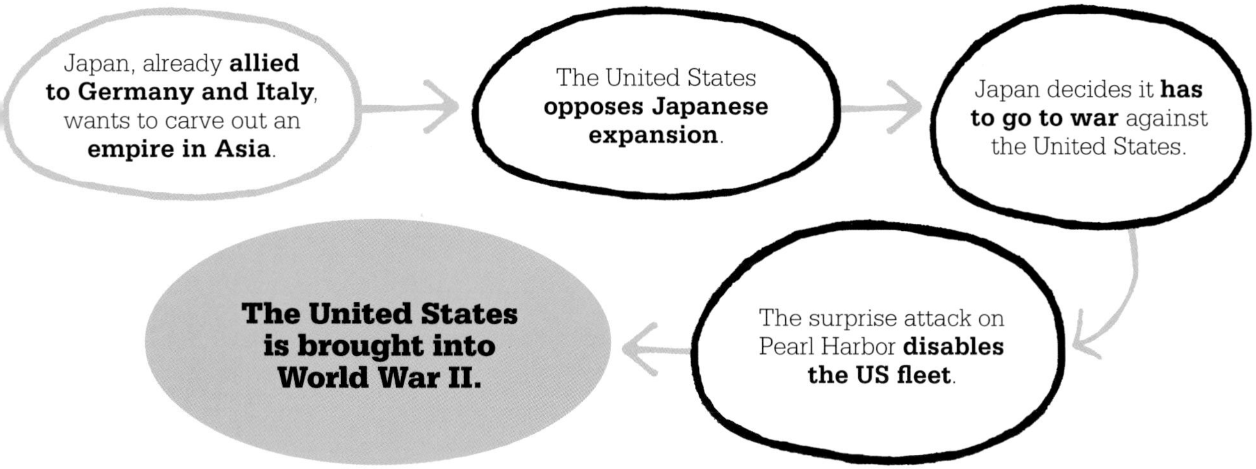

ACCEPT NO RESULT SAVE VICTORY

AMERICA AT WAR (1941–1945)

IN CONTEXT

FOCUS
The American home front

BEFORE
1919 The US Senate refuses to ratify the Treaty of Versailles, excluding the United States from the League of Nations.

1940 In the presidential election, Roosevelt is accused by his Republican opponent of secretly planning to take the US into war.

November 1941 The US government repeals most of the provisions in the Neutrality Acts after a German torpedo sinks the American destroyer USS *Reuben James*.

AFTER
August 1945 The United States becomes a founding member of the United Nations.

1948 The Marshall Plan provides foreign aid to help rebuild war-torn Europe.

> We will not only defend ourselves to the uttermost but will make it very certain that this form of treachery shall never again endanger us.
>
> **Franklin D. Roosevelt**
> **Speech to the nation, December 7, 1941**

Japan's assault on the US naval base at Pearl Harbor in Hawaii on December 7, 1941, thrust the United States instantly and unexpectedly into World War II. The attack was a complete surprise, as negotiations between both countries' diplomats concerning Japan's aggressive actions and intentions in the Pacific and east Asia were still ongoing. Japan declared war on the US (and Britain) hours after the attack, prompting the US Congress to respond in kind on December 8. Three days later, both Germany and Italy, allied with Japan under the Tripartite Pact of 1940, declared war on America. The United States was now at war around the world.

An end to isolationism

The US had made some preparations for a potential conflict, such as moving the Pacific Fleet from San Diego, California, to Pearl Harbor in mid-1940 and reinforcing its troops in the Philippines. New military bases and shipyards had been built and conscription introduced for the first time in peacetime. However, America was not yet ready for immediate, outright war.

An overwhelming majority of American people were opposed to any involvement in the war, preferring a policy of isolationism and nonintervention in all overseas conflicts. The four Neutrality Acts passed by Congress from 1935–1939 had limited American support for countries under attack, whether from Japan to the west of the US, or from Germany and Italy to the east. This policy only changed in March 1941 when President Franklin D. Roosevelt approved the Lend-Lease Act—an agreement with allies such as Britain, its Commonwealth, Free France, and China (at that time fighting Japan) to lend them military equipment in return for America receiving leases on the use of their military bases.

The War Powers Act

The Japanese attack on Pearl Harbor changed American minds. To win this war, the US had not only to send its troops into battle, but also to mobilize its people at home. This required government intervention on a scale unknown in American history. The War Powers Act that became law on December 18, 1941, gave the president huge powers to prosecute the war in an expedient manner. It allowed him to reorganize the government and set up new government agencies and other bodies to further the war effort. He could also censor mail and other communications. A second Act in March 1942 enabled the government to acquire land for military purposes and, among many other measures,

American ration books were issued by the Office of Price Administration from May 1942 until 1946. Each book contained removable stamps to be exchanged for rationed goods.

See also: A flawed peace 20–21 ▪ Dictators and fragile democracies in Europe 34–39 ▪ The end of US neutrality 108 ▪ The Japanese attack Pearl Harbor 138–145 ▪ Allied summits 225 ▪ Aftermath 320–327

Uncle Sam flies the flag on a patriotic poster encouraging the public to buy war bonds. More than 84 million Americans bought them, raising around $185 billion for the US government.

repealed the confidentiality of census data, allowing the FBI to round up suspected aliens and other potential enemies.

The war economy

The government urgently needed money to fight the war. Taxes were raised to a top marginal rate of between 81–94 percent, the threshold for the highest tax rate lowered from $5 million to $200,000, and the tax base enlarged by lowering the minimum income eligible to pay taxes and getting rid of many exemptions and deductions against tax. Caps on executive pay were also imposed. By 1944, nearly every employed person was paying federal income taxes, as opposed to just 10 percent of people in 1940.

Numerous controls were placed on the economy. Wages and prices were regulated, and rationing was introduced to preserve raw and scarce materials. Tires were the first rationed items, restricted in January 1942 to save imported natural rubber. Gas soon followed. Within a year, shoppers needed ration coupons to buy coffee, sugar, meat, cheese and other dairy products, canned foods and dried fruits, bicycles, fuel oil, clothing, nylon and silk stockings, and much more. Ration cards were issued to each household member, including babies and children. Ration stamps were valid for a set period to prevent hoarding. Items such as cars and home appliances were not rationed because they were no longer manufactured, as factories were turned over to war production. Second-hand cars rose so rapidly in price that they became almost unaffordable. Driving for pleasure was banned, as were all motor races.

The war bond challenge

With little available to purchase, personal income, and therefore savings, rose substantially, threatening inflation as more money chased fewer goods. Encouraged by the government, and endorsed by Hollywood movie stars, people poured their money into war bonds issued by the government to fund the war. The American people were challenged to put "at least 10 percent of every paycheck into bonds," allowing around 40 percent of American GDP to go into military spending »

Japanese internment

At the outbreak of war against Japan in 1941, racism led people to question the loyalty of the 127,000 Japanese Americans living in the US—most of them second- or third-generation US citizens. The US Secret Service raised fears by reporting that many of the Japanese in California were supporters of Japan in its war against China, and that those in the Philippines collaborated with Japanese troops who invaded the islands in December 1941.

On February 19, 1942, President Roosevelt signed Executive Order 9066 that forcibly relocated 120,000 Japanese Americans, mostly from the Pacific coast, and incarcerated them inland in concentration camps. A far smaller Japanese population in Canada was similarly interned. In Hawaii, where Japanese Americans made up more than a third of the population, about 1,500 were imprisoned. The Japanese Americans were finally allowed to return to their homes in December 1944.

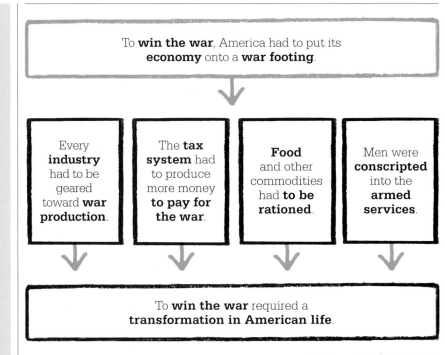

Japanese Americans arrive at the Santa Anita Assembly Center, a former race track in Los Angeles, before moving to camps inland.

To **win the war**, America had to put its **economy** onto a **war footing**.

- Every **industry** had to be geared toward **war production**.
- The **tax system** had to produce more money **to pay for the war**.
- **Food** and other commodities had **to be rationed**.
- Men were **conscripted** into the **armed services**.

To **win the war** required a **transformation in American life**.

with only moderate inflation. There were seven major war loan drives, and every one exceeded the government's expectations.

The workforce

The war transformed the labor market. Unemployment fell from 7.7 million (out of a 54-million strong workforce) in spring 1940 to 3.4 million by the end of 1941, and to 1.5 million by the fall of 1942. Two years later, it hit an all-time low of just 700,000. Skilled laborers were in high demand, and trucks armed with megaphones drove around the streets of towns producing war material begging people to apply for jobs. Millions of retired people returned to work, while students and housewives went to work for the first time. Labor shortages were common: grocery-store assistants, for example, were in such demand that retailers moved from counter- to self-service, while most retailers stopped home deliveries, which increased sales, as customers who bought products in person generally took the opportunity to stock up. To replace male farm laborers sent to war, some 290,000 *braceros* ("strong arms," in Spanish) were recruited from Mexico to work on farms in Texas and the Pacific Northwest.

Introducing conscription

The first peacetime draft in US history began in September 1940. The Selective Training and Service Act limited the number of men in training to 900,000 at any one time, and fixed their service at 12 months, rising to 18 months in August 1941. Initially men aged between 20 and 45 years had to register, but after Pearl Harbor, the age range was expanded to men between 18 and 64 years, although military service was not mandatory after the age of 45. The term of service was also extended to the duration of the war plus six months, and the president was given greater power over the deployment of draftees, including the authority to send them to fight anywhere in the world—their use had previously been restricted to the western hemisphere. To make sure there were enough people to work in factories, men aged 18 to 37 years were not allowed to volunteer. Sufficient manpower was provided by drafting up to 200,000 men a month.

American communists initially opposed the draft, and indeed the war, but their opposition ended when Germany attacked the USSR in June 1941. More than 72,000 men registered as conscientious objectors (COs), although only two-thirds of these were granted CO status: 25,000 entered the military as noncombatants, 12,000 worked in civilian roles, and nearly 6,000 went to prison. Draft avoidance was extremely low, at about 4 percent of those inducted. During the course of the war, a total of 49 million men were registered, and some 10 million actually served. Racial discrimination resulted in reduced numbers of Black recruits, and opposition to the draft was strong among Black Americans.

Working women

American women contributed to the war effort on the home front. Overall, the proportion of women in the labor force rose from 25.2 percent (14.1 million) in 1940 to a peak of 29.2 percent (19.3 million) in 1944 and 1945, many working in munitions and machine factories, and aircraft and ship production, and other war-related work. Most of them already had low-paid jobs or were returning to work after the Great Depression. Although only three million new women workers joined the workforce during the war, working married women outnumbered those who were single for the first time ever. Those with husbands away at war were more than twice as likely to seek war work. The majority did this for financial reasons, but patriotism also played an important role.

Rosie the Riveter, immortalized in a 1942 poster by J. Howard Miller, originated in a popular song. Her image soon fronted campaigns encouraging women to join the American war effort.

For many women, war work was empowering and rewarding. It gave them greater autonomy, and extended their horizons. Many were mothers, who worked together with friends and neighbors, sharing shifts to manage their childcare responsibilities and other needs. Yet in 1944, when victory was all but assured, US government propaganda began to urge women back into their homes. When the men returned from the war, the women lost their jobs.

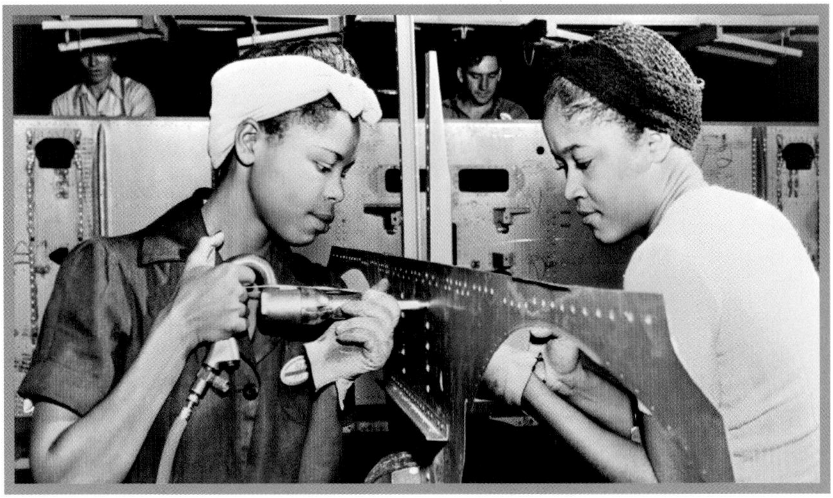

Two women at work at the Douglas Aircraft Company factory in California, during World War II. By 1943, women accounted for nearly two-thirds of all employees in the US aircraft industry.

Female volunteers

Not all women worked for money. The American Women's Voluntary Services, formed in January 1940, organized 18,000 volunteer women who were prepared to drive ambulances, fight fires, deliver first aid, operate mobile kitchens, and perform other emergency services. By the end of the war, its ranks numbered more than 325,000 women. Others joined the Red Cross or volunteered as nurses. Housewives were encouraged to collect materials needed for the war effort, such as scrap metals » and fats rendered during cooking, and helped their children make balls of rubber bands and balls of foil from chewing gum wrappers. Those with land dug "victory gardens" to grow vegetables and other produce. Many joined civil defense units to prepare for bombing raids, and the Women Airforce Service Pilots mobilized 1,000 women to fly new planes from factories to airfields. However, no women flew warplanes in combat. Children helped out on farms and in gardens, while many states changed their labor laws to allow teenagers to work. The number of students in public high schools dropped from 6.6 million in 1940 to 5.6 million in 1944.

Black America

The war affected Black Americans in different ways. Segregation was still in place and, throughout the war, Black Americans remained second-class citizens in their own country, despite the desperate need for labor in every sector. Until 1942, only a tiny number were accepted in the US Army Air Corps, none joined the US Marine Corps, and those enlisting in the US Navy were required to join the all-Black messmen's branch. The US armed forces remained totally segregated throughout the war. Some Black servicemen, however, did get the chance to fly. One groundbreaking group was the Tuskegee Airmen, whose training Roosevelt had approved in 1940. Flying thousands of sorties during the war, they were pioneers of Black aviation and served with distinction; 95 Tuskegee Airmen were awarded medals for heroism.

The official policy of segregation in the US armed forces was retained until 1948, and during the war Black American servicemen were the subject of constant slights and overt racism. Feeling largely marginalized in the war effort, Black Americans became increasingly assertive in the fight for civil rights. The *Pittsburgh Courier*, a large circulation Black newspaper, mounted a "Double V" campaign—V for victory in war, and V for victory in the campaign for equality at home. A proposed march on Washington in 1941 under the slogan "We loyal negro American citizens demand the right to work and fight for our country" was only called off when President Roosevelt signed an executive order creating the Fair Employment Practices Committee, which was dedicated to investigating complaints about discrimination and taking appropriate action. While active, the Committee enjoyed some success in compelling wartime employers to treat Black workers fairly; however, the committee was dissolved in 1946.

> I want to get my family out of this accursed Southland. Down here a Negro man's not as good as a white man's dog.
>
> **Letter to the *Chicago Defender* newspaper**

A Black American flees his pursuers during the Detroit Race Riot of 1943, sparked by tensions when thousands of Black and white migrants arrived from the South to work in the city's factories.

The war had a major impact on the South, where around 40 percent of the budget for military installations was spent as the US geared up for war. New army training camps and airfields were built. New shipyards were constructed in Charleston, Virginia, and along the Gulf Coast, together with new military aircraft factories in Georgia and Dallas-Fort Worth. Around $4 billion was spent on military facilities in the South, with a further $5 billion on defense establishments. As a result, the number of production workers, Black and white, doubled during the war. Many left their farms to work in new factories and bases.

War-prompted migrations

Despite the boost to local Black employment, more than five million Black Americans joined a mass migration from the South to urban centers in the North, Midwest, and West to seek better-paid war work. Millions of women, both Black and white, also followed their husbands to military camps on the West Coast. The vast population shifts led to confrontations over jobs and housing.

Although large-scale nationwide race riots did not break out, there were localized incidents. In Detroit, for example, the arrival of Black workers to take up jobs in the city's growing defense manufacturing industry was met with hostility, which spilled over into rioting and violence in June 1943. Over the course of two days, 34 people died. Similar events occurred in four other cities in the same year, including the Zoot Suit Riots in Los Angeles, which broke out when Latino and Mexican men were targeted and attacked by white people for wearing fashionable, baggy zoot suits, viewed as "unpatriotic" for the amount of fabric used.

Controlling information

Throughout the war, the media worked alongside the American government to disseminate an official version of events. The Office of Censorship was established in December 1941, and published a code of conduct for broadcasters, newspapers, and magazines, relying on their voluntary cooperation to avoid subjects such as troop movements, presidential travels, and other sensitive items of news. It was also given the power to examine and censor any communications between the United States and other countries.

Although the end of hostilities led to the closure of institutions that were created to respond to the emergency, such as the Office of Censorship, many of the social, industrial, and economic advances the US achieved during the war helped firmly establish it as a major global power in the post-war world. ■

> [Actor Clark Gable] was assigned to our squadron … He stayed with us right up from 1942 to 1945 and I can tell you, they didn't put him on the milk runs. He took a lot of pictures of flak bursting beside his aircraft.
>
> **Sgt Ralph Cowley**
> **351st Bombardment Group, USAAF**

Franklin D. Roosevelt

Born in 1882 in Hyde Park, New York, Franklin Delano Roosevelt, often known simply as "FDR," first entered politics when he was elected to the New York Senate in 1910. He then served as assistant secretary of the Navy under President Wilson during World War I. In 1920, he ran as a vice-presidential candidate for the Democratic Party, but the Republicans won that election. The next year he contracted a paralytic illness, thought then to be polio but more probably Guillain-Barré syndrome, that left him paralyzed from the waist down. He returned to politics as governor of New York state in 1928 and promoted policies to tackle the Great Depression.

In 1932, Roosevelt ran successfully for president and was reelected three more times—a US record. A charismatic politician, he led the country through almost all of World War II, using regular "fireside chat" radio broadcasts to communicate directly to the nation. He died in Warm Springs, Georgia, in April 1945, five months before the surrender of Japan signaled the end of the war.

I SHALL DIE ONLY FOR THE EMPEROR

JAPANESE ADVANCES (DECEMBER 1941–MAY 1942)

IN CONTEXT

FOCUS
Japanese expansion in Asia

BEFORE
July 1937 Japan invades China, beginning the Second Sino-Japanese War.

July 1941 Japanese forces occupy bases in southern French Indochina.

December 7 1941 Japanese carrier aircraft attack the US base at Pearl Harbor, Hawaii.

AFTER
May 7–8, 1942 The drawn carrier battle of the Coral Sea slows Japan's southward advance.

February–July 1944 A Japanese offensive from Burma into British India is defeated.

August 15, 1945 Japan surrenders with its troops still occupying much of southeast Asia and China.

Japan's plan for war in December 1941 required its forces to seize control of southeast Asia and the western Pacific before its enemies could organize their defense. The military onslaught began on December 8 and ended the following May with Japanese troops reaching the border of British India, having humiliated the forces of the British and Dutch empires as well as the Americans in the Philippines.

Sea and air dominance

Japan's army had no significant advantage in either numbers or equipment—its infantry progressed

See also: Japan on the march 44–45 ▪ Japan's dilemma 137 ▪ The Japanese attack Pearl Harbor 138–145 ▪ India in World War II 158 ▪ Defending Australia 159 ▪ China and Japan at war 250–253 ▪ The Allies fight back in Burma 290–293

> Our empire, for its existence and self-defense, has no other recourse but to appeal to arms and to crush every obstacle on its path.
>
> **Japanese Imperial edict**
> **December 7, 1941**

through Malaya (part of modern Malaysia) on bicycles. Although their soldiers' morale and fighting spirit were outstanding, the key to Japan's success was control of the sea and the air. On December 10, Japanese aircraft stunned the British government by sinking the battleship HMS *Prince of Wales* and the battle cruiser HMS *Repulse*, sent to reinforce the British base at Singapore. In the Philippines—an unofficial American colony—more than 100 US aircraft were destroyed on the ground by bombers on the first day of the war. Along with the Pearl Harbor raid, these actions ensured that Japan could carry out seaborne landings and reinforce and resupply their troops, while their enemies' land forces were cut off and immobilized.

Some of the territories Japan targeted would have been impossible for the Allies to defend. In the Pacific, the British-controlled islands of Tarawa and Makin were immediately occupied, as was the American territory of Guam. The US base on Wake Island fell soon afterward. British and Canadian troops in Hong Kong, surrounded by the Japanese army occupying China, surrendered on Christmas Day. Although Britain expected to be able to defend Malaya and Singapore, the speed of Japan's offensive revealed defects in the British planning and leadership. Japanese troops swiftly penetrated overland from French Indochina into northern Malaya and Thailand, while others were able to land unopposed along the coasts of Malaya and Burma. By December 16, bewildered Allied forces—chiefly Indian and Australian troops—were in retreat south along the Malaysian peninsula with Japanese forces in pursuit.

Singapore falls

The brand-new Singapore naval base, off the southern tip of the Malaysian peninsula, had been built in the 1930s to affirm British prestige in Asia. Yet as the Japanese army approached, British commander Arthur Percival shocked his government with a wholly pessimistic assessment of his ability to hold Singapore against attack from the mainland. The Japanese general Tomoyuki Yamashita, despite having fewer than half Percival's number of troops, seized the initiative. On February 8, 1942, the Japanese crossed the Straits of Johore and established a foothold on Singapore. A week later, ignoring instructions from London to fight to the death, Percival surrendered. More than 80,000 soldiers were taken prisoner, half of them Indian. The humiliation of the British Empire was complete.

Japanese seaborne landings on Luzon in the Philippines were simultaneous with their advance into Malaya. To resist them, US general Douglas MacArthur had 20,000 US and 100,000 Filipino troops, mostly poorly trained and equipped. MacArthur's strategy »

British women and children prepare to evacuate Singapore—then a British colony—by boat prior to the Japanese invasion in early 1942.

By December 1941, Japan had already invaded Indochina and parts of China. Following the attack on Pearl Harbor, Japan launched a series of amphibious and airborne attacks to extend its control over southeast Asia.

Key:
- Japan and vassal states
- Invasions July 1940–December 1941
- Invasions December 1941–May 1942
- Thailand (Japan's ally)
- Allied territory

was to withdraw to a defensive position on the Bataan peninsula and await reinforcements and supplies. Japanese domination of sea and air ensured that neither came.

Bataan turned into a trap from which the defenders could not escape. By March, the besieged troops were surviving on one-third rations. Beriberi and other diseases resulting from malnutrition became rampant. On March 12, General MacArthur was flown out to Australia, famously promising: "I shall return." The troops at Bataan surrendered on April 8. Some 80,000 of them, already weakened by disease and hunger, were severely mistreated while they were marched to a distant POW camp. An estimated 650 Americans and 10,000 Filipinos died on this "Bataan Death March." American and Filipino resistance ended with the surrender of the fortress at Corregidor on May 6.

Raw materials

For Japan, the biggest prize in the region was Indonesia. Rich in natural resources, these Dutch-ruled islands offered a solution to Japan's chronic shortage of raw materials and food. With Dutch forces unable to offer serious resistance on the ground, the Allies placed their hopes in preventing seaborne landings. In February 1942, a combined American-British-Dutch-Australian force of 14 warships was sent to intercept Japanese troopships heading for Java. In a series of encounters in the Java Sea, the Allies lost five cruisers and five destroyers, leaving the Japanese navy in total control. The Dutch surrendered Java on March 12 and Sumatra two weeks later.

British-ruled Burma was the last country to fall to Japan's initial surge. It was strategically important because it provided the main Allied supply routes to the Nationalist armies in southwest China. Moving through Thailand, the Japanese army entered the lightly defended territory in December. Britain's Indian soldiers retreated and their Burmese troops deserted in droves. Japan took Rangoon, the capital, in March, reaching Mandalay at the start of May. The British fell back into India, before the monsoon ended the campaigning season.

Nationalist movements

Burma was one of the countries in which the Japanese forces were greeted with most enthusiasm as

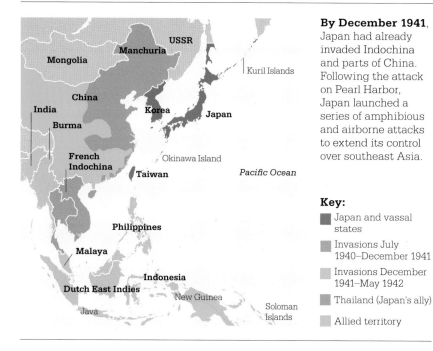

Citizens flee in Rangoon, Burma, as Japanese war planes approach in December 1941. Many civilians and troops fled northwest toward the Indian border to escape the conflict.

1

Western colonial powers suffer defeats in battle in Europe, **weakening their dominance** in Asia.

↓

Japan **seeks to evict** Western colonial powers from Asia.

↓

Rapid Japanese **victories give Japan control** of southeast Asia.

↓

Exploitative **Japanese imperial rule** temporarily **replaces Western colonial rule**.

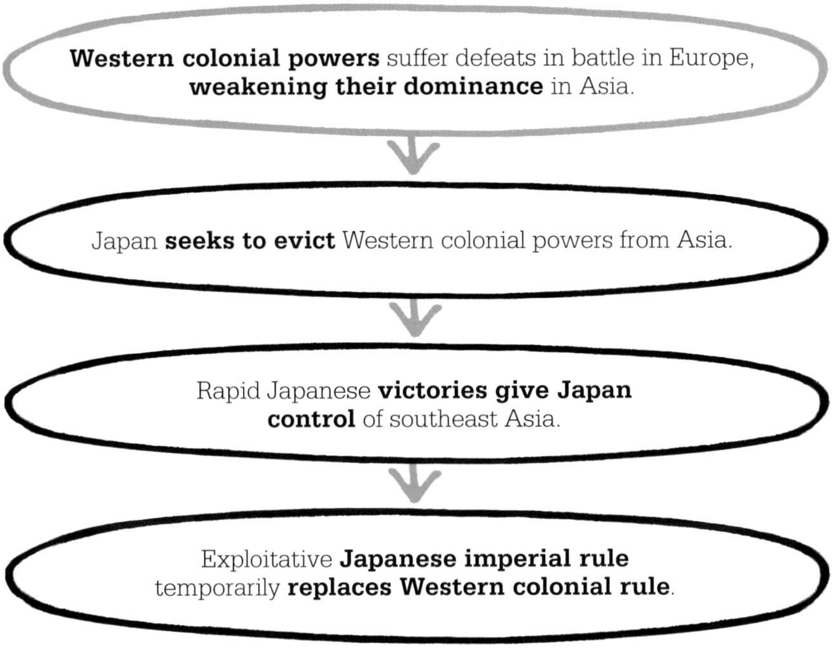

Douglas MacArthur

Born in 1880, Douglas MacArthur graduated top of the class at the West Point Military Academy in 1903 and joined the army, serving in the Philippines. After service in Mexico and on the Western Front during World War I, he returned to the Philippines in 1922, and became the army's youngest major general in 1925. He was promoted to Chief of Staff of the US Army in 1930, serving until 1935, when he returned to the now semi-independent Philippines to organize their army.

In June 1941 he became commander of US Army Forces in the Far East and led the campaign against the Japanese invasion of the Philippines in 1942. Defeated and forced to evacuate, he returned to free the islands in 1944–1945. As Supreme Commander Southwest Pacific Area, MacArthur officially accepted the surrender of Japan and oversaw its occupation until 1951. After the Korean War broke out in 1950, he also led the UN Command, but was dismissed by President Truman in April 1951 for proposing full-scale conflict with China. He died in Washington, D.C., in 1964.

liberators. As early as 1940, political activist Aung San had formed a Burma Independence Army with Japanese backing. After the invasion, the nationalist politician Ba Maw, who had been imprisoned by the British, agreed to head a pro-Japanese administration. In Indonesia the nationalist leaders Mohammad Hatta and Sukarno, who had also been detained by the colonial authorities, were freed and allowed to return to politics in exchange for aiding Japanese rule. Followers of the anti-British Indian nationalist Subhas Chandra Bose were permitted to recruit an "Indian National Army" from Indian prisoners taken at Singapore to fight alongside the Japanese army.

The notion of Japan leading their fellow Asian nations in a Greater East Asia Co-Prosperity Sphere did not materialize. Instead, Japan exploited the resources of occupied countries, and conscripted civilians into forced labor. Massacres of the local Chinese population by Japanese troops took place after the fall of Hong Kong and Singapore. Women from Korea, China, the Philippines, and elsewhere were forced to work as sex slaves for soldiers. Hundreds of thousands of men died working on projects such as the Burma Railway.

An opportunity missed

Although Japan's triumphs and ruthlessly executed tactics shocked Allied leaders, military success did not bring as much advantage to Japan as it might have hoped. US Navy submarines threatened sea transportation between southeast Asia and Japan, which restricted exploitation of the resources that had been captured. The war in China remained unwinnable, and the Japanese navy made little use of its control of the Indian Ocean. The critical question for Japan was whether or not it could defeat the United States. The war would be settled not in Asia, but in the Pacific. ∎

HOW DOES INDIA PROFIT ... IN BRITAIN'S WAR?

INDIA IN WORLD WAR II (1939–1945)

IN CONTEXT

FOCUS
Impact on colonies

BEFORE
1858 After the Indian rebellion, Britain assumes full control of India.

1876 Queen Victoria is given the title of empress of India.

1939 British viceroy Lord Linlithgow unilaterally declares war on Germany without consulting Indian leadership.

AFTER
February 1947 Britain announces that Indian independence will take place no later than June 30, 1948.

July 1947 Agreement to partition India is announced.

August 15, 1947 The Indian Independence Act establishes India and Pakistan as separate countries, no longer under British rule.

When Britain declared war on Germany in September 1939, it did so on behalf of its colonies as well as itself. British-ruled India therefore found itself at war in Europe.

Opinions about the war divided Indians. The Muslim League, which advocated a Muslim-majority nation state in Pakistan, approved. But the Indian National Congress demanded full independence before it would help Britain. When that demand was refused, on August 8, 1942, Congress leader Mahatma Gandhi launched the Quit India campaign to force the British out. Next day, Gandhi and future prime minister Jawaharlal Nehru, along with more than 100,000 other campaigners, were arrested. Heavy-handed British suppression defeated the Quit India campaign.

Appeal to Japan

Indian nationalist Subhas Chandra Bose chose a different route for the independence struggle and in May 1943 sought help from Japan. He took control of the unofficial pro-Japanese "Indian National Army," formed from Indian POWs of the British Army captured at the fall of Singapore. With the support of Japan, he set up the Provisional Government of Free India in the Andaman and Nicobar Islands.

Despite this opposition, Indian support was vital for the Allies. Some 2.6 million Indian troops fought in Europe, Africa, the Far East, and Middle East. They played a major role in preventing the Japanese from invading India, and in expelling them from Burma. ■

Indian troops leaving their desert camp in Egypt, led by two British officers. The Indian 4th Infantry Division played a key role in defeating Rommel's Axis forces in North Africa.

See also: Japan on the march 44–45 ▪ Colonial ties 90–93 ▪ Japan's dilemma 137 ▪ Japanese advances 154–157 ▪ The Allies fight back in Burma 290–293

THE PACIFIC STRUGGLE

DEFENDING AUSTRALIA (JANUARY–MAY 1942)

IN CONTEXT

FOCUS

Japanese expansion in the Pacific

BEFORE

1901 Australia becomes an independent dominion within the British Empire.

September 1939 As Britain enters the war, Australia declares war on Germany.

December 1941 Japanese forces attack Pearl Harbor and sweep through southeast Asia.

AFTER

August 1942 Australian and US forces retake Guadalcanal, one of the Solomon Islands.

November 1942 Australian forces play a major role at the Battle of El Alamein.

June 1943–January 1944 Australians join with New Zealand and US forces to dislodge the Japanese from New Guinea, New Britain, and the Solomon Islands.

The Japanese needed to isolate Australia from the United States, and to this end they planned to capture Midway Atoll; the Solomon Islands; and Port Moresby, the Australian base on New Guinea. In January 1942, they began by taking the Australian garrison at Rabaul on New Britain, an island part of New Guinea, and advancing through the Solomon Islands, taking Guadalcanal in May. They also bombed Darwin, a city in north Australia, on February 19, the first of more than 100 raids on the country, and launched submarine attacks on Sydney Harbour in May and June.

The Japanese planned to capture Port Moresby by landing troops from an invasion fleet. On May 7, as this fleet headed south from Rabaul, it was intercepted in the Coral Sea by a US and Australian task force. The next day, the forces clashed again in the first true carrier battle in history. Although the Americans lost more ships, the Japanese suffered heavier aircraft losses and called off their naval assault.

> Without a doubt … the Coral Sea was the most confused battle area in world history.
>
> **H. S. Duckworth**
> **US vice admiral**

Still anxious to capture the base, the Japanese landed troops at Buna on the north coast of New Guinea on July 21. Using the tortuous Kokoda Trail to cross the island, they came within sight of Port Moresby by early September before being beaten back by Australian and American troops. To the east, a Japanese onslaught against the Allied air base at Milne Bay from August 25 was also defeated, the first land battle won by the Allies in the Pacific. ■

See also: The Japanese attack Pearl Harbor 138–145 ▪ The Battle of Midway 160–165 ▪ The Battle for the Solomons and New Guinea 212–213

A MOMENTOUS VICTORY IS IN THE MAKING

THE BATTLE OF MIDWAY (JUNE 2–4, 1942)

IN CONTEXT

FOCUS
War at sea

BEFORE
1859 Midway Atoll is claimed for the United States by Captain N.C. Brooks of the sealing ship *Gambia*.

1867 The US Navy takes formal possession of the island.

December 7, 1941 Japan attacks Pearl Harbor, bringing the United States into the war.

May 6, 1942 Japanese carrier-based planes severely damage USS *Yorktown* in the Battle of the Coral Sea.

AFTER
July 1942 A submarine tender is stationed at Midway to support US submarines patrolling Japanese waters.

Midway Atoll is a tiny North Pacific island with an area of just 2.4 sq miles (6.2 sq km), yet its position at the most westerly part of the Hawaiian archipelago, equidistant between North America and Asia, gave it strategic importance out of proportion to its size. One of the most important naval battles in military history took place off its shores in June 1942. The decisive result of this battle marked a turning point in the Allies' war against Japan.

Next steps for Japan

After the unexpected attack on Pearl Harbor in December 1941, Japan quickly achieved its main territorial goals by taking the Philippines, Malaya, Singapore, and the oil-rich Dutch East Indies. The Japanese then debated and agreed a follow-up strategy in April 1942, strongly influenced by an American retaliatory raid on April 18. Carried out by 16 carrier-launched US Army Air Force Mitchell bombers, this Doolittle Raid bombed Tokyo and other mainland Japanese targets. While of limited military value, the raid raised US morale after Pearl Harbor and shocked the Japanese by revealing the vulnerability of their home islands to US bombers.

The Japanese follow-up plan, formulated by Admiral Yamamoto, commander-in-chief of the Japanese combined fleet, identified as its strategic goal the elimination of

> One of the most consequential naval engagements in world history … both tactically decisive and strategically influential.
> **Craig Symonds**
> **American historian, 2018**

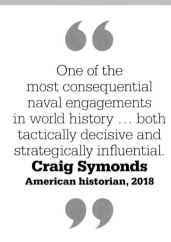

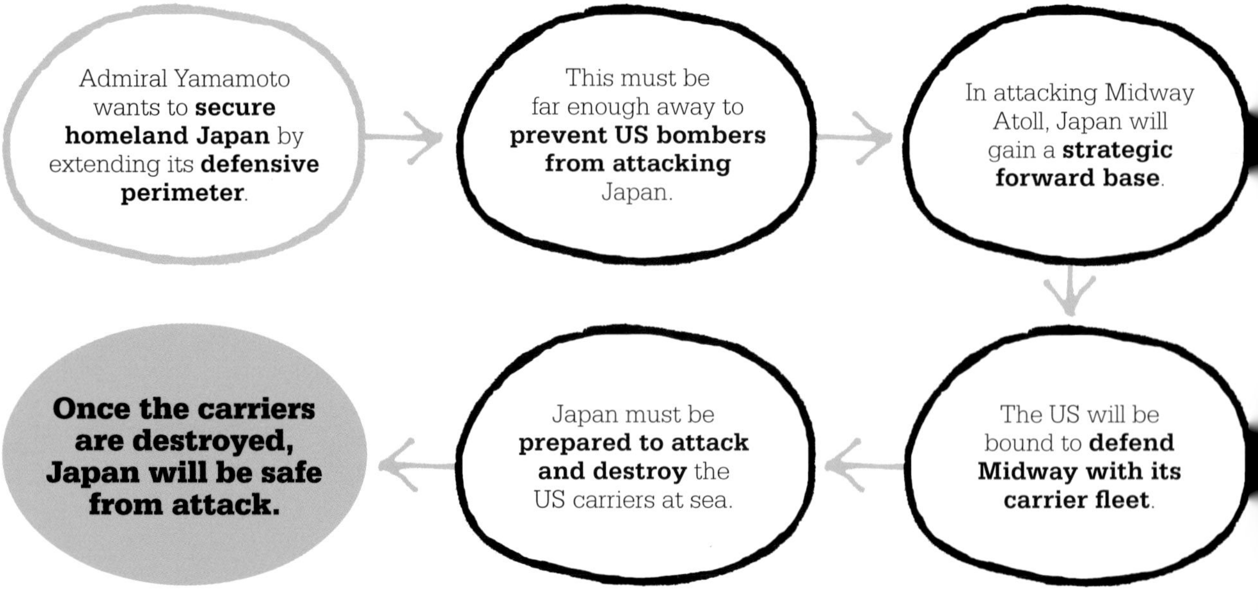

Admiral Yamamoto wants to **secure homeland Japan** by extending its **defensive perimeter**.
This must be far enough away to **prevent US bombers from attacking** Japan.
In attacking Midway Atoll, Japan will gain a **strategic forward base**.
The US will be bound to **defend Midway with its carrier fleet**.
Japan must be **prepared to attack and destroy** the US carriers at sea.
Once the carriers are destroyed, Japan will be safe from attack.

See also: Japan on the march 44–45 ▪ Japan's dilemma 137 ▪ The Japanese attack Pearl Harbor 138–145 ▪ Japanese advances 154–157 ▪ Defending Australia 159 ▪ The battle for the Solomons and New Guinea 212–213 ▪ The western Pacific 244–249

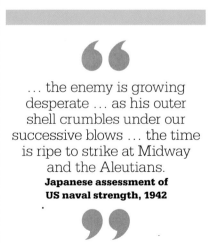

Japanese Zero fighter aircraft on the deck of the aircraft carrier *Akagi*. Zeros were unmatched in aerial combat until 1943, but the *Akagi* was scuttled during the Battle of Midway.

the US carrier fleet in the Pacific. This was seen as the principal threat to Japanese control of the region. Aircraft carriers were vitally important in the Pacific theater, because they gave both sides forward, mobile bases from which to launch air attacks. If it could destroy the US fleet, Japan would be able to extend its defensive perimeter further out across the Pacific, taking Fiji, Samoa, and Midway, and seizing the outer Aleutian Islands, part of the US territory of Alaska. It would also place Japan out of reach of any US bombers.

Yamamoto's plan

Yamamoto had reasoned that attacking Pearl Harbor once again would produce a devastating US response. Judging such an attack to be too risky, he therefore directed primary operations against the strategic US-controlled airbase and refueling station on Midway Atoll. He believed such an attack would draw out the US carrier fleet into what he hoped would be a decisive—and victorious—naval battle.

Yamamoto's plan of battle was extremely complex, as his various battle groups had to be organized across vast expanses of ocean. His plan was based on the fact that the US Navy had only two carriers available, the USS *Enterprise* and *Hornet*, both of which he believed to be in the Solomon Islands. The third carrier, USS *Yorktown*, he believed to have been sunk in the Coral Sea, whereas in fact it had been badly damaged but then speedily repaired at Pearl Harbor and was now back in service. Crucially, Yamamoto did not know that US code breaker Joseph Rochefort at the Station HYPO signals monitoring and intelligence unit in Hawaii had cracked the main Japanese naval code, dubbed JN-25 (Japanese Navy 25) by the Americans, and that the Americans were thus prepared for any attack on Midway. He also grossly misjudged American morale, which he wrongly believed to have weakened after recent Japanese successes.

> … the enemy is growing desperate … as his outer shell crumbles under our successive blows … the time is ripe to strike at Midway and the Aleutians.
>
> **Japanese assessment of US naval strength, 1942**

To ensure maximum deception, Yamamoto sent his four-strong First Carrier Striking Force and its 248 aircraft more than a hundred miles ahead of the supporting 2 battleships, 2 cruisers, 12 destroyers, and 13 submarines. Further back, a support fleet of four heavy cruisers and two destroyers was to destroy any US ships that came to Midway's defense. A further occupation force brought up the rear, ready to occupy the island once the battle was over.

Let battle commence

By June 2, two US naval task forces assembled by Admiral Chester Nimitz lay in wait for the Japanese over the horizon some 350 miles 560 km northeast of Midway. From there, search planes scoured the ocean for the incoming Japanese fleets. Task Force 16 consisted of »

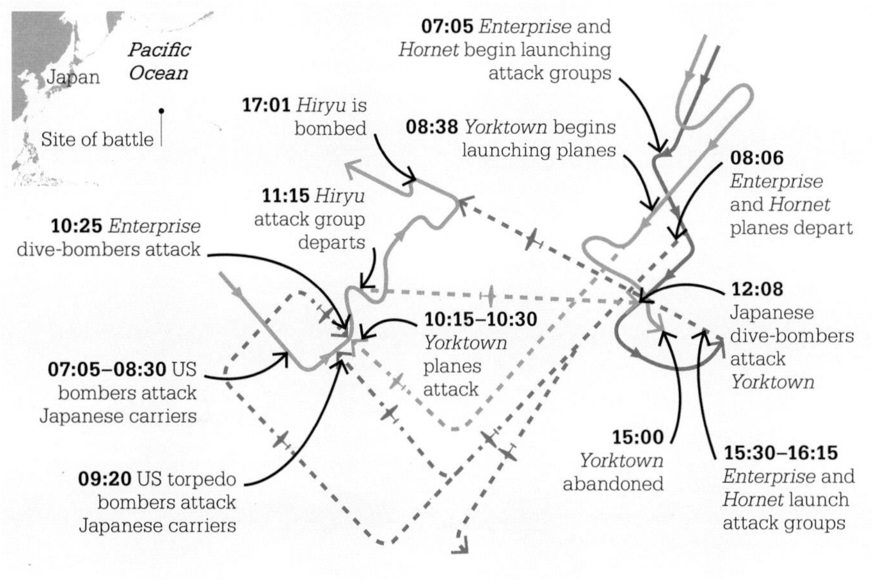
Pacific Ocean
Japan
Site of battle
17:01 Hiryu is bombed
07:05 Enterprise and Hornet begin launching attack groups
08:38 Yorktown begins launching planes
08:06 Enterprise and Hornet planes depart
11:15 Hiryu attack group departs
10:25 Enterprise dive-bombers attack
12:08 Japanese dive-bombers attack Yorktown
10:15–10:30 Yorktown planes attack
07:05–08:30 US bombers attack Japanese carriers
15:00 Yorktown abandoned
15:30–16:15 Enterprise and Hornet launch attack groups
09:20 US torpedo bombers attack Japanese carriers
Key:
Japanese strike force
Japanese carrier air strikes
USS Enterprise/Hornet group
Enterprise/Hornet air strikes
USS Yorktown group
Yorktown air strikes

By 10:30 am on June 4, 1942, dive-bombers from USS *Enterprise* and USS *Yorktown* had hit three Japanese carriers: the *Kaga*, *Soryu*, and *Akagi*. After Japanese aircraft bombed the *Yorktown* at 12:08 pm, the US retaliated with a devastating attack on the *Hiryu*, securing victory.

the carriers *Enterprise* and *Hornet*, 6 cruisers, 9 destroyers, and 152 carrier-based aircraft. Task Force 17 consisted of the repaired carrier *Yorktown*, 2 cruisers, 5 destroyers, and 73 aircraft. Midway itself was defended by 127 land-based aircraft and 16 submarines.

At 4:40 am on June 4, 108 aircraft from the Japanese carriers launched an air attack against Midway. The raiders were soon spotted and US interceptors were quickly scrambled. The Japanese offensive failed to disable Midway's defense systems and lost or suffered damage to around one-third of its assault force to US aircraft fire and antiaircraft attack from the island.

> I saw this glint in the sun and it just looked like a beautiful, silver waterfall, these dive-bombers coming down. I'd never seen such superb dive-bombing.
>
> **Jimmy Hatch**
> **US pilot, recalling the Battle of Midway**

Fierce fighting

Battle intensified during the morning when the Japanese carriers were targeted by US torpedo planes, which were in turn attacked by faster Japanese Zero fighters. These, however, were out of position and low on ammunition after their morning missions, so were unable to prevent a further attack by US dive-bombers. These hit two Japanese carriers, the *Kaga* and *Soryu*, both of which sunk later the same day; the flagship *Akagi* which was scuttled the next day; two battleships; and a cruiser.

Late in the morning, US radar detected Japanese aircraft from the carrier *Hiryu* approaching the *Yorktown* from the west. The raiders were soon intercepted, but some broke through, hitting the *Yorktown* with three bombs at around noon. The resultant fires were soon put out but torpedo planes hit it again during the afternoon. By 3 pm, the *Yorktown* was badly listing and the order was given to abandon ship. Taken in tow, it was hit again by a torpedo from a Japanese submarine on June 6 and sank the next day.

The US response to this blow was emphatic. A scout plane from *Yorktown* spotted the remaining Japanese carrier, *Hiryu*, at around 2:30 pm. Just after 5 pm, it was attacked by 40 US dive-bombers, hit many times, and set ablaze. It was scuttled the next day as B-17 bombers from Midway pursued the now retreating Japanese fleet.

Aleutian sideshow

The Japanese bombing of Dutch Harbor in the Aleutians on June 3–4, 1942, and the occupation of two small islands, Attu and Kiska, on June 6–7—the first time US territory had been invaded and occupied since 1812—shocked American public opinion. At the time, it was thought that this attack was a deliberate ruse to confuse the Americans and draw their attention away from Midway. This was far from the truth, however. For the Japanese, the Aleutians were a target in their own right, not a sideshow to Midway, and they were supposed to be attacked on the same day. But delays in getting the main carrier fleet underway to Midway meant that the Aleutian attack took place the day before. The US would not take back control of Attu and Kiska until mid 1943.

Total victory

The American victory at Midway was total. The Japanese had lost all four fleet carriers, with one heavy cruiser sunk and one damaged; 248 of its aircraft were destroyed; and 3,057 servicemen were killed and 37 captured. In response, the United States had lost one fleet carrier, one destroyer, and around 150 aircraft, with 307 men killed.

In Japan, news of the defeat was kept secret, with Japanese news announcing a great victory. Only the emperor and the highest naval personnel were accurately informed about the losses of ships and men. Having lost their four main carriers, the Japanese also lost their air superiority. Never again would they be capable of launching a major offensive in the Pacific.

For the Americans, the victory was decisive. It was their first major naval victory against the Japanese, and gave them control of the Pacific. They could now dictate the terms of the war, taking the initiative to seize Guadalcanal and regain the rest of the Solomon Islands in 1943. Midway Atoll was indeed a turning point in the war in the Pacific. ■

The *Hiryu* burns after being set ablaze by US dive-bombers during the Battle of Midway. The Japanese aircraft carrier eventually sank with the loss of 389 lives.

Chester Nimitz

Born in Texas in 1885, Nimitz studied at the US Naval Academy in Annapolis, Maryland, and first went to sea in 1905. In 1909, he took command of his first submarine flotilla, rapidly becoming the leading US Navy authority on submarines. Nimitz was involved in World War I and, in 1917, led the development of at-sea replenishment techniques, allowing the transfer of fuel, munitions, and supplies from one ship to another while underway at sea.

Nimitz was appointed commander-in-chief of the US Pacific Fleet 10 days after the attack on Pearl Harbor in 1941, later taking part in the crucial battles of the Coral Sea, Midway, Philippine Sea, and Leyte Gulf. After World War II, he gained approval to build the world's first nuclear-powered submarine, which had its maiden voyage in 1955, several years after he retired from active service. Having been made a fleet admiral—a lifetime appointment—in 1945, he remained on inactive duty until his death in 1966. The US Navy's *Nimitz* supercarrier class is named after him.

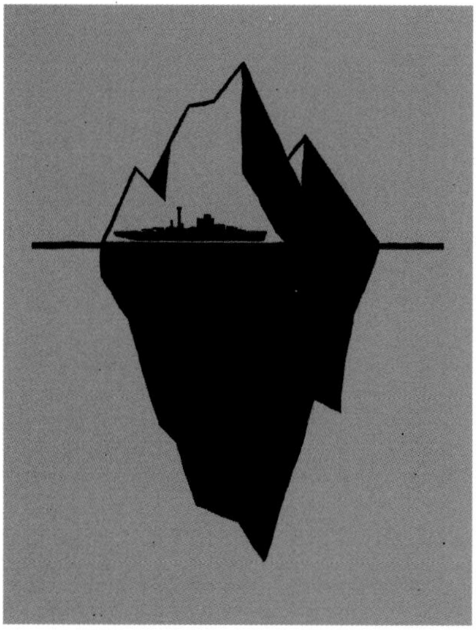

A NORTHERN SAGA OF HEROISM, BRAVERY, AND ENDURANCE

ATTACKS ON ARCTIC CONVOYS (JULY 1942)

IN CONTEXT

FOCUS
War at sea

BEFORE
August 12, 1941 The first Arctic convoy leaves Liverpool for Iceland in Operation Dervish, then delivers dozens of Hurricane fighter planes to northern Russia on August 31.

September 1941 Arctic convoys receive codes PQ for outbound, QP for homebound.

March 28–30, 1942 German aircraft, U-boats, and a destroyer flotilla attack 19-ship convoy PQ13, sinking five.

May 25–30 1942 PQ16 loses seven ships after nearly 250 bomber and torpedo sorties.

AFTER
December 1942 Arctic convoys are recoded JW for outbound, RA for homebound.

May 1945 JW67, the last Arctic convoy of the war, leaves the Firth of Clyde.

After June 1941, the USSR became Britain's ally. To sustain it in the fight, Churchill initiated convoys through the icy Arctic Ocean to Murmansk and Archangel in northern Russia. The journey skirted occupied Norway, which meant running a gauntlet of German U-boats, aircraft, and formidable warships. After initial successes for the convoys in 1942, Germany realized the route's strategic importance, and the Arctic became one of the war's great battlegrounds.

Ice forms on a signal projector on the cruiser HMS *Sheffield* while escorting an Arctic convoy to Russia. Occasionally, bad weather forced merchant ships to turn back.

Heavy losses

The experience of convoy PQ17 highlighted the risks of operating without air cover during summer's continuous daylight. It left Iceland with 35 merchant ships and six naval auxiliaries on July 1, 1942. Three days later, halfway to Russia, believing that the German battleship *Tirpitz* would attack, the British Admiralty ordered the close escort to "withdraw westward" to engage the enemy—and the convoy ships to scatter. By July 10, 24 merchant vessels, abandoned by their escorts, had been sunk. Only 11 vessels reached Russian ports. The worst convoy loss of the war was the result of an Admiralty blunder.

Between August 1941 and May 1945, 1,400 merchant ships in 78 convoys delivered 4 million tons of supplies. The Arctic operation was invaluable but perilous—3,000 Allied seamen and 85 merchant and 16 Royal Navy vessels were lost. ■

See also: The end of US neutrality 108 ▪ The U-boat war intensifies 110–113 ▪ Operation Barbarossa 124–131 ▪ A showdown in the Atlantic 214–219

THE MOST BOMBED PLACE ON EARTH

THE SIEGE OF MALTA (JUNE 1940–NOVEMBER 1942)

IN CONTEXT

FOCUS
Strategic territories

BEFORE
1800 After the eviction of French forces, Malta becomes a British protectorate.

1814 Malta officially becomes part of the British Empire.

June 10, 1940 Italy declares war on Britain.

AFTER
1942 King George VI awards Malta the George Cross to honor the bravery of its people under siege.

July 1943 Fighter cover for Operation Husky, the Allied invasion of Sicily, is provided by aircraft flown from Malta.

July 20, 1943 Malta suffers its last air raid.

1964 Malta gains independence from Britain.

The island of Malta lies astride the main shipping lanes that cross the Mediterranean Sea. During World War II, it served as a British air, naval, and submarine base from which to attack and disrupt Axis supply lines. Mussolini had long coveted the British colony, and its importance became clear once fighting began in North Africa. Without seizing control of Malta, Axis forces in North Africa would be unlikely to succeed. On June 11, 1940, the day after Italy declared war on Britain and France, its air force launched its first attack on the island. For more than two years, Malta was under siege. During this time, the Italians and Germans bombed it 3,343 times. It became the most bombed place on Earth.

Operation Pedestal

The islanders sheltered in caves and tunnels, but food, fuel, and other supplies soon ran short. British naval convoys to Malta from Egypt or Gibraltar were under constant attack, with many ships sunk. In August 1942, the 53-strong convoy of Operation Pedestal set out for Malta, escorting 14 merchant ships. Only five of these survived a concentrated Axis assault, but they included the oil tanker SS *Ohio*, which delivered the fuel the islanders needed to survive.

The British victory at El Alamein and Operation Torch in November 1942 lifted the threat to the island, and the great siege ended—but it had been a close-run thing. ■

> This tiny island is a vital feature in the defense of our Middle East position.
>
> **Hastings Ismay**
> **British general, 1942**

See also: Italy enters the war 88–89 ▪ North Africa and the Mediterranean 118–121 ▪ Victory in the desert 208–209 ▪ The invasion of Italy 210–211

MIGHT MAKES RIGHT

NAZI EUROPE (1942)

IN CONTEXT

FOCUS
Greater German Reich

BEFORE
1924 In *Mein Kampf*, Hitler advocates a racially ordered Europe with living space for Germanic peoples.

March 1938 Austria is incorporated into the Reich.

1939 Germany invades Poland.

1941 Germany captures huge swathes of Soviet territory.

AFTER
July–August 1945 The Potsdam Conference sets the Oder-Neisse line as Germany's eastern border.

1998 The principles for returning stolen artworks to their rightful owners are set out in the Washington Declaration on Nazi-Confiscated Art.

By 1942, Germany dominated almost the whole of continental Europe. Apart from a handful of neutral countries, every nation was either under direct German rule or occupied by, allied to, or dependent on the Third Reich. German forces controlled territory from the Arctic Circle to the Greek islands, and from the Atlantic coast of France to the northern Caucasus, a vast area rich in resources, manpower, industry, agriculture, and cultural wealth.

The Nazi vision of Europe had been forged over several decades. As set out in Hitler's manifesto, *Mein Kampf*, published in 1924,

See also: The Great War 18–19 ▪ German expansion 46–47 ▪ The destruction of Poland 58–63 ▪ The fall of France 80–87 ▪ Operation Barbarossa 124–131 ▪ Nazi massacres 136 ▪ The Holocaust 172–177

> When this war is over, we want to be masters in Europe.
> **Joseph Goebbels**

it maintained that there was a hierarchy of races, closely associated with ideas about land and destiny.

German expansion

Central to the Nazi vision was the doctrine of *Lebensraum* ("living space"), which claimed that superior races are destined to expand their geopolitical and cultural range by settling land cleared of inferior races. An associated concept was *Grossraum* ("great space"): the notion that the Nazis would colonize and reorder the whole of continental Europe, moving and eradicating peoples and populations to fit preordained notions of economic, cultural, and geographical destiny.

Hitler's first priority was to annex those areas that were culturally aligned with Germany—such as Austria and Bohemia—to create a *Grossdeutschland* ("Greater German Reich"), which would then expand through the longer-term process of settling lands to the east, cleared of their "inferior" Slavic and Jewish populations. Addressing a convocation of leading Nazis on July 16, 1941, Hitler proclaimed: "We must make of the newly acquired eastern areas a Garden of Eden." Nazi doctrines also envisaged incorporating Nordic races, such as the Scandinavians and Dutch, into the German state, while the rest of the continent—primarily southern Europe—would serve the needs of Germany.

Prioritizing the war effort

Hitler and other leading figures were prepared to be pragmatic in their pursuit of the ideological reshaping of Europe. Winning the war took precedence over realizing this Nazi utopia. Speaking on October 26, 1940, Joseph Goebbels, Hitler's minister of propaganda, said, "If anyone asks me what do you really want, I cannot give him an answer … We want living space. Yes, but what does that mean? We will provide a definition after the war." To this end, the Nazis were intent on exploiting conquered territory to further their war effort, using any means necessary to extract the maximum benefit.

By 1942, different forms of German colonization existed across Europe. Some areas, such as Austria and Prussian parts of Poland, had already been annexed to create an enlarged German state. Others, including Alsace-Lorraine and Moravia, were earmarked for annexation. Elsewhere, German civil administrations were introduced, such as the General Government area of Poland; the newly constituted *Reichskommissariats* of Ostland and Ukraine, carved from territory conquered from the USSR; and in Denmark, Hungary, and Norway. Other territories were under direct military government. These included occupied France, Belgium, and parts of the USSR behind the frontlines. »

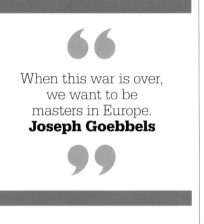

By 1942, the Axis powers and their satellites dominated Europe. Germany and Italy placed some regions under military occupation, while others were absorbed to create the "Greater German Reich."

Lastly, there were nominally independent states, such as Vichy France and Italy, which were little more than puppet regimes. Raw materials, including food, from countries in all the categories of German control were channeled into the Nazi war effort; factory machinery was often dismantled and sent to Germany.

The Nazi flag flies from the Arc de Triomphe in Paris in June 1940, days after the German invasion. Swastikas were hung from all public buildings in occupied France.

Stolen riches

In addition to plundering the raw materials of the territories they conquered, the Nazis looted their artistic treasures on a vast scale. In western Europe, they rationalized their looting by claiming to be repatriating "Germanic" art to its homeland, or removing art in order to protect it. Where these justifications did not apply, the Nazis would simply "purchase" the art at dramatically deflated valuations.

In eastern Europe and Russia, art was simply taken. According to museum authorities in Warsaw, the Nazis looted 2,774 paintings of the European School, 10,738 Polish paintings, and 1,379 sculptures, while the *Soviet War News* reported, in September 1944, that 34,000 museum pieces, including "14,950 pieces of unique furniture," had been plundered from four former palaces around Leningrad (now St. Petersburg). These included the jewel-encrusted Amber Room, removed from the Catherine Palace and never recovered.

Special offices were set up to oversee the looting. Art expert Hans Posse was commissioned to head *Sonderauftrag Linz* ("Special Operation Linz"), with the aim of collecting the cream of Europe's art treasures for a planned grand museum. Herman Göring and Joachim von Ribbentrop had their own rival organizations, which appropriated whatever Posse left behind. Göring was the power behind the *Einsatzstab Reichsleiter Rosenberg*, a special taskforce under Alfred Rosenberg, which confiscated works of art and manuscripts from Jewish people. Its records reveal that the looted artworks filled more than 1.4 million railroad trucks.

The Nazis also looted the gold reserves of the countries they occupied, seizing $625 million (worth around $12.5 billion today) in gold bullion and coins from their central banks. This included $103 million from Austria, $163 million from the Netherlands, and $223 million from Belgium. Just over half of this was found and recovered after the war—some hidden in a mine in western Thuringia—but much of it had

Alfred Rosenberg

Born in Estonia in 1893, but of German descent, Alfred Rosenberg was a key ideologue in the early days of the Nazi Party. From 1923, he edited the party's newspaper, *Völkischer Beobachter*.

Hitler personally championed Rosenberg, making him caretaker leader of the Nazi Party during his imprisonment following the failed Munich Beer Hall Putsch in 1923, and imbibing the anti-Semitic ideas Rosenberg expressed in his book *Der Mythus des zwanzigsten Jahrhunderts* (*The Myth of the Twentieth Century*), published in 1930. Rosenberg held a series of important posts in the party, including a leading role in foreign policy and head of the taskforce charged with confiscating works of art from Jewish owners.

In July 1941, Rosenberg became Reich Minister for the Occupied Eastern Territories (the *Reichskommissariats* of Ostland and Ukraine), where some of the worst atrocities were carried out. After the war, he was sentenced to death at the Nuremberg Trials and executed by hanging in 1946.

A US soldier surveys piles of Jewish-owned art and documents in a church in Ellingen, Germany, in April 1945. Mines and castles were also used to store such materials.

been paid to Switzerland, in exchange for traded goods, and was never recovered.

Reign of terror

In 1942, Nazi hegemony in western Europe was relatively benign for people who were not Jewish, Roma, disabled, or any other persecuted minority. In occupied Paris, for instance, cultural figures such as Henri Matisse and Jean-Paul Sartre continued to work more or less freely. In the eastern territories, however, the full horror of Nazi ideology quickly became clear. Mass murder had begun with the slaughter of Poland's intelligentsia and priests from 1939, and continued with the killing of hundreds of thousands of Soviet prisoners of war (POWs) and others deemed to be enemies of the German state, who were starved to death or shot by death squads. Jewish populations in both west and east were rounded up and herded into concentration camps, as Hitler's "Final Solution to the Jewish Question"—the systematic murder of all Jews—began to unfold.

At first, this reign of terror was implemented specifically by German paramilitary *Schutzstaffel* (SS) and their *Einsatzgruppen* (mobile killing units). From the outset, the SS was able to draw upon the enthusiastic services of right-wing zealots recruited from occupied and conquered territories such as the Ukraine and Estonia. By the end of the war, around 500,000 SS members—more than half the total number—were non-Germans.

In areas under German occupation, local authorities often collaborated with the Nazis to implement their racial policies. Client states such as Vichy France, Hungary, and Norway were also expected to help round up and transport Jews. Millions of eastern Europeans, including POWs, were forced to work for the Nazis as enslaved labor and, later in the war, as auxiliary troops. There were resistance movements throughout Europe, but the primary response of most Europeans was to survive as bystanders, keeping their heads down or looking the other way. ■

Soviet women and the elderly are forced to clear roads for a German army convoy. Thousands of enslaved laborers died of starvation and overwork over the course of the war.

THE FINAL SOLUTION

THE HOLOCAUST (1942–1945)

IN CONTEXT

FOCUS
Persecution and genocide

BEFORE
1918 Right-wing German political parties initiate the myth that left-wing groups and especially Jews betrayed Germany in World War I.

1920 The Nazi Party declares that only those of German blood can be German citizens and specifically excludes Jews.

1933 A Nazi concentration camp—initially for political prisoners—opens at Dachau.

September 1935 The two Nuremberg Laws deprive Jews of rights, legalizing Nazi racist and anti-Semitic ideology.

November 9–10, 1938 Nazi thugs instigate a pogrom against Jews and their property throughout Germany, in what is known as Kristallnacht.

AFTER
January 27, 1945 Soviet troops liberating Auschwitz concentration camp find 7,000 prisoners abandoned by the Nazis because they were too weak to walk.

Nov. 20, 1945–Oct. 1, 1946 Leading Nazis are tried for crimes against humanity at the Nuremberg Trials.

2005 The United Nations adopts a resolution to designate January 27, the date of the liberation of Auschwitz, as International Holocaust Remembrance Day.

The systematic slaughter of European Jews by the Nazis is now commonly known as the Holocaust; the Nazis themselves called it the *Endlösung* ("Final Solution"). The Final Solution was implemented from late 1941, although Jewish organizations date the start of the Holocaust to 1933, when Hitler came to power. Nazi ideology saw the Jews as an alien strain, "polluting" the pure Aryan bloodline, and they proposed a series of "solutions" to solve what they called the *Judenfrage* ("Jewish Question"). These solutions became worse as Nazi Germany conquered more territory, bringing ever more Jews under their control.

Emigration and ghettos

In 1933, the Jewish population of Germany was around half a million, 80 percent of whom held German citizenship. That number increased from 1935 after the passage of the Nuremberg Laws, which defined Jewishness as having one Jewish grandparent. The Nazis' initial strategy was concentration. Jews were moved into cities and large towns from the countryside, villages, and small towns. The preferred solution was emigration; racist laws, harassment, and anti-Semitic propaganda forced out German Jews, mostly to the US, South America, Britain, and Palestine, but also to Poland, France, and other parts of Europe. By 1938, more than half of German Jews had emigrated. The *Schutzstaffel* (SS), under the violent anti-Semite Heinrich Himmler, now ran purpose-built concentration camps, though these primarily held political prisoners.

> In large labor columns, separated by gender, able-bodied Jews will be brought … to build roads, whereby a large number will doubtlessly be lost through natural reduction.
>
> **Reinhard Heydrich**
> **speaking at the Wannsee Conference, 1942**

A Jew from Vinnitsa, Ukraine, is shot by a member of an *Einsatzgruppen* killing squad in 1941. On the back of the photo, probably taken by a Nazi soldier, was written "Last Jew in Vinnitsa."

After the annexation of Austria and parts of Czechoslovakia in 1938, another 250,000 Jews came under Nazi control, even as the abuse of German Jews reached a new pitch with the Kristallnacht pogroms across the country. Around this time, it became increasingly difficult for Jews to emigrate. Many destination states had begun to restrict Jewish immigration, while the German invasion of Poland in September 1939 trapped 1.5 million Polish-Jewish residents. Elsewhere the start of

See also: Kristallnacht 48–49 ▪ The destruction of Poland 58–63 ▪ Nazi massacres 136 ▪ Nazi Europe 168–171 ▪ The Warsaw Ghetto Uprising 242–243 ▪ Liberating the death camps 294–295 ▪ The Nuremberg Trials and denazification 318–319

World War II made travel more difficult as borders closed, the British mounted a naval blockade, and civilian transportation was rationed.

In Poland, the Nazis developed a new approach, herding Jews into ghettos. While some were forced to labor, the overcrowded and poorly supplied areas served to perpetuate the myth that Jews were inherently inferior and a source of diseases such as typhus. The largest ghetto was in Warsaw, where an initial Jewish population of 138,000 in November 1940 rose to almost half a million in April 1941. By July 1942, 92,000 of the ghetto's residents had died of disease, cold, and starvation.

Hundreds of thousands more Jews suffered as the Nazis occupied Denmark, Norway, Belgium, the Netherlands, Luxembourg, France, Yugoslavia, and Greece in 1940–1941.

The Final Solution

In 1941, at some point still not determined by historians, Hitler decided on what the Nazis referred to as the Final Solution—the systematic, deliberate, physical »

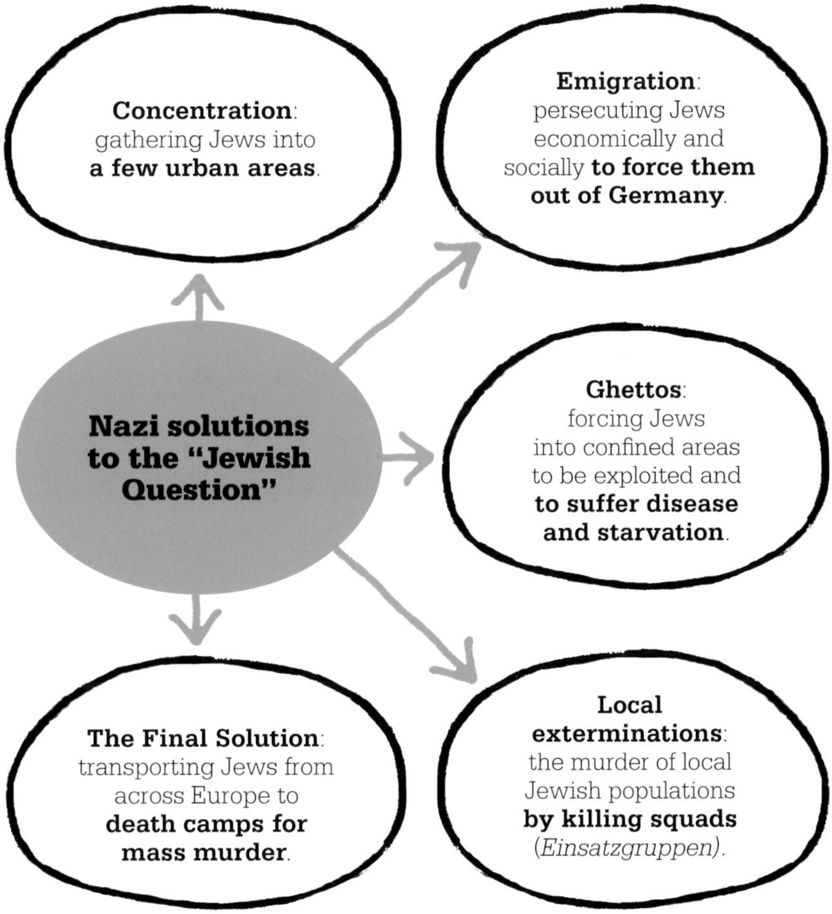

Nazi solutions to the "Jewish Question"
Concentration: gathering Jews into a few urban areas.
Emigration: persecuting Jews economically and socially to force them out of Germany.
Ghettos: forcing Jews into confined areas to be exploited and to suffer disease and starvation.
The Final Solution: transporting Jews from across Europe to death camps for mass murder.
Local exterminations: the murder of local Jewish populations by killing squads (Einsatzgruppen).

Heinrich Himmler

Born in 1900 in Munich, Germany, the son of a Catholic schoolmaster, Heinrich Himmler became an officer cadet in World War I, but never saw service. In 1923, he joined the Nazi Party, which encouraged his nationalist and anti-Semitic views. In 1929, he was appointed head of the SS.

By 1933, when the Nazis came to power, Himmler had built up SS numbers from a few hundred to more than 50,000; they later rose to a million. His SS soon had its own army, oversaw racial issues, the German police, and ran all concentration camps. In 1941, Himmler deployed killing squads (*Einsatzgruppen*) and, from 1942, was entrusted with the Final Solution. From 1943, as minister of the interior, he organized and publicly justified the mass murder of Jews and other groups, such as Roma.

As the war turned against the Nazis, Himmler hoped to broker peace and succeed the Führer. Hitler learned of the plan and ordered his arrest in April 1945. Himmler tried to escape, but was captured by the Allied forces, and poisoned himself in custody in Lüneburg in 1945.

The Bielski Partisans

Former Bielski Partisan and Holocaust survivor Aron Bell (formerly known as Aron Bielski) holds a photo of his father, David Bielski.

Throughout occupied Europe, Jewish people tried to resist the Nazi genocide. One group that had considerable success was the Bielski Partisans, operating from forests in Western Belorussia (now Belarus) from 1941 to 1944.

After their parents and siblings were killed by Nazis, the Bielski brothers escaped with other Jews from the Nowogródek ghetto in December 1941. The eldest brother, Tuvia, a veteran of the Polish army, was chosen to head the group. They carried out raids, sabotaging German trains and bridges, but their principal mission was to help Jewish women, children, and the elderly escape the ghettos and live free in the forest.

In 1943, when the Germans launched a huge offensive to track them down, the Bielskis led their group to a swampy, less accessible refuge in the Naliboki Forest, where they established a self-sufficient community. By the summer of 1944, when the Soviet Army reclaimed Belorussia, the group numbered more than 1,200. Tuvia emigrated to Israel and later the US. He died in 1987.

annihilation of all European Jews. On January 20, 1942, at a conference in the Berlin suburb of Wannsee, SS general Reinhard Heydrich and 14 other high-ranking SS officers and German officials met to discuss how to apply the Final Solution to the 9.5 million Jews across Occupied Europe.

Mass killings

Extermination methods were already in operation at this point, having begun in the wake of the June 1941 German invasion of the USSR. Following close behind the frontline, special killing squads (*Einsatzgruppen*) had immediately set about eliminating local Jewish populations, with the assistance of local security forces and other paramilitaries. Through a combination of mass shootings, burnings, beatings, and gassing, around a million Jews would be murdered by *Einsatzgruppen*. The Wannsee Conference signaled the shift to a more organized, industrial genocide, with mass deportations of Jews to remote camps where they would be gassed, either in special vans or in gas chambers disguised as shower rooms.

From December 1941, Jews were systematically killed at five death camps—Chelmno, Sobibor, Majdanek, Treblinka, and Belzec, while a sixth, Auschwitz-Birkenau, equipped with gas chambers and attached to the concentration camp at Auschwitz, opened in March 1942. On the pretext of resettlement, trains brought Jews from all over Europe to German-occupied Poland. Up to 1.5 million people were killed at the Auschwitz complex, including at least 960,000 Jews; as many as 865,000 were murdered as soon as they arrived. In many parts of Europe, local state authorities and populations assisted the Nazis by rounding up Jews and loading them on to trains, but some countries, such as Finland, Albania, and Denmark, refused to cooperate, saving many thousands of Jewish lives.

Children are rounded up on their way to Chelmno concentration camp in 1942. Among those murdered there were 593 Jewish children, aged under 12, from the Polish town of Bełchatów.

Final days and Jewish toll

From January 1945, the SS evacuated Auschwitz-Birkenau, as Soviet forces approached. They forced inmates to trudge huge distances, dubbed "death marches" as many perished or were shot en route. Most survivors were worked to death, starved, or tortured in labor camps such as Bergen-Belsen and Dachau, which had until then held mostly criminals and political prisoners. It was at such camps that the Western Allied forces—and through them the wider world—first began to comprehend the full horror of Nazi Germany's "solutions."

The Holocaust claimed the lives of six million Jews, including more than a million children. It wiped out one-third of the Jewish population in the world, and two-thirds in Europe. Just over 300,000 Jews survived the camps and death marches.

Other victims

While Jews suffered by far the highest death toll, they were not the only communities targeted in the Holocaust. In the Nazi bid to create its pure Aryan state, millions deemed racially inferior—not just Jews but also Slavic people, including Poles, other central and eastern Europeans, or anyone with "Asiatic" features—were deported from occupied territory to concentration and forced labor camps, or murdered. Nazis killed up to 1.9 million non-Jewish Polish civilians during World War II. More than 200,000 Roma and Sinti peoples were murdered or died from disease and starvation in a genocide they called *Porajmos* ("the Devouring"). Many more were forced to labor or subjected to sterilization and medical experimentation. Others targeted included the gay community, disabled people, and religious minorities.

The Nazis imprisoned more than 50,000 gay men, and sent up to 15,000 to concentration camps, where most perished. Many gay men remained in prison after the war, as the Allies refused to repeal the German penal code outlawing homosexuality. The Nazis also murdered around 250,000 disabled people in euthanasia programs. Jehovah's Witnesses were among the religious groups persecuted; more than 8,000 were sent to camps and around 1,500 killed.

Tens of thousands of people were complicit in the Holocaust, but just 199 Nazis were tried for war crimes at Nuremberg. Of those, 161 were convicted, 37 of whom were sentenced to death. ■

Haggard Auschwitz survivors—a few in the striped uniform of inmates—peer through barbed wire as Soviet forces arrive at the camp in 1945.

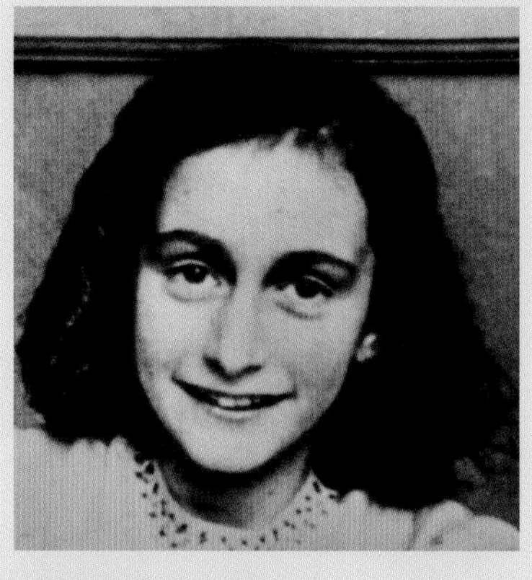

Anne Frank

Born in 1929 in Frankfurt, Germany, Anne Frank fled with her German-Jewish family in 1933, moving to Amsterdam where her father had business connections. In 1940, Germany occupied Holland, and in 1942, as the Nazis began to transport Jews to forced labor camps, Anne and her family went into hiding. For two years they lived in a secret attic apartment behind the office of the family-owned business at 263 Prinsengracht.

Anne kept a diary, (which she addressed to "Kitty"), referring to their cramped living space as the Secret Annex. In August 1944, the Nazi SS and Dutch police discovered Anne's family; the next month, the Franks were sent to Auschwitz. Anne and her sister Margot were then transported to labor at the Bergen-Belsen camp, where they died of typhus in 1945. Of the family, only their father survived. After the war, he worked hard to have his daughter's writing published as *The Diary of Anne Frank.* It was later translated into 65 languages; Anne's personal Holocaust account became known around the world.

WE MUST DEFEND THE CITY OR DIE IN THE ATTEMPT

THE BATTLE OF STALINGRAD (SEPTEMBER 1942–FEBRUARY 1943)

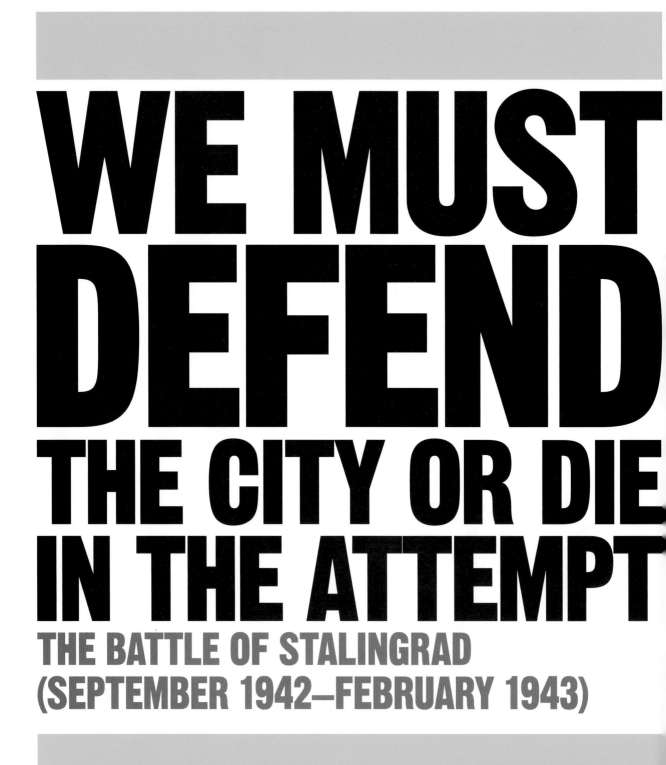

IN CONTEXT

FOCUS
German advances in the USSR

BEFORE
June 22, 1941 Germany attacks the USSR in Operation Barbarossa, ending the Nazi-Soviet nonaggression pact.

June–December 1941 The German invasion of the USSR fails to defeat the Red Army.

AFTER
February–March 1943 Germany wins one of their last major victories on the Eastern Front at the Third Battle of Kharkov.

July–August 1943 Germany is defeated at the Battle of Kursk, their last major offensive on the Eastern Front.

1945 In post-war agreements, Stalin demands a Soviet-friendly buffer zone against any future German aggression.

> During the battle for Stalingrad we came to feel that everybody in the world was watching us—and hoping for something heroic, a turning point.
>
> **Vladimir Turov**
> **Defender of Stalingrad**

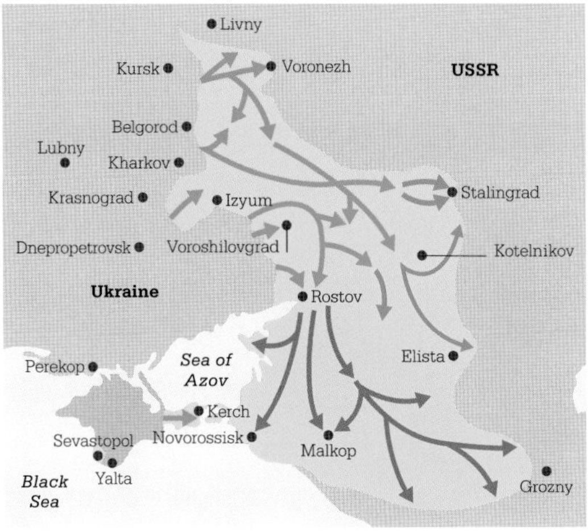

From June 1942, the Axis powers advanced on the Caucasus, a region rich in resources that Hitler hoped would help fuel the German war effort in Europe. Their invasion of Stalingrad proved to be a costly diversion from this strategic aim.

Key:
German advance, June–November 1942
Army Group South
Army Group A
Army Group B

For the 1942 summer campaign, Hitler and his generals planned to target the Caucasus. The region was the source of most of the USSR's oil reserves and also contained mineral resources, industry, and farmland. If it captured the Caucasus, Germany would not need to rely so heavily on Romanian oil fields or their own synthetic fuel production.

The plan for the German offensive, code-named *Fall Blau* ("Case Blue"), was for the Army Group South to advance southeast of the Don River and then into the Caucasus. To hide their goal, the Germans launched a deception campaign called Operation Kremlin to give the impression that their aim was to capture Moscow. It included increasing Luftwaffe reconnaissance flights over Moscow and distributing maps of the city to German soldiers.

The offensive begins

On June 28, 1942, Case Blue swung into action. German forces, reinforced with soldiers from Hungary, Romania, and Italy, made rapid gains, partly because the majority of Red Army troops were guarding Moscow, still believing it was the offensive's objective. By early July, Axis progress had begun to slow due to supply problems and increased Soviet resistance. To regain momentum, on July 23, Hitler directed Army Group South to split into two: Group A, on the right flank, would conduct Operation Edelweiss and thrust toward the Caucasus, aiming to capture the oil fields of Maikop, Grozny, and Baku. On the left flank, Group B would conduct Operation Fischreiher, an advance toward the Volga River that would help to screen Group A.

New priority

Operation Edelweiss initially went well for the Germans. On August 9, they captured the oil fields at Maikop, only to find they had been wrecked so severely by the retreating Red Army that it would take a year to repair them. Although Axis forces made some gains to the south after this, their progress slowed as the terrain became more mountainous and the weather worsened. In the winter of 1942–1943, the Soviets pushed them back, denying the Germans access to the oil fields of the Caucasus.

There was, however, another reason why Operation Edelweiss failed. Another priority had emerged that was draining German

See also: The destruction of Poland 58–63 ▪ Operation Barbarossa 124–131 ▪ The Great Patriotic War 132–135 ▪ Prisoners of war 184–187 ▪ The Battle of Kursk 232–235 ▪ Operation Bagration 266–269

reinforcements, supplies, and air support: the assault on Stalingrad (today's Volgograd). Originally named Tsaritsyn but renamed in honor of the Soviet leader in 1925, Stalingrad was an industrial city and transportation hub on the west bank of the Volga River. The city's association with Stalin gave it a symbolic value to Hitler that far outweighed its strategic importance.

Not a step back!

Group B began to advance toward Stalingrad on July 23, and within two days had pushed Soviet forces back to the Don. To galvanize the Red Army, Stalin issued Order No.227, known for its slogan "Not a step back!" on July 28. Penal units (consisting of convicts) were sent to dangerous areas of the front, while regular army detachments at the rear were ordered to shoot or arrest "defeatists." Any commander who allowed an unauthorized retreat was to be stripped of their position and court-martialed.

Renewed Soviet resistance slowed Group B, who were further delayed when Hitler diverted their Panzer units to support Group A's offensive in the Caucasus. As a consequence, Axis forces did not begin crossing the Don until August 11. These delays gave the Red Army time to retreat toward Stalingrad and prepare for German onslaught. Women and children were evacuated to the east bank of the Volga and 7,000 workers were formed into a militia. On August 23, the Luftwaffe began their massive aerial bombardment of Stalingrad. The German Sixth Army, led by General Friedrich Paulus, fought their way into Stalingrad itself on September 14. The man charged with planning Stalingrad's defense, General Vasily Chuikov, ordered his men to "hug" the enemy forces—advance and remain so close to them that the Germans would not be able to use artillery or aerial bombardment for fear of hitting their own men. He also created "storm groups," heavily armed mobile formations that specialized in house-to-house fighting. The combat amid the ruins that Stalingrad had become was among World War II's most brutal. Individual buildings were ferociously fought over, sometimes changing hands several times in one day. German veterans described the fighting in Stalingrad as the *Rattenkrieg* ("Rat War") because of its savagery. By early November, the Axis forces had pushed the Red Army back to the Volga, leaving them in control of only isolated strips along the riverbank.

Soviet reinforcements

The sacrifice of Chuikov's men at Stalingrad had bought the Soviets a vital commodity: time. Hitler had poured manpower and resources »

> Rubble became fortresses, destroyed factories harbored deadly sharpshooters, behind every lathe and every machine tool lurked sudden death.
>
> **Colonel Herbert Selle**
> **Engineer, German Sixth Army**

A German tank from the 14th Panzer Division advances on Stalingrad in October 1942. Although the division was destroyed in the Battle of Stalingrad, it reformed and later returned to the Eastern Front.

Friedrich Paulus

Born in 1890 in Breitenau, Germany (now in Austria), Friedrich Paulus served as a junior officer in World War I. By 1939, he had gained a reputation as a diligent and intelligent staff officer.

In January 1942, Paulus was promoted to general and given command of the Sixth Army, based in southern Russia. This was his first experience as a battlefield commander. That August, he led his men into Stalingrad.

By November, Paulus's forces were surrounded by the Red Army. Rejecting his request for permission to surrender, Hitler promoted him to field marshal, wrongly expecting Paulus to die by suicide rather than surrender.

In Soviet captivity, Paulus became a member of the National Committee for a Free Germany, an anti-Nazi organization, and urged Germans to surrender. After the war, he was a witness for the prosecution at the Nuremberg Trials. Freed in 1953, Paulus was allowed to settle in East Germany, where he died four years later of motor neuron disease.

into the city, hoping to score a major symbolic victory there. But while the fighting at Stalingrad raged on, Soviet reinforcements had arrived in the region: one million soldiers, 13,500 artillery pieces, 900 tanks, and 1,000 aircraft.

Axis forces surrounded

The advance on Stalingrad created a 400-mile- (640-km-) long bulge, or "salient," in the Axis lines. The Soviet general staff planned to use the reinforcements to attack the salient flanks, thus encircling Axis forces in Stalingrad. On November 19, the Red Army launched Operation Uranus, a pincer attack targeting the Romanian, Italian, and Hungarian forces guarding the flanks of the Axis salient.

After four days of fighting, the Soviet forces completed the encirclement, trapping at least 250,000 Axis soldiers in the "pocket" in and around Stalingrad. Now surrounded, Paulus requested permission from German high command for his forces to break out from the city and fight their way back to the Axis lines. Hitler's advisers urged him to agree to the request, not least because the only way their forces at Stalingrad could now be resupplied—they needed more than 440 tons of supplies per day—was by air, which required countless risky flights over Soviet lines. However, Göring vainly boasted that the Luftwaffe could achieve this, so Hitler ordered Paulus to hold his position and fight on.

> For us, it was life and death which met on the Volga. And it was life which won the fight.
> **Konstantin Rokossovsky**
> **Marshal of the USSR**

Luftwaffe transport planes began landing at Stalingrad on November 25, but were never able to supply the amount Göring had promised. The Luftwaffe also lost around 500 aircraft in the doomed provisioning of "Fortress Stalingrad," weakening their aerial operations elsewhere on the Eastern Front.

Desperate plight

On December 12, the Germans launched their relief effort, Operation Winter Storm. Panzer units attempted to create a land corridor to Stalingrad but by December 23 they had been beaten back by Soviet forces. The Soviets then followed

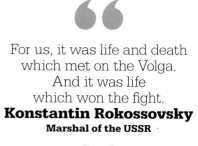

A Soviet sniper picks off Axis soldiers amid the rubble of Stalingrad. The most successful sniper, Vasily Zaytsev, of the 284th rifle division, killed 225 enemy soldiers.

German captives become prisoners of war near Stalingrad. Many German POWs went on to die in labor camps. Some of those who survived were not released until 1955.

this success with Operation Little Saturn, which succeeded in pushing back Axis forces and severely hampering any further attempts at relief. The beleaguered soldiers trapped inside Stalingrad were by now in dire straits. Temperatures had plummeted to –22°F (–30°C), and lice, scabies, fever, and dysentery were endemic. Only one-tenth of the supplies they had requested had arrived, creating desperate shortages of food and ammunition. The starving forces resorted to eating rats, wallpaper paste, and sawdust.

The final Soviet push into Stalingrad, Operation Ring, was launched on January 10, 1943. Within two weeks the Axis had lost their last airfield in the city, completely cutting them off from any outside support. Despite the hopelessness of the situation, Hitler forbade any surrender and ordered Paulus to instruct his men to fight to their last round.

By January 27, the Soviets had split the Axis forces into two groups. On January 31, Paulus surrendered himself and the southern group. The other pocket of Axis soldiers, to the north, fought on for two more days before also surrendering.

Axis forces reach the Volga, north of Stalingrad. They **bombard the city by air**, reducing it to rubble.

↓

Axis troops **break into Stalingrad**.

↓

The Soviet **Red Army encircles** Axis troops in a **pincer movement**, cutting off supplies and reinforcements.

↓

Axis forces **attempt to break** the Soviet encirclement but fail.

↓

The trapped Axis forces surrender.

A Soviet turning point

Around 91,000 German and Romanian soldiers, who were mostly wounded, sick, starving, and frostbitten, were taken into Soviet captivity. The vast majority of these men died in forced marches or prisoner of war (POW) camps; only 6,000 of them survived to return home. Around 150,000 Axis soldiers had died in the city of Stalingrad, adding to the 480,000 Red Army dead.

Overall, the brutal struggle for Stalingrad led to some 2 million casualties (including 40,000 civilians). The defeat was a devastating blow to Germany's hopes for victory in the war, and fatally weakened their strength on the Eastern Front. In contrast, for the Soviets it was a major turning point; proving they could win a major victory over the Axis and leaving them in a strong position to advance west and push back the invaders. ■

WE WERE NOT JUST PRISONERS BUT SLAVES

PRISONERS OF WAR

IN CONTEXT

FOCUS
Humanitarian crises

BEFORE
April 1863 US president Abraham Lincoln signs the Lieber Code, which sets out, among other things, the legal principles governing the treatment of prisoners of war (POWs).

1899 The First Hague Convention agrees international law on warfare and treatment of POWs.

1929 The Convention Relative to the Treatment of Prisoners of War is signed at Geneva.

AFTER
1949 The Third Geneva Convention on the treatment of POWs is signed.

1956 The last surviving German POW returns home from the USSR.

More prisoners were taken during World War II than in any other conflict in history. The experience and fate of these prisoners varied massively, from Italian prisoners of war (POWs) in Britain, who ended up inheriting the farms on which they had worked, to the millions of captured Soviets, Filipinos, and other nationalities murdered by their captors. So much depended on the nationality and rank of the prisoner, but even more on the nationality of their captors, and on whether the nation in question had signed and was willing to respect the Geneva Convention of 1929. Rules governing the treatment of enemy

See also: The destruction of Poland 58–63 ▪ The fall of France 80–87 ▪ Operation Barbarossa 124–131 ▪ Nazi massacres 136 ▪ The Holocaust 172–177 ▪ Liberating the death camps 294–295 ▪ Victory in Europe 298–303 ▪ Aftermath 320–327

Death rates among prisoners of war

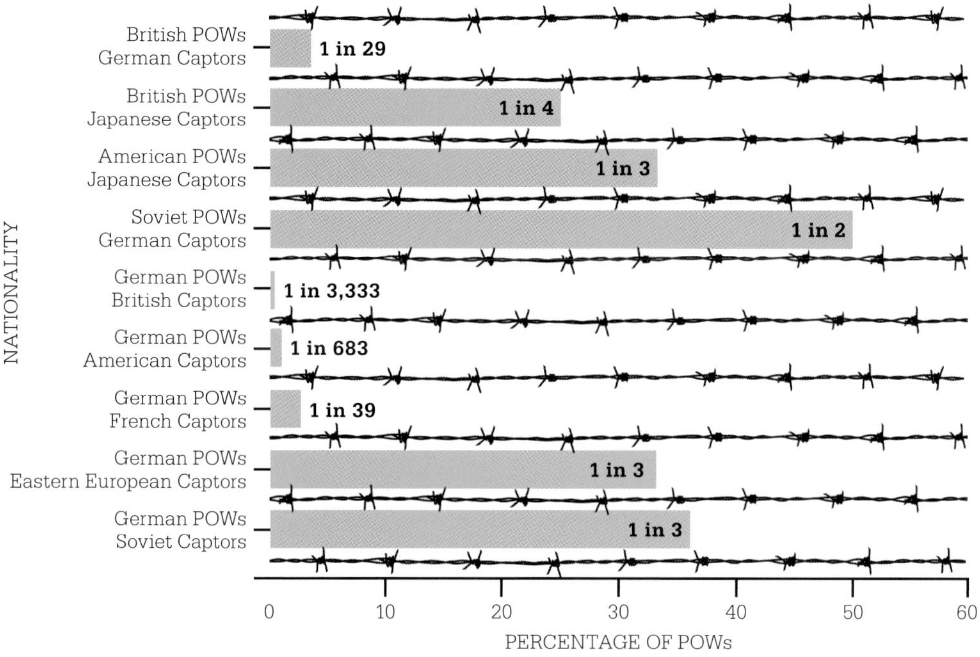

Percentage of POWs dying in captivity during World War II. Survival rates for POWs captured by the Japanese or the Soviets were lower, as a result of the failure of those nations to sign up to the Geneva Convention. Germany used the USSR's refusal to sign the convention as justification for the mistreatment of captured Soviet troops.

combatants taken prisoner had evolved in the 19th century, and the Hague Conventions of 1899 and 1907 spelled out the principle that fighting men who laid down their arms were to be well-treated. In July 1929, these principles were expanded in the Geneva Convention, which set out the duties of care owed to surrendered soldiers. POWs were to be safeguarded from battle, cared for if wounded, and housed and fed no worse than the garrison troops of the power that had captured them. The only information they were obliged to provide under interrogation was their name and rank, or service number. The International Red Cross was supposed to be allowed to inspect camps regularly. All the principal combatant powers involved in World War II had signed and ratified the Geneva Convention, except for Japan, which had signed but not ratified it, and the USSR, which had not signed on the ideological basis that no Red Army soldier would ever surrender. This had fateful consequences for Soviet POWs captured by German troops, as the Germans concluded that they were not bound by the convention in respect to Soviet prisoners.

Treatment of POWs

German treatment of POWs was broadly informed by the racial theories of the Nazis, which viewed Slavic peoples, such as Poles and Russians, as racially inferior, and therefore less deserving of humane treatment than Anglo-Saxon POWs, such as the British and Americans. The Japanese forces took an even harsher view of those soldiers they captured, viewing surrender as the ultimate disgrace; their treatment of POWs and interned civilians was cruel and inhumane. Allied nations generally treated their prisoners well. This disparity is starkly reflected in the death rates suffered by POWs under the different powers. A German POW held by the British had just a 1 in 3,333 chance of dying, compared to 1 in 3 for an American POW in Japanese hands, and 1 in 2 for a Russian POW in German hands.

The POW experience

The fate of POWs was significantly impacted by their unprecedented numbers. The lightning success of the German offensives at the start of the war delivered immense »

> Prisoners of war … shall at all times be humanely treated and protected, particularly against acts of violence, from insults, and from public curiosity.
> **Geneva Convention of 1929**
> **Article 2**

numbers of enemy captives into their hands: over 2 million Polish and French POWs by mid-1940. The Germans themselves lost 4.5 million men to captivity during the war, while the Italians had so many troops captured in North Africa that a communiqué from the British Coldstream Guards in the Western Desert on December 9, 1940, reported that they had not yet had time to count their prisoners, but had captured "about five acres of officers and two hundred acres of other ranks."

POW camps

Airmen shot down over enemy territory might expect a rough reception; in some areas of Germany they were likely to be lynched by mobs of angry civilians, or they might try to evade capture and sneak back across the frontlines. On the battlefield, men taken prisoner were likely to be subjected to a brief interrogation by the intelligence officer of the capturing unit, in an attempt to glean useful tactical information, before being transported away from the frontline for further interrogation. Both the Germans and the British set up holding camps in which intelligence might be extracted from prisoners in possession of strategically important information. In Cockfosters, in London, for instance, German officers had their cells bugged and their conversations analyzed by German speakers.

Eventually a POW would be sent to a permanent camp. For the vast majority on the Western Front there was little to do but wait out the war. The main focus for most prisoners was getting enough to eat, with Red Cross food and comfort parcels supplementing meager rations for British and American POWs in Germany, at least up until the fall of 1944, when the Allied invasion of Europe disrupted the Red Cross supply chain. Apart from hunger, the concern for most Allied POWs on the Western Front was boredom—much effort went into entertainment and education. The Geneva Convention asserted that officers were not to be made to labor, but enlisted men could be put to work (supposedly to be paid after hostilities had ended).

Escapes and executions

Although the majority of POWs made no attempt to escape, more than 33,000 British, Commonwealth, and American prisoners succeeded in escaping captivity. The Germans even set up a special prison, Colditz in Saxony, to contain "difficult" Allied prisoners, but even from there a few prisoners managed to escape. However, only a single German POW, German fighter ace Franz von Werra, escaped from British custody, jumping off a train in Canada in early 1941, and returning to Germany by way of the still-neutral US, Mexico, and Spain.

In some theaters of war, however, prisoners were executed on the spot. In May 1940, in what became known as the Wormhoudt Massacre, a Waffen-SS unit threw grenades

British POWs play music in a German prison camp. In addition to military bands, other POW entertainments included staging plays for fellow inmates.

Soviet POWs captured by Germans in the south of Ukraine in June 1942. Order No.270, issued by Stalin in 1941, effectively designated surrender as an act of treason.

and opened fire on a barn into which they had corralled 100 British POWs. Soviet POWs taken by the Germans were systematically starved and often left prey to the elements, ravaged by exposure, lice, and serious diseases such as dysentery and typhus. So desperate were their conditions that many of them "volunteered" to join an anti-Stalinist army led by the renegade Russian general Andrey Vlasov. Those soldiers that survived capture and fell back into Soviet hands were likely to be rewarded for their travails by being transported to the network of gulags (slave labor camps) in the USSR.

> … [murdered Filipinos] suffered slow and painful death in dark, foul, and lice-infested cells.
>
> **Pedro Lopez**
> **Philippine counsel at the Tokyo War Crimes Tribunal, 1946**

POWs in the Far East

Conditions for prisoners of the Japanese were appalling. In 1942, 61,000 Allied POWs were forced to construct the Burma-Thailand railroad, alongside nearly 300,000 laborers from southeast Asia. Working in horrific conditions, many succumbed to disease and starvation; up to 12,000 Allied prisoners and 90,000 native laborers may have died. Another Japanese war crime was the Bataan death march. Some 12,000 American and 64,000 Filipino troops, taken prisoner while defending the Philippines in 1942, were marched 60 miles (95km) in the heat, without adequate shelter or sustenance, and killed or abandoned if they fell behind. Nearly half of the Americans died; how many Filipinos perished is unknown. ■

Anders' Army

Following the carving up of Poland by Germany and the USSR, over a million Polish civilians and 250,000 Polish POWs found themselves in Soviet custody, languishing in prison or the gulags. After the German invasion of the USSR, the Polish government-in-exile and Stalin agreed on the creation of an army of exiled Poles, led by former cavalry officer Wladysław Anders.

Polish men from all over the USSR tried to reach the mustering points, although many died on the journey due to starvation or exhaustion. As relations with Stalin turned sour, Anders evacuated 77,000 troops and their dependents to British-controlled Persia (modern-day Iran). Elements of what became known as Anders' Army went on to win fame at the Battle of Monte Cassino in Italy. After the war, unable to return safely to communist Poland, many settled in Britain. Testimony from members of Anders' Army helped reveal the horror of Stalin's prison camp system.

A tomb for Polish soldiers at Monte Cassino, Italy. Many of the soldiers who died there had reached Italy from the gulags via central Asia, Persia, Palestine, and north Africa.

THE CRUEL REALITY

GERMANY AND THE REALITY OF WAR

IN CONTEXT

FOCUS
The German home front

BEFORE
1933 Nazi Robert Ley creates the German Labor Front (*Deutsche Arbeitsfront*) to control industrial relations and monopolize control of workers.

1934 Albert Speer oversees the Nuremberg rallies.

1936 The Nazis implement a four-year plan intended to accelerate rearmament.

AFTER
1946 Speer avoids a death sentence at Nuremberg.

1948 Infant mortality among Germans is twice that of other western European nations.

2011 The Quandt family of wealthy German industrialists admits to having benefited from the slave labor of 50,000 prisoners during World War II.

Eventually, Germany would be consumed by the conflagration it had ignited, but for a surprisingly long time the German people were relatively insulated from the effects of war. All-encompassing sociocultural control, cruel repression, clever economic management and, above all, ruthless exploitation of the rest of the continent helped shield much of the population from hardship. But the collapse, when it came, was brutal.

Unity at all costs

One of the lessons Hitler learned from the aftermath of World War I was the revolutionary potential

See also: Establishing the Nazi state 30–33 ▪ German expansion 46–47 ▪ Nazi Europe 168–171 ▪ The Holocaust 172–177 ▪ Germany's war industry 224 ▪ The destruction of German cities 287 ▪ The Soviets push into Germany 288–289

> We, the boys of Berlin … thought … the Battle of Britain was a jousting match. … War, no, that wasn't a word we used.
>
> **Wolf Jobst Siedler**
> **German writer**

unleashed by inflicting hardship on a population. The Nazis were determined to avoid anything that might upset the carefully constructed dispensation of *Gleichschaltung* ("coordination," i.e. national regimentation and conformity). Accordingly, in the first year of the war, many of their policies sought to avoid upsetting the domestic population. They resisted military demands for compulsory auxiliary service for youth, and measures such as across-the-board rationing and wage and price freezes were not introduced until 1944.

Economic resilience

Until late in the war, the most striking feature of German domestic consumption was its stability. Per capita, it fell only slowly each year, and even in 1944 was still at 70 percent of 1938 levels. The per capita food budget remained steady until 1944, even increasing in some years. Industrial production, which did not function in a command economy in the early years of the war, increased hugely after Albert Speer executed the plans laid out by Organization Todt—a military-engineering group created by Fritz Todt, Speer's predecessor as minister for armaments and ammunition. Technocratic management of the wartime economy led to a huge surge in armaments production. For instance, aircraft construction increased nearly fourfold between 1941 and 1944.

This apparent miracle was achieved in the face of a massive blockade by the British and (later) American navies. Resources were redirected from civilian consumption to the military, quotas and rationing ensured the efficient distribution of resources between the military and industry, and military interference in industry was stamped out. Substitution (the use of synthetic oil instead of petroleum products, for example) helped make up for blockaded resources, and German industry became hugely more efficient. By 1944, it took 46 percent less raw material to produce a BMW aero-engine compared to 1941.

The spoils of war

Ultimately, however, Germany was only able to negate the naval blockade by exploiting resources that came via other routes—specifically, conquest. Its rapid achievement of continental hegemony brought access to oil from Romania, coal from Poland, iron ore from France, and manganese from the USSR, among others. By 1944, Germany had access to 60 percent more coal than in 1936 and 140 percent more iron ore. Food, too, could be sourced from conquered territory, or simply bought in. After all, Germany had plenty of money, thanks to looting of invaded nations. In the early part of the war, access to many imports from the USSR counteracted the effects of the blockade. In fact »

German domestic consumption

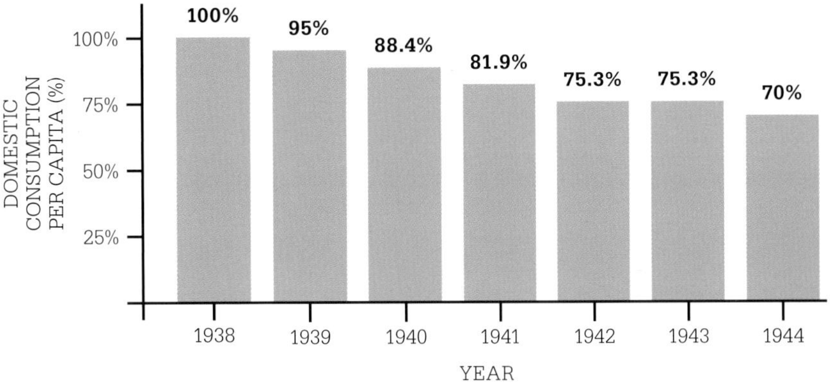

Despite the war, German consumption of domestically produced goods and services (based here on 1938 levels as 100 percent) declined only gradually until 1944. Imports from captured territory, looted resources, and forced labor kept domestic consumption relatively high.

Walther Funk, the economics minister of the Third Reich in 1941, argued strongly that, in the face of the British blockade, Germany's increasing dependence on imports from the USSR was a compelling reason to invade and thus secure permanent supply lines.

Apparent German economic resilience depended to a large degree on human misery, with millions of prisoners used as forced or slave labor. At the start of the war, Germany was effectively already at full employment. The demands of military conscription threatened to cause labor shortages. More women were recruited into the workforce in Britain and the US, but Nazi ideology restricted the role of women to the domestic and reproductive spheres. For instance, while all young men aged 18 to 25 were obliged to spend six months in the Reich Labor Service (RAD) and then join the military, for young women of the same age bracket, a voluntary labor service was restricted to just 50,000 "work maidens," serving for around 26 weeks at a time.

Soviet men and women at Kovel station in Ukraine, awaiting transportation to work as forced labor in Germany. Almost 5 million citizens of the USSR were drafted in this way.

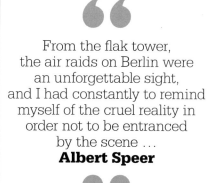

Forced labor

Instead of compromising their patriarchal ideology, the Nazis used foreign workers to resolve their labor shortages. By 1944, a quarter of the German labor force were foreign workers, including 5.3 million forced laborers and 1.8 million prisoners of war. This figure increased still further as the number of concentration camp inmates forced to work in armaments factories increased tenfold during 1944. Conditions for these foreign workers varied considerably according to their ethnicity and nationality, but the majority—including Jews, Slavs, and those from occupied parts of the USSR—were treated appallingly. They were barely sustained by starvation rations and worked to death, or to the point at which their health was ruined.

> From the flak tower, the air raids on Berlin were an unforgettable sight, and I had constantly to remind myself of the cruel reality in order not to be entranced by the scene …
>
> **Albert Speer**

Largely cushioned from the ill winds of war by looting and slave labor, the German public continued to support Hitler until deep into the war. In 1939, public sentiment had been tuned to a fine pitch by Nazi propaganda, with a widespread belief that the German cause was righteous. Breathtaking successes in 1939–1940 raised Hitler's popularity still further. He was lauded as a military genius, and the invasion of Russia in 1941 seemed, at least to begin with, to fit the authorized script.

The tide begins to turn

The course of the war began to turn with the Battle of Moscow over the winter of 1941–1942, but back in Germany the fiction of a victorious crusade was maintained. Wolf Siedler, a Berlin teenager during the war, observed that German public sentiment, fed only "reports about millions of prisoners of war," was divorced from the reality of the faltering campaign in the east: "What the average German did not see was that not a single great battle was fought after [Moscow]." Siedler did observe, however, that

US planes drop bombs on the docks and shipyards of Bremen, Germany. One raid, on March 11, 1945, involved more than 400 US Air Force bombers and seriously damaged the city.

during 1942 reports from the Eastern Front became steadily less specific and less boastful.

The change in German public morale came with news of the defeat at Stalingrad in 1942–1943, and the increasingly vicious Allied bombing of German cities. The actual economic impact of the bombing is much debated. War production was not seriously impaired until late in 1944, when the US began to target oil and transportation infrastructure in earnest, although there is a case to be made that the impact of their bombing was mitigated by the astonishing increase in productivity that had already been achieved. Attacks on industrial areas made many workers homeless, causing labor shortages and absenteeism, as workers had to take care of their families, or stayed with relatives in the countryside, where food security was greater.

Desperate defense

In the closing months of the war, what Speer called "the cruel reality" bit deep. He could have been referring to the devastating diktats of the beleaguered Führer and his coterie. Victor Klemperer, a Jewish-born scholar and diarist who survived the war in Germany, recorded desperate Nazi jargon from the last days of the war. Propaganda papers spoke about fantastical *neue Eingreifkräfte* ("new interventionary forces"). Boys and old men were forced into suicidal service as part of a national press-ganging called the *800,000 Mann-Plan*. Adolescent members of the *Volkssturm* (German home guard) were armed with just a *Volkshandgranate 45*—a "people's hand grenade"—in reality a chunk of concrete packed with explosives, which was as likely to kill the thrower as the target. Squads of *Panzerjagdkompanie* (Panzer tank companies) dispatched to tackle Soviet tanks were in reality just boys on foot or on bicycles.

Final sacrifice

This hopeless resistance was the result of Hitler's final betrayal of his own people, when he issued his *Nerobefehl* ("Nero Decree") on March 19, 1945. This ordered a scorched-earth policy in which everything and everyone was to be sacrificed. "You must not worry about what will be needed for rudimentary survival ...," he wrote to Speer. "... the best thing is to destroy that as well ... Those who remain after this struggle will in any event be inferior, for the good will all be dead." Thus Germany's citizens were forced to sacrifice their lives in a hopeless cause. ■

A Woman in Berlin

One of the most harrowing accounts of the fate of German civilians, particularly women, at the end of the war is an anonymous diary published in the US in 1954 under the title *A Woman in Berlin*.

It recounts the weeks from April 20 to June 22, 1945, and the horrific rapes and privations suffered by the diarist and others as Berlin falls to the Russians. Later revealed to have been journalist Marta Hillers, the diarist describes herself as "a pale-faced blonde always dressed in the same winter coat," and begins the memoir desperately searching for food and battling constant hunger. When the Russians arrive, the rapes begin, and the diarist realizes that she must move in with an officer for protection, although she continues to be raped by others. When her German boyfriend eventually returns, he scorns her sufferings and compromise, leaving her to reflect that, "to the rest of the world we're nothing but rubble women and trash."

THE END OF THE BEGINNING

FROM GAZALA TO EL ALAMEIN (MAY–NOVEMBER 1942)

IN CONTEXT

FOCUS
Decisive battles

BEFORE
June 10, 1940 Italy declares war on Britain and France.

February 6–7, 1941 Italian troops suffer heavy defeat in eastern Libya.

February 12, 1941 Rommel and the Afrika Korps land in Libya to support the Italians.

AFTER
November 8, 1942 US and British troops land in Morocco and Algeria at the start of Operation Torch.

May 6–13, 1942 Axis troops surrender in Tunisia.

July 9, 1943 Allied troops launch Operation Husky, landing on Sicily to begin the invasion of Italy.

At the start of 1942, Axis troops were engaged in heavy fighting in the USSR. That brutal campaign was the main focus of Hitler's attention, but the campaign in North Africa remained important. Here, however, by January 6, the Allied Operation Crusader had forced Rommel's German and Italian troops back from the Egyptian border to El Agheila on the Gulf of Sirte in Libya. The retreat had left Rommel's forces exhausted and his supply lines disrupted.

The British then assumed that Rommel would be unable to take the initiative for some time, and so took the time to rest their troops

See also: Italy enters the war 88–89 ▪ War in the Balkans 114–117 ▪ North Africa and the Mediterranean 118–121 ▪ Operation Torch 196–197 ▪ Victory in the desert 208–209 ▪ The invasion of Italy 210–211

and overhaul their equipment. Rommel, however, almost immediately proved them wrong.

Success and stalemate

After swiftly restoring his troops to fighting order, on January 21 Rommel began to advance once again. He quickly took Benghazi, forcing the Allies to regroup behind the 60-mile- (95-km-) long Gazala Line, which stretched inland from the Mediterranean coast. The line was heavily fortified with a defensive barrier of minefields interspersed with small, fortified "keeps"—concentrations of tank obstacles and mines. Despite some fierce resistance, notably from a Free French force at Bir Hakeim to the south, and heavy losses on both sides, Rommel outwitted his enemy by taking his troops around the southern end of the line. Axis forces then bunkered down within a defensive perimeter that became known as The Cauldron.

Despite constant Allied attacks, Rommel managed to break out on June 11 and headed east before turning north to attack British-held Tobruk on June 20. This was one of the key ports on the North African coast because large ships could dock in its natural deepwater harbor and deliver both troops and equipment in relative safety. Rommel captured two airfields and breached the perimeter defenses before his Panzer divisions entered the town. At 8:00 the following morning, South African general Hendrik Klopper, commander of the British garrison, surrendered. Tobruk was in Axis hands for the first time since the Allies had taken it on January 22, 1941. Rommel's capture of the port was probably his greatest achievement.

> Am sending mobile troops out tonight. Not possible to hold tomorrow … Will resist to the last man and last round.
>
> **Hendrik Klopper**
> **while in charge of the Tobruk garrison, June 21, 1942**

Faced with this major setback, the British Eighth Army quickly withdrew from the Gazala Line, first to the port of Mersa Matruh and then, when that was overrun, across the Egyptian border toward the small railroad halt of El Alamein. The First Battle of El Alamein took place about 9 miles (15km) to the west of the town. It began on July 1 when Rommel attacked the Allied lines.

Rommel rebuffed

British General Claude Auchinleck held back the German advance for two days, while New Zealand forces repelled an assault by the Italian Ariete Armored Division, and Australian units resisted an Axis breakthrough. After two British attacks across the Axis defensive lines on July 14–16 and 21–22, Rommel abandoned his attack.

On August 30, Rommel made another attempt to break through the British lines, launching a feint attack to the north, close to the coast, and directing his main attack to the south. The Allied troops, now under the command of Lieutenant-General Montgomery, held firm and forced Rommel to »

Free French soldiers celebrate after successfully defending the desert oasis of Bir Hakeim in June 1942. Their efforts bought the Allies time to safely retreat back to Egypt.

Axis v. Allies: relative strength of forces

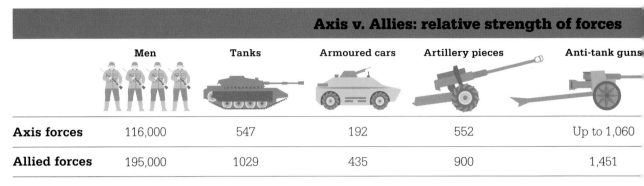

	Men	Tanks	Armoured cars	Artillery pieces	Anti-tank guns
Axis forces	116,000	547	192	552	Up to 1,060
Allied forces	195,000	1029	435	900	1,451

> In the situation in which you find yourself there can be no other thought but to stand by your post, not to take even one pace back, and to throw every available weapon and every available solider into battle.
>
> **Adolf Hitler**
> **to General Rommel, November 3, 1942**

swing north toward the Alam Halfa position. Running short on fuel and vehicles, Rommel withdrew on September 5 and prepared to fight a defensive campaign to hold back the British. Yet again, he had failed to break through, and his eastward advance was now halted.

The second battle

Some battles are won by initiative and daring, while other battles are won by meticulous planning. The Second Battle of El Alamein was definitely in the latter category. Axis forces were on the defensive, having failed to breach British lines, and their supply lines were seriously overstretched. Above all, they were outnumbered and also outgunned. The combined Axis forces, made up of German and Italian troops, numbered fewer men, and had fewer tanks, armored cars, artillery pieces, anti-tank guns, and serviceable aircraft than the Allies. Despite his superior weaponry, Montgomery did not rush to go on the offensive. He slowly built up and trained his forces, gained intelligence, and continued to choke off Axis supplies by land and sea. Rommel had expected a major British attack, so had dug deep into the desert behind an array of minefields known as the Devil's Gardens. Weaker Italian troops settled in between them for support. Meanwhile, Montgomery resorted to subterfuge, running a number of operations to confuse and mislead his enemy. With the time gained, he meticulously planned the two phases of his attack, code-named Operations Lightfoot and Supercharge.

Only when Montgomery was ready did he strike. On October 23, the British Thirtieth Corps launched an artillery offensive against the north of the Axis line. Fortuitously, Rommel was away in Germany for medical treatment and did not return until the third day of the battle. Allied infantry began by advancing through the minefields and eventually broke through after some delays, particularly in the misleadingly named Kidney Ridge (in fact a depression). Meanwhile, to confuse the enemy, the British Thirteenth Corps staged a diversionary assault to the south, and an amphibious assault was launched on the coast near Sidi Abd Rahman on November 1. German resistance was strong, and the fighting was fierce everywhere. However, ultimately Operation Lightfoot had gone according to Montgomery's plan.

Operation Supercharge

On November 2, Montgomery unleashed Operation Supercharge. Aware that Rommel was now short on fuel, he dispatched his forces to break through the final German defenses. Fierce and protracted

> It may almost be said: "Before Alamein we never had a victory. After Alamein we never had a defeat."
>
> **Winston Churchill**
> ***The Hinge of Fate, 1950***

Aircraft

350

530

A comparison between Axis and Allied forces in the Second Battle of El Alamein shows that Rommel's *Panzer Armee Afrika* was heavily outnumbered in every department.

bombardments of Tel el Aqqaqir to the west and Sidi Abd Rahman helped British forces break through in the north. Rommel informed Hitler that his troops faced annihilation; Hitler responded that they must stand firm or die. On November 4, however, Rommel withdrew.

The Second Battle of El Alamein was a turning point for the Western Allies, who had suffered defeat in most previous ground confrontations with the Axis. It was a massive boost to flagging morale, and for Britain, a major success that enhanced Montgomery's reputation. Previously silenced church bells rang out across the land. The tide of battle had now swung in Britain's favor.

Retreat to Tunisia

In defeat, Rommel rapidly withdrew to the west, pursued by Allied troops. The Allies recaptured Tobruk on November 13 and then Benghazi on November 20, before Rommel halted behind a defensive line at El Agheila from November 24 to December 13. He then set off again, establishing a line beyond Sirte, which he would hold until January 13. Such was Rommel's speed of retreat that Allied supply lines became too stretched to follow him closely. On January 23, 1943, as Libya's capital Tripoli fell to the Allies, Rommel crossed the border into Tunisia. ■

British infantry advance at El Alamein. They were part of an Allied coalition that included Australian, Free French, Greek, Indian, New Zealand, Polish, and South African troops.

Bernard Montgomery

Born in London in 1887, Bernard Montgomery served throughout World War I. He was shot by a sniper at the first Battle of Ypres in 1914 and ended the war as chief of staff in the 47th (2nd London) Division. Between the wars he rose to become general officer, commanding the 8th Infantry Division. As commander of the British Eighth Army from August 1942, he led his troops to victory at El Alamein and on to the final Allied victory in Tunisia in May 1943. He subsequently led the Eighth Army during the Allied invasion of Italy and was in command of all Allied ground forces in Normandy after D-Day.

By the end of the war, the troops under Montgomery's command had liberated northern France, Belgium, and the Netherlands and captured much of northern Germany. On May 4, 1945, he accepted the surrender of German forces in northwest Europe. Often criticized for his arrogance and lack of tact and diplomacy, he was described by Winston Churchill as "in defeat, unbeatable; in victory, unbearable." He died in Hampshire, UK, in 1976.

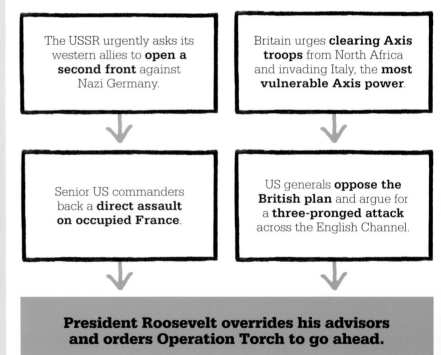

AT LAST WE ARE ON OUR WAY

OPERATION TORCH (NOVEMBER 1942)

IN CONTEXT

FOCUS
The North African front

BEFORE
June 1940 After the fall of France, French North Africa is controlled by the pro-Axis Vichy government.

December 1941 The Axis declares war on the US after Japan attacks Pearl Harbor.

AFTER
November 1942 After Vichy forces fail to resist Operation Torch, German and Italian troops occupy Vichy France. The French navy scuttles almost all of its fleet at Toulon.

January 1943 Roosevelt and Churchill meet in Casablanca to plan strategy, agreeing a "Mediterranean First" policy to drive the Axis out of North Africa and Italy.

May 1943 Axis troops surrender in Tunisia. Two months later, Allied troops land in Sicily.

On paper, Operation Torch—the Allied invasion of French North Africa—was a straightforward operation. Its ultimate aim was to seize Tunisia and attack Rommel and the Axis forces from the west, while the British Eighth Army pursued him from the east, clearing the way for the invasion of Italy. In reality, the entire operation was a compromise that risked going horribly wrong.

Complex planning

When Germany invaded the USSR in June 1941, Stalin urged the Allies to open a European front against Hitler. After entering the war that

The USSR urgently asks its western allies to **open a second front** against Nazi Germany.

↓

Senior US commanders back a **direct assault on occupied France**.

↓

Britain urges **clearing Axis troops** from North Africa and invading Italy, the **most vulnerable Axis power**.

↓

US generals **oppose the British plan** and argue for a **three-pronged attack** across the English Channel.

↓

President Roosevelt overrides his advisors and orders Operation Torch to go ahead.

See also: Italy enters the war 88–89 ▪ North Africa and the Mediterranean 118–121 ▪ The Japanese attack Pearl Harbor 138–145 ▪ From Gazala to El Alamein 192–195 ▪ Victory in the desert 208–209 ▪ The invasion of Italy 210–211 ▪ Allied summits 225

François Darlan

Born in 1881, François Darlan served in the French navy from 1902, rising through the ranks to become admiral of the fleet in 1939. Commander-in-chief of the French navy at the outbreak of war, he was de facto head of government in Marshal Pétain's Vichy French administration from 1941.

Although forced by the Nazis to resign his various ministerial positions in April 1942, Darlan was made overall commander-in-chief of the entire Vichy French armed forces. French North Africa was nominally loyal to the pro-Axis Vichy government—which was recognized by the US but not by Britain, which supported General de Gaulle's Free French—but Darlan convinced the Vichy forces to agree to an armistice and cooperate with the Allies. Many Free French, however, later criticized Darlan for his previous collaboration with the Axis, and he was assassinated by a Resistance fighter on December 24, 1942.

December, the US was torn between whether to fight Japan in the Pacific or aid the USSR via a three-pronged attack from Britain into northern Europe. The British were cautious, lacking the resources to support such a bold move. Churchill argued instead for driving Axis troops from North Africa. After prevarication among his generals, President Roosevelt gave a rare direct order in favor of the invasion of North Africa at the earliest possible date.

Once strategic disagreements were overcome, military planning also faced problems. US forces were untested in battle, let alone in amphibious assault. Axis airfields in Italy made Tunis too dangerous for landing, while Mediterranean Morocco or Algeria risked Spain joining the Axis and blocking the Straits of Gibraltar. The Moroccan port of Casablanca was risky due to dangerous Atlantic swells, and ruled out the early capture of Tunisia.

The landings commence

On November 8, 1942, the US Western Task Force landed near Casablanca. Although the US had probed local resistance and amenable French officers to sound out support for the Allied landing, the reception was far from certain. In the end, Vichy forces put up strong artillery opposition, while a major naval battle broke out at sea. Further east, the Central Task Force that had sailed from Britain landed near Oran in Algeria after an attempt to seize the harbor failed. The Vichy fleet intervened but its ships were sunk or driven ashore.

More successful was the Eastern Task Force landing by British forces at Algiers, where 400 French Resistance fighters (mainly from the Jewish "Géo Gras Group") seized key targets early on November 8. Heavy artillery fire prevented a British destroyer from landing its troops, but the city surrendered the same evening. On November 10, an armistice was agreed with the Vichy French. Operation Torch had succeeded—the Allies had secured their position in North Africa. ■

US troops from the Central Task Force land near Oran, Algeria. Supporting naval fire was initially withheld in the hope of French support, but forces loyal to Vichy soon mounted a defense.

THE GEESE THAT LAID THE GOLDEN EGGS AND NEVER CACKLED

THE SECRET WAR (1939–1945)

IN CONTEXT

FOCUS
Espionage and intelligence

BEFORE

1909 The British government formally constitutes its Military Intelligence (MI) agencies, MI5 and MI6.

1938 In the USSR, the much-feared Lavrentiy Beria becomes head of the NKVD.

July 1939 Polish intelligence officers give British and French agents a replica Enigma, the German electromechanical enciphering machine.

AFTER

September 1945 The US government dissolves the Office of Secret Services (OSS). The newly formed Central Intelligence Agency (CIA) takes on many of its agents in 1947.

1946 Reinhard Gehlen, a former major general in German army intelligence, becomes head of a US-sponsored anticommunist spy network in eastern Europe.

1951 The Cambridge Spy Ring, a UK-based network of Soviet informers, is exposed.

1952 British mathematician and computer pioneer Alan Turing, a hero of the wartime code-breaking operation, is convicted of gross indecency for having a homosexual relationship. Forced to undergo chemical castration, he also loses his government security clearance. He dies by suicide two years later.

In **the secret war**, the tools available include …

Signals intelligence ("sigint") …

… intercepted data that **reveals the enemy's strategy or tactics**, often after cryptanalysis (decrypting enemy codes and ciphers).

Human intelligence ("humint") …

… **eyewitness descriptions**, stolen or copied documents, personal interventions, and covert actions.

Intelligence is analyzed and **informs military strategy** and future **covert operations**. It may also draw upon …

… **counterintelligence**, such as intercepting or disrupting enemy operations, "turning" agents, and influencing the enemy's intentions.

Effective gathering and use of intelligence sways the course of World War II.

As armies clashed on the battlefields of World War II, a secret war was fought in the shadows. Its operatives included housewives, code breakers, spies, and diplomats, while its weapons ranged from the latest technology to homing pigeons—distributed in occupied Europe to enable locals to file reports, such as passing ships—and even semen as invisible ink. All the warring powers used their intelligence agencies, covert operations, and counterintelligence forces, the effectiveness of which greatly affected the course of war.

Japanese humint

The Japanese authorities regarded spying as integral to warfare. A military "spy school" in Tokyo taught espionage, sabotage, and subversion techniques, and by the outbreak of war, Japan had a significant intelligence network across southeast Asia. Senior

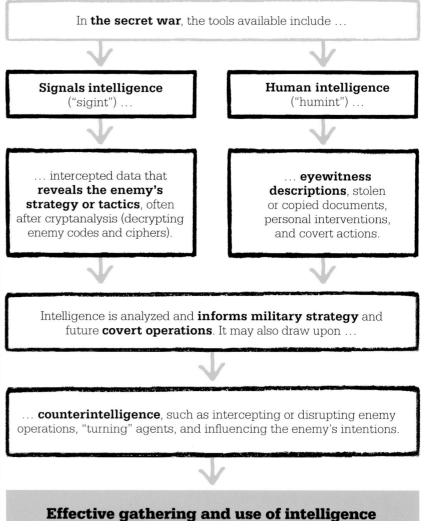

See also: The U-boat war intensifies 110–113 ▪ The Japanese attack Pearl Harbor 138–145 ▪ Operation Torch 196–197 ▪ A showdown in the Atlantic 214–219 ▪ The D-Day landings 256–263 ▪ The plot to kill Hitler 270

Enigma and ULTRA intelligence

Enigma was the code device used by the German military to encrypt all its communications. Portable and easy to use, its cypher wheels achieved encryption that Germany believed could not be broken. But when a German working for French intelligence informed the Poles, three Polish cryptographers set to work on cracking Enigma. In 1939, the operation was passed to the UK's Government Code and Cypher School at Bletchley Park.

Code named ULTRA, the resulting sigint was of great value because it came straight from the horse's mouth. But it could only be trusted if Germany remained unaware the code had been cracked. The task of obtaining it was in constant evolution, with code breakers battling to crack the ever-changing encryption fast enough for the intelligence to be useful. Under British mathematician Alan Turing, by 1944 the "Colossus" digital computer was used at Bletchley to speed up decryption. ULTRA intelligence was key to many Allied triumphs, from the 1942 victory at Alam el Halfa, Egypt, to the ending of the U-boat threat in the Atlantic in May 1943.

Japanese army officers posed as waiters in British service clubs in the Malay states, where they collected intelligence from gossip. An espionage ring run by naval commander Yamamoto Hirashi extended across the Pacific, ranging from a chain of "comfort houses" (brothels) in Los Angeles to agents operating from New York to Mexico.

Japan's biggest intelligence coup was arguably the easiest to achieve. A ring of spies posing as diplomats in Honolulu built up detailed intelligence on US military installations, timetables, air defenses, topography, and security measures at Pearl Harbor naval base. They collated newspaper reports, made personal observations, and even used postcards—copies of a postcard with an aerial view of the harbor were used by Japanese pilots in the shock attack of 1941.

The success of Japan's humint may have led to discounting the value—and threat—of sigint. Following Pearl Harbor, the US "MAGIC" cryptanalysis operation broke Japanese diplomatic codes, while the US arm of ULTRA (see box, above) broke the key Japanese naval code JN-25. This prevented a Japanese victory at the Battle of the Coral Sea in May 1942, foiling Japan's plan to invade Port Moresby in New Guinea and sever supply lines with Australia. ULTRA also discovered Midway as a Japanese target en route to Hawaii, helping US forces to win the decisive Battle of Midway.

Stalin's spy apparatus

In the USSR, a climate of paranoia and purges prompted frequent reorganization of Soviet intelligence institutions. But throughout, the *Narodnyi Komissariat Vnutrennikh Del* (NKVD; "People's Commissariat for Internal Affairs") remained the key agency. Although in charge of state security, the NKVD also operated in occupied territories. It was responsible for numerous atrocities, such as purging and banishing Soviet citizens to gulags (prison camps), and the massacre of Polish army officers at Katyn. Notable successes included planting moles in the British intelligence services and the theft of top-secret US atomic bomb plans.

The *Glavnoye Razvedyvatel'noye Upravleniye* (GRU; "Main Intelligence Directorate of the General Staff of the Red Army") gathered intelligence at the battle fronts and had successes against Germany on the Eastern Front. Although it was subsidiary to the NKVD, the GRU operated a number of spy rings; its best-known agent was German–Russian journalist and Nazi Party »

> Secret operations are essential in war—upon them the army relies to make its every move.
>
> **Sun Tzu**
> **6th-century BCE Chinese general**

member, Richard Sorge. Close to the German military attaché in Tokyo, Sorge acquired intelligence—including dates—of Operation Barbarossa, the German invasion of the USSR. However, Stalin was so convinced of an Anglo-American plot that Sorge was threatened with recall and punishment. Sorge later uncovered Japan's plan to move its forces away from the USSR's border, rehabilitating him in the eyes of Stalin, who was able to divert Red Army forces to fight the Germans.

Soviet counterintelligence was handled by SMERSH, an acronym for *Smert Shpionam* ("Death to Spies"). Since Stalin suspected almost anyone of being a potential traitor, SMERSH had a wide remit that included the armed forces. In total, an estimated 3–4 percent of military personnel were directly employed in intelligence or counter-intelligence, while another 12 percent were sub-agents or informers.

German in-fighting

The primary arms of German intelligence were the Abwehr (the military intelligence agency) and the *Reichssicherheitshauptamt* (RSHA; "Reich Security Main Office"), which was controlled by Himmler and the SS. Rivalry between Nazi leaders and institutions impaired the effectiveness of German intelligence, although SS suspicion of the Abwehr was eventually borne out when the latter was involved in the 1944 plot to kill Hitler. Germany's intelligence was also hampered by the fact that its ultimate consumer was Hitler himself. While often shrewd and insightful, he could also be limited by preconceptions, blind spots, and overconfidence.

Counterintelligence

The Abwehr had most success in counterintelligence. The Soviet GRU spy rings *Rote Drie* ("Red Three") in Switzerland and *Rote Kapelle* ("Red Orchestra") in Germany were both discovered, while in Holland, the Abwehr and RSHA jointly ran the *Englandspiel* ("English game"). Having captured agents in the Netherlands, the Germans fooled the British into thinking that they were still active, enabling them to capture every agent sent by the British Special Operations Executive (SOE). British handlers repeatedly failed to spot the warnings built into their own communication system, and over the course of two years, their incompetence—and the Germans' cunning—led to the loss of 54 agents, at least 50 RAF personnel, and large numbers of resistance fighters. Eventually, the Abwehr was dissolved after the 1944 plot to kill Hitler, with many of its leaders executed and most of its organs subsumed into the RSHA. The latter oversaw state security—including the Gestapo (political police)—counterintelligence, and occupied and conquered areas. It was also integral in the Holocaust.

> “ British agents secretly buying French francs—landing expected. ”
>
> **German intelligence report of faked Allied invasion plans, March 1944**

Notably, German intelligence failed to run any successful agents in Britain, while many agents sent to the US and Canada were quickly picked up. It also failed to detect ULTRA, arguably the most valuable secret of the war, or to detect the Allies' deception around D-Day.

US intellectual sweat

Founded in 1942 and led by General "Wild Bill" Donovan, the Office of Strategic Services (OSS) was the US equivalent of Britain's MI6 and

Personal effects, official documents, and other belongings of Polish officers massacred by the Soviet NKVD at Katyn, Russia, are displayed in this Nazi propaganda photograph.

SOE combined. Although the US domestic agency, the Federal Bureau of Investigations (FBI), jealously guarded many areas of counter- and domestic intelligence, the OSS oversaw field operations and counterintelligence. Its largest branch was Research and Analysis: Donovan believed that "good old-fashioned intellectual sweat" was the heart of modern intelligence practice. Accordingly, he assembled a staff of experts—many from academia—to analyze and report on different regions and topics.

OSS accomplishments included Operation Torch in North Africa, although Polish spymaster "Rygor" Slowikowski's "Agency Africa" spy ring—which he ran under the cover of a porridge-making business—supplied much of the intelligence. The OSS also introduced economic theory to military intelligence in its planning of US bombing campaigns; carried out extensive covert ops and network-building in Italy, Greece, and the Balkans; and worked to counter Soviet influence in the post-war world. In the Far East, the OSS trained a large force of Burmese guerrillas, and disrupted Japanese air defenses to allow air supply of Chinese forces in the region. Perhaps most spectacularly, from 1944, the OSS infiltrated agents into Germany itself, where their intelligence provided invaluable confirmation of other channels.

Painted black for nocturnal pickups, the Westland Lysander—the workhorse of SOE secret ops—was among the dozen British aircraft downed during the German *Englandspiel* deception.

British espionage

Intelligence agencies in Britain included the SOE, Military Intelligence (MI) directorates MI5 and MI6, and the Bletchley Park code breakers. Key MI5 successes included the XX-committee—which oversaw domestic intelligence and counterintelligence—intercepting and turning or imprisoning every German spy sent to Britain. Notable double agents included the Dane Wulf Schmidt (code named TATE), whose report of a minefield off the south of Ireland kept U-boats at bay, and was so trusted that he was naturalized as a German in order to receive the Iron Cross. MI5 also ran the Spaniard Juan Pujol (code named GARBO), who helped invent a fictional spy ring that duped the German high command into thinking D-Day would occur not in Normandy, but near Calais.

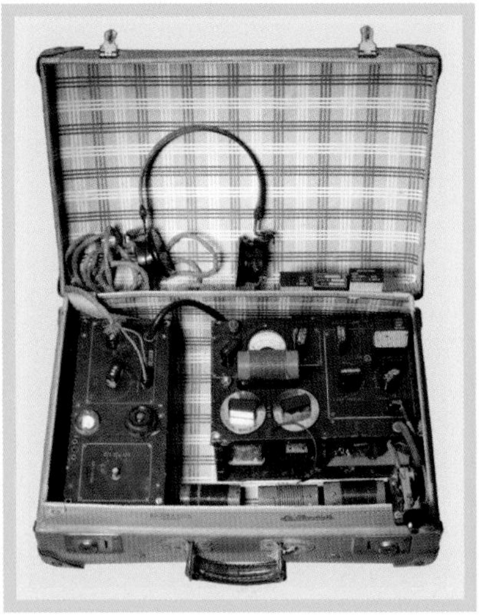

Undercover agents working for the Allies' SOE and OSS were issued with special equipment, such as this radio disguised as a briefcase, for sending humint from occupied territory.

Successes overseas

MI6 oversaw foreign operations, including breaking the Abwehr's codes and providing tactical intelligence from occupied Europe. It also gave targeting information against German radar installations and V-weapons development and launch sites, which saved many lives. SOE conducted espionage in occupied territories, from commando raids and sabotage to intelligence-gathering and POW escape lines. Notable successes included Operation REMORSE, a smuggling and currency-dealing venture in China that made a sizable profit. ■

TURNING TIDE 1943–1944

THE

FEB 9, 1943
After a long and bitter struggle with Japanese forces, the **US gains control of Guadalcanal** in the Solomon Islands in the Pacific.

MAY 13, 1943
The **last Axis forces** in Tunisia **surrender** to the Allies. More than 250,000 Italian and German soldiers enter **POW camps**.

MAY 16–17, 1943
The **RAF's 617 Squadron** mounts what becomes known as the **Dambusters Raid**, a precision attack on dams on the Möhne and Eder rivers.

MAY 22, 1943
Admiral Karl Dönitz, the German U-boat chief, **orders his submarines to break off operations** in the north Atlantic, an admission of defeat.

JUL 1943
During the **Battle of Kursk**, **German tank forces** drive a wedge into the Soviet lines. They are later **forced to withdraw**.

JUL 10, 1943
The **Allies** open an **attack** on **Sicily**, followed by a **full-scale invasion** of the Italian mainland two months later.

JUL 24, 1943
British and US aerial forces mount a major **raid** on the German port of **Hamburg** that creates a "firestorm." Around 50,000 civilians die.

NOV 1943
In the Pacific, **US marines capture the Tarawa atoll** in the Gilbert Islands. The Japanese fight to the death. The only POWs are 17 wounded men.

By the spring of 1943, it was clear that the course of the war was turning irrevocably in favor of the Allies. Earlier gains by both Germany and Japan were being reversed. The German defeat at Stalingrad in February 1943 was followed a few months later by the surrender of Axis troops in north Africa. In the Pacific, the strategic initiative lay in the hands of the US.

Sea and air

Whereas Axis triumphs in the first part of the war had been achieved through military brilliance, Allied strategy relied on superior resources to grind down their opponents. Reflecting a business-like approach to the war, Allied leaders met regularly to resolve any differences, clarify their goals, and develop a unified strategy.

Despite the change in the balance of fortune between the two sides, the Axis powers would prove to be masters of defensive warfare, managing to hold off superior Allied forces far longer than anticipated. The Allied strategy would eventually culminate in the occupation of Germany and Japan, but before this could happen the Allies had to gain mastery of the sea and air.

In the war against Germany, a first step was victory in the Battle of the Atlantic, achieved in mid-1943. This made the Atlantic safe for the millions of US troops crossing to Britain in preparation for the attack on Europe and also guaranteed food and material supplies would reach Britain safely. In the air, from as early as February 1942, Britain mounted a nighttime strategic bombing offensive against Germany, designed to destroy its economic resources and undermine the will of its civilian population. The US air force made its presence felt from the middle of 1943, flying in daylight from bases in Britain.

The Allies advance

In September 1943, the Allies invaded southern Italy. Mussolini had been deposed in a coup in July, and a new Italian government came to terms with the Allies. However, Hitler's reaction was swift and ruthless: German forces took over Italy in a matter of days and introduced a defensive strategy that brought the Allied advance to a crawl.

It would only be through an invasion of northern France that the Allied armies could defeat the

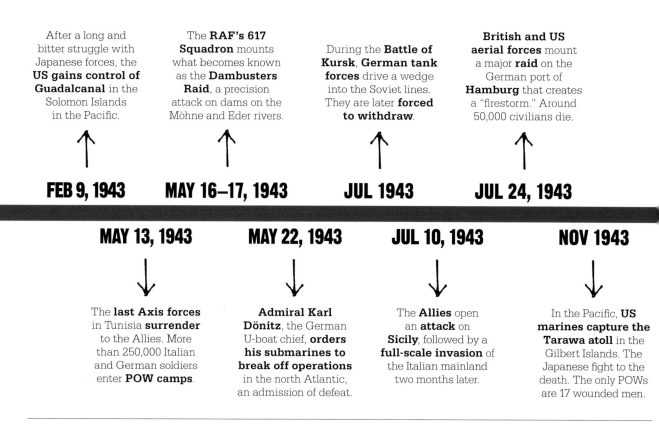

MAR 8, 1944

The **Japanese army in Burma launches its U-Go offensive**, designed to capture the British strongholds at Imphal and Kohima.

MAY 18, 1944

Monte Cassino, the **German stronghold** in Italy, **falls** to the Allies after weeks of fighting. The way is now open for the Allied drive on Rome.

JUN 6, 1944

The Allies launch **Operation Overlord**, the **invasion of Normandy**, the largest amphibious operation ever mounted.

JUL 20, 1944

An **attempt to assassinate Hitler** by detonating a bomb at his headquarters **fails**. The conspirators, who are mainly army officers, are executed.

AUG 30, 1944

Soviet forces capture the **Romanian oil fields** at Ploesti, further depriving the Germans of the fuel needed for the conduct of military operations.

OCT 20, 1944

US troops land in the Philippines and begin the process of liberating the islands from Japanese control.

OCT 23–26, 1944

The **US inflicts a crushing defeat** against the Japanese navy at the **Battle of Leyte Gulf**.

DEC 1944

In the Ardennes, in Belgium, the Western Allies **push back a major German offensive**, known as the **Battle of the Bulge**.

Germans in open warfare. Within Europe, the civilian populations groaned under the oppressive Nazi occupation. During 1944—when hope grew that Germany faced defeat—resistance movements gained traction. The French resistance provided intelligence of German troop dispositions and instigated a sabotage campaign to prevent their free movement during the invasion period.

In eastern Europe and the Balkans, resistance movements tied down large numbers of German troops. Members of the Polish resistance, for example, wrestled control of central Warsaw and fought a bloody seven-week battle before defeat by the Germans; in Yugoslavia, Marshal Tito's partisans engaged German soldiers in open combat.

On June 6, 1944, the Allies launched Operation Overlord, known as D-Day, the invasion of Normandy. Central to their success was their vastly superior intelligence and air supremacy, which ensured the uninterrupted movement of soldiers and armaments. Without these two advantages it is unlikely that the invasion would have succeeded.

On the Eastern Front, the Red Army went on the offensive after their victory at Stalingrad. In July 1943, it won a dramatic tank encounter at the Battle of Kursk, in Ukraine. In 1944, it turned its attention to the northern sector, destroying the German Army Group Center during Operation Bagration, before turning southward and clearing the Balkans. By the fall of 1944, Soviet forces had expelled the invaders from their country and were poised to cross the border into Germany itself.

Stopping Japan

In the Pacific theater, US submarines played a vital role in sinking merchant vessels transporting oil and other vital resources from China and the Pacific Islands to Japan. US aircraft also played a growing role in disrupting these vital trade routes. By mid-1944, Japan's economy was being slowly strangled to death, and an island-hopping campaign conducted by the US armed forces brought Japan within bombing range. The decisive factor, however, was the US's development of a new terror weapon, which would bring the Pacific war to a terrifying conclusion—the atom bomb. ■

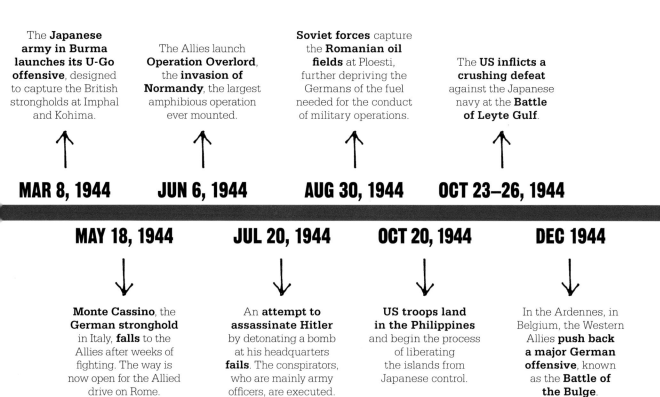

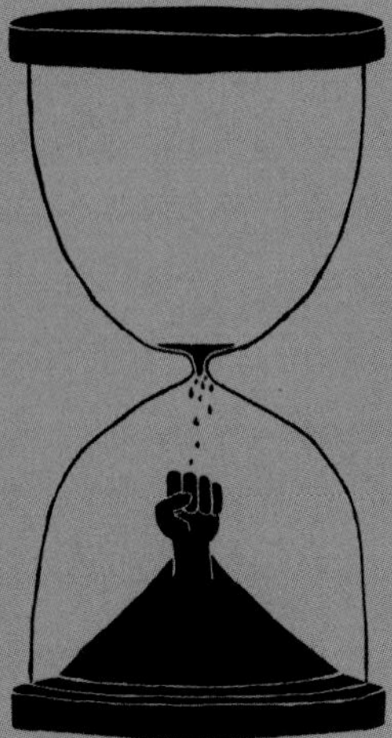

THEY ARE FINISHED

VICTORY IN THE DESERT (FEBRUARY–MAY 1943)

IN CONTEXT

FOCUS
Tunisian campaign

BEFORE
1942 Rommel is defeated by British and Commonwealth forces at El Alamein, Egypt, on November 4. He begins to retreat westward into Tunisia.

1942 From November 8, Allied forces commence Operation Torch, a series of landings on the Mediterranean and Atlantic coasts of North Africa.

1942 German forces fortify Tunisia against Allied attack from November 9.

AFTER
1943 The Allies begin their invasion of Sicily in July.

1944 After being implicated in a plot to assassinate Hitler, in July Rommel dies by suicide.

The Tunisian campaign in the first half of 1943 brought the war in North Africa to an end. The fighting was intense in a contest that could have been better handled by both sides. While the Allies were slow to reach Tunisia, the Axis made a huge mistake in risking all to defend it.

The rush to Tunisia

On November 9, 1942, one day after the Allied landings of Operation Torch, German forces landed in Tunisia to protect Rommel's rear as he retreated west from El Alamein. As they did so, British forces advanced 500 miles (800 km) west from Algiers toward Tunis, their paratroopers landing at Bône airfield near the Tunisian border on November 12 just minutes before the Germans made their own attempt to land. British forces advancing from Bône encountered German patrols on November 18, and heavy fighting broke out as they attempted to seize Medjez el Bab, west of Tunis.

By the end of 1942, the Germans had established a series of strong points around Tunis. Their efforts in Tunisia were helped by the French Vichy governor, Admiral Jean-Pierre Esteva, who allowed German aircraft to land additional troops and new Tiger tanks. By the start of 1943, the Germans and their Italian allies had amassed around 250,000 troops there, supported by the close proximity of airfields in Sicily.

> The decision to reinforce North Africa was one of the worst of Hitler's blunders … it placed … Germany's best troops in an indefensible position from which … there would be no escape.
>
> **Williamson Murray**
> **American historian, 1995**

Battle of Kasserine Pass

The first major battles broke out on February 14, 1943, when, determined to take the initiative, the German Fifth Panzer Army launched Operation *Frühlingswind* ("Spring Wind"), pushing west across the

Mediterranean Sea

Chased by the Allies, the Germans begin retreat to Enfidaville in northern Tunisia.

El Hamma

Gabes

Zarat

Tebaga Gap

Mareth

AFRICA

German Afrika Korps

Medenine

British Eighth Army

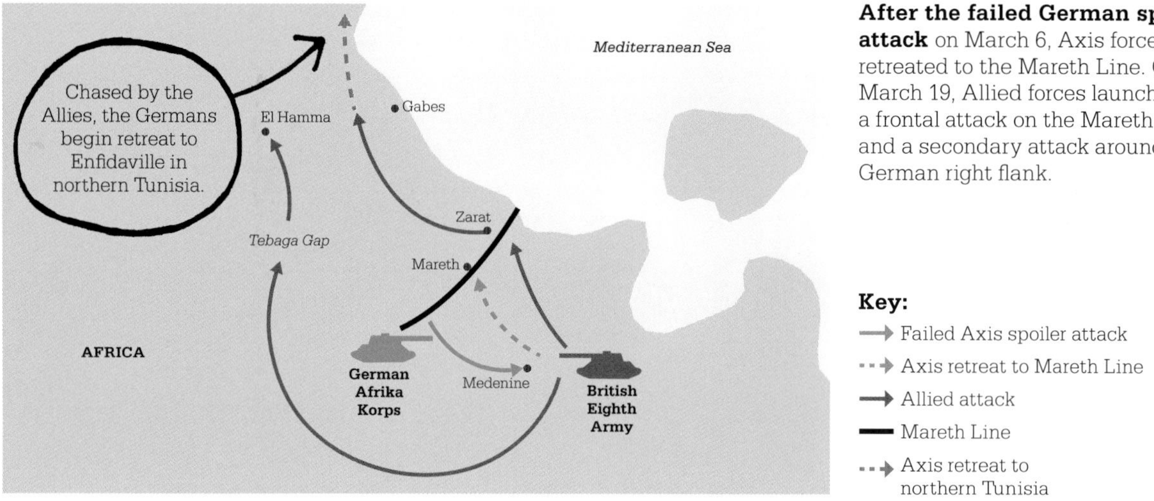

After the failed German spoiler attack on March 6, Axis forces retreated to the Mareth Line. On March 19, Allied forces launched a frontal attack on the Mareth Line and a secondary attack around the German right flank.

Key:

→ Failed Axis spoiler attack

- - → Axis retreat to Mareth Line

→ Allied attack

▬ Mareth Line

- - → Axis retreat to northern Tunisia

center of Tunisia. A day later, Rommel and his Afrika Korps began Operation *Morgenluft* ("Morning Air") to threaten the flank of the Allied First Army heading west from Algeria. After a pitched battle at the Kasserine Pass, the Axis armies were forced to withdraw.

Breaking the Mareth Line

To the south, the British Eighth Army pursuing Rommel tried to break through the Mareth Line— a former French defense running 22 miles (35 km) from the coast to the mountains—near Tunisia's southern border with Libya. After intelligence revealed British plans for an offensive, the Germans launched a spoiler attack, code named Operation Capri, but it failed, with the loss of 55 Axis tanks.

Montgomery ordered a frontal attack on the line, supported by a second attack around the German right flank by New Zealand and Free French forces. This secondary attack achieved its aim, forcing the Axis to abandon the Mareth Line and retreat north on March 28. On

April 7, the Allied reinforcements from Operation Torch finally reached the British Eighth Army, rendezvousing at El Hamma.

With Axis forces hemmed in on the coastal plain of northeastern Tunisia, the Allies moved north on April 20. Progress was slow, and the fighting often hand-to-hand, but on May 7 the Allies finally entered Tunis. Axis troops surrendered en masse, and once Italian General Messe finally surrendered on May 13, the

battle for Tunisia was over. Around 250,000 Axis troops surrendered—a needless sacrifice of experienced fighters by Hitler, who had blundered in keeping them in an indefensible position. For the Allies, the war in Africa was over, but the delays of Operation Torch proved costly. ▪

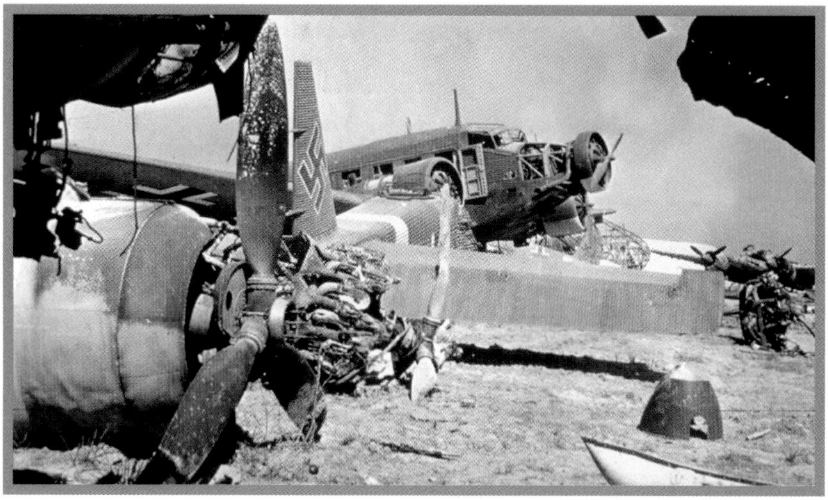

Luftwaffe planes lie wrecked at El Aouina airfield near Tunis, destroyed by fragmentation bombs from US B-17 bombers in February 1943.

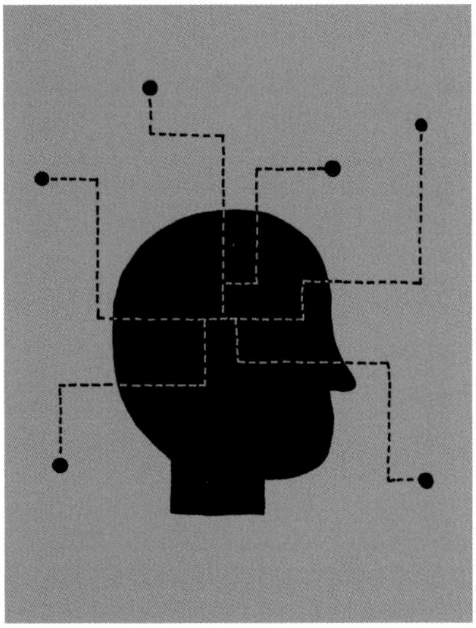

THE ENEMY IS VICIOUS, CLEVER, AND RUTHLESS

THE INVASION OF ITALY (JULY–DECEMBER 1943)

IN CONTEXT

FOCUS
The Mediterranean Front

BEFORE
June 1940 Italy joins World War II as part of the Axis.

January 1943 Britain and the US agree a "Mediterranean First" policy at Casablanca, Morocco, to drive the Axis from North Africa and Italy.

June 1943 The Allies invade the Italian island of Pantelleria, giving them control of a crucial Mediterranean airbase.

AFTER
January–May 1944 The Battle of Monte Cassino rages. The Allies are victorious after four costly assaults.

June 5, 1944 Rome is liberated by Allied soldiers.

April 28, 1945 Mussolini is captured and killed by Italian resistance fighters.

May 2, 1945 German forces in Italy surrender to the Allies.

The Allies defeated Axis forces in Tunisia in May 1943, giving them control of North Africa. The next step was the invasion of Italy, after Allied disagreements on strategy were resolved when Roosevelt and Churchill met at Casablanca.

Operation Husky

Amphibious assaults and airborne landings marked the beginning of Operation Husky, the invasion of Sicily, on July 10. Allied forces fought their way north, and Palermo surrendered on July 22. Although Axis command of the island was nominally in Italian hands, in practice Marshal Albert Kesselring—leader of German forces—was dominant. Realizing that the situation was untenable, he coordinated the successful evacuation of 100,000 Axis soldiers.

British troops wade ashore off the coast of Sicily. Operation Husky was almost postponed due to a summer storm, but the Allied forces landed on July 10, 1943, with only light casualties.

See also: Italy enters the war 88–89 ▪ North Africa and the Mediterranean 118–121 ▪ From Gazala to El Alamein 192–195 ▪ Operation Torch 196–197 ▪ Victory in the desert 208–209 ▪ The fall of Rome 254 ▪ Last stand in Italy 296–297

American soldiers hand out candy to children in the port town of Agropoli. Three years of wartime privations had left little support for the fascist regime among Italian civilians.

The final units left on August 17; Messina, the last Axis stronghold, surrendered that morning.

Events in Sicily persuaded Italian leaders that a new regime was needed. Military commitments in Greece, the Balkans, France, and Russia were becoming increasingly costly, and food shortages and air-raids were wearing down the people. On July 25, Mussolini was forced to resign and was arrested. Pietro Badoglio, an ambitious general, became prime minister, and a secret armistice was signed with the Allies on September 3. When it was publicly announced five days later, Germany was quick to neutralise the Italian military, forcibly disarming 600,000 in Italy and 400,000 elsewhere in Europe.

On September 12, German commandos rescued Mussolini, who was installed as leader of the Italian Social Republic, a German puppet state in northern Italy.

A difficult campaign

Meanwhile, the Allies had begun the invasion of mainland Italy with landings at Calabria on September 3. On September 9—by which time the Allies only faced German units—further landings at Salerno resulted in fierce fighting. Only last-minute reinforcements saved the Allies from having to retreat. German forces disengaged on September 16 and retreated north.

Allied advances

In Naples, the largest city in southern Italy, a popular uprising occurred against German forces and their Italian fascist supporters from September 27–30. The Neapolitan people and resistance fighters held out until the Allies arrived to liberate the city (and its vital port) on October 1. Badoglio declared war on Germany on October 13, bringing the forces he controlled over to the Allied side.

Despite the Allied advances, German forces had not suffered overwhelming losses. Rome, bravely defended by the Italian army, fell to Kesselring, who disarmed the Italian military and withdrew to the Winter Line, a well-prepared network of fortifications in central Italy. The Allies first attacked the German defensive line in December; the formidable fortified positions and mountainous terrain proved difficult to overcome. There would be no quick Allied victory in Italy. ■

> “The city of Naples smells of charred wood, with ruins everywhere, sometimes completely blocking the streets, bomb craters, and abandoned trams.”
>
> **Norman Lewis**
> **British intelligence officer, October 1943**

Deceiving the Axis

Central to Operation Husky's success was the duping of Axis leaders, particularly Hitler, into believing the invasion would be elsewhere in the Mediterranean.

A key factor was Operation Barclay, a web of misdirection spun by British intelligence. They invented the fictional "Twelfth Army," transmitted fake radio signals with plans of a Balkan invasion, and created inflatable vehicles to fool German reconnaissance. In Greece, the British recruited local interpreters and—together with Greek resistance forces—attacked railroads and roads.

The most audacious deception was Operation Mincemeat. The corpse of a recently deceased man was dressed in the uniform of a Royal Navy Marines officer and furnished with plans for an Allied invasion of Greece and Sardinia. On April 30, 1943, a submarine released the corpse off the coast of Spain. The papers were passed on to the Germans who, believing the intelligence was genuine, sent reinforcements to both Greece and Sardinia.

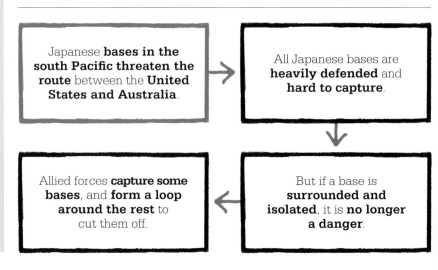

THE GRAVEYARD OF THE JAPANESE ARMY

THE BATTLE FOR THE SOLOMONS AND NEW GUINEA (1942–1943)

IN CONTEXT

FOCUS
War in the Pacific

BEFORE
January 23, 1942 Japanese forces take Rabaul on the island of New Britain from Australia, and establish it as their main base in the south Pacific.

March 8, 1942 Japanese forces begin attacks on New Guinea.

May 3, 1942 The Japanese reach Guadalcanal in the Solomon Islands, where they begin construction of a large airfield.

AFTER
November 20, 1943 US troops begin attacks on Tarawa and Makin in the Gilbert Islands.

January 31, 1944 US troops begin their assault on the Marshall Islands.

June 1944 US forces begin to attack Japanese positions on the Mariana Islands and Palau.

After naval victories against Japan in the Pacific theater, in the Coral Sea and off Midway, the United States went on the offensive again in August 1942. Japanese forces had reached Guadalcanal and Tulagi in the Solomon Islands on May 3, and had begun to build an airfield on Guadalcanal and a seaplane base at Tulagi. The threat these posed to communications between the US and Australia prompted the Allies to attack both islands on August 7, with 11,000 US Marines landing on Guadalcanal almost unopposed. On the night of August 8–9, the Japanese navy countered, sinking four cruisers off Savo Island. The Allied fleet withdrew, leaving the marines to fend for themselves without the heavy equipment that had yet to be landed.

The Battle for Guadalcanal

The marines soon completed construction of the airfield begun by the Japanese on the north coast of Guadalcanal. Once operational, US forces used it to stop Japanese naval operations around the island. The Japanese responded by moving troops to the island from their large base at Rabaul, New Britain, on fast

Japanese **bases in the south Pacific threaten the route** between the **United States and Australia**.

All Japanese bases are **heavily defended** and **hard to capture**.

But if a base is **surrounded and isolated**, it is **no longer a danger**.

Allied forces **capture some bases**, and **form a loop around the rest** to cut them off.

See also: Japan on the march 44–45 ▪ Japan's dilemma 137 ▪ The Japanese attack Pearl Harbor 138–145 ▪ Japanese advances 154–157 ▪ Defending Australia 159 ▪ The Battle of Midway 160–165 ▪ The western Pacific 244–249

Navajo code talkers at work during the assault on Bougainville Island in December 1943. Japanese code breakers could not understand them.

The code talkers

Code talkers in the US military used little-known Indigenous languages to communicate confidential military information. During World War II; 400–500 Indigenous troops were recruited into the US Marines.

Code talkers sent messages over military telephones or radio using two main types of code. Type One codes were based on the languages of the Comanche, Hopi, Meskwaki, and Navajo peoples, using words for each letter of the English alphabet. Such messages were encoded and decoded using a simple substitution cypher. Type Two codes were more informal, translating English words into the Indigenous language. If there was no existing word or phrase, one was created: for example, Navajo code talkers translated "submarine" as "iron fish." The Navajo language was well-suited to code talking as it was not mutually intelligible with even its closest relatives, and was unwritten. The code talkers' role in the campaign in the Pacific was invaluable.

destroyers—a system of transportation known as the "Tokyo Express"—and by mid-September they were ready to attack the airfield. The marines were forced to repel these attacks while staging patrols in the surrounding jungle.

On November 13, Japanese warships bombarded the airfield and landed more troops. In two nights of chaotic fighting, Japan lost two battleships and four other warships. The US had comparable losses, but managed to stop the Japanese troop landings. As more US reinforcements arrived, the Japanese withdrew, and had left Guadalcanal by February 7, 1943.

Operation Cartwheel

The brainchild of General Douglas MacArthur, Operation Cartwheel was a series of operations against Japanese forces in the southwest Pacific. Cartwheel had two wings: one moving up the coast of New Guinea, the other island-hopping through the Solomons. The aim of the operation was to encircle and neutralize the Japanese base at Rabaul—the main obstacle to the Allies retaking the Philippines.

Operation Cartwheel was launched on June 29 with the first attacks on New Guinea. Further landings throughout the year on Bougainville Island allowed the Allies to move in a large loop around New Britain, which they began to assault in March 1944. This resulted in the Japanese bases at Rabaul and Kavieng on New Ireland becoming surrounded and isolated. At great cost to Allied lives and shipping, Operation Cartwheel had succeeded. ■

US Marines land at Cape Gloucester on the island of New Britain. The Pacific theater required mastery of amphibious warfare, including landing mechanized transport in difficult conditions.

THE ENEMY'S NEW LOCATION DEVICES MAKE FIGHTING IMPOSSIBLE

A SHOWDOWN IN THE ATLANTIC (MARCH–MAY 1943)

IN CONTEXT

FOCUS
Battle of the Atlantic

BEFORE
1918 As captain of a U-boat during World War I, Dönitz launches a daring nighttime surface raid on a convoy.

1940 From July, U-boat crews enjoy a "happy time" of relative success in the Atlantic.

AFTER
Early 1944 U-boats are fitted with *Schnorchels* ("snorkels") that allow their engines to take in air while submerged, vastly improving performance.

1944 The Colossus computers enter service at Bletchley Park in June, enabling real-time deciphering of German codes.

1944 In August, Dönitz ends U-boat attacks on the Allied invasion force's supply lines after losing more than half his vessels in the English Channel.

The Battle of the Atlantic was an extended conflict that lasted for almost the whole of the war, but its climactic struggles were fought in the spring of 1943. That was when the seesaw nature of the battle, in which one side and then the other gained the upper hand, tipped decisively in the Allies' favor. In early 1942, however, the outlook had been very different, as events had combined to inflict heavy losses on the Allied shipping and give the U-boats the advantage. Crucial factors in influencing outcomes included the number of operational U-boats, range of Allied air cover, detection and antisubmarine technology, escort numbers and tactics, and, above all, the ability of each side to read the other's encrypted signals.

> The U-boat at sea must be hunted, the U-boat in the building yard or dock must be bombed.
> **Winston Churchill, 1941**

Intelligence wars

Germany believed the encrypted messages used by the Kriegsmarine (German navy) were unbreakable. Assessing the Enigma machines that were used to create these messages, Spanish intelligence officer Antonio Sarmiento reported in the 1930s: "To give an idea how secure these machines are, suffice to say that the number of combinations is a remarkable 1,252,962,387,456." But in 1941, the Allies broke the code. At one point, signals could be read within an hour of their transmission—a breakthrough so valuable that up to 1.7 million tons of shipping was saved between July and December 1941. While Germany investigated the security of Enigma, the Kriegsmarine did not abandon it, merely adding another wheel to the configuration in February 1942.

However, this small change was a disaster for the Allies, blinding the ULTRA intelligence operation

Karl Dönitz

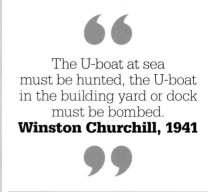

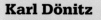

A brilliant U-boat captain, Dönitz (1891–1980) turned conventional submarine wisdom on its head in World War I. Instead of attacking when submerged by daylight, he launched a surface attack at night, slipping past the convoy's escort and sinking a merchant ship.

In 1935, inter-war appeasement allowed Germany to build U-boats once more. Dönitz was made commander-in-chief of U-boats by Hitler, of whom he was a fervent admirer. For overseeing the sinking of British battleship HMS *Royal Oak* in Scapa Flow in October 1939, he was promoted to rear-admiral. Dönitz oversaw a brilliant U-boat campaign, introducing tactics such as "wolf packs" and his signature nighttime surface attack, which saw him promoted twice more.

In January 1943, Dönitz was handed command of the Kriegsmarine, but he proved an ineffective naval chief. He still retained the confidence of Hitler, who made him his successor, and Dönitz was the president of Germany when arrested on May 22, 1945. Found guilty of war crimes at the Nuremberg Trials, he served 10 years in prison.

See also: Britain organizes for total war 100–103 ▪ The end of US neutrality 108 ▪ The U-boat war intensifies 110–113 ▪ America at war 146–153 ▪ Attacks on Arctic convoys 166 ▪ The secret war 198–203 ▪ Germany's war industry 224

A British ship in the Atlantic Ocean deploys a depth charge. Depth charges were initially the only weapon for countering U-boats, which sank huge amounts of Allied shipping until 1943.

at a stroke. The tables turned still further as, in the same month, the German *Beobachtungdienst* ("radio monitoring service") cracked most of Naval Cypher No.3 (NC3), a code used for routing Allied convoys. While only 10 percent of intercepts were cracked in time to be useful, this small success was enough to build up accurate pictures of the timing and routes of convoys. Just as the Germans were overconfident in the security of Enigma, the British were overconfident in NC3, persisting with it until June 1943.

Dark days at sea

In the meantime, Germany scored a string of devastatingly successful blows. The July 1942 attack on Arctic Convoy PQ-17 resulted in the loss of 24 of the 35 merchant ships and two-thirds of the armaments being carried to Russia, while convoy PQ-18 in September 1942 lost 13 of 40 ships. Just as Germany later mistakenly blamed naval technologies for its losses, the British believed that the alarming German success rate was due to advanced U-boat hydrophones, which were believed to be capable of detecting a ship's propeller noise from more than 80 miles (130 km). Arctic convoys were temporarily suspended, and it would be a year before Allied shipping could safely pass east and west without losses.

Desperate to redress the balance, the Allies added several innovations to their existing maritime defenses. These new capabilities included ASDIC (sonar) detection technology; rear- and side-firing depth charges; "huff-duff" (high frequency/direction finding, or HF/DF) apparatus, which enabled the position of U-boats to be triangulated from their radio signals; "Leigh" floodlights to spot U-boat periscopes and conning towers, even at night; airborne radar; and Anti-Surface-Vessel radar, which the Germans falsely believed was responsible for Allied success at predicting U-boat movements. In fact, one of the most effective means of denying U-boats tactical and strategic advantage was the threat of aerial spotting and attack. This forced U-boats to operate submerged—reducing their speed considerably—but depended for its success on the range of the available Allied aircraft.

Improved defenses

The "Mid-Atlantic Gap" in air cover that had plagued the Atlantic convoys was eventually closed with the development of Very Long Range (VLR) bombers. The escort services available to the convoys also improved dramatically, as the »

Royal Canadian Navy was enlarged 50-fold over the course of the Battle of the Atlantic, with special focus on its antisubmarine division, the Canadian Escort Force.

The American B-24 Liberator VLR bomber was modified to increase its range to 2,300 nautical miles (2,650 miles/4,250 km), enabling it to offer cover to convoys in the Mid-Atlantic Gap.

Tipping the balance

In addition to the Allies' new technology, two intelligence coups were instrumental in swaying the course of the submarine war. In December 1942, the Royal Navy changed its codes for directing convoys (although a complete change of codes—which blinded German naval intelligence—did not occur until June 1943). Around the same time, Bletchley Park began to have real success decrypting naval Enigma codes. This was thanks to the heroic recovery of codebooks from the scuttled U-559 on October 30. As 1943 dawned, the stage was set for a massive showdown in the Atlantic. Churchill told his War Cabinet there was "no doubt about the gravity of the U-boat war" on January 11. Germany's war industry was producing 17 U-boats a month, and by spring of 1943, Dönitz had 400 submarines (although only around one-third were operational at any one time). But the Allies had ULTRA back in service, and at the Casablanca Conference of January 1943, Roosevelt and Churchill made dealing with the U-boat menace a top war aim. Combined sea and air attacks harried the U-boats at their bases on the Bay of Biscay, and by employing long-range bombers, detection technologies, and improved escort tactics—directed with the help of ULTRA intercepts—the Allies turned the Battle of the Atlantic decisively in their favor in the space of four months.

Advances in weaponry—such as the "Hedgehog" forward-facing antisubmarine mortar launcher—and intelligence breakthroughs enabled the Allied convoys to gain the edge in 1943.

Climax of the conflict

The Battle of the Atlantic reached its climax with the passage of the 43 merchant ships of Convoy ONS-5, which sailed west across the North Atlantic in late April. The U-boat attacks began as the convoy passed south of Iceland, and over the next nine days the Royal Navy escorts—fluctuating between 7 and 16 warships—fought off three wolf packs with a combined strength of around 50 U-boats. But by May 6, when Dönitz called off the hunt, 6 U-boats had been sunk and 7 damaged, for the loss of 13 Allied merchant ships. Despite the heavy losses on both sides, the Allies' success at inflicting damage showed they had gained the upper

U-boat success and Allied defense

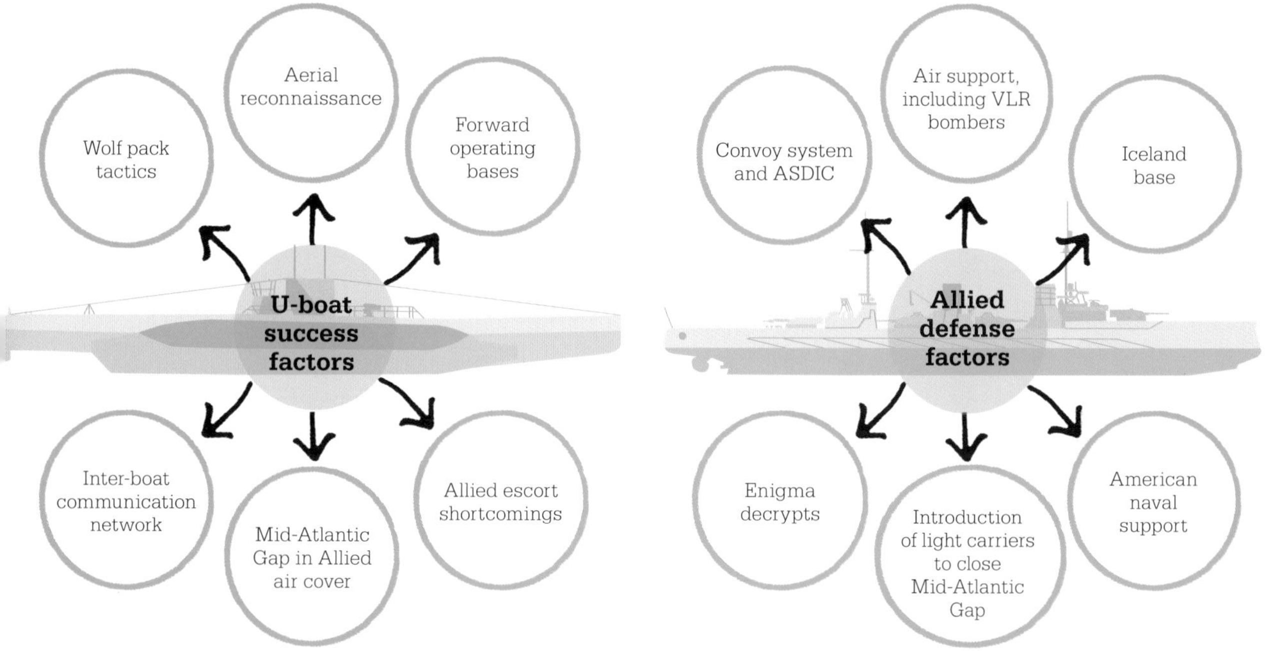

hand. Peter Gretton, commander of ONS-5, later wrote: "The longest and fiercest convoy action of the war had ended with a clear-cut victory."

In what the Kriegsmarine described as "Black May," Dönitz lost 41 U-boats—almost one-third of his operational fleet—including U-954, on which his son Peter was serving. "The enemy, by means of new location devices … makes fighting impossible" he complained. On May 24, Dönitz withdrew all U-boats from the North Atlantic, and, despite Hitler's direct order of June 5 that "There can be no let up in submarine warfare," June was the first month of the war in which no Allied convoys were attacked. The Allies were confident enough to decree that ships capable of sailing at 15 knots or faster could make their passage without escort.

Ending the U-boat threat

By September 1943, increased rationalization of German war industries under Albert Speer had cut the build time of a U-boat from 42 weeks to just 16. However, the space for U-boat deployment was rapidly diminishing. That month, 28 U-boats returned to the North Atlantic but only sank 9 of the 2,468 Allied ships afloat. In August 1943, more U-boats were sunk than Allied vessels—"news which stirred a thousand hearts, afloat and ashore," wrote British novelist and naval officer Nicholas Monsarrat. "For the first time in the war, the astonishing balance was struck." ■

Minelayer U-118, sunk on June 12, 1943, after attacks by Avenger aircraft from the carrier USS *Bogue*, was one of 242 U-boats lost that year—a rate of attrition judged too high by Dönitz.

A MIGHTY FIRE HURRICANE RACED THROUGH THE STREETS

BOMBING OF GERMANY (MARCH–DECEMBER 1943)

IN CONTEXT

FOCUS
Impact on civilians

BEFORE
April 1, 1918 The British Royal Air Force (RAF) is created, achieving full independence from the British Army.

June 1938 British prime minister Chamberlain states that it is "against international law to bomb civilians …."

September 7, 1940 The Luftwaffe starts bombing British cities (the Blitz).

AFTER
1945 The US drops two atom bombs on Japan, wiping out two cities at a stroke and forcing Japan's surrender.

1992 A statue of Arthur Harris is unveiled in London.

2005 Reconstruction of Dresden's historic Frauenkirche church is finally complete.

Even before the Blitz, Churchill was considering an "absolutely devastating exterminating attack by very heavy bombers … upon the Nazi homeland." Other than its bombers, Britain had few other means of striking back at the Germans, and accordingly RAF Bomber Command started raids in 1940. Soon realizing that daytime operations made its aircraft vulnerable to enemy fighters, the RAF switched to night bombing. This protected the bombers but rendered them highly ineffective—they missed most of their targets.

Thus, in February 1942, Bomber Command was instructed to make the "morale of the enemy civil

See also: The Phony War 64–65 ▪ The Blitz 98–99 ▪ Germany and the reality of war 188–191 ▪ Germany's war industry 224 ▪ The destruction of German cities 287 ▪ The bombing of Hiroshima and Nagasaki 308–311

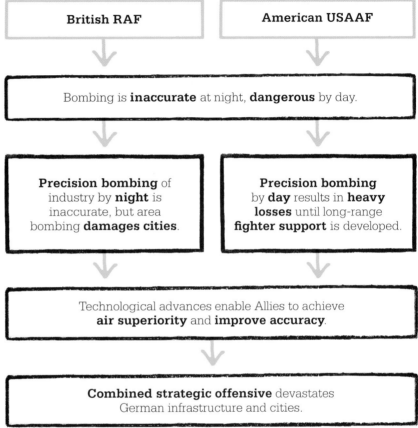

The crew of a Lancaster bomber stand by as their plane is prepared for an operation in 1942. The Lancaster was the RAF's principle heavy bomber from 1942–1945.

British RAF | **American USAAF**

Bombing is **inaccurate** at night, **dangerous** by day.

British RAF: **Precision bombing** of industry by **night** is inaccurate, but area bombing **damages cities**.

American USAAF: **Precision bombing** by **day** results in **heavy losses** until long-range **fighter support** is developed.

Technological advances enable Allies to achieve **air superiority** and **improve accuracy**.

Combined strategic offensive devastates German infrastructure and cities.

population" the target of the strategic air offensive, in a policy that came to be called "area bombing." Arthur "Bomber" Harris was appointed the new head of Bomber Command one week after this directive was issued. He was motivated by a desire to avoid the slaughter of British soldiers that he had witnessed in the trenches in World War I, and proved to be a merciless exponent of the doctrine, launching raids with ever larger numbers of bombers.

Cologne was the first target, in May 1942, but Berlin soon became the main one—it was both the seat of government and a major center for war industry. In a memorandum of November 1943, Harris claimed that "we can wreck Berlin from end to end if the USAAF (US Army Air Force) will come in on it. It will cost between us 400–500 aircraft. It will cost Germany the war." Harris' motivation was to end the war without the massive cost in Allied blood of an amphibious invasion—the same calculation that would later be made by the US in Japan. Yet German morale and the German war economy proved highly resilient: its armaments production continued to rise until mid-1944.

Precision bombing

The USAAF joined the campaign in summer 1942. In contrast with the British, it insisted that it would focus on precision bombing. This in turn necessitated daylight raids. After practicing over France with fighter cover, the US attempted to carry out precision bombing over Germany, beyond fighter range. The USAAF suffered a series of terrible maulings, which culminated in a raid on factories at Schweinfurt on October 14, 1943, in which 60 US bombers were lost and 100 more damaged out of a force of 291.

Yet out of this disaster came the strategic shift that would tip the air war decisively in the Allies' favor. Rather than accepting that its bombers had to attack by night because fighter cover was not available, the USAAF determined to find fighter support, even for long-range attacks on Berlin.

Accordingly, they pressed into service a previously overlooked aircraft, the P-51 Mustang, designed by the US but previously used only by the British. With the »

Aircraft of the USAAF's 401st Bomb Group drop their deadly load on the railroad marshaling yard and road junction at Lohne, in northern Germany, in March 1945.

addition of extra fuel tanks that could be jettisoned, the Mustangs could accompany bombers all the way to Berlin. Luftwaffe fighters, forced into action by the arrival of the bombing fleets, found themselves outmatched by the Mustangs. From January 1944, the Allies began, slowly but surely, to grind down the Luftwaffe and achieve air superiority and eventually almost complete control of the air.

Staying on target

The accuracy of Allied bombers was also enhanced by significant developments in electronic navigation technology. Bomb sighting was effectively a precise form of navigation, so a device that enhanced one also improved the other. The first advance was the Oboe system, which used radio waves broadcast from the ground to set a guide path for bombers. At first, Oboe could only be used to guide a single aircraft at a time, so it was used by "pathfinder" aircraft that could mark the target for the main force. Subsequent technological advances meant it could handle multiple planes.

Then, in early 1943, the invention of a device called a cavity magnetron (a kind of microwave generator) led to the development of the HS2 centimetric radar. Carried by the aircraft, this device bounced microwaves off the surface below, distinguishing between water, open ground, mountains, and urban areas, and could thus, if used in conjunction with good maps, provide accurate long-distance navigation and bombing.

The combined air offensive

With increasing air superiority and ever-improving accuracy, Allied bombing became steadily more effective. Strategic bombing over France and the Low Countries helped the Allies prepare for and execute Operation Overlord, the D-Day landings. British Bomber Command developed night bombing to high levels of accuracy.

Of more lasting significance was the demonstration that true precision bombing was possible, and from June 1943 the British and US joined forces in the Combined Bombing Offensive to apply all the advantages they had developed. In attacks on Germany, US daylight bombing focused mainly on oil infrastructure and successfully produced an oil famine. Meanwhile, British night bombing continued to target German cities, and with devastating consequences. This culminated in the firebombing of Dresden in February 1945, raising serious moral issues.

Operation Thunderclap

Dresden was targeted as part of Operation Thunderclap, designed to demonstrate support for the Soviet offensive into Germany and clog up German transportation infrastructure. On the night of February 13, 796 Lancaster bombers of Bomber Command attacked in two waves, dropping

> There are a lot of people who say that bombing can never win a war. Well, my answer to that is that it has never been tried yet, and we shall see.
>
> **Arthur Harris, 1942**

1,500 tons of high explosive bombs and 1,200 tons of incendiaries, a combination specially selected to cause a firestorm, the impact of which was worsened by a follow-up US attack the next day. Estimates of the death toll vary wildly, from 20,000 to 100,000; they included many refugees.

Controversial strategy

Accusations of Allied "terror bombing" caused even Churchill, who had previously supported Thunderclap, to question the ethics of area bombing. On March 28, 1945, perhaps seeking to shield his own reputation against post-war revision, he wrote to the chiefs of staff to put on record that: "The destruction of Dresden remains a serious query against the conduct of Allied bombing …." Harris was unmoved, stating that he did not regard "the whole of the remaining cities of Germany as worth the bones of one British grenadier." The strategic air offensive against Germany cost the lives of about 50,000 British aircrew and a similar number of Americans. It also caused the deaths of between 750,000 and 1 million Germans. What had this terrible expenditure of blood bought? It is commonly argued that the objective of the strategic air offensive was not achieved, so it did not justify the expenditure of bomber crew and planes, let alone the tragic cost in civilian lives. This argument points to the resilience of German war production up until mid-1944.

However, although German armaments production remained relatively stable, its rate of increase, which had been truly extraordinary in 1942–1943, was dramatically curtailed. Speer himself, the architect of much of Germany's industrial resilience, calculated that, because of the air offensive, the armed forces received around a third fewer tanks and aircraft than he had planned to build. So there is a strong case to be made that the bombing was a success, dramatically curtailing Germany's ability to resist invasion and thus shortening the war by months and perhaps even years. ■

Operation Gomorrah, an Allied bombing campaign, virtually destroyed the city of Hamburg in the last week of July 1943, killing many thousands of civilians and damaging industry.

Arthur Harris

Born in Cheltenham, England, in 1892, "Bomber" Harris was a controversial figure whose dogged support for area bombing, combined with an abrasive personal style, colored his reputation even during the war. Aged 17, he emigrated to Rhodesia, where he became a farm manager. He fought in southern Africa and Europe in World War I. Before joining the Royal Flying Corps (RFC), he served in the infantry, an experience that motivated many of his later beliefs.

The Royal Flying Corps evolved into the RAF in 1918, and Harris remained. At the outbreak of World War II, he was a senior officer and was brought in as the new head of Bomber Command in early 1942. He inspired fierce loyalty and operated his strategy of bombing German cities with equally strong conviction. This bombing campaign proved to be popular with the British public although its effectiveness has been fiercely debated ever since. He retired from the RAF in 1946 and lived in South Africa for several years before returning to the UK. Harris died in 1984.

WE MUST USE OUR FULL RESOURCES

GERMANY'S WAR INDUSTRY (1943–1945)

IN CONTEXT

FOCUS
The German home front

BEFORE
March 1935 Hitler declares that Germany will rearm, disregarding the Treaty of Versailles.

October 1936 Hermann Göring's Four Year Plan aims to make Germany self-sufficient in raw materials.

July 1941 Two-thirds of Germany's industrial workforce is engaged in war-related production.

AFTER
August 1945 After the Potsdam Conference, Stalin, Churchill, and Truman call for the complete disarmament and demilitarization of Germany.

April 1948 The Economic Cooperation Act (Marshall Plan) provides US funds for West Germany and other European powers to rebuild their industries.

In 1942, Hitler's architect Albert Speer became minister for arms and ammunition, after the death of his predecessor, Fritz Todt, in a plane crash. Speer continued Todt's efforts to streamline war production and, in 1943, he took charge of all industries and the production of raw materials, implementing a number of changes. He centralized the allocation and distribution of resources, reduced military interference in industry, and enhanced the roles of engineers and industrialists in the war economy.

The Heinkel factory in Rostock, on Germany's Baltic coast, produced military aircraft—specializing in bombers, but also making seaplanes—for the Luftwaffe throughout the war.

From 1942 to 1945, arms production tripled, and Speer gained a reputation as an organizational genius—although recent historians have cast doubt on how much he actually influenced the already high levels of output.

To solve the labor crisis created by the drafting of millions of men into the army, Speer appointed the politician Fritz Sauckel to find one million workers. By 1944, 5.7 million civilians from 20 European nations, including France and Italy, resided in the Reich's 30,000 forced labor camps.

Allied disruption

Despite Allied bombing, the output of German factories remained steady until mid-1944. However, distribution was disrupted by the attacks, and Germany was forced to focus on antiaircraft measures at the expense of other areas. In March 1945, as Allied troops approached Berlin, Hitler ordered the destruction of German infrastructure. Mindful of Germany's future, Speer succeeded in opposing the drastic measure. ■

See also: German expansion 46–47 ▪ Preparations for war 66 ▪ Blitzkrieg 70–75 ▪ Nazi Europe 168–171 ▪ Germany and the reality of war 188–191

FRIENDS IN FACT, IN SPIRIT, AND IN PURPOSE

ALLIED SUMMITS (1943)

IN CONTEXT

FOCUS
Allied cooperation

BEFORE
August 1941 Roosevelt and Churchill meet to issue the Atlantic Charter, a joint statement of post-war goals.

January 1942 In a United Nations joint declaration, China, the US, UK, and the USSR pledge full resources to defeat the Axis powers.

August 1942 Churchill and Stalin meet for the first time at the Moscow Conference.

AFTER
February 1945 The "Big Three"—the leaders of the US, UK, and the USSR—meet at Yalta on the Black Sea to plan the final defeat of Germany.

July–August 1945 At the Potsdam Conference, the "Big Three" demand unconditional surrender from Japan, and agree their policies on occupied Germany.

As 1942 ended, the USSR and the Western Allies were still separated by ideological and strategic differences. In 1943, a series of meetings between them strengthened bonds, shaped their strategy, and laid out a vision for the post-war world.

British prime minister Winston Churchill and US president Franklin D. Roosevelt met in January and May to make plans for Allied military actions, including the invasion of Italy later in the year, and further offensives against Japan in the Pacific. The foreign ministers of Britain, the US, and the USSR convened in Moscow in October to discuss restoring Austrian independence and plan strategies for occupied countries.

Shaping the future

After many delays, Soviet leader Josef Stalin agreed to a November summit with the leaders of Britain and the US in Tehran. Prior to this, Churchill and Roosevelt met the Chinese leader, Chiang Kai-shek, in Cairo to agree on post-war goals in Asia. The Tehran Conference, from November 28 to December 1, was the first meeting of the "Big Three." They addressed a range of topics, including the post-war division of Germany, and Soviet support of the war against Japan. The major outcome was that the US and UK would invade France in June 1944. ■

> "If we do not … avail ourselves of the present moment to further our common interests, it may so happen that the Germans, having obtained a breathing-spell and gathered their forces, will be able to recover."
>
> **Joseph Stalin**
> **Letter to Roosevelt, February 1943**

See also: A flawed peace 20–21 ▪ Failure of the League of Nations 50 ▪ The invasion of Italy 210–211 ▪ The D-Day landings 256–263 ▪ Aftermath 320–327

AWAKE AND FIGHT!

RESISTANCE MOVEMENTS

IN CONTEXT

FOCUS
Civilian and guerrilla opposition

BEFORE
1939–1941 Germany launches its Blitzkrieg air and ground offensives across Europe.

July 1940 Britain sets up the Special Operations Executive (SOE), an agency dedicated to coordinating the work of resistance fighters in Europe.

AFTER
March 1945 The Soviets round up and imprison 16 leaders of Polish underground groups, including Home Army commander Leopold Okulicki.

November 1945 Communist revolutionary Tito, leader of the Yugoslav Partisans, the most effective anti-Axis resistance group in Europe, is elected premier of Yugoslavia.

December 1958 Insurrection in Algiers brings de Gaulle back into politics, and he is elected as French president.

Every occupied and Axis country had its resistance fighters. Spontaneously, or with the prompting, guidance, and funding of outside forces such as the USSR's NKVD (Soviet police and secret police) or the British Special Operations Executive (SOE), they formed groups, organizations, and eventually entire armies. The primary impetus, however, was from the grassroots up. There was never just a single, coherent resistance or underground movement, but rather a shifting tapestry woven from disparate and evolving groups, each with their own agendas, methods, capabilities, and ideologies. The nature of resistance also varied immensely, from the guerrilla warfare and sabotage raids of the popular imagination, to mass strikes or workers deliberately misperforming their jobs. Among the most notable theaters of resistance were Poland, France, Germany, and Yugoslavia.

> “For seven hours I was tortured physically and mentally. I know that today I went to the limit of resistance.”
>
> **Jean Moulin**
> **French resistance leader (1940)**

Poland's patriots

In terms of armed fighters engaged in the struggle, Poland's resistance was the largest in Europe, involving 400,000 people by some accounts—partly due to the brutality of the German occupation. Even before the fall of Warsaw, Polish forces had set up an underground organization. As the country moved from partition between the Nazis and the Soviets in 1939 to outright Nazi occupation in 1941, it evolved into what became known as the Home Army (*Armia Krajowa*, or AK). From 1942, it sought to sabotage German infrastructure in Poland and fiercely resisted Nazi attempts to erase Polish culture by establishing secret schools and university courses, underground theater, and music and science activities. The Poles referred to these activities collectively as the “Underground State.”

From 1942, communist groups, mainly concentrated in the marshes and forests of the east, joined the Polish resistance, but soon clashed with the Polish government-in-exile, the so-called “London camp.” The Home Army's principal aim was to wait until conditions were right to launch a general uprising, with the goal of restoring the pre-war Polish state. Attempts to forge alliances between the London camp, the communist partisans, and their Soviet masters foundered, however, and it became increasingly clear that Stalin did not share the goals of the Polish government-in-exile. Some cooperation continued, but there were also chilling incidents of Polish resistance commanders being “disappeared” after going to meet their Red Army counterparts. The tensions reached a terrible climax when the Home Army

Polish fighter Zdzich (Zdzisław de Ville), from the Jedrusie underground guerrilla group of the Home Army, keeps watch, armed with his automatic rifle, in the forests of southeastern Poland.

See also: Establishing the Nazi state 30–33 ▪ Dictators and fragile democracies in Europe 34–39 ▪ German expansion 46–47 ▪ The Fall of France 80–87 ▪ Nazi Europe 168–171 ▪ The secret war 198–203 ▪ Propaganda 236–241 ▪ The Warsaw Uprising 271

launched the Warsaw Uprising of August 1, 1944—a last attempt to exert domestic agency over the outcome of the war in Poland. As the Nazis levelled Warsaw and perhaps as many as a quarter of a million Poles perished, the Soviets chose not to intervene.

Diverse French opposition

There never was a single French resistance, but rather disparate groups with diverse methods and intentions, each trying to do their part to resist the German occupation and Vichy collaboration. After the fall of France in 1940, many different people called for resistance—most notably Charles de Gaulle, who broadcast from London—while other groups circulated clandestine tracts and anti-Nazi newsletters.

Alongside such ideological and propagandist acts of resistance were active and passive attempts to sabotage the occupation and the German war effort. These included reconnaissance, spying, helping POWs and downed Allied airmen to escape, guerrilla warfare, and sabotaging war industries and infrastructure. Among the most effective saboteurs were the *cheminots*—railroad employees who crippled German communications and transportation. Their *Résistance-Fer* ("railroad resistance") was bankrolled by the British SOE, who were on the lookout for effective groups to sponsor but found it in different French resistance groups.

The communist *Front National* and *Francs-Tireurs et Partisans* (FTP) had an organized structure from the start, but only in January 1943 did noncommunist groups begin to come together. In the north, a coordinating committee was established, while in the south de Gaulle's representative, Jean Moulin, led the *Mouvements Unis de la Résistance* (MUR). Charged with unifying the groups across France, Moulin established the *Conseil national de la Résistance* (CNR) in May 1943, weeks before his capture, torture, and death in custody. In January 1944, the *Mouvement de libération nationale* (MLN) further unified the principal noncommunist groups.

The imposition from mid-1942 of the hated labor conscription (*Service du travail obligatoire* or STO), with its enforced deportation of French workers to Germany, spawned the *Maquis*—rural bands of guerrilla resistance fighters, »

Polish Home Army sabotage

An extensive campaign of sabotage was carried out by the Polish Home Army between January 1, 1941, and June 30, 1944, against transportation and infrastructure, seeking to disrupt and weaken the Nazi occupation.

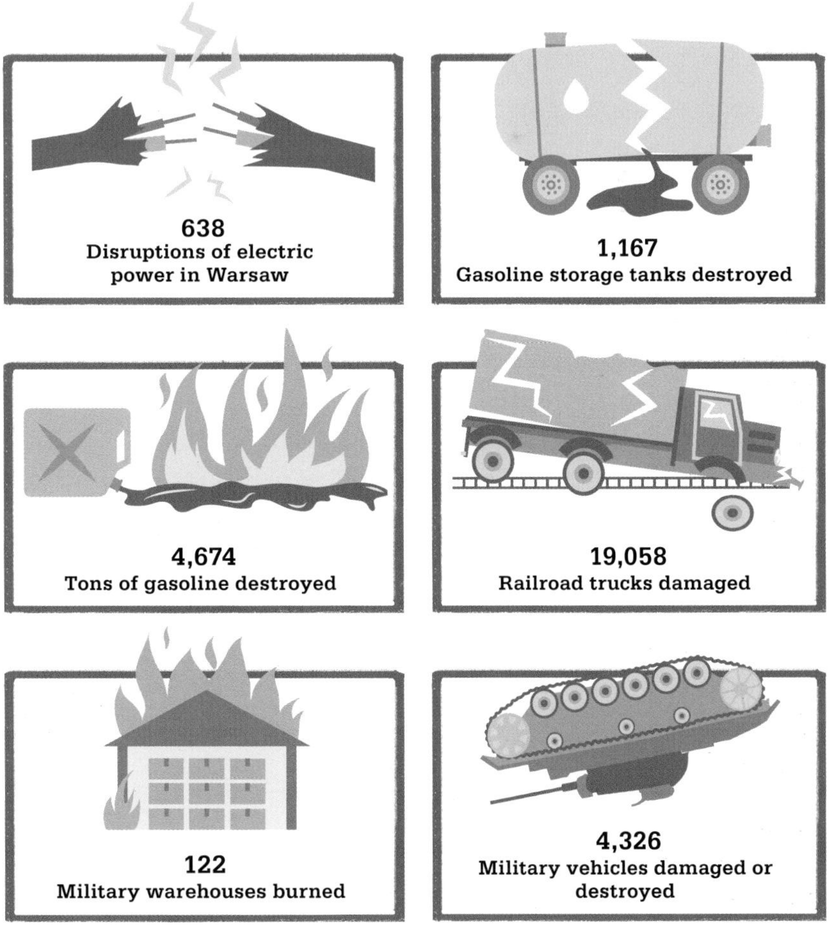

named after the bandit-infested bush of the Corsican interior. By the fall of 1943, the number of active *maquisards* was estimated at 15,000, though spread among many diverse groups, each with its own individual approach and sphere of influence. British philosopher A. J. Ayer, who arrived as a secret agent in 1944 to liaise with the resistance fighters in southwest France, described the region's colorful *maquisards* as "a series of feudal lords."

Attempts at coordination

In early 1944, in a bid to coordinate the Allies' planned invasion with resistance forces on the ground, de Gaulle attempted to subsume all resistance groups (some 200,000 fighters) under the label of the French Forces of the Interior (FFI) Throughout France that year, the FFI's tactical intelligence and acts of sabotage smoothed the path of the advancing Allied forces. In August, however, concerned about the FFI's increasing influence, de Gaulle insisted that its units should all become part of the French regular army—a process that was gradually enacted between October 1944 and March 1945.

Reprisals for resistance actions often exacted a terrible toll. Among the worst atrocities was the Oradour massacre of June 10, 1944, four days after the D-Day landings, when the SS murdered 643 people, from babies to old women, ostensibly to revenge the capture of a Panzer battalion commander. During the course of the war, more than 90,000 French resistance fighters were tortured, executed, or deported, together with thousands more civilians murdered in reprisals by the Gestapo; SS; or Milice, the Vichy paramilitary force.

At the war's end, France took great pride in its resistance fighters, who helped obviate the shame of collaboration and occupation, and raised its standing with other Allies.

Resistance within Germany

In Germany on September 1, 1939, it became a capital crime to criticize the Nazis' conduct of the war. This, however, did not deter some communists and social democrats who, despite the danger, persisted with acts of resistance, as did some members of the clergy, military, and civil service, together with students.

Among the bravest were those in the White Rose student group at Munich University in 1942–1943, who distributed anti-Nazi pamphlets, but were denounced by a university staff member in February 1943, tried, and executed. The *Schwarze Kapelle*, a loose group that included anti-Nazi military leaders, came close to assassinating Hitler in July 1944. Many of the conspirators were from the conservative military class, who realized that the Nazis were destroying Germany. The plot's failure led to the execution of around 5,000 opponents of the regime and, at the time, increased popular support for Hitler.

> Whatever happens, the flame of the French Resistance must not be extinguished and will not be extinguished. Tomorrow, as today, I will speak on Radio London.
>
> **Charles de Gaulle**
> **First London speech, June 18, 1940**

White Rose resistance core members Hans Scholl (left) and his sister Sophie. Along with Christoph Probst, they were guillotined for their nonviolent anti-Nazi resistance in 1943.

George Elser, a factory worker and communist sympathizer, was the first to attempt to assassinate Hitler on November 8, 1939. He spent the rest of the war in custody, and was executed at Dachau on April 9, 1945. Hanged on the same day were several more high-profile German anti-Nazis: Pastor Dietrich Bonhoeffer, Admiral Wilhelm Canaris, General Hans Oster, and the German army jurist Karl Sack.

Female Yugoslav guerrillas from Tito's communist Partisan forces train for battle. Women, mostly aged under 20 years, were both fighters and leaders in the communist resistance movement.

Yugoslavia—torn apart

The German conquest of Yugoslavia in April 1941, and its rushed and partial occupation as Hitler's troops were redeployed to the Eastern Front, caused the fragile, unstable state to fracture into ethnic and sectarian rivalries. Two primary resistance forces emerged to oppose the Germans, but they often fought against each other and other ethnic groups in a bitter civil war. Former paramilitary and military forces organized themselves under the banner of the Chetniks, a royalist and Serbian nationalist group, led by Colonel Draža Mihailovic. Opposing them were the communist Partisans under Josip Broz Tito. The Chetniks were initially supported by the Western Allies, but both the Soviet and Western leaders transferred their support to the Partisans, rebranded as the People's Liberation Army (PLA), after Tito's military successes in 1943.

Tragically, most of the 1.2 million Yugoslavs killed in the war died at the hands of their compatriots. Yet the Allies also credited Yugoslav forces—especially the Partisans—with pinning down 35 Axis divisions that might otherwise have fought Allied forces. As elsewhere, determined resistance fighters frustrated Germany's armed forces. ■

Josip Broz Tito

Born Josip Broz in Zagreb in 1892 to a Croat father and Slovene mother, Tito fought in World War I in the Austro-Hungarian army. In 1920, he joined the Communist Party of Yugoslavia (CPY), which became an underground group after its suppression a year later. Imprisoned from 1928–1934, he took the name Tito and rose through CPY ranks to become the group's secretary-general in 1939.

Following the German invasion of April 1941, Tito's communists became the Partisan resistance movement, espousing an ideology of pan-Yugoslav liberation. After considerable military successes and with Allied support from 1943, Tito marched into Belgrade in 1945 as leader of Yugoslavia.

Tito soon assumed complete control of the country, ruthlessly extinguishing any opposition. He rejected Stalin's demands for total obeisance, skillfully forging a unique path for Yugoslavia, which hosted the first summit of the Non-Alliance Movement in 1961. At home, Tito contained ethnic, sectarian, and nationalist tensions, maintaining relative unity and stability for 35 years. He died in Ljubljana in 1980.

THEY WERE AROUND US, ON TOP OF US, AND BETWEEN US

THE BATTLE OF KURSK (JULY 1943)

IN CONTEXT

FOCUS
Defense of Soviet territory

BEFORE
December 1942–February 1943 Operation Little Saturn, a Red Army offensive in Ukraine, is successful.

February–March 1943 Germany wins the Third Battle of Kharkov, stabilizing the German frontline in the Ukraine region.

AFTER
August 1943 A Soviet offensive in Ukraine forces the retreat of German troops behind the Dnieper River.

August–October 1943 The Red Army wins a hard-fought victory in the Battle of Smolensk.

November–December 1943 Soviet troops liberate Kiev and hold it, despite a German counteroffensive.

In January 1943, with the German forces at Stalingrad on the verge of defeat, the Stavka (the USSR's high command) decided to press its advantage. The Red Army launched a series of offensives in southern Russia and Ukraine. They took back the cities of Voronezh, Kharkov, and Kursk, advancing around 300 miles (480 km). However, the main Axis formation in the area, Army Group South, had recently been reinforced by the arrival of elite Waffen-SS Panzer tank units, and it was led by Marshal Erich von Manstein, who was a capable strategist. He had allowed the evacuation of Kharkov

See also: Operation Barbarossa 124–131 ▪ The Great Patriotic War 132–135 ▪ The Battle of Stalingrad 178–183 ▪ The invasion of Italy 210–211 ▪ Operation Bagration 266–269 ▪ The Soviets push into Germany 288–289 ▪ Victory in Europe 298–303

on February 16—despite Hitler's order to hold it at all costs—in the expectation that he could lure Soviet forces forward and launch a counteroffensive.

Manstein acted on this plan on February 19. German forces retook Kharkov on March 15 and the city of Belgorod three days later. This created a "salient," or bulge, of Soviet territory around the city of Kursk. It stretched 160 miles (256 km) north to south and around 100 miles (160 km) east to west; Axis-controlled territory surrounded it to the north, south, and west.

Intending to continue his advance to capture Kursk, Hitler ordered Manstein to halt, primarily because he wanted to strengthen German forces so they could launch a massed attack later in the year. In addition, Manstein's forces were exhausted, and the muddy conditions created by the spring thaw made Panzer warfare near-impossible. After weeks of movement, both sides had time to consolidate, amass forces, and prepare for the next phase of conflict.

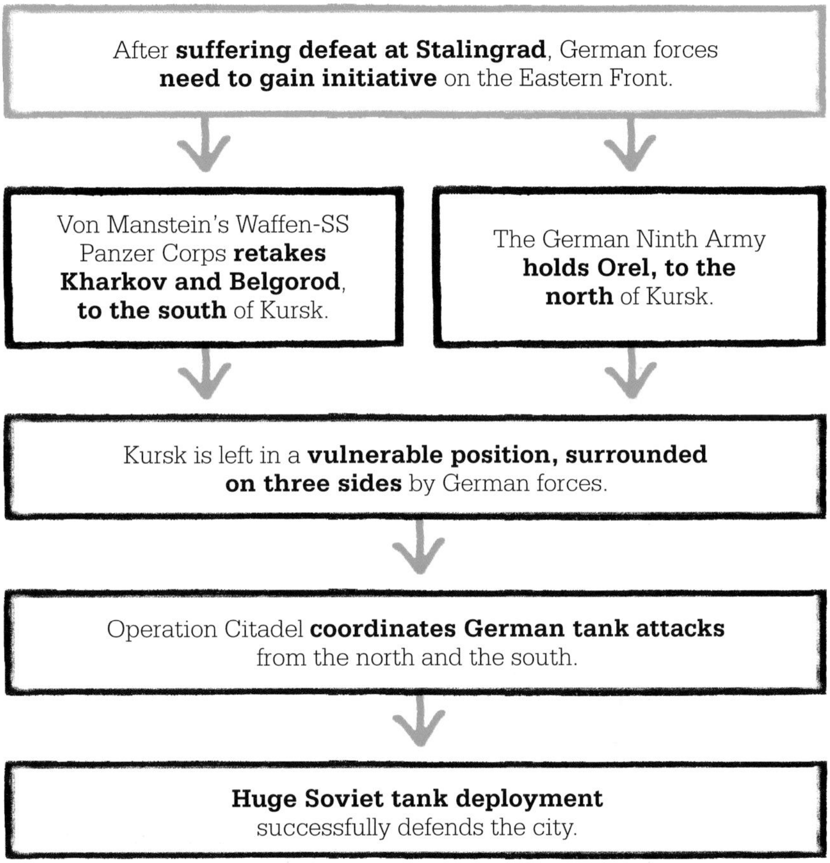

After suffering defeat at Stalingrad, German forces need to gain initiative on the Eastern Front.
Von Manstein's Waffen-SS Panzer Corps retakes Kharkov and Belgorod, to the south of Kursk.
The German Ninth Army holds Orel, to the north of Kursk.
Kursk is left in a vulnerable position, surrounded on three sides by German forces.
Operation Citadel coordinates German tank attacks from the north and the south.
Huge Soviet tank deployment successfully defends the city.

Preparing for battle

On April 15, 1943, Hitler formally approved Operation Citadel. This was a pincer strike on the Kursk salient, with simultaneous attacks from the north and south. Hitler and the German high command hoped victory would reverse the losses of Stalingrad and end the deadlock on the Eastern Front. Time was of the essence—the Germans had to attack before the Soviets could strengthen their defenses. Hitler was urged to begin in early May, but he delayed several times, hoping for better weather, and eventually settled on July 5.

Hitler also stalled Operation Citadel to wait for newer tanks to be delivered to the Eastern Front. In 1942, a new German tank, the Tiger, had gone into production. Heavily armored and armed, it had already been successfully used in North Africa. Despite its strengths, the Tiger was prone to breakdowns and was fuel-inefficient. Joining the Tiger for Operation Citadel was the Panther, making its combat debut. It had been rushed into service without full testing—numerous mechanical flaws emerged in the field. Problems with the Tigers and Panthers meant that at Kursk the Germans would have to rely primarily on the comparatively outdated Panzer III and Panzer IV tanks.

Advance warning

German delays gave the Red Army time to prepare fearsome defenses around Kursk. The Stavka hoped that "defense in depth" would blunt the initial German strike, draw them into a trap, and enable a counterattack. As a result of intercepted messages decoded by British Intelligence at its Bletchley Park code-breaking center, the Soviets knew that the Germans were planning an offensive around Kursk at some time between »

> We were advised to fight to the last man, defend our comrades from these fascists. It fell to us … to stop Nazism rampaging across Mother Russia.
> **Red Army gunner**

July 3 and 6. For every mile of front the Soviets assembled 4,500 soldiers, 45 tanks, and more than 100 artillery pieces, along with an array of blockhouses, trenches, and antitank ditches. They also laid more than 1 million mines and thousands of barbed-wire snares.

Mass production of tanks

Essential to Soviet preparations was assembling enough tanks to outnumber those of the Germans. Their main battle tank was the T-34, the most widely produced of all tanks of World War II. It was resilient, heavily armed, had a top speed of 34 mph (54 km/h), and was fitted with wide tracks that prevented it from getting bogged down in muddy or snowy ground. These benefits made up for its deficiencies, which included a cramped cabin, poor interior visibility, and mechanical problems. The greatest strength of the T-34 was its simple design, which meant it could be mass-produced quickly. By June 1943, while the Germans were producing around 500 tanks per month (half of which were Panzer IIIs), Soviet factories were churning out more than 1,000 T-34s every month.

German advances thwarted

Prior to the Battle of Kursk, Soviet intelligence had conducted a successful deception exercise through false radio transmissions and the creation of dummy airfields, as well as conducting troop movements at night or times of limited visibility. Consequently, many German generals were ignorant of the strength of the Red Army and did not know where their forces were massed. More cautious voices, aware of the scale of Soviet fortifications around Kursk, urged Hitler to call off Operation Citadel. He did not heed them.

On July 5, the Germans launched Operation Citadel. They attacked with around 900,000 men, against the Soviet force of 1.3 million (plus around 500,000 in reserve). The attack was met by a sustained and immediate Soviet artillery barrage, making it clear that it had been anticipated. Despite this, and the mechanical problems of many tanks, Operation Citadel initially went according to Germany's plan. However, it was soon disrupted by the Soviet defenses and the bravery of Red Army soldiers, who often ran out in the face of advancing Panzers, laying mines in their path, or throwing grenades or Molotov cocktails at them. In addition, for all the firepower and mobility that Panzer tanks provided, infantry support was needed to guard their flanks and hold the ground they seized, and the Germans had a major shortage of foot soldiers, as well as aircraft and artillery.

In the northern part of the Kursk salient, General Konstantin Rokossovsky's Central Front halted the German Ninth Army on July 10 after an advance of just 8 miles (13 km). German

A Russian T-34 tank rolls into a burning village after the Germans launched Operation Citadel. The innovative sloping steel armor of the T-34 increased its resilience to shells.

German infantry during the Battle of Kursk, 1943. Troops from Army Group Center and Army Group North were deployed to squeeze Soviet forces from both north and south.

forces made greater gains against General Nikolai Vatutin's Voronezh Front in the south. The Stavka sent reserves there, but the advance had pushed forward more than 20 miles (32 km) by July 10. Two days later, the Germans approached Prokhorovka, just 50 miles (80 km) from Kursk.

German withdrawal

As hundreds of tanks clashed, the Red Army suffered huge losses but prevented a German breakthrough. It became clear that the plan to envelop Soviet forces at Kursk had failed. With the start of the Allied invasion of Sicily on July 10, Hitler ended Operation Citadel, redirecting troops to the new threat in western Europe. Some German forces carried on fighting in the southern part of the salient, but operations were halted completely on July 17.

On July 12, the Red Army launched a counteroffensive in the northern part of the Kursk salient. Central Front troops, joined by those from the Bryansk and Western fronts, aimed to capture a German salient around the city of Orel. The heavier fighting in the southern part of the Kursk salient meant that the counteroffensive there was delayed until August 3. Orel was liberated on August 5, followed by Belgorod on August 6, and Kharkov on August 23.

Turning point

Kursk was one of the largest tank battles in history—about 6,000 tanks were deployed, along with 2 million troops and 4,000 aircraft. Germany failed to achieve its objectives and the Battle of Kursk marked the end of its ability to attack the Eastern Front. Germany lost an estimated 200,000 men through death and injury at Kursk and in the subsequent fighting. Although the Soviet forces suffered perhaps five times as many casualties, by the fall of 1943, the initiative on the Eastern Front was firmly in their hands. The Red Army was poised to advance farther west. ■

The "Flying Tank"

Although Kursk is primarily known as a tank battle, one of the other factors behind the Soviet victory was aerial superiority. Central to this was the Ilyushin Il-2, an attack aircraft designed to provide air support for ground forces. It was known as the "Flying Tank" because its steel armor could withstand heavy enemy fire. The Il-2 was produced in high numbers—more than 36,000 of these machines were built during World War II. Armed with two cannons and two machine guns, and with a bomb load of 1,000 pounds (450 kg), the Il-2 helped repel the German onslaught at Kursk.

By the time of the Battle of Kursk, the Soviets had developed fighter airplanes that were more than a match for German designs, and their pilots had developed greater skill and experience over the course of the war. Most importantly, they possessed a huge numerical advantage in the air, which meant they could stage far more sorties than the Luftwaffe. This helped them deny critical air support to the German forces on the ground.

The Ilyushin Il-2, seen here in flight, first entered service in 1941. It would drop low across the field of battle to provide cover for the ground troops of the Red Army.

LOOSE LIPS MIGHT SINK SHIPS

PROPAGANDA

IN CONTEXT

FOCUS
Controlling public opinion

BEFORE
1914–1918 The British popular press makes effective use of anti-German propaganda during World War I.

1935 Leni Riefenstahl's *Triumph of the Will*, a film celebrating the 1934 Nazi Party Congress in Nuremberg, is released.

1938 Years of anti-Semitic propaganda culminates in Kristallnacht, in which Jewish communities in towns and cities in Germany, Austria, and the Sudetenland are attacked—people are killed and synagogues destroyed.

AFTER
2016 Online "fake news" propaganda is cited as a factor influencing the outcome of the US presidential election.

The experience of World War I had proved the value of propaganda, as a means of boosting or attacking public and military morale, encouraging desired behaviors and discouraging undesired ones, and disseminating ideology. These lessons had been studied by dictators. Stalin enforced a ruthless rewriting of history and truth in the USSR during the 1930s, while Hitler wrote at length about the potential power of propaganda, devoting two chapters of *Mein Kampf* to the topic. Hitler blamed Britain's highly effective use of propaganda during World War I for poisoning the morale of the German people. But he also saw that propaganda could be a potent tool in bending the will of the people to his own, urging the use of simple slogans that would appeal to "the primitive sentiments of the broad masses."

"Big lies"

In his project to make propaganda a weapon of war, Hitler found a willing and able collaborator in Joseph Goebbels. Although Goebbels is most famous for a quote he never said, about the value of "big lies," he endorsed wholeheartedly Hitler's own beliefs on the topic. In *Mein Kampf*, Hitler argued that "the big lie"—a lie so audacious that it seems beyond fabrication—could be used to shape public opinion through the manipulation of deep-seated emotions.

Goebbels had become the Nazi propaganda chief in 1929, and was appointed as the head of the new Reich Ministry of Information and Propaganda in March 1933, after Hitler took power. Under Goebbels, the Nazis used every form of media

> The essence of propaganda consists in winning people over to an idea so sincerely, so vitally … they succumb to it utterly and can never again escape from it.
> **Joseph Goebbels**

Joseph Goebbels

Born to a strict Roman Catholic family, Goebbels was studious and clever, but insecure and resentful, partly as a result of a deformity of the foot which had seen him rejected by the military in World War I, and partly because of his non-Aryan appearance.

Goebbels found his niche in the Nazi Party. After Hitler made him propaganda chief, Goebbels created a heroic Führer myth, forging a cult of personality and Nazi ideology that won over the majority of Germans. At the same time, Goebbels gave free reign to his vitriolic anti-Semitism, demonizing Jewish people and validating violence. He orchestrated the anti-Jewish violence of Kristallnacht, and was involved in the Final Solution genocide.

The war brought him even closer to Hitler—even when it turned against Germany. Goebbels was given more power, but as the nation collapsed, he succumbed to apocalyptic thinking. He ignored Hitler's testament naming him as successor, and chose death for himself, his wife Magda, and his six young children.

See also: Rise of the Nazis 24–29 ▪ Dictators and fragile democracies in Europe 34–39 ▪ Kristallnacht 48–49 ▪ Preparations for war 66 ▪ The Great Patriotic War 132–135 ▪ America at war 146–153

БУДЬ НА ЧЕКУ,
В ТАКИЕ ДНИ
ПОДСЛУШИВАЮТ СТЕНЫ.
НЕДАЛЕКО ОТ БОЛТОВНИ
И СПЛЕТНИ
ДО ИЗМЕНЫ.
НЕ БОЛТАЙ!

A Soviet poster from 1941 that says, "Don't chatter, gossip is almost treason!" Propaganda often used images of ordinary people to encourage identification with the message.

and culture to push propaganda, including art, film, theater, radio, music, literature, the popular press, and posters. By the outbreak of World War II, his propaganda skills had been used to impose a uniform national culture, demonize Jewish people, and indoctrinate the German public to believe that the war in which they were engaged was not only justified but sacred.

Once the war started, this armory of propaganda was deployed to portray the German military as all-conquering and noble, while enemies were depicted either as depraved and cowardly, or brave but misled by their leaders. Particular vitriol was reserved for the Soviet enemy, with Russians depicted as sub-humans bent on rape and despoliation. Soviet propaganda, in the form of posters, newspapers, and leaflets, attacked the Nazi high command in kind, condemned atrocities committed by German soldiers in occupied countries, depicted the Red Army as heroes, and exhorted civilians to carry out their patriotic duty in daily life.

Responding to events

After 1941, reverses in Germany's fortunes in the war, especially on the Eastern Front, along with heavy Allied bombing of German cities, challenged Goebbels' presentation of events. With characteristic adeptness, he used these blows as provocation, inflaming German public morale and stiffening resolve by depicting the war as a struggle for survival against the threat of complete destruction. In a famous speech at the Sportpalast in Berlin, on February 18, 1943, Goebbels used every oratorical trick to whip up an atmosphere of hysterical emotion, along with wild promises of secret weapons and impregnable fortress redoubts, winning widespread acceptance for the total mobilization of Germany in pursuit of victory. In the aftermath of this, the Nazis' hold on German public opinion strengthened still further, and it was not until late 1944 that its grip would loosen. By then, even Goebbels believed that the enemy »

Types of propaganda

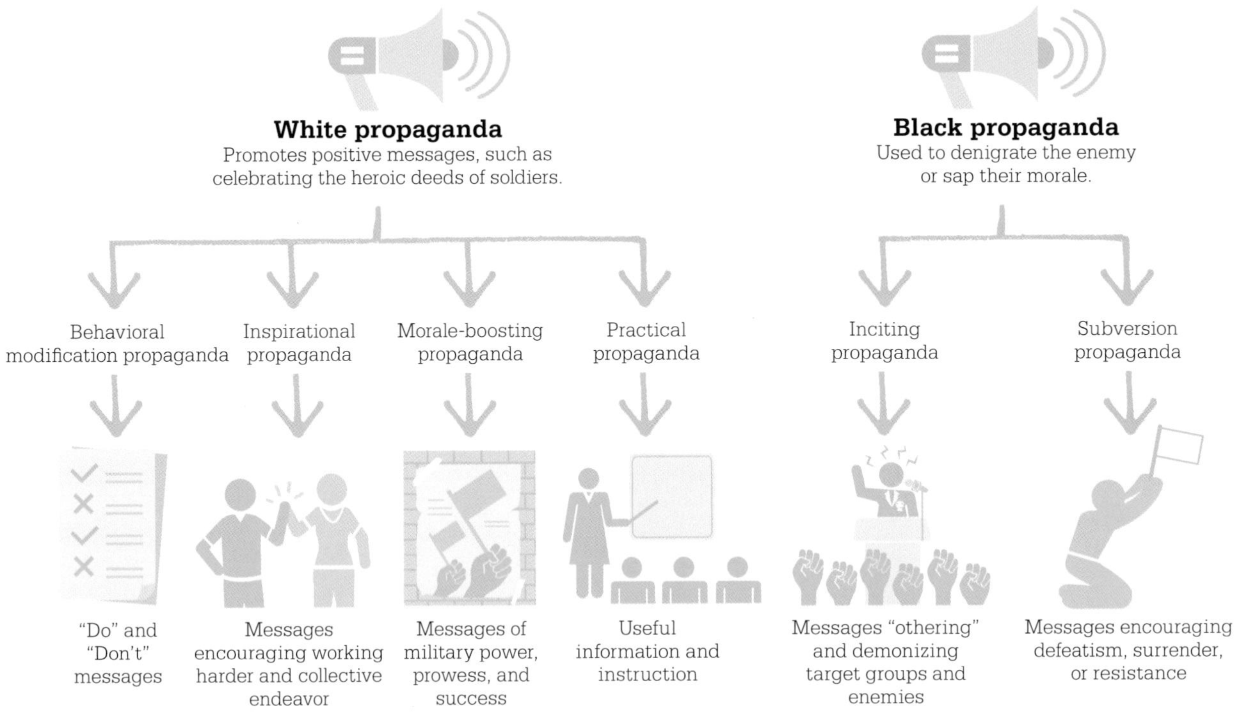

White propaganda
Promotes positive messages, such as celebrating the heroic deeds of soldiers.
Black propaganda
Used to denigrate the enemy or sap their morale.
Behavioral modification propaganda
Inspirational propaganda
Morale-boosting propaganda
Practical propaganda
Inciting propaganda
Subversion propaganda
"Do" and "Don't" messages
Messages encouraging working harder and collective endeavor
Messages of military power, prowess, and success
Useful information and instruction
Messages "othering" and demonizing target groups and enemies
Messages encouraging defeatism, surrender, or resistance

propaganda that reached German civilians had begun to have a negative effect on morale, with Allied leaflets "no longer carelessly thrown aside but … read attentively."

British propaganda

Britain ran a sophisticated and multi-faceted propaganda operation. Its most obvious expression was in the work of the British Broadcasting Corporation (BBC), which broadcast all over the world, walking a difficult path between maintaining its reputation for truthfulness and pushing the British line. A British diplomat in Italy wrote home pointing out that while Mussolini's radio broadcasts simply lied, the BBC reported the news "objectively and factually, though favorably by a process of selection and omission." This reputation for objectivity enhanced the "soft power" of BBC broadcasts, which were viewed as a source of reliable information by both Allied and Axis populations. Tensions inevitably arose, however, between the desire to control information and to maintain the freedom of the press. A system of censorship for both newspapers and the BBC was implemented, overseen by the Ministry of Information, a government department led by Sir John Reith, himself a former head of the BBC. Editors were required to pre-censor stories they judged a potential threat to national security or public safety, and submit those they were unsure about to the ministry for vetting. Failure to comply with this left journalists open to prosecution.

BBC output was seen by Winston Churchill as "white propaganda"—overt and relatively transparent. What Churchill termed "black propaganda" was assigned to a covert operations department, the Political Warfare Executive (PWE), formed in 1941 to create and distribute propaganda that would damage enemy morale. The PWE worked closely with the BBC, and

> Words are ammunition. Each word an American utters either helps or hurts the war effort.
>
> ***Government Information Manual for the Motion Picture Industry,* US Office of War Information**

also established, with American technology, a network of clandestine German-language radio stations—40 of them by 1945—to shape German public opinion. PWE broadcasts satirized Axis leaders and propaganda and, thanks to signals interception, were able to use information from Goebbels' own twice-daily German press briefings to add authenticity to their offerings. PWE agents were even parachuted into occupied France to help set up newspapers and printing presses.

Influencing US opinion

Although American propaganda was also directed at occupied and enemy populations, with a particular emphasis on the air-dropping of leaflets, perhaps the primary target of American output was the domestic audience. The experience of World War I and the subsequent Great Depression had intensified an isolationist trend in American popular opinion. To help rally the country behind the war effort, President Franklin D. Roosevelt established in June 1942 the Office of War Information (OWI). The OWI fought subversion at home, pushed a message of racial unity in an attempt to counteract some of the most damaging effects of racism on the workings of the economy and the military, and worked to undermine enemy morale. Its greatest focus, however, was on increasing production and reducing waste, whether through loose talk, inefficient use of resources, or time off work. Alongside in-house efforts from industry, the OWI sought to bring women into the workforce through its Womanpower department, the Basic Program Plan of which baldly stated: "These jobs will have to be glorified as a patriotic war service if American women are to be persuaded to take them and stick to them."

The film industry

The OWI worked with Hollywood to produce propagandist content, such as cartoons featuring Donald Duck throwing tomatoes at Hitler. Frank Capra, best known today for directing films such as *It's a Wonderful Life*, directed an Oscar-winning series of documentary films called *Why We Fight*, featuring xenophobic and racist depictions of Axis nationals. The OWI reviewed scripts, even rewriting dialogue, and issued film studios with guidance based around a single mission: "Will this movie help win the war?" Despite this highly intrusive supervision, the OWI held no formal powers of censorship. ■

A 1943 recruitment poster for the US Army Air Corp. The patriotic design was intended to inspire men to enlist, although Congress also introduced conscription to draft military personnel.

Iva "Tokyo Rose" Toguri Ikoku

Tokyo Rose was the collective nickname given by US troops in the Pacific to the female DJs on the Japanese radio show *Zero Hour*, which was well-liked by them for its combination of popular music and ridiculous propaganda.

There was no single Tokyo Rose, but after the war the name became linked to the Japanese-American Iva Toguri (later Iva Toguri Ikoku). American-born Toguri had been visiting relatives in Japan when war broke out; despite pressure, she refused to give up her American citizenship. However, during the course of the war she was forced to work on *Zero Hour*, playing music and telling jokes, while illicitly helping American POWs working at the station.

After the war, Toguri was initially cleared of wrongdoing, but in 1948, when she tried to return to the US, a media campaign led to her indictment for treason. After a trial that featured witnesses pressured into perjury by the state, she was jailed. In 1977, she received a presidential pardon and won back her citizenship.

THE MAGNIFICENT HEROIC STRUGGLE

THE WARSAW GHETTO UPRISING (APRIL–MAY 1943)

IN CONTEXT

FOCUS
Resistance movements

BEFORE
October 2, 1940 The German governor of Warsaw signs the order to establish a Jewish ghetto, sealed from the rest of the city.

1940–mid-1942 Around 83,000 Jews die of starvation and disease in the ghetto.

July–September 1942 In what the Nazis call the "Great Action," around 265,000 Jews are deported from Warsaw to the Treblinka death camp.

AFTER
November 1943 Around 42,000 Jews, deported from Warsaw after the ghetto uprising, are murdered in a two-day operation known as Operation Harvest Festival.

August 1, 1944 A city-wide uprising against the German occupiers begins in Warsaw.

The Warsaw Ghetto Uprising in 1943 was the largest act of Jewish resistance in Nazi Europe. When the ghetto was established in 1940, more than 400,000 Jews were crammed into an area barely more than 1.3 sq miles (3.4 sq km), with more than seven people on average in each available room. At first, the Nazis starved the population, then they deported more than half to labor and death camps. Thousands also succumbed to disease. By April 1943, only around 60,000 Jews remained.

> The Jewish women took an active part in the fighting … pouring boiling water on the attacking Germans. Such an embittered and unequal battle is unprecedented in history.
>
> **Mary Berg**
> **Survivor and diarist of the Warsaw ghetto**

Although the Nazis framed deportation as a "resettlement" policy, it was increasingly clear to the Jews that this was an extermination, and resistance groups inside the ghetto banded together into two forces, the Jewish Combat Organization (*Żydowska Organizacja Bojowa*; ŻOB) and the Jewish Military Union (*Żydowski Związek Wojskowy*; ŻZW). Through fleeting contact with the Polish resistance, the two forces acquired a few weapons and improvised others, so that by January 1943, when the Germans were threatening to complete their deportations, around 750 young men and women were prepared for armed resistance. "Awake and fight!" the ŻOB exhorted ghetto residents, urging them to "put an end" to their "terrible acceptance" of a death sentence.

Unequal battle

On January 18, 1943, German *Schutzstaffel* (SS) and police units arrived at the ghetto to begin another round of deportations, but quickly withdrew when their operation was disrupted by resistance fighters who had infiltrated the column of deportees. The rest of the ghetto

See also: Kristallnacht 48–49 ▪ The destruction of Poland 58–63 ▪ The Holocaust 172–177 ▪ Resistance movements 226–231 ▪ The Warsaw Uprising 271

took heart from this fleeting success and began to dig bunkers and gather weapons in preparation for the return of the SS.

The Germans brought in an experienced SS commander, Jürgen Stroop, to oversee their next attempt to clear the ghetto, and on April 19, 1943, the eve of the Passover holiday, a force of more than 2,000 German troops moved in, supported by a tank, armored vehicles, heavy machine-guns, and artillery. They were met by fierce resistance and forced to retreat, but soon returned with orders to burn down the ghetto.

Mordecai Anielewicz

Born in Wyszków, near Warsaw, in 1919, Mordecai Anielewicz (also spelled Anilowitz) was an activist for Jewish self-defense from an early age. In Warsaw, he joined a pro-Soviet Jewish resistance group and fled to Soviet-controlled territory when the Germans took the city.

Anielewicz infiltrated the Warsaw ghetto, setting up a newspaper, but was in western Poland in 1942 when the mass deportation of Jews was carried out. He rushed back to convince the ghetto elders to embrace armed resistance. At first, they were reluctant, but with the support of other activists, and with intelligence of the fate of "resettled" Jews, Anielewicz prevailed and the ŻOB was set up under his command. He was the de facto leader of the ghetto and led the resistance until May 8, 1943, when the Germans surrounded the ŻOB command bunker. Anielewicz either died by suicide or from gas pumped into the bunker.

Death and destruction

With their intimate knowledge of the streets and buildings, Jewish fighters waged guerrilla warfare, while civilians holed up in bunkers hid from deportation. Against all odds, the resistance continued for almost a month, but on May 8, 1943, German forces managed to seize the ŻOB headquarters at 18 Mila Street, where 24-year-old ŻOB commander Mordecai Anielewicz and many of his comrades died. Eight days later, Stroop ordered the destruction of the Great Synagogue on Tłomackie Street and reported back to Berlin that "The former Jewish Quarter in Warsaw is no more." Surviving individuals continued to hold out amid the ruins into July. About 50 ŻOB fighters escaped through the sewers, some later joining the Warsaw Uprising of 1944. In the battle and the fires, around 7,000 Jews had been killed, while another 7,000 were captured and sent to death camps, mainly Treblinka. The surviving population of the ghetto was deported en masse and murdered a few months later. ■

German SS troops round up members of the Jewish resistance during the suppression of the Warsaw Ghetto Uprising. Women helped organize the revolt and fought alongside the men.

> Although we will not survive to see it, our murderers will pay for their crimes after we are gone. And our deeds will live forever.
>
> **Izhak Katznelson**
> **Jewish poet and uprising activist**

EVERY MAN SHOULD DO HIS UTMOST

THE WESTERN PACIFIC (NOVEMBER 1943–AUGUST 1944)

IN CONTEXT

FOCUS
War in the Pacific

BEFORE

1892 Britain proclaims a protectorate over the Gilbert and Ellice Islands in the central Pacific.

1920 Japan receives a League of Nations mandate to administer the Marshall, Caroline, and Mariana islands in the western Pacific.

1930s Japan builds major military bases on many of its Pacific islands.

December 1941 Two days after the attack on Pearl Harbor, Japanese forces occupy the Gilbert Islands.

AFTER

1947 The United States establishes the Trust Territory of the Pacific Islands under United Nations trusteeship, taking over the earlier Japanese mandate.

1968 The Ogasawara Islands (Bonin Islands) of Micronesia are restored to Japan.

1972 The US administration of the Ryukyu Islands (centered on Okinawa) ends, and they are returned to Japanese rule.

1979 Renamed Kiribati, the Gilbert Islands receive independence from Britain.

1986 The Marshall Islands and Micronesia (the Caroline Islands) become independent states; the Marianas remain in political union with the US.

During 1943, the American strategy toward Japan became clear. To attack the Japanese home islands, the bombers of the United States Army Air Forces (USAAF) required Pacific-island bases from which to launch their attacks. Building on the successes of the ongoing Operation Cartwheel—a bid to take out the major Japanese air base in Papua New Guinea in the South Pacific—American military chiefs decided to island-hop into the thinly spaced Japanese-occupied Gilbert, Marshall, Caroline, and Mariana islands in the central western Pacific.

The campaign's aim was to comprehensively breach the defensive perimeter in the Pacific Ocean erected by Japan in the early weeks of 1942. With the Marianas under Allied control, the US would be able to launch expeditions against the Philippines and Japan itself. A lack of naval resources initially delayed the American attack on the islands, but in November 1943, US Admiral Chester W. Nimitz was ready to take the offensive.

The Gilbert Islands assault

Nimitz's first targets were the two tiny coral atolls of Tarawa and Makin in the Gilbert Islands. His total fleet comprised 7 aircraft carriers, 12 battleships, 12 cruisers, and 66 destroyers—more than enough to prevent attacks by the Japanese navy—plus a flotilla of landing craft and other amphibious vehicles developed for Pacific

To **attack Japan**, the USAAF needs **island bases** within bomber range of the nation's home islands.

↓

The nearest air bases to Japan are in the **Mariana Islands and under Japanese control**, as are all the neighboring island groups.

↓

American forces are located far to the south, in New Guinea and the Solomon Islands.

↓

Their best option is to **island-hop and conquer** the Gilberts, Marshalls, and Carolines **to reach their target, the Marianas**.

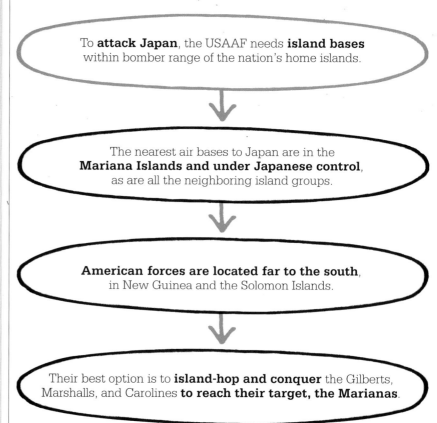

See also: Japan's dilemma 137 ▪ The Japanese attack Pearl Harbor 138–145 ▪ Japanese advances 154–157 ▪ The Battle of Midway 160–165 ▪ Battle for the Solomons and New Guinea 212–213 ▪ The Battle of Leyte Gulf 276 ▪ Japan under siege 304–307

operations. He was ready to attack. Tarawa was defended by fewer than 5,000 Japanese soldiers, but the defenses of the island had been strengthened. On November 20, 18,000 American marines attacked and were met by fierce resistance from Japanese forces. It took the marines four days to seize the atoll, at a cost of more than 1,000 dead and 2,000 wounded. The Japanese fought almost suicidally to the end; only 17 of their men were captured alive. A further 66 American marines died in the simultaneous assault on Makin Atoll, while the navy lost 644 men when the USS *Liscome Bay* escort carrier was sunk by a Japanese submarine. Such losses were a great shock to the Americans and an indication of the carnage to come.

Attacking the Marshalls

With the Gilberts captured, the way was clear to the Marshall Islands. Many were bypassed, and of the seven targeted, the strategic atolls of Kwajalein and Eniwetok were key objectives as both had airfields, and naval and submarine bases. Kwajalein was taken by February 3, 1944, Eniwetok by February 23, and the remaining target islands by the end of the month. Fighting was fierce on both Kwajalein and Eniwetok, but the Americans had learned some lessons from Tarawa, and kept their casualties down to around 450 deaths. The Japanese, however, again fought almost to the last man, losing all but 400 of their combined strength of 12,000 men.

> The capture of Tarawa knocked down the front door to the Japanese defenses in the Central Pacific.
> **Admiral Chester Nimitz**

Operation Hailstone

Further west, a major US naval and aerial assault was launched on February 17–18 against the islands of the Truk atoll in the Caroline Islands. Truk was the main Japanese naval base in the south Pacific and of huge strategic importance. Code named Operation Hailstone, the American attack was highly successful, destroying 15 Japanese naval ships and 32 merchant ships, together with more than 250 Japanese aircraft. Around 4,500 Japanese troops were killed. Of the 40 Americans who died, 29 were aircrew members and the rest were sailors. In contrast to the Marshall and Gilbert islands, where the Americans had proceeded to build military bases, Truk atoll was left to the Japanese after the »

Japanese vessels off Dublon Island, Truk Lagoon, trail clouds of smoke during Operation Hailstorm as USAAF aircraft bombard the heavily fortified Japanese naval base on February 17.

> The entire island [Kwajalein] looked as if it had been picked up to 20,000 feet and then dropped.
> **American soldier**
> **Official US Army Task Force 51 report**

crippling of its naval base and bypassed and isolated as the American forces continued to advance toward their goal—the Mariana Islands.

The Marianas—at a price

Much of the Marianas had been controlled by Japan since World War I, except the island of Guam, which came under US rule in 1898. Japan seized Guam at the same time as its attack on Pearl Harbor in December 1941, heavily fortifying the island, alongside its other key settlements on Saipan and Tinian. Seizing these islands would give the US the crucial bases it needed to bomb the Japanese mainland, and would also cut off Japan from the Philippines and its other gains in southeast Asia.

A Grumman TBF Avenger, the most widely used torpedo bomber of the war, prepares for take-off from USS *Bunker Hill* to launch an aerial attack on Japanese vessels defending Saipan.

The attack on the Marianas began on June 15, 1944, with a marine assault on the west coast of Saipan. By June 27, occupation of the island was complete, except for the far south. A Japanese counterattack began on July 7 but failed to dislodge the American forces. The Japanese surrendered on July 9. Casualties were immense: 3,426 American servicemen died and 10,364 were wounded. For Japan, around 29,000 of a fighting force of 32,000 died, together with 7,000 Japanese civilians on the island and 22,000 local people. But the capture of Saipan now put Japan within range of US B-29 heavy bombers.

The Philippine Sea battle

The American assault on Saipan prompted the Japanese First Mobile Fleet under Admiral Jisaburo Ozawa to sail east across the Philippine Sea toward the Marianas to give battle. The fleet was heavily outnumbered, its five aircraft carriers, 20 main ships, 31 destroyers, 6 oilers, and 24 submarines fighting the larger US Fifth Fleet of 7 aircraft carriers, 36 main ships, 68 destroyers, and 28 submarines. The Japanese could launch around 450 aircraft from its carriers and 300 from its base in Guam against a total of some 900 American carrier-launched aircraft.

> Why, hell, it was just like an old-time turkey shoot down home!
>
> **Pilot from USS *Lexington***
> **describing aerial engagements during the Battle of Philippine Sea**

The battle began on June 19 to the west of the Marianas, with four major Japanese air-raids against US Task Force 58. The raid was intercepted with the loss of two Japanese carriers—the flagship carrier *Taiho* and the *Shokaku*—sunk by submarines, and 200 aircraft downed. By the day's end, the Japanese had lost 300 aircraft and the Americans just 23.

Japanese defeat

The following day, the battle continued farther west, as the US fleet chased the Japanese away from the Marianas. The Japanese carrier *Hiyo* and two oil tankers were sunk, and some 340 aircraft were downed. That day, the Americans lost 110 aircraft, 80 of which ran out of fuel on their return journeys. Facing defeat, Admiral Ozawa retired west to Okinawa. The two-day conflict was the largest carrier battle in history and the last of

American marines wade ashore on the island of Tinian in July 1944. While the northwest had two small beaches and low coral, the coral cliffs of the south had to be scaled with ramps.

the five major carrier-versus-carrier battles that so defined the Pacific naval war.

As a result of their defeat, the Japanese lost 90 percent of their carrier airpower in two days. Of the roughly 450 aircraft with which they had begun the battle, they returned home with only 35; some 200 of their 300 land-based aircraft were also lost. The trained pilots who died in the battle were a further irreplaceable loss to the already outnumbered Japanese fleet air arm. As it had done with its previous losses, the Japanese military concealed its casualties from the Japanese public.

Taking Tinian and Guam

On July 16, American forces began a naval bombardment of Tinian, an island just to the south of Saipan. After mounting a feint attack to the south to mislead the Japanese, marines landed on the northwest of the island on July 24 and took it on August 1. Here, the Japanese lost 5,542 soldiers, and up to 4,000 Japanese civilians died, some of whom took their own lives.

Resistance on Saipan and the naval battle had set back the offensive against Guam by a month. American forces finally landed on two beaches on the island's west coast on July 21 after sustained air and naval bombardments. Although the patrols that moved south met no organized resistance, those advancing toward the Japanese lines in the north, amid rain and thick jungle, were engaged in fierce fighting and endured nightly attack. The Japanese, running out of food and ammunition, finally surrendered on August 10, 1944. Casualties were high, the Japanese suffering 18,337 deaths with 1,250 taken prisoner, and the Americans 1,783 deaths and 6,010 wounded.

Maneggon March

Prior to the American assault, the Japanese forced most of the indigenous Chamorro people to walk to six concentration camps in the south of Guam, on what became known as the Maneggon March. The sick and starving were left to die en route, while Japanese troops massacred another 600 during the march. As many as a tenth of the Chamorro population of 20,000 are thought to have been killed during the Japanese occupation.

From late 1944, Guam became a major air base for bombing attacks against Japan, while Tinian would be the future launching point for the atomic bombs that ended the war. ■

Japanese holdouts

Resisting their official defeat in the Mariana Islands in July and August 1944, some Japanese troops refused to give up. One group held out on Tinian until September 4, 1945, two days after Japan's official surrender. On Saipan, others held out until December 1. On December 8, a further group, in hiding on Guam, ambushed and killed three American marines.

Captain Sakae Oba, the resistance leader on Saipan, was so elusive that the marines nicknamed him "the Fox" and admired him, despite his group's raids to steal the Americans' food or blow up B-29 bombers.

Some resisters held out for many years. Murata Susumu survived on Tinian until 1953, while Private Bunzo Minagawa and Sergeant Masashi Ito surrendered within days of each other in May 1960. Sergeant Shoichi Yokoi was only found by hunters on Guam on January 24, 1972. He had lived alone in a cave for 28 years.

KILL ALL, BURN ALL, LOOT ALL

CHINA AND JAPAN AT WAR (1941–1945)

IN CONTEXT

FOCUS
War in China

BEFORE
1928 Chiang Kai-shek's nationalist Kuomintang government unites most of China under its rule.

1931 Japanese forces occupy Manchuria in northern China.

July 1937 Clashes between Chinese and Japanese troops outside Beijing trigger full-scale war.

1938 After a series of severe defeats, Kuomintang armies withdraw to Chongqing in southwest China.

AFTER
1945–1946 The Japanese surrender is followed by civil war between Chinese nationalists and communists.

October 1949 Victorious in the civil war, communist leader Mao Zedong proclaims the People's Republic of China.

When Japan attacked Pearl Harbor in December 1941, provoking war with the Western powers, its ongoing conflict with China—the Second Sino-Japanese War—became another arena of World War II. Although victories in 1937–1938 had left the Japanese in control of China's major cities and economic resources, opposition came from two sources: Chiang Kai-shek's nationalist Kuomintang government in the remote southwest, and the communists based at Yan'an in rural Shaanxi province. Seeking to

See also: China in turmoil 42–43 ▪ Japan on the march 44–45 ▪ Japanese advances 154–157 ▪ The Allies fight back in Burma 290–293 ▪ Japan surrenders 312–313 ▪ Aftermath 320–327

stabilize their occupation, from 1940 the Japanese established several puppet Chinese regimes, the most ambitious headed by Wang Jingwei in Nanjing. However, none of these ever won recognition from the Chinese people as legitimate governments. Although Japan succeeded in exploiting some of China's economic potential, the need to maintain a very large military presence imposed a severe strain on Japanese resources.

Even before Pearl Harbor, the United States had openly sided with China in its struggle against Japanese occupation. And once it found itself at war with Japan, the United States enthusiastically embraced China as an ally. Military aid was sent to the Kuomintang government in Chongqing, and American propagandists hailed China as one of the major Allied powers. American General Joseph Stilwell was sent to liaise with Chiang Kai-shek.

Chinese response

American relations with the Chinese nationalists were flawed by a fundamental conflict of interests. While the United States wanted to use the Kuomintang's nationalist National Revolutionary Army (NRA) to help win its war against Japan, Chiang preferred to let the Americans defeat Japan and preserve his own forces so he could gain control of China after the war. In contrast to Chiang's inactivity, Mao Zedong's communists actively pursued guerrilla warfare against the Japanese in northern China while extending their political support among the rural population, equally with an eye to winning control of the country after Japan had been defeated.

"Three Alls" policy

From 1941 through to spring 1944, Japanese occupation forces made no serious effort to attack the Chinese nationalist army, apart from a failed assault on Changsha in early 1942. Their major operations were punitive campaigns targeting Chinese civilians. Across a swathe of northern China, from Hebei and Shandong on the coast to inland Shaanxi, the Japanese conducted the brutal "Three Alls" policy ("Kill All, Burn All, Loot All"), designed to crush the communist guerrilla movement. They laid waste to rural areas that supported the guerrillas. In their brutal campaign of burning villages, destroying crops, and killing or forcibly relocating the population, Japanese troops are reckoned to have killed almost 3 million Chinese civilians.

The Japanese launched another ruthless operation, the Zhejiang-Jiangxi campaign, in the aftermath of the Doolittle Raid on Tokyo by American bombers in April 1942. »

Japanese troops march through Saigon. By occupying Vietnam, Japan hoped to close China's southern border and cut off supplies of weapons and materials to the Kuomintang.

Some of the bomber crews landed in Zhejiang and Jiangxi provinces in eastern China. As punishment for aid given by Chinese civilians to these airmen, the Japanese sent an army to devastate the region. Chinese estimates put the death toll at 250,000. In this operation and in their counterinsurgency in northern China, the Japanese employed biological warfare, releasing fleas infected with bubonic plague bacilli, as well as spreading cholera and typhoid.

Supply routes

United States support for the Chinese nationalists was restricted by the Japanese conquest of Burma in spring 1942, which cut the Burma Road, the only land link to nationalist Chongqing. Following this, all US supplies had to be flown in by transport aircraft via a hazardous route from British India over the Himalayas. Under Joseph Stilwell's direction, NRA troops trained in India were used to combat the Japanese in Burma while a new road was built through difficult terrain to link India and China. Stilwell developed an acrimonious relationship with both Chiang Kai-shek and the US air commander in the region, Colonel Claire Chennault. This friction did nothing to help operations, especially as the three men had different priorities. Chennault was pressing for the establishment of air bases in nationalist-controlled areas of China; Stilwell focussed primarily on Burma; and Chiang was trying to impose his authority on Xinjiang in western China, which had become a client state of the Soviet Union. None of them reacted adequately when the Japanese launched a new offensive in spring 1944.

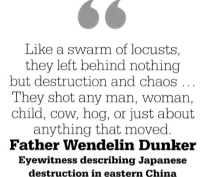

US planes drop supplies for Chinese nationalist forces. Air drops of military supplies and fuel were needed after the overland route through Burma was cut by the Japanese.

> Like a swarm of locusts, they left behind nothing but destruction and chaos … They shot any man, woman, child, cow, hog, or just about anything that moved.
>
> **Father Wendelin Dunker**
> **Eyewitness describing Japanese destruction in eastern China**

Operation Ichi-Go

The largest Japanese military campaign of the war, Operation Ichi-Go aimed to seize large areas of central and southeast China that it had previously not occupied. The primary goal was to establish a continuous north–south rail route across China, linking northern ports with southeast Asia. This had become urgent since US submarines had made the sea route along the Chinese coast almost unusable. Ichi-Go was also designed to overrun the US air bases that Chennault had established. These were used to raid Taiwan and, with the arrival of new long-range B-29 bombers in June 1944, were able to target the Japanese mainland.

Involving more than 600,000 Japanese troops, the Ichi-Go offensive began with an attack on landlocked Hunan province in May, rapidly capturing the provincial capital Changsha. The Japanese then thrust south into Guangxi and Guizhou provinces, seizing air bases at Guilin and Liuzhou, and threatening Chongqing itself. The practical impact of Operation Ichi-Go was limited. The United States established new air bases further east and, in any case, began bombing mainland Japan from the Marianas Islands.

Tarnished image

The poor performance of Chinese nationalist troops in the fighting had a critical impact on the standing of the Kuomintang regime. Chiang Kai-shek had risen to be a lauded hero in America. In November 1943, he attended a summit conference with Roosevelt and Churchill in Cairo. But the spectacle of NRA soldiers in headlong retreat from Hunan, an event reported by American journalists, severely tarnished Chiang's image. Starving Chinese peasants harassed NRA conscripts, themselves often ragged and barefoot, whom they regarded with hostility after years of extortion and oppression. Reports of the corruption and incompetence of senior NRA officers led to calls for a withdrawal of US aid. In October 1944, Roosevelt made the difficult decision to continue his support for Chiang; he also removed Chiang's bitterest critic, Stilwell. However, the Kuomintang leader would never fully recover his status in American eyes.

The Americans tentatively explored the idea of backing the Chinese communists, who by 1945 were reaping the benefits of years of tough fighting and ruthless political action. Their influence over the rural population of northern China had grown enormously, and 95 million people lived in their "liberated areas." Their guerrilla armies, largely equipped with captured Japanese weaponry, could field some 900,000 troops. Although some suggested arming and training the communists, US hostility to their ideology—and Chiang's bitter opposition—meant this would never happen.

Japanese surrender

In early 1945, Kuomintang forces began to perform better, but this tentative revival was cut short by the sudden Japanese surrender in August of that year. Despite its vast cost in human lives, the fighting in the Chinese theater was revealed to have been a sideshow. It was the war in the Pacific and in Japan itself that determined the latter's fate. More than 2 million Japanese soldiers who were still occupying Chinese territory laid down their arms because of events elsewhere.

The end of the conflict with Japan did not bring peace to war-ravaged China. While the US ferried Kuomintang forces around China to accept the Japanese surrender in major cities, the communists took advantage of the support of the USSR, which had occupied Manchuria in the final days of the war. Allowed to establish themselves in secure Manchurian bases, armed with equipment surrendered by the Japanese to the Soviet occupiers, the Chinese communists were able to shift from guerrilla warfare to full-scale conventional military operations against the NRA. The scene was set for the Chinese Civil War. ■

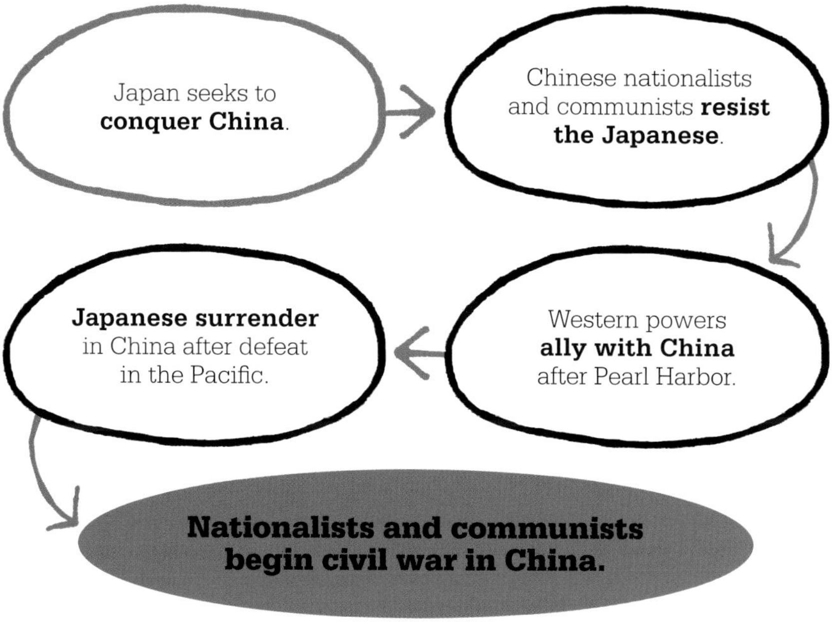
Japan seeks to **conquer China**.
Chinese nationalists and communists **resist the Japanese**.
Western powers **ally with China** after Pearl Harbor.
Japanese surrender in China after defeat in the Pacific.
Nationalists and communists begin civil war in China.

Chiang Kai-shek (1887–1975)

Born in Zhejiang province in 1887, Chiang Kai-shek emerged as a prominent member of Sun Yat-sen's nationalist Kuomintang regime in Guangzhou in the 1920s. He founded the Whampoa Military Academy, which trained officers for the nationalist NRA. After Sun Yat-sen's death in 1925, he assumed leadership of the Kuomintang.

In a series of successful campaigns against regional warlords, Chiang extended nationalist rule into northern China, taking Beijing in 1928, but his efforts to eradicate the Chinese communists failed. Despite military defeats, the war with Japan from 1937 increased Chiang's prestige abroad. By 1943, he was being treated as one of the "big four" Allied war leaders. Soon, however, the corruption and military incompetence of his regime alienated foreign opinion, as well as support within China. Defeated by Mao Zedong's communists in the Chinese Civil War, in 1949 he was forced to flee with his followers to Taiwan, which he ruled until his death in 1975.

ROME IS MORE THAN A MILITARY OBJECTIVE

THE FALL OF ROME (JUNE 1944)

IN CONTEXT

FOCUS
The Mediterranean front

BEFORE
Sixth century CE Benedict of Nursia founds a monastery on Monte Cassino.

September 1943 German forces occupy northern Italy after it surrenders to the Allies.

October 13, 1943 Liberated Italy declares war on Germany.

December 1943 Eisenhower signs the Protection of Cultural Property Order to protect cultural sites from attack.

AFTER
August 1944 The Allies invade southern France, capturing the ports of Toulon and Marseille.

April–May 1945 As part of the Spring Offensive, the 15th Allied Army Group penetrates the Gothic Line, leading to the defeat of German forces in Italy.

When Italy surrendered to the Allies in September 1943, the country was divided between German forces in the northern and central regions (including Rome) and Allied forces in the south. The Allied advance north was halted by the Gustav Line, a network of German defenses masterminded by Field Marshal Albert Kesselring. Attempting to outflank this line, the US 36th and 45th infantry divisions landed at Anzio, 30 miles (51 km) south of Rome, on January 25, 1944, but they failed to move on rapidly.

Monte Cassino

In February, the Allies became bogged down at Monte Cassino, inland from Anzio. In the belief that it was a German command post, and claiming "military necessity," they bombed the monastery above the town—a mistake that damaged their reputation. After failed British and Indian attacks on Monte Cassino, Polish troops finally captured it on May 18 after months of fierce German resistance.

The spring thaw allowed the Allies to advance, and on June 4, 1944, the US Fifth Army, supported by British and Canadian troops, liberated Rome. Kesselring retreated to the northern Apennines to establish a 200-mile (322-km) defensive position, known as the Gothic Line. In difficult terrain, Field Marshal Harold Alexander's Allied forces faced a desperate enemy, but they had started down the road to victory. ■

> The most grueling, the most harrowing, and in one aspect the most tragic of any phase of the war in Italy.
>
> **General Mark Clark**
> **on the battle for Monte Cassino**

See also: Italy enters the war 88–89 ▪ North Africa and the Mediterranean 118–121 ▪ Operation Torch 196–197 ▪ The invasion of Italy 210–211

OVERPAID, OVERSEXED, AND OVER HERE

US TROOPS IN BRITAIN (1942–1945)

IN CONTEXT

FOCUS
GIs in the UK

BEFORE
December 1940 President Roosevelt proposes the Lend-Lease initiative to assist the UK's war effort.

December 8, 1941 The US declares war on Japan. A few days later, Germany declares war on the US.

February 1942 In the US, the *Pittsburgh Courier* launches the Double V Campaign, urging Black servicemen to seek victory in war—and in the fight against discrimination at home.

AFTER
May 1945 By the end of the war in Europe, there are more than 200 US air bases in Britain, each housing around 2,500 US personnel—several times the population of most British villages.

Once America had entered the war in December 1941, it did not take long for US troops to arrive in Britain in order to support Allied operations in Europe. Between January 1942 and December 1945, about 1.5 million US troops spent time in Britain.

Each serviceman, known as a GI, was given "Instructions for American Servicemen in Britain," a pamphlet that introduced them to British life, including Britain's history, culture, and even its slang.

The people of Britain received a culture lesson in return, in the form of Coca-Cola, candy, nylon, jazz, and free-flowing cash. GIs were paid up to five times more than their British counterparts, and their generosity was renowned. Around 70,000 British women became GI brides, and thousands of babies fathered by GIs were born out of wedlock.

A US soldier hands out candy to a group of children in London's East End. With food strictly rationed in Britain, treats from the GIs were welcomed.

Black GIs

The US forces in Britain included around 150,000 Black Americans, who served in Black-only units, initially mainly in service roles, reflecting the racial segregation and discrimination that was still rampant in the US at this time.

Black American servicemen were generally welcomed into British pubs and homes. This often antagonized white GIs. In June 1943, violence broke out between white and Black GIs in the Lancashire village of Bamber Bridge after local pub owners refused a US military police request to segregate their establishments. ■

See also: The end of US neutrality 108 ▪ The Japanese attack Pearl Harbor 138–145 ▪ America at war 146–153 ▪ Bombing of Germany 220–223

THE TIDE HAS TURNED

THE D-DAY LANDINGS (JUNE 6, 1944)

IN CONTEXT

FOCUS
Liberation of France

BEFORE
May 26–June 4, 1940
Hundreds of naval and civilian vessels evacuate more than 338,000 Allied soldiers from the French port of Dunkirk.

June 25, 1940 France formally surrenders to Germany. Fifteen days later, the Nazis establish Vichy France, a puppet government headed by Marshal Philippe Pétain.

November 8–16, 1942 The Allies invade French North Africa in Operation Torch.

AFTER
August 15, 1944 The Allies launch Operation Dragoon, their successful invasion of southern France.

August 25 French and US troops liberate Paris after four years of German occupation.

Before 1944, the Allies were divided as to the wisdom of opening a second front in Europe. Stalin was eager for this, as it would relieve pressure on the Red Army. The US was also keen, and in early 1942 developed Operation Roundup, a plan to invade France in spring 1943 (it even considered bringing the date forward to fall 1942). However, the British were reluctant. Churchill remembered the failure of the Gallipoli Campaign, in World War I, and was aware of the perils of a seaborne invasion. Believing the Western Allies were not yet ready, the British proposed first focusing on North Africa and the Mediterranean.

The British view prevailed and in November 1942, British and US troops launched Operation Torch, the invasion of French North Africa.

Operation Overlord

In May 1943, Roosevelt and Churchill met at the Third Washington Conference and decided to invade France 12 months later. The planned invasion was confirmed at the Tehran Conference, attended by Stalin, at the end of November. It was code named Operation Overlord.

> Unless we can go and land and fight Hitler and beat his forces on land, we shall never win this war.
> **Winston Churchill**

The newly established Supreme Headquarters Allied Expeditionary Force, led by Dwight Eisenhower, coordinated the planned invasion. It rejected the idea of invading the Calais region; even though the area was closest to Britain, it was heavily fortified. They decided to invade Normandy, which was farther away, but more lightly defended.

The sea crossing, landings, and establishment of beachheads were code named Operation Neptune. It was envisaged that the invasion would be preceded by an aerial and naval bombardment and consist of seaborne troops landing on five

Dwight Eisenhower

Born in Denison, Texas, in 1890, and a graduate of the US Military Academy at West Point, New York, Dwight Eisenhower served in the US Army from 1915. He was made commander of American troops in Europe in June 1942 and led the Allied invasions of North Africa and Sicily before commanding the Normandy landings.

Possessing sound strategic vision and organizational skills, Eisenhower was able to balance the different personalities of the other Allied military leaders, as well as navigating the logistical and political difficulties of such a vast and complex enterprise. Following the success of the Battle of Normandy, he led the Allies in the liberation of the rest of France and western Europe.

After Germany's surrender in May 1945, Eisenhower governed the American occupation zone in Germany for six months, and later became the first supreme commander of NATO from 1951–1952, building relationships across western Europe.

Eisenhower went on to serve as US president from 1953–1961, winning two landslide election victories. He died in 1969.

See also: The fall of France 80–87 ▪ Allied summits 225 ▪ V-weapons 264–265 ▪ The Allies sweep eastward 272–273 ▪ Operation Market Garden 274 ▪ Battles at the border 275

A series of Allied operations seeks to mislead the German high command about the time and place of the D-Day landings.

Diplomatic meetings are held to make Germany believe that the **Allies are about to invade Norway**.

A **General Montgomery look-alike** is flown to North Africa in May 1944 to suggest that **no invasion is imminent**.

Fake army groups are created in Britain, apparently **poised to invade Norway and the Calais region**.

The Allies **disseminate rumors** that they will **attack in Greece and the Balkans**.

An invasion fleet is sent toward **Genoa** in Italy, **fooling Germany** into believing that a **major operation is likely** around there.

beaches (code named Sword, Juno, Gold, Omaha, and Utah) along an 50-mile (80-km) stretch of coastline. Airborne troops would then land on their left and right flanks.

Preparations for Operation Overlord were exhaustive. The proposed date, D-Day, was pushed back to June 1944 to allow more time to build up stocks of landing craft. Huge efforts were made to gather information about Normandy. Around 16,500 homing pigeons carrying questionnaires for local people to fill out were dropped over France (only 12 percent of the pigeons returned; many of them were shot down by German snipers). The Allies also collected millions of postcards and tourist photographs of potential landing sites in order to gain a clear understanding of the topography. These were supplemented by reports from the French resistance and aerial reconnaissance.

Meanwhile, British intelligence planted misinformation about the invasion. A string of deception operations, collectively code named Operation Bodyguard, misled German leaders, particularly Hitler, into thinking Normandy was a feint and that the Allies would invade elsewhere. Consequently, the Germans spread their defenses thinly, keeping thousands of their troops in Norway, Greece, and the Balkans.

Ingenious inventions

The Allies developed new technology and equipment in preparation for D-Day. The »

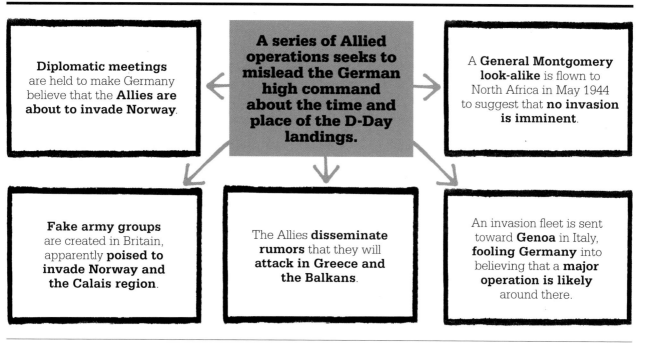

US forces rehearse the landings on an English beach. At one point, the exercise caught the attention of German fast attack craft, leading to frantic efforts to repel them—and Allied casualties.

Canadian army tanks lie wrecked and abandoned on Dieppe beach after the failure of Operation Jubilee in August 1942.

The Dieppe Raid

Before D-Day, another, more limited, Allied operation took place in northern France: a raid on the port city of Dieppe. Code named Operation Jubilee, its purpose was to gauge the difficulty of a cross-Channel invasion. The Allies planned to land troops in Dieppe, destroy its harbor and defenses, gather intelligence, and then evacuate.

The Dieppe Raid was launched on August 19, 1942, with around 5,000 Canadian soldiers, plus 1,000 British commandos and 50 US Army Rangers. Following an ineffective naval bombardment, Allied troops began to land at 6:20 am. The German garrison had received warning of a possible attack and rained machine gun fire on the infantry as they landed. Allied tanks were held up by the soft sand and concrete obstacles.

The order to withdraw was given less than five hours after the landing. The operation had achieved almost none of its objectives, and 3,642 Allied soldiers were killed, captured, or wounded.

"swimming tank," which could be launched near the shore and landed on the beach, had an inflatable canvas screen to make it buoyant and propellers on the rear, enabling it to move at 4 mph (6.4 km/h). The British also added long-range flamethrowers, mortars, and mine-clearing devices to regular tanks, and developed armored bulldozers.

A major logistical problem was how to fuel these, and other, Allied vehicles. Through Operation Pluto (which stood for "Pipeline Under the Ocean"), British engineers modified underwater telegraph cables to deliver fuel. Once deployed in Normandy, they could pump 8,800 tons of oil per day. Even more important was the "Mulberry," a prefabricated, portable harbor that could be towed across the English Channel and assembled. This would allow the Allies to unload cargo without having to capture a port first. The Allies planned to establish two Mulberry harbors, at Omaha and Gold beaches.

German defenses

Field Marshal Gerd von Rundstedt had commanded German forces in the west since March 1942. He had served on the Eastern Front until Hitler had relieved him of his command for allowing a withdrawal in the face of a Soviet advance. By 1944, Rundstedt had only 850,000 men to call on. Believing it was impossible to stop an Allied landing, he made the decision to concentrate his forces inland, so they could counterattack if an invasion did take place.

Beach fortifications

The main German coastal defense was the Atlantic Wall, a series of fortifications extending for around 2,000 miles (3,200 km) from western France to Norway. Construction of the "wall" had started in 1942, and in November 1943 Field Marshal Erwin Rommel was charged with strengthening the defense system.

Rommel was at odds with Rundstedt, as he believed the best way to defeat the Allies was to concentrate forces on the coast, preventing them from securing a beachhead. Rommel had set about improving coastal defenses by adding thousands of concrete strongpoints and had millions of mines laid offshore and in coastal areas. To disrupt the passage of tanks and aerial landings, he set up obstacles and traps on beaches and in coastal fields.

Sea crossing

Eisenhower had earmarked June 5 for the D-Day landings, but on the previous day he was warned of high winds and overcast conditions, which would disrupt aerial and naval operations. He therefore postponed the invasion for 24 hours.

Allied ships began leaving from various points along England's coast at 9 am on June 5. The crossing took 17 hours. Shipping an invasion force

> "Our only possible chance will be at the beaches – that's where the enemy is always weakest."
> **Erwin Rommel**

of more than 150,000 men across the English Channel was a huge logistical challenge. The landings, the largest seaborne invasion ever, required nearly 7,000 ships. Airborne Allied forces began to land in Normandy just after midnight. Some parachuted down, while others landed in gliders that had been towed and released by aircraft. British and Canadian airborne forces landed to the east of Sword Beach, near the city of Caen, while US forces arrived to the west of Utah Beach, in the southern part of the Cotentin Peninsula.

Airborne successes

Bad weather and antiaircraft fire disrupted the landings, scattering paratroopers and gliders. Despite this, airborne operations were mostly successful. The British and Canadians severely damaged a major German gun battery and captured two strategically vital bridges. US airborne forces faced greater difficulties but achieved many of their objectives, such as capturing the town of Sainte-Mère-Église, on the main road between Cherbourg and Paris.

Britain's RAF conducted another deception—Operation Titanic. From 2 am on June 6, they parachuted 500 dummies over Normandy, joined by British commandos who were ordered to briefly engage Germans and use amplifiers to play recordings of gunfire and shouted orders. This diverted German forces away from the real landing zones and made them waste time searching for nonexistent soldiers. Before the beach landings, the Allies also bombarded German defenses and fortifications along the Normandy coast. Starting at midnight, Allied aircraft dropped 7.2 million tons of bombs on D-Day, but cloud cover meant many fell wide of their targets. At around 5:45 am, the naval bombardment commenced. Thousands of shells and rockets rained down on fortifications but the results were mixed. When the Allied landings began, many German defensive positions were still intact.

The landings begin

At 6:30 am on June 6, US forces landed on Utah and Omaha beaches, the first Allied forces to come ashore. At Utah, little went to plan initially. Many infantry and swimming tanks failed to keep to the planned schedule or landed off course. Despite this, they rallied and regrouped, and by 9 am had begun to push off the beach. By the end of the day, they had advanced 4 miles (6.4 km) inland.

The situation at Omaha was more chaotic. Rough seas and high winds, compounded by navigational errors, resulted in only 2 out of 29 swimming tanks making it ashore. Without their support, the US infantry faced high casualties at the hands of the entrenched Germans firing from the cliffs. Many units were scattered and leaderless, and officers considered a withdrawal from Omaha. However, by noon, the Americans had fought their way off the beach, and by the end of D-Day had advanced 1 mile (1.6 km) inland.

British forces commenced their landing at Gold Beach at 7:25 am on June 6. The preliminary bombardment had succeeded in neutralizing many of the German defenses. With infantry and armor working closely together, by mid-afternoon the British had established a substantial beachhead and advanced 2 miles (3.2 km) inland.

On Juno Beach, the Canadians began landing at 7:50 am; none of the German positions there »

A US landing craft approaches Omaha Beach, where some 3,000 US troops were killed or wounded. Some of them drowned in the strong swell, weighed down by heavy equipment.

had been seriously damaged by the preliminary bombardment, and rough seas delayed the swimming tanks. Suffering heavy casualties, the Canadians fought their way up and off the beach, managing to link up with British forces from Gold Beach. By midnight the Canadians had advanced 6 miles (10 km) in some places.

The first wave of British troops landed at Sword Beach at 7:25 am. Their objective was to win the high ground above Caen and perhaps even assault the city itself. The British secured the beach in just over an hour and began advancing inland. At 4 pm, German Panzers and infantry counterattacked, pushing some British forces back to the beach. However, by 9 pm, the only major counterattack of D-Day had been defeated and the Germans had been forced to withdraw. Although congestion and German resistance prevented an advance on Caen, the British had still established a beachhead.

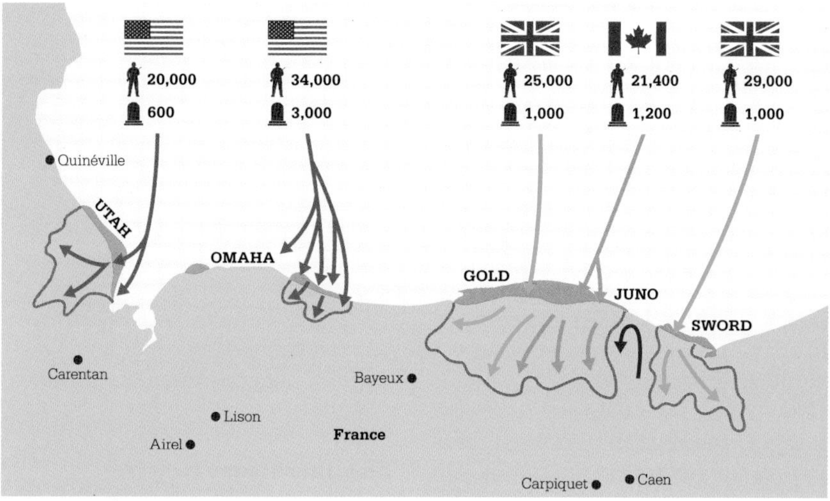

Five beaches, code named Sword, Juno, Gold, Omaha, and Utah, were targeted during the D-Day landings. The first task for troops after landing on each beach was to secure and reinforce a beachhead—a stronghold from which attacks could be launched. The second task was to link the five beachheads.

German confusion

The German response to the Normandy landings was confused. Rommel, who would have been central to any counterattack, had returned to Germany to celebrate his wife's birthday. Rundstedt struggled to impose his authority. The scale of the airborne landings in Normandy convinced him it was the main invasion site, and at 4 am he tried to order armored reserves to the area. He was told that only Hitler had the authority to do this, and the Führer was asleep and not to be disturbed. Hitler did not rise until noon, by which time the Allies were already establishing a beachhead. While the Normandy landings were taking place, French resistance and British commandos disrupted the German counterattack. They cut railroad lines to hamper the arrival of German reinforcements, and RAF bombers dropped aluminum strips over the sea north of the invasion site, creating the illusion on German radar of an entire fleet.

Immediate objectives

By the end of D-Day, the Allies had landed 156,000 soldiers. One major objective was to take Caen. After bombing the city to rubble for two

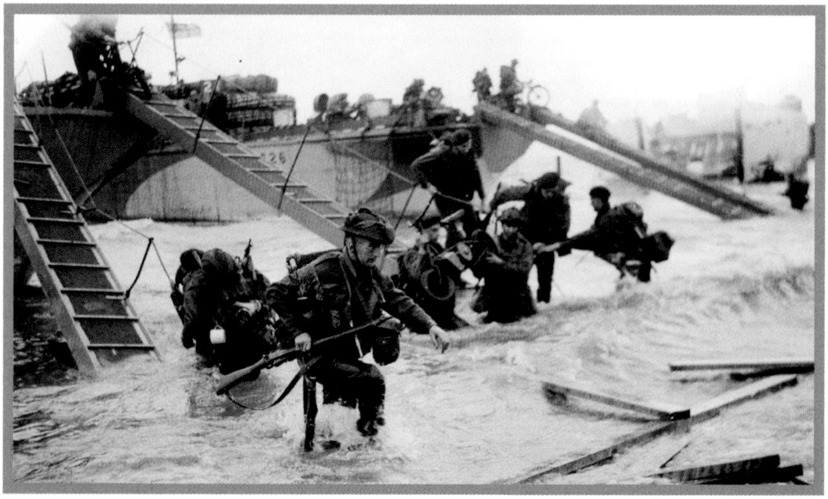

Landing on Juno Beach are British commandos from the 48th Royal Marines. Their allotted objective was to take and hold the flanks of the beach to allow other troops to advance.

days, killing 2,000 civilians, British forces tried to capture it on June 7, but were pushed back.

On June 9, the Allies began building Mulberry harbors at Saint-Laurent-sur-Mer on Omaha Beach and Arromanches on Gold Beach. Although the former was wrecked by a storm, the other was completed. Known as "Port Winston," it was used for 10 months to land 2.5 million men, 500,000 vehicles, and 4 million tons of supplies. On June 12, American troops captured the town of Carentan on the Cotentin Peninsula, connecting all the Allied beachheads for the first time.

The Battle of Normandy

Hitler flew to France on June 16 and held a conference with his generals outside Paris the next day. He tore into Rundstedt and Rommel, blaming them for the Allied advances. They warned him that the German position in Normandy was untenable and asked to withdraw east to form a defensive line. Hitler flatly refused. During the second half of June, the Allies made steady progress through Normandy. On June 22, the Americans attacked Cherbourg, capturing the city after eight days.

> Normandy had been a shattering experience for us. We hadn't realized the Germans were quite that good, even though they had nothing like what we had.
>
> **Interview with a British Army company commander**

Equipment and supplies are unloaded from naval vessels following the D-Day landings. It was vital for the Allies to reinforce their advantage as quickly as possible.

However, Allied hopes of using its port were dashed when they saw that the Germans had dumped masonry into the waters around it. In July, the Allies captured Caen and advanced into the interior of Normandy. Much of the fighting took place amidst the bocage, dense hedgerows 15 ft (4.5 m) high in places, which hampered movement, especially of tanks.

By mid-July, the Americans had captured the town of Saint-Lô, which they used as the launch-point of Operation Cobra, an advance southwest toward Brittany. Operation Cobra lasted from July 25–31 and was a total success for the Allies. With the help of a British attack that tied down German forces, the Americans advanced 40 miles (64 km) and broke out of the bocage and into Brittany.

Counteroffensive

Despite being warned that the position in Normandy was hopeless, Hitler ordered a major counteroffensive, code named Operation Liège. The attack on American positions near the town of Mortain was launched on August 7. The Allies, who had intercepted and decoded orders for the attack, quickly gained aerial supremacy in the area. The next day, the Germans were outflanked to the north by Canadian and Free Polish forces and to the south by US troops.

By August 13, Operation Liège had failed, leaving 80,000 German soldiers trapped in a pocket around the town of Falaise. There was a small exit from the Falaise Pocket through which 20,000 Germans escaped before it was closed by the Allies, now joined by Free French troops, on August 21.

Victory at Falaise essentially ended the Battle of Normandy, although the final German forces did not retreat until August 30. Operation Overlord had been a triumph. Normandy had been liberated, and the Allies were poised to advance into occupied Europe. ■

DAWN BROUGHT NO RELIEF, AND CLOUD NO COMFORT

V-WEAPONS (JUNE 1944–MARCH 1945)

IN CONTEXT

FOCUS
Weapons and warfare

BEFORE
September 1940–May 1941 Germany directs an intensive bombing campaign against Britain's infrastructure and urban areas, targeting historic towns and cities a year later.

March–December 1943 The RAF and US Air Force bomb Germany by day and by night.

AFTER
August 6, 1945 The first atom bomb ever used in warfare is detonated by Allied forces over Hiroshima, Japan.

August 21, 1957 The USSR successfully launches the first intercontinental ballistic rocket, the R-7, influenced by the German V-2.

July 16, 1969 Apollo 11 is launched by a rocket designed by German missile engineer Wernher von Braun and lands on the moon four days later.

Germany deploys "reprisal weapons," seeking **to avenge** heavy bombing raids carried out by the Allies.

The missiles often **fail to hit their targets** as a result of malfunction or interception, but **their innovative technology is admired**.

So late in the war, **the weapons have little impact** on its outcome, but many of **the scientists** who devised them go on to **work as aerospace engineers** in the United States.

In 1944, as German cities faced further devastating aerial bombardment from the Allies, in retaliation, the Nazi leadership deployed their *Vergeltungswaffen* ("reprisal weapons"), designed to inflict maximum damage.

Deploying the V-weapons

The two principal V-weapons, as they were commonly known, were a jet-powered flying bomb and a long-range ballistic missile—the V-1 and V-2. They were developed at the Peenemünde research center on the Baltic Sea island of Usedom. The first V-1 was fired at London on June 13, 1944. Reaching speeds of up to 400 mph (644 km/h), it carried some 2,000 lb (900 kg) of explosives. Its engine's buzzing, droning sound earned it the nickname in Britain of the "doodlebug." Nearly 10,000 V-1s were fired at London and targets in Belgium, killing around 6,000 people, but fewer than a quarter of them reached their targets. Some suffered technical or navigational

See also: The Blitz 98–99 ▪ Bombing of Germany 220–223 ▪ Germany's war industry 224 ▪ The destruction of German cities 287 ▪ The Soviets push into Germany 288–289 ▪ The bombing of Hiroshima and Nagasaki 308–311

Wernher von Braun

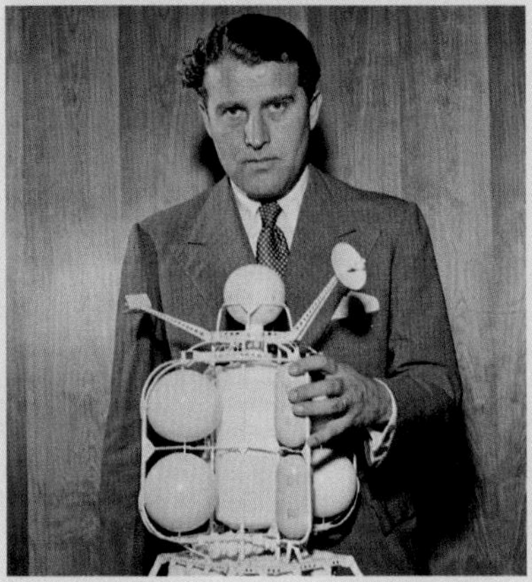

Born into a rich, aristocratic family in 1912, Wernher von Braun was enthused by space and astronomy at a young age. When he received his doctorate in physics in 1934, he was already involved in Germany's experimental rocketry program. In 1937, Braun was named technical director of the newly founded research and testing facility at Peenemünde, where he was central to the development of the V-2 rocket.

A member of both the Nazi Party and the *Schutzstaffel* (SS), Braun claimed to have joined both only because it was politically expedient to do so and claimed he was never an enthusiastic follower of Hitler.

In May 1945, Braun and many of his team surrendered to the Americans. As part of the secret scheme Operation Paperclip, they were moved to the US to develop its rocket technology. Braun worked for the US Army's ballistic missile program and became an American citizen in 1955. In 1960, he was transferred to NASA and played a major role in the success of the American space program. He died in 1977 in Alexandria, Virginia.

problems, while Allied antiaircraft guns, barrage balloons, and fighter planes brought down hundreds more.

Largely developed by engineer Wernher von Braun, the V-2 had its test launch in 1942. It had a range of 200 miles (322 km), and could reach an altitude of 50 miles (80 km) and a top speed of 3,580 mph (5,760 km/h). On September 6, 1944, the first V-2s struck Paris, then London two days later. They were directed against targets in Belgium, the Netherlands, and even Germany, in the bid to slow Allied advances.

Too little, too late

Over 1,000 V-2s were fired, causing 5,000 civilian deaths; more than twice as many concentration and forced-labor camp inmates died while manufacturing them. To seek out and destroy their production and launch sites, the Allies launched Operation Crossbow and, by March 1945, they had captured all the launch-sites for the V-1s and V-2s in northern France, Belgium, the Netherlands, and Luxembourg.

The V-weapons were two of several *Wunderwaffen* ("wonder weapons") the Nazis developed and deployed in an attempt to turn the course of the conflict. Innovative as the weapons were, however, they cost Germany dearly for relatively little gain. After World War II, the Americans estimated that, with the resources devoted to their production, the Germans could have built 24,000 conventional aircraft.

Another of the *Wunderwaffen* was the Messerschmitt Me-262 "Swallow," the first-ever operational jet-powered fighter aircraft, with a top speed of 540 mph (870 km/h). Due to production delays, it was not used until August 1944. The same year, the Messerschmitt Me-163 "Comet," a rocket-powered fighter plane that could reach speeds of over 596 mph (960 km/h) made its debut. Both arrived too late and in too few numbers to have a major impact on the course of the war. At its end, however, all the Allies vied to secure the brilliant minds behind *Wunderwaffen* technology. ■

The V-1 flying bomb was launched initially from a ramp and later from specially adapted bomber aircraft. It was guided by an automatic navigation system within the body of the missile.

THE ROAD OF REVENGE!

OPERATION BAGRATION (JUNE–AUGUST 1944)

IN CONTEXT

FOCUS
Soviet strategy

BEFORE
July–August 1943 Repelling a German attack, the Red Army is victorious at the Battle of Kursk in the USSR.

November 1943 A Red Army offensive leads to the liberation of Kiev, Ukraine.

AFTER
October 1944 The Warsaw Uprising against Germany, led by the Polish underground resistance, is defeated.

September–November 1944 The Red Army launches successful offensives in the Baltic and Balkans.

February 13, 1945 The Soviet assault on Budapest ends in victory, and the fall of Hungary's pro-Nazi regime.

Following their devastating defeat at the Battle of Kursk in the summer of 1943, the Germans were unable to launch a concerted offensive on the Eastern Front. Lacking resources, they could only hold a defensive line against the advancing Red Army. During the fall and winter of 1943–1944, the Soviets forced the Germans out of most of Ukraine, and gained control of Crimea in spring 1944, after a month-long campaign.

Strategic deception

On May 1, 1944, Stalin and his Red Army commanders began to plan a summer offensive. As the most direct route to Germany was

See also: Operation Barbarossa 124–131 ▪ The Great Patriotic War 132–135 ▪ The Battle of Stalingrad 178–183 ▪ The Soviets push into Germany 288–289

Significant losses force the **Germans to adopt a defensive strategy** on the Eastern Front.

↓

Soviet leaders covertly **amass troops for an attack on German forces** through Belorussia.

↓

Germany, stretched by Allied advances in the west, is **unable to hold back the Red Army assault**.

↓

Soviet forces **drive the Germans out** of Belorussia and Romania, and **advance into** both **Poland** and **the Balkans**.

↓

The future dominance of the USSR in central and eastern Europe is established.

through western Ukraine and Poland, Hitler and his generals anticipated an attack on the city of Lvov (now Lviv, Ukraine). The Soviet leaders, however, were planning a massed frontal assault through Belorussia (present-day Belarus), where the German position was surrounded on three sides by Soviet territory. Supervised by Marshals Georgy Zhukov and Aleksandr Vasilevsky, the plan was approved on May 30 and was code named Operation Bagration after Pyotr Bagration, a distinguished Russian general in the Napoleonic wars.

The Soviets initiated an elaborate program to disguise their intentions. Soldiers were moved to their staging areas at night, and concentrated in woodland to minimize the risk of detection. Soviet aircraft patrols were increased to deter or destroy any Luftwaffe reconnaissance missions. The Red Army units involved in Operation Bagration were moved to the frontline only one or two nights before the attack, and had to observe radio silence and use camouflage. As a final touch, the Red Army reinforced the frontline »

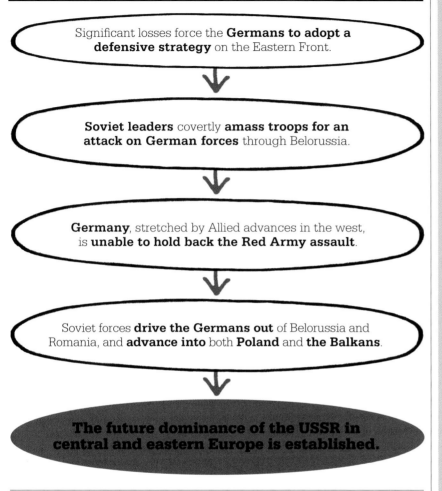

Georgy Zhukov

Born in 1896 into a peasant family in Kaluga, western Russia, Georgy Zhukov was conscripted into the Imperial Russian Army in 1915 and served with distinction in World War I. He joined the Bolshevik Party in 1917, and fought with the Red Army cavalry in the Russian Civil War (1918–1920). By 1939, he was head of Soviet forces in Manchuria and led them to victory against Japan. In 1941, he was made chief of staff of the Red Army. Though fired in the aftermath of Operation Barbarossa, he remained influential, overseeing the defense of Stalingrad and subsequent counteroffensives.

Promoted to marshal in 1943, Zhukov helped win the victory at Kursk, coordinated Soviet forces for Operation Bagration, then commanded the First Belorussian Front. In 1945, he led the final assault on Berlin.

After World War II, Zhukov was sidelined by Stalin, who viewed him as a threat. In 1955, he returned to a position of influence as minister of defense under Khrushchev but clashed with him and was forced to retire in 1957. Zhukov died in Moscow in 1974.

Soviet Katyusha rockets soar from launchers in the Carpathian Mountains. The Dnieper-Carpathian offensive that ended in May 1944 had left German forces in Belorussia vulnerable to attack.

with huge bundles of barbed wire to make the Germans think they were simply defending it. In just six weeks, the USSR had deployed 2.3 million men for the offensive and delivered several million tons of supplies, making this one of the largest operations of World War II.

German lack of resources

The Soviet deception was effective. Hitler and his generals kept their Panzer reserves concentrated in the south, in the Ukrainian area of the Eastern Front. The sector around Belorussia was held by the German *Heeresgruppe Mitte* (Army Group Center), under Field Marshal Ernst Busch, a veteran of Operation Barbarossa. As the frontline his troops held was fairly stable, they had been able to build defenses and broad trenches, and create strategic strongpoints around fortified towns.

By June 1944, however, Busch lacked manpower, as many German forces had been transferred west to fend off the Normandy landings. He could call on only 400,000 combat troops and roughly the same number of support and noncombat personnel to defend the 180-mile (290-km) frontline. Additional Hungarian units fighting with them were undermanned and underpowered. Busch also lacked significant aerial strength, strategic reserve, and sufficient armored support, making his infantry highly vulnerable. As a further complication, local partisans had cut railroad lines, which would disrupt the German ability to bring up reinforcements, forcing them on occasions to use horses to deliver supplies to the frontline.

The Soviets advance

Operation Bagration was launched on June 22, the third anniversary of Operation Barbarossa, Germany's surprise invasion of the USSR. More than 1.2 million Red Army soldiers went into battle that day, supported by 5,200 tanks and assault guns, and over 5,000 aircraft. The First Baltic and Third Belorussian Fronts advanced in the north, while the First and Second Belorussian Fronts attacked in the south. In some areas, the Germans were outnumbered by more than eight to one and could call on only 900 tanks and assault guns, and 1,350 aircraft. As Hitler had ruled that there should be no retreat from their strongpoints, Busch forbade a strategic withdrawal to the Dnieper River.

German prisoners of war—more than 57,000 men—are paraded through Moscow on July 17, 1944, to mark the end of Operation Bagration and the Soviet retaking of Belorussia.

Red Army tanks advance through Bucharest, the capital of Romania, on August 31, 1944, meeting no resistance as Michael I of Romania had already negotiated peace with the Allies.

Facing waves of attack, his men were encircled and brutally killed; survivors fled west. Summer daylight was also 18 hours long, giving the Soviet air forces ample time to target German positions.

The Germans retreat

On June 28, Busch was replaced by Field Marshal Walter Model, who had risen to fame as a Panzer commander and was known as the Führer's troubleshooter. But Model could do little to stem the Soviet onslaught. The Germans had hoped that the vast Pripet Marshes might prove an obstacle, but the Red Army crossed them in four-wheel-drive trucks supplied under the American Lend-Lease program; these also carried equipment for constructing temporary bridges to maintain the pace of their advance. The Soviets steadily closed in on Minsk, the capital of Belorussia, which was liberated on July 4.

> The nearer the Soviet armed forces came to the borders of Fascist Germany, the more desperate the resistance of the enemy forces became.
>
> ***Operation Bagration***
> **Report by Soviet General Staff**

Model's attempts to establish a new defensive line in western Belorussia had little effect. By July 11, his forces were retreating into Lithuania. The Red Army pursued them, capturing Vilnius two days later. By July 17, they had cleared Belorussia of German troops.

The Soviets sweep on

The Red Army moved into eastern Poland, reaching the Vistula River on August 15 and halted to await supplies. In five weeks they had advanced 450 miles (724 km), within striking distance of Warsaw.

It was Hitler's costliest defeat. Army Group Center had been torn apart, losing over 300,000 men, and the Germans had been forced to divert soldiers and Panzers to Belorussia from elsewhere on the Eastern Front. The Red Army seized the opportunity for further gains. On July 13, they attacked in western Ukraine. Here, Marshal Ivan Konev's First Ukrainian Front enjoyed massive superiority and advanced into eastern Poland, taking the city of Lvov. By late August, his men had established bridgeheads on the west bank of the Vistula. Further to the south, in eastern Romania, the Red Army attacked on August 20. Three days later, the Nazi-aligned government was overthrown, and Romania switched allegiance to the Allies. The Red Army was now well placed for an advance into the Balkans.

Meanwhile, on July 24, the Red Army's Leningrad Front had attacked the weakened German Army Group North around Narva in Estonia. Here, the outnumbered Germans fought a strong rearguard action, retreating to prepared defensive lines and delaying the Soviet bid to recapture Estonia. As a result, the Soviet forces could not use Estonia as a base to attack Finland, which successfully negotiated peace with the USSR during August, signing the Moscow Armistice on September 19, 1944.

The success of Operation Bagration, subsequent gains, and devastating German losses on the Eastern Front set the Soviets firmly on the path to Berlin and gained them territory they would occupy post-war for more than 40 years. ■

IT IS TIME THAT SOMETHING WAS DONE

THE PLOT TO KILL HITLER (JULY 20, 1944)

IN CONTEXT

FOCUS
Assassination attempts

BEFORE
1938 German army officers form a plan to overthrow Hitler but abandon it when war is averted by the Munich Agreement on September 30.

1941 Major General Henning von Tresckow establishes Operation Spark, a plan to assassinate Hitler and then launch a coup to overthrow the Nazis and end the war.

March 13, 1943 A plot to kill Hitler by placing a bomb on his airplane fails when low temperatures cause the detonator to ice up.

AFTER
August 1944 The first trials of those involved in the July 20 plot are held.

October 14, 1944 Field Marshall Erwin Rommel dies by suicide after being implicated in the July 20 plot.

Since 1938, figures within the German army had plotted to kill Hitler. A small network of senior officers believed the Nazis were leading Germany to oblivion. Of the many attempts on Hitler's life, the one that came closest to success was carried out on July 20, 1944.

After assassinating Hitler, the plotters aimed to coordinate with civilian opposition groups and use Operation Valkyrie—an existing plan to restore order in Germany in an emergency—as a pretext to seize power. Central to the plot was Lieutenant Colonel Claus von Stauffenberg, an officer seriously wounded while fighting in North Africa, who now worked in a post that gave him access to Hitler.

The briefcase bomb

On July 20, Stauffenberg flew to the *Wolfsschanze* ("Wolf's Lair"), Hitler's headquarters in East Prussia, for a meeting that Hitler was due to attend. He left his briefcase, with a bomb inside it, under the conference table. A few minutes after the meeting began, he left to receive a telephone call. The bomb went off at 12:42 pm, leaving four dead but Hitler only wounded because the briefcase had earlier been moved behind a table leg. Stauffenberg, believing the blast had killed Hitler, flew to Berlin but was soon arrested. He and three other ringleaders were executed by firing squad on July 21. The Gestapo then carried out a sweeping purge of other suspected political opponents, during which around 5,000 were killed. ■

Bomb damage in the Wolf's Lair is inspected by Hermann Göring (center) and Nazi official Martin Bormann (left) following the July 20 plot.

See also: Germany and the reality of war 188–191 ▪ Resistance movements 226–231 ▪ The D-Day landings 256–263 ▪ The Allies sweep eastward 272–273

WARSAW WAS TO BE RAZED TO THE GROUND

THE WARSAW UPRISING (AUGUST 1944)

IN CONTEXT

FOCUS
Polish resistance

BEFORE
September 1939 Germany invades Poland and its troops enter Warsaw.

1942 Polish resistance forces are amalgamated into the Home Army.

April–May 1943 Residents of the Warsaw Jewish ghetto rise up against German forces.

AFTER
October 1944 Captured Home Army fighters are treated as prisoners of war, but thousands of Warsaw civilians are sent to concentration camps.

January 1945 Soviet troops enter Warsaw. They find only 174,000 people left in the city, less than 6 percent of the pre-war population.

2004 The Warsaw Rising Museum opens, marking 60 years since the revolt.

In 1944, the Home Army (the Polish resistance) began a series of uprisings across Poland. This formed part of Operation Tempest, which aimed to drive out the Germans while asserting Polish claims to post-war independence in the face of the Soviet advance. On August 1 at 5 pm ("W Hour"), around 40,000 Home Army insurgents in Warsaw launched an uprising—the biggest act of resistance in the war. It was planned to last just 10 days but raged instead for 63 days.

> The first days of the uprising were successful, and we were given hope.
> **Sylwester "Kris" Braun**
> **Photographer and resistance member**

Defeat and Nazi revenge

At first, the Germans lacked the forces to suppress the revolt, but the poorly equipped insurgents (they had only one rifle for every 12 soldiers) failed to secure enough strategic targets. However, with strong support from the civilian population of Warsaw and an expectation of Allied backup, the Polish commander, General Tadeusz Bór-Komorowski, decided to fight on. He hoped to link up with the Red Army, but the Soviet advance had been halted on the outskirts of eastern Warsaw. Stalin made little effort to intervene as German forces battered the city, massacring Polish civilians and beating back the insurgents street by street. On October 2, Bór-Komorowski was forced to admit defeat, by which time 18,000 insurgents and more than 130,000 civilians had been killed. The Germans drove out the survivors and eventually levelled around 85 percent of the city. ■

See also: The destruction of Poland 58–63 ▪ Resistance movements 226–231 ▪ The Warsaw Ghetto Uprising 242–243 ▪ The Soviets push into Germany 288–289

NONSTOP CONVOYS OF TRUCKS OF ALL SHAPES AND SIZES

THE ALLIES SWEEP EASTWARD (AUGUST–SEPTEMBER 1944)

IN CONTEXT

FOCUS
Liberation of France

BEFORE
May–June 1940 France, Belgium, Luxembourg, and the Netherlands surrender to Germany.

June 6, 1944 On D-Day, the Allies invade France from the English Channel, securing a foothold in Normandy.

AFTER
September 1944 Allied forces fail to secure a position on the eastern side of the Rhine River, between France and Germany, dashing hopes of a speedy end to the war in Europe.

September–October 1944 Allies advance from southern France into the Vosges mountains but face fierce resistance there.

November 1944 General Allied offensive makes gains on the Western Front.

By the middle of August 1944, the Western Allies had established a strong beachhead in Normandy, France—a secure position on the beaches where they had landed—and were on the verge of breaking out of the region. With the Germans on the defensive in northern France, the Allies launched another invasion, this time far to the south.

Rapid advances

Code named Operation Dragoon, the invasion of southern France began on August 15, with US and Free French soldiers landing on the Côte d'Azur in Provence. It quickly established a beachhead. German forces lacked quality, numbers, and firepower, and Allied paratroopers and French resistance fighters caused havoc behind enemy lines. The Allies made rapid gains; crucially, Marseille and Toulon were liberated on August 27, with both opened to Allied shipping within a month. The Allies then swung north. By mid-September, the Germans had been forced back to the Vosges mountains in the east of the country, next to the German border.

Meanwhile, momentous events had taken place in Paris. On August 19, the city had revolted

With footholds in both the north and south of France, **Allied forces move east across France**, liberating Paris.

→

Unable to hold on to their territory in the south of France, the **German army retreats to the Vosges mountains**, near the Franco-German border.

↓

Sweeping across France, **Allied troops progress into neighboring Belgium** and **prepare to advance into Germany**.

See also: The D-Day landings 256–263 ▪ Operation Market Garden 274 ▪ Battles at the border 275 ▪ The Battle of the Bulge 280–281 ▪ The Allies invade the Reich 286

Allied troops are welcomed by Parisians after the liberation of the city in August 1944. After over four years of occupation, German forces surrendered within 24 hours of the Allies' arrival.

and, within a few days, the German authorities there had lost control. The Allies had not sought to capture the city, planning to encircle and contain it so they could avoid a potentially costly street battle and focus on advancing east. Under pressure from Charles de Gaulle, however, Dwight Eisenhower allowed a contingent to advance into the city. They arrived at dawn on August 24 and by the next day the German military governor there had surrendered. Paris was liberated.

Progress on all fronts

On August 30, all the remaining major German forces in Normandy retreated from the region. The leading Allied generals had differing views about what to do next, though. British general Bernard Montgomery and US commander Omar Bradley wanted a "narrow thrust" east, believing this would quickly defeat Germany. Eisenhower was more cautious, and instead adopted a "broad front" strategy, with Allied forces advancing across all sectors through France and the Low Countries. To ensure they were supplied, the Americans instituted the Red Ball Express, a truck convoy system named after the red-ball-topped bollards that marked out the two routes. They ran from Normandy to the forward supply base in Chartres. Operations began on August 25 and continued for 83 days. During that time, the drivers of the Red Ball Express, three-quarters of whom were Black Americans, delivered over 400,000 tons of supplies.

From France into Belgium

Canadian and British forces, under the command of Montgomery, made progress in the north of the Allied advance, liberating the Channel ports of Dieppe, Ostend, Le Havre, Boulogne, and Calais. After advancing into Belgium on September 2, Brussels was freed from German occupation the next day. The crucial port of Antwerp was captured two days later, but it could not be opened to Allied shipping for another five weeks. In the center of the Allied "broad front," Bradley's American troops were also successful, although fuel shortages sometimes stalled their advance. Despite such problems, in mid-September they were still able to link up with the Allied forces that had advanced from southern France near Dijon. By that time, the Allies were poised to advance into the Netherlands as well as make serious incursions into Germany itself. ■

Omar Bradley

Central to leading the Allied advance east was Omar Bradley. Born in Missouri in 1893, his military career began in 1915, when he graduated from the US Military Academy. World War I ended before his deployment to Europe, however. Between the wars, Bradley rose through the ranks and built a reputation as a dependable organizer and tactician.

Bradley gained his first World War II experience as a frontline commander in North Africa in 1943, then played a major role in the successful Allied invasion of Sicily. Later, he led American ground forces during the Battle of Normandy. In August 1944, he was given command of the US 12th Army Group, placing him in charge of 1.3 million men. Under his leadership, they advanced through France, the Low Countries, and into Germany, playing a crucial role in defeating the Nazis. Popular with officers and enlisted soldiers alike, he retired from active duty in 1953. He later advised President Lyndon Johnson on strategy in the Vietnam War and died in 1981.

I THINK IT IS A SUICIDE OPERATION

OPERATION MARKET GARDEN (SEPTEMBER 1944)

IN CONTEXT

FOCUS
Strategic failures

BEFORE
May 1940 Dutch forces surrender, marking the start of the German occupation of the Netherlands.

June–August 1944 During Operation Overlord, following the D-Day landings, the Allies first establish a beachhead in Normandy and then break out of the region.

September 4, 1944 After four years of German occupation, Montgomery leads the capture of the Belgian port of Antwerp.

AFTER
October 20–November 4, 1944 In Operation Pheasant, Allied soldiers liberate much of the southern Netherlands.

May 4, 1945 The last German forces in the Netherlands surrender unconditionally.

Following Operation Overlord, General Montgomery lobbied for a daring plan to bring the war to a swift end. His strategy was to create a bridgehead over the Rhine from the Netherlands into northern Germany—bypassing the heavily fortified Siegfried Line. It was planned as an operation in two parts: "Market," an airborne assault by troops landing in the Netherlands to seize bridges over the Rhine; and "Garden," a ground attack by British armored divisions, linking up with the airborne forces at Arnhem. Allied intelligence had warned that the Germans had reinforced the invasion area, but Montgomery persevered and, on September 10, 1944, Eisenhower approved the plan.

Operation Market Garden began on September 17 with the daylight landings of 35,000 parachute and glider troops, together with vehicles and artillery pieces, around Arnhem, Nijmegen, and Eindhoven. The same day, British armored forces advanced into the Netherlands, aiming to link up with the airborne troops. After initial Allied successes, the operation stalled. Outnumbered and outgunned, on September 25, Montgomery called off the operation.

The Allies gain ground

Despite their strategic failure, the Allies liberated southern Netherlands by early November. Those who remained under German occupation faced the "Hunger Winter" of 1944–1945. Freezing weather and a German blockade led to food shortages and the deaths of 20,000 people. ■

> If the operation had been properly backed . . . it would have succeeded in spite of my mistakes.
> **Bernard Montgomery**

See also: Blitzkrieg 70–75 ▪ The D-Day landings 256–263 ▪ The Allies sweep eastward 272–273 ▪ Battles at the border 275 ▪ The Battle of the Bulge 280–281

IT IS JUST A QUESTION OF CROSSING THE RHINE

BATTLES AT THE BORDER (SEPTEMBER–DECEMBER 1944)

IN CONTEXT

FOCUS
Allied advances

BEFORE

June–August 1944 After landing in northern France on D-Day, the Allies break out of Normandy and into the French interior.

August 15, 1944 Allied forces land in southern France as part of Operation Dragoon.

August 19–25, 1944 Following a resistance uprising, Allied forces liberate the French capital, Paris.

AFTER

December 1944–January 1945 In the Battle of the Bulge, the Allies repel a surprise German counterattack in the Ardennes.

February–March 1945 The Allies launch the Rhineland Offensive, which enables them to occupy the west bank of the Rhine River.

Despite their successes in summer 1944, the Allies' victory on the Western Front was by no means inevitable. The Lorraine Campaign, fought by the Third US Army, highlighted their difficulties. Although it liberated Nancy and Metz, in France, in September and November, a combination of overstretched supply lines, wet weather, and stiff German resistance delayed its advance.

Meanwhile, the US First Army pushed into Belgium and, from September 9–12, liberated most of Luxembourg. On September 19, seeking to bypass the Siegfried Line protecting the German interior, US troops assaulted the German defensive positions in Hürtgen Forest. Other parts of the US First Army targeted Aachen, the first major German city the Allies had reached, attacking on October 13, following an 11-day aerial and artillery bombardment. After two days of brutal street-fighting, they were forced back, despite heavily outnumbering the city's defenders, many of whom were civilian militia.

US soldiers advancing through Hürtgen Forest, close to the German border. After three months of bitter fighting, they had still not removed its German defenders.

The Americans attacked again on October 19, forcing the Germans to surrender two days later.

On November 16, the Allies launched Operation Queen, which they hoped would allow them to cross the Roer/Rur River into the Rhineland. Although they reached the river after four weeks, they couldn't establish a bridgehead and had to postpone their efforts to advance east because of a big new threat—a German counteroffensive in the Ardennes. ■

See also: The D-Day landings 256–263 ▪ The Allies sweep eastward 272–273 ▪ The Battle of the Bulge 280–281 ▪ The Allies invade the Reich 286

WE MUST BE SUPERHUMAN TO WIN THE WAR

THE BATTLE OF LEYTE GULF (OCTOBER 23–26, 1944)

IN CONTEXT

FOCUS
Control of the Pacific

BEFORE
December 7, 1941 Japanese naval aircraft devastate the US fleet at Pearl Harbor.

January 2, 1942 Japan occupies Manila and drive US forces out of the Philippines.

August–November 1942 Japanese and US fleets fight a series of fierce battles around Guadalcanal in the Solomon Islands.

June 1944 Japan's naval aviation is decimated at the Battle of the Philippine Sea.

AFTER
March 26–April 30, 1945 Japanese kamikazes sink or damage 177 US warships off Okinawa Island, Japan.

April 7, 1945 US aircraft sink *Yamato*, Japan's last battleship, off Japan's Kyushu island.

By autumn 1944, the Japanese Imperial Navy knew it was outclassed by the US Pacific Fleet. Japan still possessed an impressive array of battleships and cruisers, but its naval aircraft were unable to protect them against the far superior American carrier-borne planes. To send the Japanese fleet into battle without good air cover was near-suicidal, but Japanese naval commanders believed the Japanese warrior spirit might achieve a miracle against all odds. If not, they would at least have gone down fighting.

Climactic showdown

In October 1944, the Americans assembled more than 200 warships to support troop landings on Leyte, an island of the Japanese-occupied Philippines. Japan gathered all their resources—some 70 ships—to mount an attack on this daunting armada. Their plan was to send separate fleets north and south of Leyte and use a decoy force to distract the US carriers. At one point they had the US troop carriers under their guns, but in the end little damage was done to the Americans. At the battle's climax, the Japanese battleship *Musashi*, one of the largest warships ever built, was sunk with all hands, helpless against US dive- and torpedo-bombers.

Japan sacrificed 28 warships and 12,000 lives in the Battle of Leyte Gulf. The US had soon regained control of the Philippines, where they were perfectly placed to attack Japanese merchant shipping. ■

A Japanese heavy cruiser tries to maneuver as it is targeted by US Navy carrier-based bombers in the Philippines in 1944. The cruiser quickly sank.

See also: Japanese advances 154–157 ▪ The Battle of Midway 160–165 ▪ The battle for the Solomons and New Guinea 212–213 ▪ Kamikaze pilots 277

THE DAILY DUTY ... IS TO DIE

KAMIKAZE PILOTS (OCTOBER 1944–AUGUST 1945)

IN CONTEXT

FOCUS
Suicide tactics in war

BEFORE
12th century Samurai develop a code of strict conduct called *bushido*—the way of the warrior.

August 1942 Japanese army on Guadalcanal begins a near-suicidal *banzai* attack—an all-out desperate charge.

July 1944 1,000 Japanese civilians die by suicide as Saipan falls.

AFTER
October 15, 1944 USS *Franklin* is the first warship to be hit by a suicide crash-dive.

August 15, 1945 The last suicide mission is flown on the day Japan surrenders.

October 23, 1983 A bomb-laden truck is driven by terrorists into a US Marine base in Lebanon, killing 241 military personnel.

Referencing the *bushido* warrior code of Japan's historic samurai, Japanese military training stressed the honor of dying for the emperor and the shame of surrender. Unable to compete with US technology and productivity, Japanese commanders theorized that warrior spirit could overcome material inferiority because their men were prepared to die.

Dispensable sacrifices

Suicide tactics were employed at times by all Japanese forces, but particularly by pilots against Allied warships. They were used during the Battle of Leyte Gulf in October 1944, when special units crashed bomb-laden aircraft onto the decks of US ships. These suicide missions were dubbed *kamikaze*, meaning "divine wind," a reference to freak weather that saved Japan from Mongol invasion in the 13th century.

Initially, kamikaze pilots were a volunteer elite, but practical sense soon dictated that experienced pilots should fly only as escorts. The suicide planes were entrusted to dispensable young men fresh from flight training. During the Battle of Okinawa (March–June 1945), thousands of pilots were sent to die in mass attacks on Allied ships. The tactic inflicted substantial losses—34 Allied warships were sunk by kamikaze strikes—but thousands of young Japanese lives were ruthlessly sacrificed. ■

Pilots salute their commander at the Chiran Air Base, on the Satsuma Peninsula. Chiran was the main departure point for kamikaze missions, including the Battle of Okinawa.

See also: Japan on the march 44–45 ▪ The western Pacific 244–249 ▪ Japan under siege 304–307 ▪ Japan surrenders 312–313

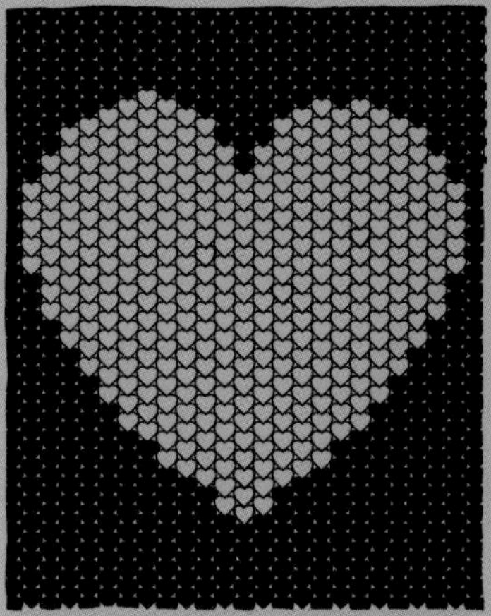

ONE HUNDRED MILLION HEARTS BEATING AS ONE

THE JAPANESE HOME FRONT (1937–1945)

IN CONTEXT

FOCUS
Japan at war

BEFORE
1931 Japanese troops occupy Manchuria after the Mukden Incident.

July 1937 Japan embarks on a full-scale war for the domination of China.

December 7–8, 1941 Japan enters World War II, attacking Pearl Harbor and invading southeast Asia.

AFTER
August 1945 Japan surrenders and is occupied by American forces.

1947 Japan adopts a new constitution that makes it a parliamentary democracy.

1968 Japan becomes the world's second largest economy after spectacular post-war growth.

Japanese society was already organized for conflict prior to the country's entry into World War II. After Japan initiated large-scale fighting in China in the summer of 1937, Japanese militarists constructed a "national defense state." Workers were conscripted into the war industries and businesses were converted from the manufacture of consumer goods to production of military hardware. Shortages became a fact of life for people in Japan from 1938 onward: food and clothes were rationed, luxury goods disappeared from the shops, and an austere attitude to life was enforced.

> Teachers drilled the idea into our brains that it was our duty to die in the war.
>
> **Tadashi Ono**
> **School pupil, 1941**

Hollywood films were banned from cinemas, dance halls were closed, and women who wore bright clothes or makeup were sometimes harangued in the street. Schools prepared their pupils for military service, teaching that readiness to sacrifice their lives in defense of the emperor was a sacred principle for Japanese subjects.

Food and labor shortages

From 1940, a single organization, the Imperial Rule Assistance Association, took complete control of the political life of the country. Its local branches were tasked with surveilling the population, reporting any dissent or defeatism to the political police. After Japan's entry into the war in 1941, propaganda was used to inflate its military victories and conceal its defeats. However, as the war continued, it could not disguise the mounting shortage of basic foodstuffs such as rice and soy beans. By 1945, individual rations officially provided 1,600 calories a day, far below the intake required for health, and in practice even this level was not met. Beriberi and other diseases of malnutrition were rife among the civilian population.

See also: Japan on the march 44–45 ▪ The Japanese attack Pearl Harbor 138–145 ▪ Japanese advances 154–157 ▪ The western Pacific 244–249 ▪ China and Japan at war 250–253 ▪ Japan under siege 304–307

Women working in a Japanese munitions factory. The increased number of women in Japan's labor force was a significant social change brought about by the war.

With 10 million men in the armed forces, labor shortages became acute. Women, students, and forced labor from Korea helped meet the demand. Students supported Japan's war efforts by undertaking a range of jobs, from working in munitions factories to gathering resin from pine trees to use as fuel for trucks.

As it became clear that Japan was going to suffer direct attack, air-raid shelters were built, and children evacuated to the countryside. Although many people had already moved out of the cities because food was more readily available in rural areas, most of the urban population remained to face the fire-bombings that razed cities, including Tokyo, in 1945. In the final stage of the war, most schools were closed and all but the youngest pupils were required to work in the fields, construct firebreaks, or serve as air-raid wardens. Young and old, men and women alike, trained for a final suicidal resistance to an Allied invasion using bamboo spears as weapons.

Social solidarity

Toward the end of the war, absenteeism in factories reduced productivity. Workers abandoned their tasks to search for food, or moved away to escape air-raids. The political police's reports from the time reveal widespread war-weariness and criticism of Japan's rulers. Despite the hardships, social solidarity held firm. When Japan surrendered, it was a disciplined population that obeyed the order to submit to American occupation. ■

The Japanese workforce during World War II

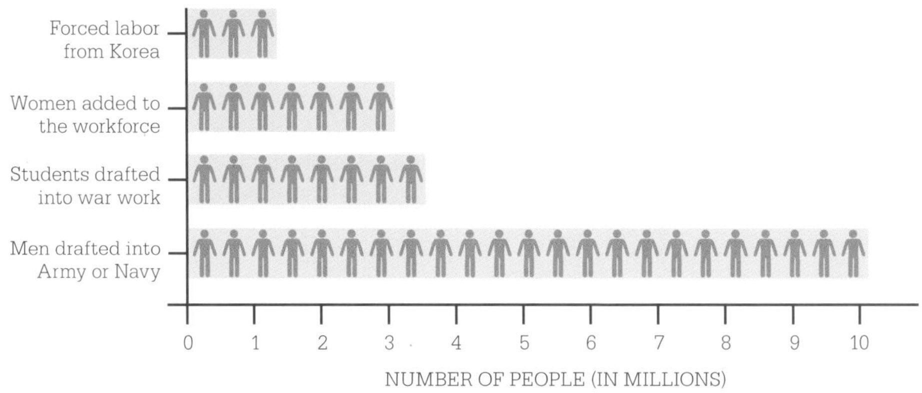

With men conscripted into military service, women and students filled gaps in the workforce, along with forced labor from Korea. Thousands of forced laborers died from exhaustion and poor working conditions.

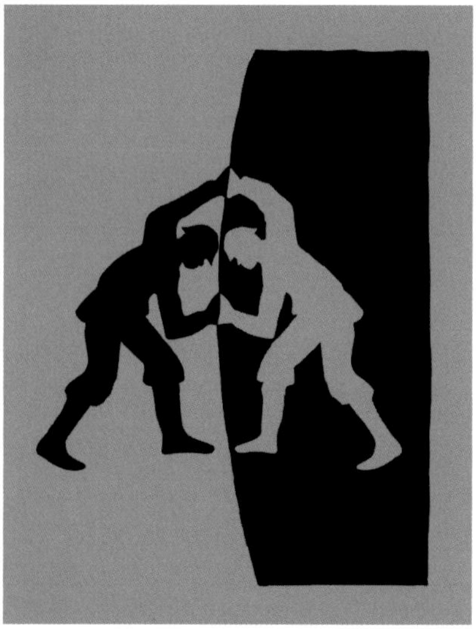

A VIOLENT AND COSTLY SORTIE

THE BATTLE OF THE BULGE (DECEMBER 1944)

IN CONTEXT

FOCUS
Hitler's last stand

BEFORE
June 1944 Allied troops invade the coast of France in the largest amphibious invasion in history.

September 3, 1944 The British Second Army liberates Brussels.

September 1944 Some 16,000 Allied parachute troops are dropped over the Netherlands, but they fail to establish a bridgehead over the Rhine.

AFTER
January 1945 The Red Army sweeps across Poland in the Vistula Offensive, capturing most of East Prussia and driving deep into Silesia, coming to a halt less than 50 miles (80km) from Berlin.

January 27, 1945 Soviet forces enter Auschwitz and liberate more than 7,000 mainly Jewish prisoners.

On December 16, 1944, more than 200,000 German troops and nearly 1,000 tanks launched Hitler's final bid to reverse the ebb in Germany's fortunes since the Allied invasion of Normandy in June of that year. Their plan was to push through to the coast around the city of Antwerp, and split the Allied armies, just as they had done in May 1940.

Aided by thick fog, which hampered Allied airpower, the German offensive achieved complete surprise and pushed westward through the middle of the American line in Belgium's wooded Ardennes, creating the "bulge" that gave the battle its name. Breaking through the American front, the Germans surrounded most of an infantry division, seized key crossroads, and advanced toward the Meuse River, which they needed to seize in order to advance on Antwerp, the main port supplying the Allies.

Rumors about the massacre of civilians and US soldiers in the Belgian cities of Malmedy and Stavelot began to trickle down the lines. English-speaking German soldiers had infiltrated the US forces, using captured uniforms and jeeps to impersonate US soldiers and sabotage communications. In a desperate attempt to distinguish between friend and foe, Americans began questioning men on their knowledge of US popular culture.

> I was from Buffalo – I thought I knew cold, but I didn't really know cold until the Battle of the Bulge.
> **Warren Spahn**
> **World War II veteran**

The clutches of defeat

By December 22, strong German armored units had encircled US forces in the town of Bastogne, on which all the major roads in the Ardennes converged. The German commanding officer sent a note addressed to the "US Commanding Officer," who was Brigadier General Anthony McAuliffe of the 101st

See also: The Japanese attack Pearl Harbor 138–145 ▪ Operation Torch 196–197 ▪ Allied summits 225 ▪ The D-Day landings 256–263 ▪ Operation Bagration 266–269 ▪ Battles at the border 275 ▪ The Allies invade the Reich 286

American soldiers of the Tenth Armored Infantry Regiment advance on German positions surrounding the critical crossroad town of Bastogne on December 27, 1944.

Airborne Division, giving him two hours to surrender. Initially confused and then enraged, McAuliffe sent a one-word reply: "NUTS!"

The Americans slowed the German advance with resilient defense of both Bastogne and the nearby town of St. Vith. The arrival of the 37th Tank Battalion of General Patton's Third Army on December 26 effectively broke through the German line, turning the Battle of the Bulge in America's favor. After initially approaching from the south of the bulge, Patton moved north, isolating German troops in the bulge, and forcing them to turn and retreat in the difficult winter weather.

The Allied armies regained the momentum. The German war machine was running out of fuel, literally and metaphorically. Improving weather conditions allowed Allied planes to support the counterattacks. With no way to continue the advance across the Meuse River, German forces began to crumble by mid-January.

End in sight

Hitler was unable to regain the initiative. The monumental defensive effort by US forces had effectively drained the Nazis' effort. They did not have the manpower or the resources to hold off two fronts. The disaster in the Ardennes fighting only served to confirm to the German high command that the war was irrevocably lost. It would be the last major German offensive in the west. ■

General Patton

Born into a wealthy California family in 1885, General George S. Patton graduated from the US Military Academy at West Point in 1909. During World War I, he headed the US Army's new tank brigade in France, winning both the Distinguished Service Cross and the Distinguished Service Medal for leading the tank units while injured.

After working through staff posts in the interwar years, Patton took over the US II Corps in Tunisia in March 1943 and went on to command the Seventh Army's invasion of Sicily later that year, when he confided in his diary that he had a "feeling of being a chip in a river of destiny." In June 1944, when the D-Day invasion was well underway, he took control of the Third Army, countering the final German offensive. He was known as "Old Blood-and-Guts" by his men.

After the Nazis had been defeated, Patton lobbied for a role in the Pacific. Instead, he was made the military governor of Bavaria. In December 1945, he died from injuries sustained in a car accident.

ENDGAM

1945

JAN 27, 1945

Soviet forces enter Auschwitz. It is the first of the Nazi death camps to be liberated.

JAN 27, 1945

Japanese forces are cleared from Mongyu **in Burma**, opening up the strategically vital Ledo Road supply route connecting Burma with China.

FEB 4–11, 1945

Churchill, Roosevelt, and Stalin meet at the Crimean resort of Yalta to **negotiate**, among other things, the post-war borders of eastern Europe.

FEB 13, 1945

Axis forces holding the Hungarian capital of Budapest **surrender to the Red Army**.

FEB 13–15, 1945

British and US planes bomb Dresden, reducing the city to rubble.

FEB 19, 1945

US marines land on Iwo Jima, Japan, beginning a bitterly contested battle for the island.

MAR 3, 1945

The US defeats the 20,000-strong **Japanese garrison** defending the Philippine capital of Manila.

MAR 6, 1945

Led by the Waffen-SS, the Germans launch a last-gasp but futile **offensive against the Red Army** in Hungary.

As 1945 dawned, World War II entered its final phase. Both Germany and Japan were staring defeat in the face, but neither Hitler nor the Japanese military government were willing to accept the humiliation of unconditional surrender, the only terms the Allies were prepared to offer. The war continued, and the Axis dictatorships forced their troops to fight to the last.

Resistance crumbles

Allied domination in the air and at sea was now almost total. In Europe, British and US air fleets roamed over Germany at will, as acute shortages of aircraft, pilots, and fuel made German opposition minimal. By early 1945, the Allied air strategists were running out of targets to bomb.

Despite the destruction meted out from the air, the German army continued its defense of the fatherland on the ground. Organized resistance only began to collapse when Anglo-American forces finally broke through the formidable Rhine barrier in March 1945, advancing deep into the German heartland.

In the east, however, the Germans fought on with fierce determination, perhaps in fear of Soviet retribution. At the same time, millions of German civilians fled from East Prussia, Silesia, and the Baltic as the Red Army continued its advance.

On April 25, Soviet and US troops met at the German port of Torgau on the Elbe River, and a few days later, Soviet tanks smashed through central Berlin. Within days, Hitler died by suicide, leaving the German people to face a bleak new future as a defeated people.

Japan falls

Victory in Germany allowed the Allies to redirect their resources toward Japan, which was already struggling to survive pressure from air and sea. The US seizure of Iwo Jima and Okinawa put Japan within reach of an amphibious US invasion, but the fanatical Japanese defense of these islands had made the US wary. Its military planners warned that an invasion of Japan could entail up to a million US casualties.

Such misgivings played their part in the decision to use atom bombs against the Japanese cities of Hiroshima and Nagasaki, although most historians now agree that the US blockade of Japan, conventional

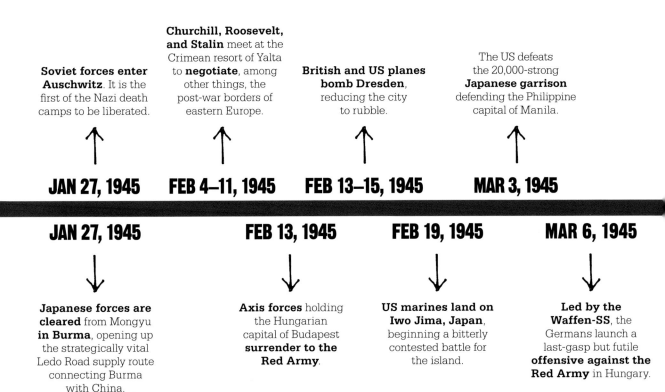

APR 1, 1945

The US initiates the **invasion of Okinawa**, the largest combined naval/land operation in the Pacific war.

APR 12, 1945

President Roosevelt dies of a cerebral hemorrhage. He is **replaced** by **Vice President Harry S. Truman**.

APR 28, 1945

Benito Mussolini and his mistress are caught and **executed** by Italian partisans as they attempt to flee to Switzerland.

APR 30, 1945

Adolf Hitler dies by suicide in his Berlin bunker as the battle for the city rages all around him. He nominates **Admiral Dönitz** as **his successor**.

MAY 7, 1945

German representatives sign **Germany's unconditional surrender** at General Eisenhower's headquarters.

JUN 26, 1945

The text for the **Charter of the United Nations is agreed** in San Francisco, a first step in attempting to create a more harmonious world order.

AUG 6, 1945

The **US drops an atom bomb on the city of Hiroshima**, heralding a new, deadly form of warfare.

SEP 2, 1945

The **Japanese surrender** is formally signed onboard the battleship **USS *Missouri*** in Tokyo Bay, bringing World War II to an end.

bombing, and the USSR's declaration of war against Japan on August 8 would have forced a capitulation without nuclear weapons.

A new world

Japan's official surrender within a month of the atom bombs being dropped gave the US total authority over the country. Under the direction of General Douglas MacArthur, a democratically based constitutional monarchy was established, which helped Japan develop into a modernized industrial nation.

Another consequence of the war in Asia was the collapse of colonial empires. The old imperial powers—Britain, France, and the Netherlands—were exhausted, and indigenous movements for national self-determination were impossible to deny.

In Europe, the political situation was more complicated. The continent was divided between the Western powers, represented by the US, Britain, and France, and the USSR and its communist allies. In the opening moves of a new conflict—the Cold War—Europe was partitioned into east and west, separated by a political boundary known as the "Iron Curtain." In some places, such as Berlin, a defensive line was built to prevent any crossing of the border.

In western Europe, the old parliamentary democracies were reestablished and reconstruction was soon underway, with US help in the form of the Marshall Plan. This financial program enabled West Germany (the Federal Republic of Germany) to become an economic and political success.

The USSR took control of eastern Europe—East Germany, Poland, Czechoslovakia, Hungary, Romania, and Bulgaria. The division between western Europe and these Soviet-dominated states was to last until the collapse of Soviet communism, signaled by the fall of the Berlin Wall in 1989.

Whatever the political system adopted in Europe, there was no disguising the fact that European dominance in world affairs had come to a close. Power was now divided between the US and the USSR, and much of the rest of the world would be an ally of one or the other. This divided world became normal, as the two superpowers fought to maintain their global influence. This was the most lasting and important legacy of World War II. ■

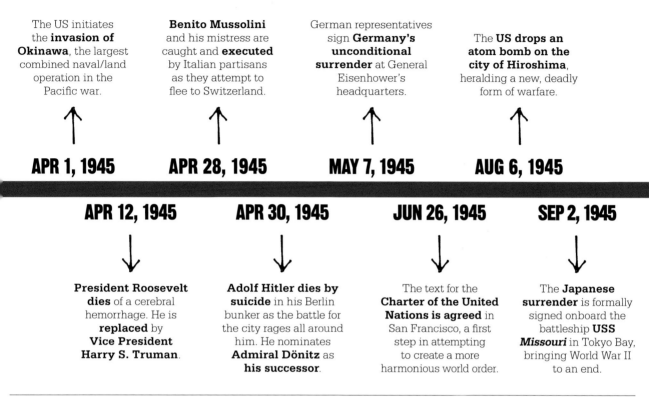

THE FINAL DEFEAT OF THE COMMON ENEMY

THE ALLIES INVADE THE REICH (JANUARY–MARCH 1945)

IN CONTEXT

FOCUS
Invasion of Germany

BEFORE
1940 The British Army's evacuation at Dunkirk and the fall of Paris give Germany control of mainland Europe.

1941 German forces launch Operation Barbarossa, the invasion of Russia.

1944 The German Army Group Center is destroyed by the Red Army, opening the way for a Soviet offensive against Germany.

1944 The Allies' D-Day landings in Normandy, France, begin the reconquest of Europe from the west.

AFTER
1945 Berlin falls to the Allies and Hitler dies by suicide, bringing victory in Europe.

1945–1946 At the Nuremberg Trials, Nazi leaders are put on trial for the atrocities.

The German bounce-back at the Battle of the Bulge was short-lived. General Montgomery's British armies swung south to the Meuse, while General Patton's US forces moved north to squeeze the Germans in the so-called "bulge." To avoid being cut off, the German armies began withdrawing on January 8, 1945, but as 5,000 Allied aircraft peppered the German forces and their supply routes, they suffered heavy casualties. Soon, the liberation of Belgium was complete.

Europe's future determined

On January 20, just days after being made US president for a unique fourth term, Roosevelt met Soviet leader Stalin and British prime minister Churchill at Yalta in the Crimea.

On the agenda was the post-war future of Poland. Against Churchill's wishes, the Polish government in London was overlooked in favor of the Lublin Committee, a Soviet-backed communist governing authority. To compensate for land lost to the USSR in the east, Poland would be given some—but not all—of its pre-war territory in the west.

By March, the Allies reached the Rhine. Extraordinarily, a bridge was still intact at Remagen, despite desperate German attempts to destroy it. US divisions crossed into Germany on March 8, and by the time the bridge collapsed 10 days later, a firm foothold had been established. Germany's defenses in the west were in tatters. ■

> Company B went on the bridge [at Remagen] and cut all the wire connections to prevent the Germans from blowing up the bridge.
> **Michael Kucirka**
> **US soldier, 1945**

See also: The D-Day landings 256–263 ▪ The Battle of the Bulge 280–281 ▪ Victory in Europe 298–303 ▪ The Nuremberg trials and denazification 318–319

NOW THEY ARE GOING TO REAP THE WHIRLWIND

THE DESTRUCTION OF GERMAN CITIES (JANUARY–APRIL 1945)

IN CONTEXT

FOCUS
Air raids

BEFORE
1849 Besieging Austrian forces send balloons fitted with incendiaries over Venice.

1914 German Zeppelin airships bomb the city of Antwerp, the first of many airship bombing raids in World War I.

1940 Germany launches the blitz against UK cities.

1942 The RAF begins "morale bombing" attacks on civilian areas in Germany, including its first 1,000-bomber raid on Cologne.

AFTER
1945 Operation Meetinghouse, the US firebombing of Tokyo, kills 100,000 people—making it the most destructive air raid in history.

1945 USAAF atom bombs devastate the cities of Hiroshima and Nagasaki.

The western Allies pushed east in spring 1945, determined to pummel Germany into collapse through massive bombing raids on German cities. In total, Allied bombers dropped more than 1.5 million tons of explosives, inflicting heavy damage on nearly every German city and killing more than 600,000 people. The raids were first ordered by British RAF chief "Bomber" Harris, and historians have argued long over the justification for such extreme attacks on noncombatants.

Allied bombing reduced Dresden to rubble, as shown in this photograph of the city's *Prager Strasse* (Prague Street), taken from the tower of the city's town hall.

Devastation from the skies

The city of Jülich suffered the most physical destruction, while Essen was reduced to rubble. But the most horrific devastation was a series of attacks on Dresden, killing around 25,000 people. On February 13, 1945, RAF Lancaster bombers dropped 880 tons of bombs in 15 minutes. High-explosives shattered buildings and sent out massive shock waves, while incendiaries torched wooden buildings. The firestorm reached unimaginable intensity, generating hurricane-force winds. Days later, US and British air-raids added to the city's torment; Dresden remained ablaze for weeks.

The target switched to Berlin in March, when 1,329 bombers and 733 fighters of the US Eighth Air Force met with fierce resistance from a small force of Messerschmitt Me-262 jet fighters. US losses were high, but the raid dropped many bombs on Hitler's capital, forcing him to take refuge in his bunker. ■

See also: The Blitz 98–99 ▪ Bombing of Germany 220–223 ▪ The bombing of Hiroshima and Nagasaki 308–311 ▪ The cost of war 314–317

THE EASTERN FRONT IS LIKE A HOUSE OF CARDS

THE SOVIETS PUSH INTO GERMANY (JANUARY–APRIL 1945)

IN CONTEXT

FOCUS
Invasion of Germany

BEFORE
September 1939 Germany invades Poland from the west; the USSR invades it from the east.

June 1941 The Germans launch Operation Barbarossa—the invasion of Russia.

1943 After major victories at Stalingrad and Kursk, the Soviet army drives the Germans out of Russia, Ukraine, and eastern Belarus.

AFTER
1945 Victory in Europe is declared on May 8 and in the USSR on May 9.

1961 The Communist German Democratic Republic builds a wall dividing East and West Berlin; it comes down in 1989.

1991 With the dissolution of the USSR, Poland finally gains full independence.

On January 12, 1945, the Soviet Red Army launched its offensive across Poland's Vistula River. At this point, most of the German forces were fighting the Allies in the Ardennes, while others were repelling Soviet advances in Lithuania, Hungary, and Yugoslavia. German troops in Poland were heavily outnumbered, and the Red Army advanced rapidly. Ignoring the advice of his chief of staff, General Heinz Guderian, Hitler sent reinforcements to Hungary's capital Budapest rather than to Poland, and refused to transfer troops from Lithuania. Within five days, the Soviet forces captured

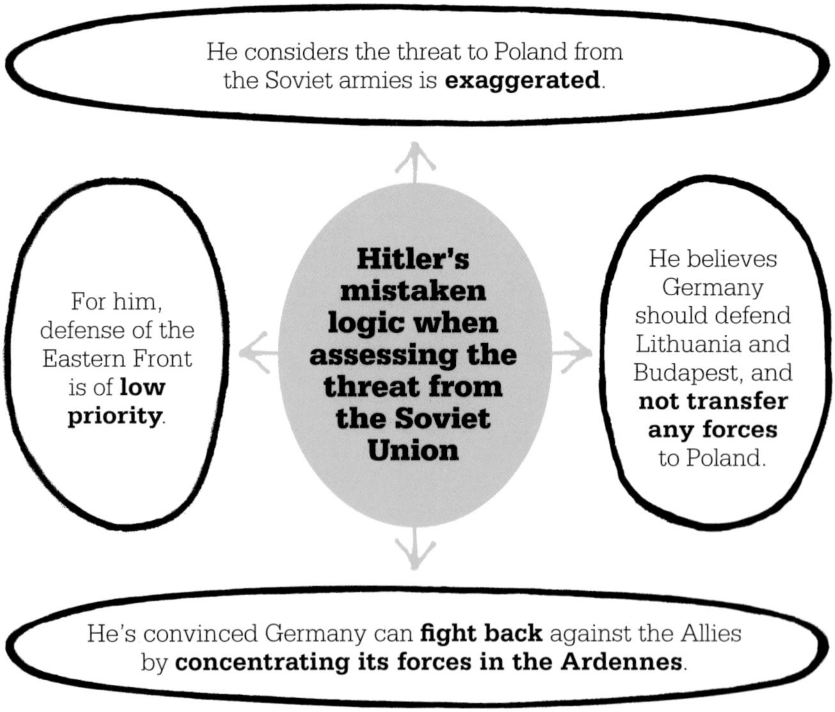

He considers the threat to Poland from the Soviet armies is **exaggerated**.
For him, defense of the Eastern Front is of **low priority**.
Hitler's mistaken logic when assessing the threat from the Soviet Union
He believes Germany should defend Lithuania and Budapest, and **not transfer any forces** to Poland.
He's convinced Germany can **fight back** against the Allies by **concentrating its forces in the Ardennes**.

See also: The destruction of Poland 58–63 ▪ Operation Barbarossa 124–131 ▪ The Battle of Stalingrad 178–183 ▪ The Battle of Kursk 232–235 ▪ Operation Bagration 266–269 ▪ The Allies invade the Reich 286 ▪ Victory in Europe 298–303

Soviet troops ride triumphantly past the Austrian Parliament Building in Vienna. Advancing toward Germany, the forces took the city on April 15, after a month-long offensive.

Warsaw and within a week, they reached Germany's pre-war eastern boundary in Silesia. In February, some 40 miles (64km) from Berlin, the Red Army halted to consolidate its gains on the Eastern Front.

Moving through Poland, Russian troops had uncovered the horrors of Auschwitz-Birkenau and liberated 7,000 prisoners—including 180 children used in Nazi medical experiments—all left to die when the Germans evacuated the camp.

The Soviets take Berlin

In April, the Soviet armies resumed the race to Berlin, determined to beat the Allied forces who were approaching from the west.

The end came swiftly, with the First Belorussian Front, led by Marshal Georgy Zhukov, advancing from the north and the First Ukrainian Front, led by Marshal Ivan Konev, from the south. In April, vastly superior Soviet forces at Seelow Heights east of Berlin and Halbe to the south destroyed the 110,000-strong German Ninth Army, and the Red Army encircled Berlin. Scores of British Mosquito combat planes also bombarded German positions inside Berlin for 36 consecutive nights until April 20, when the Soviet artillery began its heavy shelling of the city.

On April 22, Hitler, admitting defeat, declared he had been failed by his generals but would remain in Berlin to the end, then die by suicide. That day, Joseph Goebbels, Hitler's propagandist, ordered Berliners to defend their city. Hastily scrawled on house walls were phrases such as "We shall stop the Red hordes at the walls of our Berlin."

Yet, within days, the Red Army—greatly feared for their record of rape and pillage—were fighting their way into Berlin street by street in close combat. On April 29, they reached the heart of the city to attack the Reichstag (parliament building). Hitler made his will and married his mistress Eva Braun. The following day, General Helmuth Weidling, the last commander of the Berlin Defense Area, informed Hitler that only a few hours' of ammunition supplies were left. Hitler and Braun died by suicide in his bunker, and Goebbels became chancellor.

Berlin lies in ruins as the Red Army advances through its streets. Since the Yalta conference had decided its future, the Western Allies were content to let the Soviets take the city.

Surrender and victory

On May 1, Goebbels sent General Hans Krebs to present his surrender terms to the Red Army's Marshal Vasily Chuikov, who refused them demanding unconditional surrender. Unable to accept, Goebbels and his wife killed their children and then themselves, leaving Weidling to acquiesce to the Soviet demands. Most German army units surrendered on May 2, but in the west of the city some German units, fearing brutal Soviet reprisals, fought their way out to surrender to the Western Allies. By May 8, the war in Europe was over. In the Far East, however, it raged on until Japan's surrender in September 1945. ■

SEIZE RANGOON BEFORE THE MONSOON

THE ALLIES FIGHT BACK IN BURMA 1943–45

IN CONTEXT

FOCUS
Jungle warfare

BEFORE
1886 Burma becomes a province of British India.

1938 The Burma Road, a supply route to aid China in the Second Sino-Japanese War, is completed.

December 8, 1941 Britain and the US declare war on Japan, a day after Japan's attack on Pearl Harbor.

1941–1942 Japanese invade Burma and capture Rangoon.

AFTER
1947 Aung Sang negotiates Burmese independence from Britain, but is assassinated months later. Burma achieves independence in January 1948.

1962 General Ne Win takes over Burma in a military coup; he remains in power until 1988.

The fight for Burma between the Japanese and the British was one of the longest struggles of World War II and involved some of the fiercest and most brutal fighting. When the Japanese, as part of their bid to control southeast Asia, invaded Burma in 1942, they had met little opposition—partly because the country was under-defended by the British, and partly because many Burmese, including communist leader Aung Sang, saw Japan as their savior from British rule.

The invading Japanese had cut off the Burma Road, a vital supply route to China, and the British BurCorps (Burma Corps), formed

See also: Japan on the march 44–45 ▪ Failure of the League of Nations 50 ▪ Japan's dilemma 137 ▪ Japanese advances 154–157 ▪ India in World War II 158 ▪ Defending Australia 159 ▪ The Battle of Midway 160–165 ▪ Japan surrenders 312–313

William Slim

Born in Bristol in 1891, William Joseph Slim joined the Royal Warwickshire Regiment at the start of World War I in 1914. Wounded at Gallipoli and awarded the Military Cross in 1918 for his service in Iraq, he was promoted to captain in the British Indian Army in 1919.

In 1939, at the outbreak of World War II, Slim was made commander of an Indian brigade that helped the British conquest of Italian East Africa. Two years later, he led an Indian Division in campaigns to secure Iraq, Syria, Lebanon, and Iran for the Allied forces. In 1942, he was moved to head the Burma Corps in a skillful retreat to India away from the invading Japanese. He then devised new tactics, including aerial support and guerrilla warfare, that helped him lead the Fourteenth Army to the reconquest of Burma in 1945.

Well respected and dubbed "the soldier's soldier," Slim was promoted to field marshal in 1948. From 1953–1960, he was governor-general of Australia and then made a viscount. He died in London in 1970 and received a full military funeral.

in March 1942, had coordinated the British, Indian, and local troops' forced to retreat into India. It would prove a long route back.

Guerrilla tactics

At first, few on the British side believed there was any hope of fighting back against the Japanese in Burma's tough jungle terrain. However, unconventional British commander Orde Wingate created a special operations group in India that he called the "Chindits." They traveled light and fast and were coordinated with air support, which was crucial, as was soon realized. In 1943, the Chindits launched their first guerrilla raids against the Japanese which, despite heavy losses, proved that such operations were viable. A similarly maverick American unit—"Merrill's Marauders" under the command of Frank Merrill—joined the fray in 1944. Both the Chindits and Merrill's Marauders would receive vital scouting aid from the Kachin Rangers, who were northern Burmese tribesmen.

By 1943, Chinese leader Chiang Kai-shek was pressing the Allied forces to retake the Burma Road supply route. Meanwhile, Aung Sang had recognized that hopes of Japanese support for Burmese independence were vain, and urged cooperation with the British. His Anti-Fascist People's Freedom League (AFPFL), founded in 1944, would play a key role in the fighting. The British began to consider the possibility of regaining Burma.

Planning for battle

In late 1943, General William Slim took charge of the Fourteenth Army, newly created in eastern India and part of the South East Asia Command under Lord Louis Mountbatten, and helped ensure better-coordinated air support. Slim stressed the importance of jungle warfare training and advocated grouping units in defensive "boxes" supplied and militarily supported from the air to encourage them to hold their ground and resist Japanese attacks.

Meanwhile, the Japanese, still intent on conquering southeast Asia, were planning the 1944 Ichi-Go offensive to take over China, eliminating American air bases in the south, and preparing Operation U-go to invade India. Japanese General Renya Mutaguchi was an »

Merrill's Marauders in the Burmese jungle. They held positions for 13 days in March and April 1944, cut off and supplied only from the air, as they advanced toward Myitkyina.

Why air support is so important in jungle warfare. → **Supply lines are slow** through jungle terrain and there is **no continuous frontline**. → Fast-moving enemy **guerrilla units** can make **surprise attacks**. → If units are **attacked by superior forces** in the jungle, they **must retreat**. → Guided by a ground signal, aircraft can **drop supplies and ammunition** by parachute. → Units can then **hold on in defense**, gaining **vital impetus**, until reinforcements arrive.

enthusiastic proponent of U-go, urging an advance from northwest Burma across the border into India's Assam Province.

The Allies push forward

On January 9, 1944, before either of the Japanese initiatives were underway, the Fourteenth Army, made up of Indian and British troops, moved in from India and captured the port of Maungdaw in western Burma. At the subsequent Battle of Admin Box at nearby Sinzweya in February, aided by air supplies of arms and rations, the army held its ground against the Japanese, forcing them to retreat—a significant win for the Allied forces.

Meanwhile, in northern Burma, American General Joe Stilwell was leading "X-Force," a Chinese army equipped and trained by the Americans in India. Its mission was to protect construction workers building the Ledo Road to carry supplies from India to China. It was also instructed to inflict maximum damage on Japanese forces and, assisted by Merrill's Marauders, to press south through the jungle to capture the town of Myitkyina and its critical air base.

X-Force drove the Japanese back, but failed to trap them. Then, in spring 1944, the Chindits, now with Stilwell's forces, led a daring raid, landing by glider behind Japanese lines to cut off the railroad supplying Myitkyina. Meanwhile, Merrill's Marauders and some of Stilwell's forces forged a path through the jungle to reach Myitkyina itself. They captured its airfield in May 1944, but the battle for the town raged on until August.

India's eastern front

Launching his U-go operation, Japanese General Mutaguchi moved his Fifteenth Army across the Chindwin River toward the Burmese border with eastern India in March 1944. His target was the Allied forces' air base at Imphal, held by IV Corps, part of Slim's Fourteenth Army. Located on a plain, flanked by mountains, the

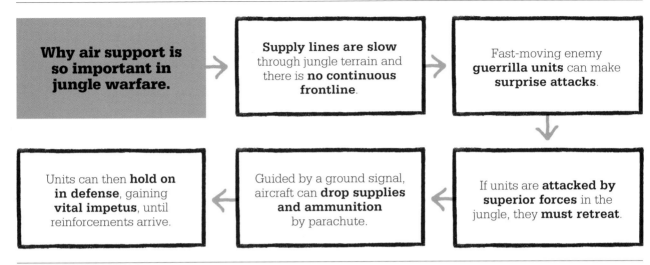

Japanese and Indian soldiers fight side-by-side in Burma. Many Indian prisoners of war, wanting to free India from colonial rule, joined their Japanese captors to fight against the British.

Two British soldiers patrol the ruins of the town of Bahe in central Burma, as General Slim's forces advance south in January 1945 toward Mandalay in the later stages of the campaign.

base supported Allied troops and sent supplies to China via the "Hump"—an air route over the Himalayan foothills. By April, the Fifteenth Army was attacking the plain from several directions.

At the same time, in a move that Slim had not anticipated, 15,000 Japanese troops advanced through the jungle to attack Kohima, an Indian hill station 85 miles (137 km) to the north, thereby cutting off the main supply route to Imphal. Allied troops arrived within days to relieve the desperate 2,500-strong Kohima garrison, but savage fighting continued until the end of May.

Thwarted by Allied resistance, Japanese attacks around Imphal had largely halted by the end of May, and a short stalemate ensued as monsoon rains slowed the Allies' counteroffensive. Yet it was lack of supplies that ultimately defeated the Japanese. Exhausted, sick, and starving, they withdrew, and British troops cleared the road to Kohima. In the two battles, the Japanese had suffered around 55,000 casualties, including 13,000 deaths—their costliest defeat to date and seen by many as the major turning point in the Burma conflict. Allied losses were far lighter, largely due to the efficiency of transport aircraft bringing in men and supplies, and flying out casualties.

> The outer part of the defenses became piled with Japanese corpses.
>
> **Major Tom Kenyon**
> **Commander of A Company, Fourth Royal West Kents, British Army**

Japanese in retreat

By early 1945, the Japanese had withdrawn to the eastern side of the Irrawaddy River, and the Allies' target was Mandalay, just east of the river in central Burma. Slim now divided his army, sending half to Mandalay and the other half on a roundabout route to launch a surprise attack on Meiktila, a city between Mandalay and Rangoon. Meiktila fell on March 3, and the British took Mandalay ten days later.

With the Japanese now in retreat, the Allied forces advanced on the port of Rangoon, anxious to take it before the monsoon season. On short notice, naval forces were diverted from Thailand to take part in Operation Dracula, an airborne and amphibious attack on May 1. Indian troops landed early the next morning, just hours before the monsoon rains, but found that the Japanese had evacuated the port.

On June 15, Supreme Allied Commander Lord Mountbatten held a victory parade in Rangoon, although fighting continued in the jungles to the north. By September, victory was complete, and Burma was once again under Allied control.

While historians debate the impact of the Burma campaign on World War II in Asia, the Allied victory boosted respect for British forces and severely dented Japanese morale. Four years of conflict also set the scene for independence in both Burma and India. ■

NO HUMAN BEING COULD THEN CONCEIVE ... WHAT WE SAW

LIBERATING THE DEATH CAMPS (JANUARY–APRIL 1945)

IN CONTEXT

FOCUS
Humanitarian atrocities

BEFORE
1900 British force 200,000 Black Africans and Boers into internment camps during the Boer War.

1914–1918 Over 800,000 people are held in concentration camps during World War I, although basic human needs are looked after in most.

1929 Stalin develops the gulag system of forced labor camps in the USSR.

1933 The first Nazi prison camp is created at Dachau.

AFTER
1946 Prominent Nazi leaders are sentenced for crimes against humanity at the Nuremberg trials.

1953 Millions of prisoners are released from Soviet gulags.

Allied forces had been made aware of the existence of death camps before they came across them on their advance into German territory. But nothing could have prepared them for the sheer horror of what they found as they passed through the camp gates. Although the camps had been liberated, many of their survivors were too shattered, physically and mentally, to feel joy, or even to recognize that they had been freed.

> [The survivors of Auschwitz] rushed toward us shouting, fell on their knees, kissed the flaps of our overcoats, and threw their arms around our legs.
>
> **Georgii Elisavetskii**
> **One of the first Red Army soldiers to step into Auschwitz**

In summer 1944, the advancing Soviet Red Army made the first concentration camp discovery, at Majdanek near Lublin. Although the Nazi SS had already evacuated many of its inmates farther west as the Soviets approached, some were still incarcerated. And there was sufficient evidence in the camp to bear witness to its horrors. The gas chambers in which so many had met their death were still intact.

As the Red Army advanced, SS commander Heinrich Himmler ordered the evacuation of all the camps in the line of advance. Tens of thousands of malnourished prisoners emptied from camps such as Auschwitz–Birkenau were simply abandoned or sent on long "death marches" in freezing weather to other camps farther west. Thousands died from cold or hunger on these marches; others were shot because they were too weak to keep up.

Auschwitz

On January 27, 1945, the Red Army came across the Auschwitz–Birkenau concentration camp and found about 9,000 weak, emaciated prisoners who were barely clinging to life. Delirious with joy at their

See also: Nazi massacres 136 ▪ Nazi Europe 168–171 ▪ The Holocaust 172–177 ▪ Prisoners of war 184–187 ▪ The Nuremberg trials and denazification 318–319

Between July 1944 and May 1945, Allied troops liberated concentration camp prisoners as they advanced across Europe. Soviet forces liberated camps in the east, US forces liberated those in the south and west, and British and Canadian forces liberated camps in the north.

Key:
- Liberated by the US
- Liberated by Britain/Canada
- Liberated by the Soviet Union
- Territory liberated prior to March 21, 1945
- Territory liberated March 21, 1945–May 9, 1945
- Territory held by Germany at surrender May 7–9, 1945
- Neutral territory

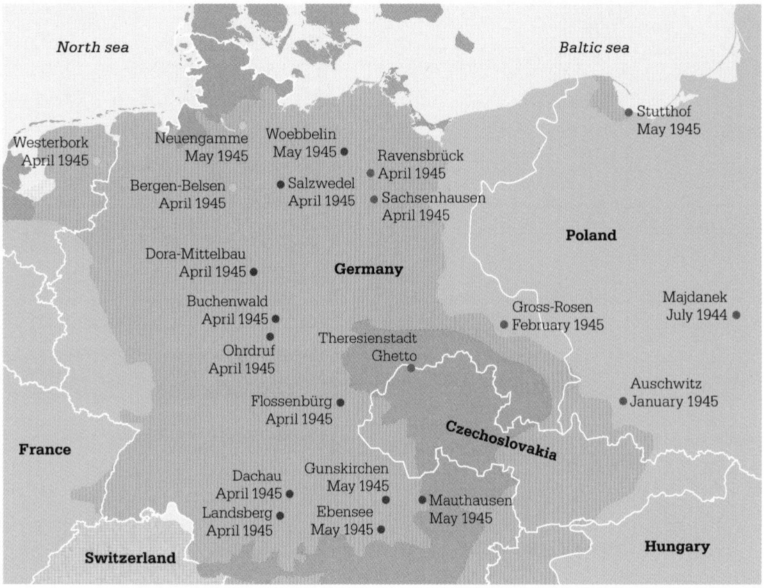

liberation, some flung themselves on the Soviet troops in desperate displays of gratitude. Some were too weak to live for much longer but about 7,500 survived after receiving food and medical attention.

Auschwitz was the biggest of all the Nazi killing centers, where more than 1.1 million people—mostly Jews, but also including 25,000 Sinti and Roma people, and prisoners of war—had been brought from all over Europe. Although the retreating Germans had destroyed much of the camp, Soviet soldiers still found hundreds of thousands of men's suits, more than 800,000 women's dresses, and over 14,000 pounds (6.3 metric tons) of human hair, all of which had been stripped from the prisoners.

In the following months, Soviet troops also liberated the Stutthof, Sachsenhausen, and Ravensbrück camps, while US forces liberated the Buchenwald, Dora–Mittelbau, Flossenbürg, Dachau, and Mauthausen camps. The British and Canadians also freed camps, including Neuengamme and Bergen–Belsen. When the British entered the latter, they found it crammed with the overflow from other prisons. Some 60,000 prisoners were critically ill with typhus, and 13,000 died from malnutrition or disease within a few weeks.

Former prisoners at the Bergen–Belsen concentration camp line up to collect bread rations following the liberation of the camp by British forces in April 1945.

Shock and retribution

Reports of the sheer horror revealed in the camps—piles of unburied corpses, the stench of death everywhere, and skeletal survivors who had been worked and starved close to death—sent shock waves around the world. Some survivors died soon after being rescued simply from the shock of their first mouthful of food.

The retreating Germans had tried desperately to cover up the evidence by murdering witnesses and destroying prison buildings, gas chambers, and prison records. But they left too much material evidence, and too many witnesses, to save Nazi leaders and camp commanders such as Auschwitz's Rudolf Höss from justice at the Nuremberg trials. ■

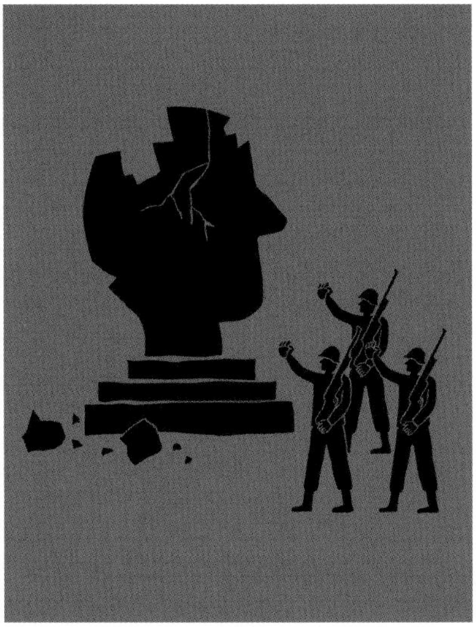

WE FOUGHT FOR A CAUSE AND NOT FOR CONQUEST

LAST STAND IN ITALY (APRIL 1945)

IN CONTEXT

FOCUS
The Mediterranean front

BEFORE

June 1940 Italy enters the war on the side of Germany to cement an "axis" of power.

July 1943 The Allies land on Sicily in Operation Husky and secure the island.

September 1943 Allied forces attack southern Italy. The Italian government surrenders but the Germans establish a puppet regime led in the north by Mussolini.

January 1944 Allied forces land at Anzio and in May capture the stronghold of Monte Cassino.

AFTER

May 1946 King Victor Emmanuel III of Italy abdicates, and his son, Umberto II, is exiled.

June 1946 Italy holds its first elections as a republic.

Frontal assaults by Allied forces **fail to break through** the well-defended **Gothic Line**.

→

Operation Grapeshot is launched, beginning with **diversionary attacks** at each end of the line.

↓

The main Allied forces then **attack through the center**, capturing key cities and cutting off German supply lines.

←

The success of Operation Grapeshot **triggers Italian partisan revolts** in Milan and Turin, ensuring complete **victory for the Allies in Italy**.

After the invasion of the southern mainland of Italy in September 1943, Allied forces fought their way north. They gradually breached each defensive line of the retreating Germans, but progress was slow. The German forces proved resilient, taking advantage of the impenetrability of the rugged Apennine Mountains that run down the spine of Italy and the easily defended strips of territory either side. By summer 1944, the Allies were held up by the Gothic Line, a German defensive system that crossed the Apennines, stretching from the Adriatic coast in the east to the Ligurian Sea in the west. The line blocked the way to the Po valley, the location of Italy's main industrial cities, such as Milan and Turin, as well as vast croplands supplying food to the German armies.

An assault by the Allies in the fall broke through the Gothic Line, but dogged German defense and poor weather halted the advance.

See also: Italy and the rise of fascism 22–23 ▪ Dictators and fragile democracies in Europe 34–39 ▪ Italy enters the war 88–89 ▪ The invasion of Italy 210–211 ▪ The fall of Rome 254

> The wretched end of Benito Mussolini marks a fitting end to a wretched life.
> ***The New York Times***
> **April 30, 1945**

The Allies decided to wait until the following spring, and in April 1945, under the command of US General Mark Clark, launched a decisive offensive, code named Operation Grapeshot.

German defenses broken

The plan was not to capture the line but to distract the Germans with small actions at either end, and punch through the center with the main forces. The Allies would then push on to capture key towns and cities behind the German line. The two main armies involved were the US Fifth Army, which would aim for Bologna, and the British Eighth Army, which would advance from the east and target Ferrara and Bondeno. Among the Allied troops were many nationalities, including New Zealanders, French, Algerians, Greeks, Indians, Poles, Brazilians, Moroccans, and Canadians.

Diversionary attacks began on April 1, followed from April 6 by the heavy bombing of German positions. The Eighth Army then advanced up the eastern flank, and on April 14, after a delay due to fog, the Fifth Army attacked through the mountainous center. On April 21, Polish troops entered and secured Bologna, and by April 25 the Allied armies had crossed the Po, breaking the German forces apart. As the Allies advanced, Italian resistance fighters, or partisans, rose up against the Germans and the puppet government of Mussolini, so that by the time the Allied forces reached many of their targets they faced little or no resistance.

The death of Mussolini

On April 25, Mussolini fled Milan with his mistress Claretta Petacci, hoping to reach the Swiss border. Historians do not know for certain what happened next, but the most widely accepted account is that the pair were captured two days later by local partisans near the village of Dongo on Lake Como and executed. On April 29, the bodies were carried back to the Piazzale Loreto in Milan where they were assaulted by angry crowds.

That day, German commanders signed a surrender document, which came into effect on May 2, with nearly 1 million German soldiers laying down their arms. By then, some 313,000 Allied troops who fought in Italy had been killed or were wounded or missing. German casualties were around 336,000. The Italian campaign is sometimes seen as a sideshow to the wider war against Germany, but it had cost the Germans enormous resources to defend Italy, making the Allied victory in northern Europe easier. ■

Italian partisans arrive in Milan after the success of Operation Grapeshot in spring 1945. Grabbing what weapons they could, thousands of partisans fought alongside the Allies.

THE WORLD MUST KNOW WHAT HAPPENED, AND NEVER FORGET

VICTORY IN EUROPE (MAY 7, 1945)

IN CONTEXT

FOCUS
Achieving peace

BEFORE
September 1939 Germany invades Poland, prompting Britain and France to declare war—the start of World War II.

1941 The USSR enters the conflict after invasion by Germany, and Japan's bombing of Pearl Harbor brings the US into the war.

1944 The Western Allies launch the D-Day landings in northern Europe.

AFTER
1945–1946 Nazi war leaders are tried for war crimes at the Nuremberg Trials.

1961 The German Democratic Republic—East Germany—builds the Berlin Wall to prevent defections to the West.

1989 The Berlin Wall falls, and Germany is reunited the following year.

Adolf Hitler's suicide on April 30, 1945, did not bring World War II to an abrupt halt. Not all Nazi commanders accepted defeat, and even among those who did, there was uncertainty about what to do. German soldiers and civilians were also terrified of reprisals from the Red Army, which captured Berlin at the start of May. After Germany's final surrender, however, the US, UK, and the USSR could finalize plans to divide up the country in a bid to establish a lasting peace.

Soviet reprisals

After General Helmuth Weidling's surrender in Berlin on May 2, a deathly calm descended on the German capital. Desperately short of food and water, Berliners emerged from their cellars to see smoking ruins and streets filled with corpses—many of teenagers and aging veterans who had supplemented the depleted German army as it mounted a final defense.

Soviet troops rounded up anyone in uniform and marched them off to an unknown fate. For many of the women and girls of Berlin, too, the nightmare was just beginning, as countless Red Army soldiers regarded them as spoils of war and objects of their revenge for the suffering the Nazis had inflicted on their home country. There are no exact figures, but as many as 100,000 Berlin women may have been raped by the Red Army in the weeks after the surrender, 10,000 of them dying as a result.

A Soviet soldier hoists the Red Flag over Berlin's ruined Reichstag on May 2, 1945. The photographer, Yevgeny Khaldei, later admitted the image was staged after the first flag was shot down.

Boxed in by the **Western Allied forces** and **Soviet forces**, Germany surrenders.

→ Victory **pits the Western powers against the USSR** as both seek lasting influence.

→ Early Soviet **promises of democracy** for eastern European countries are **not honored**.

↓ Western Allies **accept Stalin's creation of an Eastern bloc** under Soviet influence **to avoid further conflict**.

← **Eastern and western Europe remain divided for more than 40 years.**

See also: The D-Day landings 256–263 ▪ Operation Bagration 266–269 ▪ The Allies invade the Reich 286 ▪ The Soviets push into Germany 288–289

Some German units tried to fight their way out to the south of the country, perhaps believing Nazi propaganda about the existence of a Bavarian stronghold. Others tried to break out to the west, in the hope of surrendering to the Western Allies, whom they feared less than the Soviets. Many German civilians attempted to follow them.

General Walther Wenck, who in early April had been appointed commander of the German Twelfth Army and charged with resisting the US and British advance, found himself administering a vast camp of fleeing German refugees south of Berlin. When the news of the Berlin surrender came through, Wenck fought his way west, linking up with the remnants of the Ninth Army to lead them and possibly as many as 200,000 refugees across the Elbe River into US occupied territory to escape the Red Army.

German forces surrender

On May 4, the German military commanders in Holland, Denmark, and northwest Germany, fearing the Soviet advance, met the British commander Field Marshal Bernard Montgomery on Lüneberg Heath in Lower Saxony to make their surrender. Montgomery sent them on to Supreme Headquarters Allied Expeditionary Force (SHAEF) in Reims, northeast France, where the Allied command, led by General Dwight D. Eisenhower, demanded an immediate unconditional surrender. The Germans requested a two-day delay, ostensibly to have the time to communicate the cease-fire to all their troops, although more likely to give more of them time to reach the Western Allies rather than be caught by the Red Army. Eisenhower agreed to the delay, and the surrender was signed on May 7, to come into effect at one minute past midnight on May 8.

To the north, Norway—still occupied by a well-equipped German army of more than 350,000 and a small fleet of U-boats—had been seen as a potential point of continued Nazi resistance by Grand Admiral Karl Dönitz, who had taken over as German head of state after Hitler's death. However, once Germany had surrendered unconditionally on May 7, Dönitz ordered the commander in Norway, General Franz Böhme, to follow suit, with all hostilities ending on May 8.

A chaotic peace

The Soviet leader, Joseph Stalin, was angered by the events in Reims, arguing that the surrender should be signed by Field Marshal Wilhelm Keitel, the supreme commander of all German forces, and take place in the German capital. The surrender was therefore restaged on May 8 in Berlin and came into effect on May 9, after a short delay brokered by »

> The Russian soldiers were raping every German female from eight to eighty. It was an army of rapists.
>
> **Natalya Gesse**
> **Soviet war correspondent**

Harry S. Truman

Born in Lamar, Missouri, in 1884, Harry S. Truman fought in France during World War I as a captain in the US Army—the only US president to have experienced combat in that conflict. A longtime member of the Democratic Party, he was elected to the US Senate in 1934, and his reputation grew during the early years of World War II thanks to his effective leadership of a committee scrutinizing defense spending.

In November 1944, Truman was elected as Franklin D. Roosevelt's vice president. When Roosevelt suffered a fatal stroke just 82 days after the election, Truman took over. He authorized the use of the atomic bomb against Japan in August 1945, forcing its surrender and bringing to a close the conflict in the Pacific.

Motivated by concern over the political influence of the USSR and its allies, Truman pursued an interventionist path after the war, exemplified by his decision in 1950 to send troops to defend South Korea from invasion by communist North Korea. In 1952, with his popularity in decline, he chose not to run for reelection. He died in 1972.

Londoners and US soldiers dance on the streets to celebrate V-E Day on May 8, 1945. The war, though, was not over and Churchill spoke the same day of "the toil and efforts that lie ahead."

Keitel to allow news of the cease-fire to reach all German units. By that time, however, news of the surrender had leaked out, and crowds poured joyfully into the streets of London, New York, and other cities. Winston Churchill announced that Victory in Europe (V-E) Day celebrations would go ahead on May 8. Stalin responded that in the USSR they would take place on May 9.

All over Europe, chaos still reigned, as pockets of fighting continued and millions of people were displaced. Many of the more than 6 million who had been dragged into forced labor by the Nazis tried to make it back to their towns and villages on foot, along with other uprooted people, including concentration camp survivors. Ethnic Germans were targeted and hounded out of formerly Nazi-held territory. Three million Germans were evicted from the Czech Sudetenland alone, and hundreds of thousands were taken into forced labor camps, known as gulags, by the Soviet armies. Meanwhile, soldiers of the Western Allied and Soviet forces were exhausted and anxious to celebrate victory and return home.

Vying for power

The Germans had been defeated by the combined efforts of the USSR and the Western Allies, but the tension between the victors was extreme. Churchill feared the US would pull out of Europe, leaving the continent defenseless against the Soviets, with Stalin's tyranny replacing that of Hitler. In February 1945, when German defeat seemed sure, Franklin D. Roosevelt, Stalin, and Churchill had met at the Yalta Conference in Crimea to discuss—among other issues—the post-war reorganization of Europe. While Churchill pressed for east European countries, such as Poland and Czechoslovakia, to determine their own futures and elect democratic governments, Stalin made it clear that political control of east and central Europe was essential for the national security of the USSR. Although Stalin promised free elections in Poland, a Soviet-backed provisional government with communist sympathies was already in place by January 1945.

Control of Poland

By May, when the Soviet intentions became ever clearer, Churchill argued for Operation Unthinkable, a rapid offensive against the Red Army to liberate Poland while US forces were still in Europe. Harry S. Truman, the new US president, recognized that attacking the Soviets would require further significant manpower and involvement in a long, costly war. He took a more accommodating line with Stalin, allowing him to install a puppet government in

> This is what we went to war against Germany for—that Poland should be free and sovereign.
>
> **Winston Churchill**
> **UK prime minister, Yalta Conference, 1945**

Harry S. Truman is flanked by Stalin (right) and Clement Attlee, UK prime minister (left), at Potsdam in late July 1945. Attlee replaced Churchill after defeating him in the July UK election.

Poland, although this left the Polish government-in-waiting abandoned in its London headquarters.

Planning post-war Europe

The Yalta Conference had achieved broad agreement on a number of areas, including the division of Germany into four occupation zones to be controlled by the US, the USSR, UK, and France. Charles de Gaulle, the leader of France's provisional government, was not, however, invited to this or the subsequent conference, held in July 1945 at Potsdam, west of Berlin. Here, three Allied leaders—Truman, Stalin, and Churchill—met to hammer out a conclusive agreement for post-war Europe.

Stalin, who already knew of Churchill's aborted Operation Unthinkable, arrived in confident mood. However, he was upstaged by Truman, who, on the eve of the conference, had received the message "Babies satisfactorily born." This was the signal that the first successful tests of the atomic bomb created by the Manhattan Project research group had been carried out at Los Alamos, in the US state of New Mexico. Churchill recognized that the Western Allies could now counter any Soviet threat. Because Soviet spies soon relayed the information to Stalin, it came as no surprise a week later when Truman informed him that the US had developed a new weapon, more powerful than any known bomb. Truman later recalled that Stalin merely said he was "glad to hear it" and hoped the Americans would make "good use of it against the Japanese."

Under the Potsdam Agreement, signed on August 1, Germany was to be disarmed, demilitarized, and split into the four occupation zones agreed at Yalta. The Western leaders also made plans to denazify German society, and arrest and try Germans who had committed war crimes. They formed a Council of Foreign Ministers to negotiate treaties on Germany's behalf and transferred considerable German territory to Poland. The agreement left the USSR essentially in control of most of eastern Europe.

Uneasy aftermath

Germany and Italy had been defeated and Europe was at peace, but on the other side of the world, Japan was still waging war and refusing to concede. For a while, the Western Allies and the USSR (lured by the promise of territories in eastern Asia) put aside their differences in order to rout the Japanese. However, it was a highly uneasy alliance riven by ideological differences and conflicting ambitions. Churchill understood the dangers of an expansionist USSR, and in March 1946 he spoke of an "iron curtain" descending across Europe. It was an early shot fired in a "Cold War" that would divide Europe for more than four decades. ■

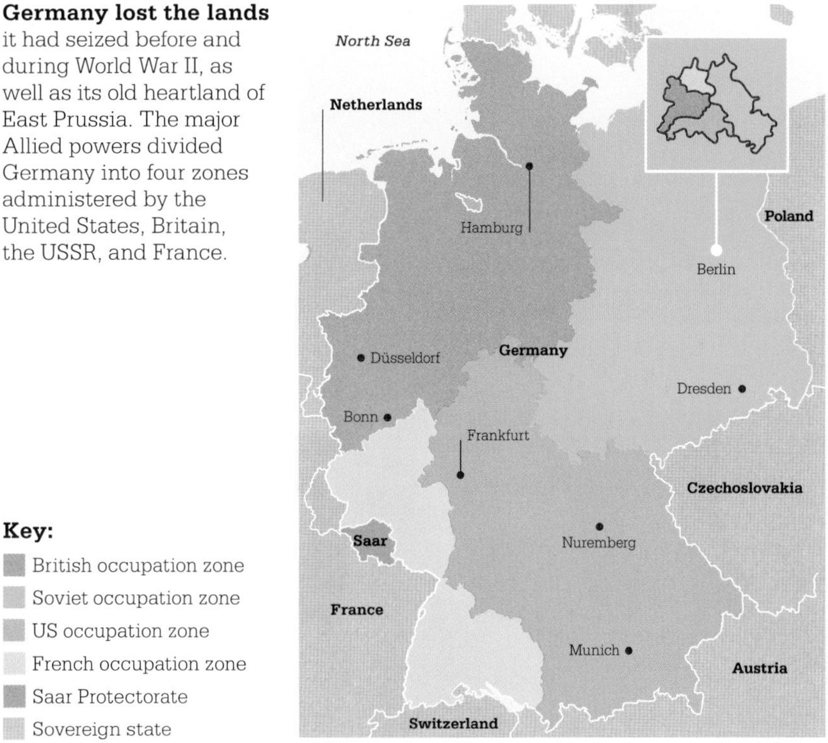

Germany lost the lands it had seized before and during World War II, as well as its old heartland of East Prussia. The major Allied powers divided Germany into four zones administered by the United States, Britain, the USSR, and France.

WE SHALL DEFEND THIS ISLAND ... TO THE END

JAPAN UNDER SIEGE (FEBRUARY–AUGUST 1945)

IN CONTEXT

FOCUS
War in the Pacific

BEFORE
December 7, 1941 The Japanese bomb Pearl Harbor, forcing the US into the war.

December 1941 Japan launches offensives against the Philippines, Burma, Borneo, and Hong Kong.

February 1942 The British surrender the stronghold of Singapore.

June 1942 US forces destroy four Japanese aircraft carriers and 248 planes at the Battle of Midway, ending Japanese dominance in the Pacific.

January 1944 The Allies begin the recapture of Burma.

AFTER
September 2, 1945 Japan finally surrenders and is occupied by American forces.

May 1947 Japan becomes a parliamentary democracy under its newly adopted constitution.

By early 1945, the American naval, army, and air forces dominated the Pacific and the skies above it, but needed to take the Pacific islands south of Japan before advancing north to attack the Japanese archipelago.

Retaking the Philippines, held by the Japanese since 1942, was the next goal. In late 1944, Allied forces under American General Douglas MacArthur had begun by capturing the Philippine islands of Leyte, and then Mindoro, just south of Luzon, the main island. Luzon

See also: Japan's dilemma 137 ▪ The Japanese attack Pearl Harbor 138–145 ▪ Japanese advances 154–157 ▪ China and Japan at war 250–253 ▪ The bombing of Hiroshima and Nagasaki 308–311 ▪ Japan surrenders 312–313

> Here on these islands, a great tragedy is about to occur. This is going to be a fight to the death.
> **Japanese press corps**
> **January 1945**

itself proved more of an obstacle. The American battle fleet suffered waves of kamikaze attacks from Japanese planes that badly damaged the battleships USS *California* and USS *New Mexico.* On January 9, 1945, a 68,000-strong American invasion force landed at Lingayen Gulf in the west of Luzon, aiming to approach the capital, Manila, from the north. American forces also landed south of Manila and to its west on the Bataan Peninsula.

The battle for Luzon

The Americans met little initial resistance as Japanese forces commander General Tomoyuki Yamashita had not anticipated the Lingayen Gulf landing site. He had divided his 262,000 troops into three groups—most of them in the north, with only 30,000 defending Bataan and the western shores, and 80,000 defending Manila and the south. MacArthur was anxious to capture Manila quickly, and three divisions reached the city in early February.

At this point, Yamashita's local naval commander Sanji Iwabuchi launched a desperate defense of the city. The Americans freed Allied prisoners held in Manila's Santo Tomas internment camp, but were unable to fully secure the city without a month of savage street fighting, by which time more than 100,000 citizens had been killed—many massacred by the Japanese. By the end of May, the conquest was largely complete, but Yamashita's forces remained entrenched in caves and tunnels in the island's northern hills. Fighting continued for months more; Yamashita did not give himself up until September 2, when Japan officially surrendered.

Targeting Japan

In May, while MacArthur's forces were retaking the Philippines, Australian units began to reoccupy Borneo. They secured it by the end of July, denying the Japanese an important source of oil as well as a key land base. The major target now was Japan itself.

From late 1944, the US Army Air Forces had begun strategic bombing raids on Japanese infrastructure. These were carried out by B-29 Superfortress aircraft based 1,565 miles (2,519 km) southeast of Japan in the Mariana Islands, which had been seized a few months earlier. General Curtis LeMay, who took charge of the operation in early 1945, deemed precision daylight bombing ineffective as, at the high altitudes required to avoid Japanese air defenses, powerful jet stream air currents blew bombs off-course, while frequent cloudy weather obscured targets. Instead, he ordered nighttime, low-altitude incendiary attacks.

On March 9, more than 300 B-29 Superfortress planes headed for Tokyo. Incendiary bombs rained down on the city, engulfing 250,000 buildings in flames and killing more than 80,000 people, with over 40,000 injured, and a million rendered »

US troops fire on Japanese positions in Manila. Unlike the army, which had obeyed Yamashita's orders to evacuate the city, the Japanese marines were determined to fight to the death.

homeless as fires burned through vast areas of the city. It was the most destructive bombing raid ever launched, and Tokyo's defenses proved wholly inadequate. LeMay judged it highly successful since American losses had been light. Similar raids targeted the cities of Nagoya, Osaka, and Kobe later in March, and more were planned.

Attacking Iwo Jima

While the firebombing operations were underway, a bloody battle was raging on Iwo Jima, a strategic strip of land between the Marianas and Japan. Just 5 miles (8 km) long, it had no native population, but was used by Japan as an air base. Defending the island were up to 20,000 heavily armed Japanese troops, commanded by General Tadamichi Kuribayashi, who had built fortified underground bunkers, command centers, and concrete guard-posts, linked by extensive tunnels. As a result, the initial, intense Allied bombardment of the island had little effect, and the first American marines landing on February 19 incurred enormous losses from Japanese mortar fire, machine guns, and land mines laid in advance.

Boeing B-29 Superfortress planes bomb Hiratsuka, Japan, in 1945, as seen from a nose cone window. Their targets were the city's naval ammunitions arsenal and an aircraft factory.

In the following days, ambushes and surprise attacks continued to exact a terrible toll on the tens of thousands of American forces engaged in the battle, who used grenades and flamethrowers to flush out the Japanese troops. Ferocious battles raged—almost nonstop—for more than five weeks.

On March 21, American forces finally blew up Kuribayashi's stronghold—a complex of tunnels around a gorge in the northwest of the island. A few days later, the Japanese survivors mounted a counterattack. It was the final battle for Iwo Jima, which ended in victory for the Americans on March 26. Scattered Japanese guerrillas continued to hold out against the garrison force left on the island, however, with two refusing to surrender until 1949.

More than 6,800 Americans died in the conflict and over 19,000 were wounded. For their courage, 27 marines and sailors were awarded the Medal of Honor, the highest American military decoration. Most of the Japanese fought bravely to the last; only 216 were taken prisoner.

The Battle of Okinawa

The costly victory at Iwo Jima was a salutary warning of the ferocity with which Japan would defend its land.

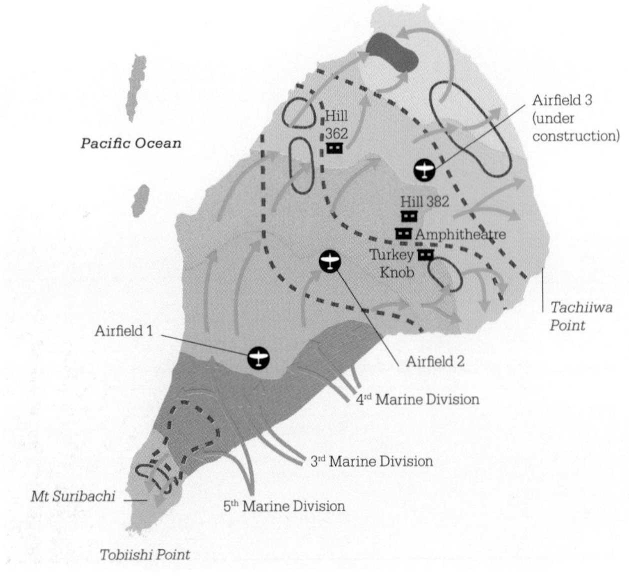

US marines spread across Iwo Jima over five weeks in February and March 1945, capturing the island in four stages. By March 14, Iwo Jima was declared secure, and by March 26, the US had taken the last Japanese stronghold.

Key:
- Airstrip
- US landings
- US advances
- Japanese lines of defense
- Japanese artillery positions
- Heavy fortified terrain/high ground
- Last Japanese stronghold until March 26, 1945

US territorial gains, 1945:
- Beachhead on February 19
- By February 24
- By March 1
- By March 9
- By March 14

Marines plant the American flag on Mount Suribachi, Iwo Jima, for a second time. Photographer Joe Rosenthal restaged the event to create this iconic image, which won him a Pulitzer Prize.

Days later, when the Allies attacked its most southerly island, Okinawa, one of the bloodiest battles of the war in the Pacific ensued.

The Allied forces planned to subdue the Japanese response with a heavy preliminary bombardment to support the initial landing on April 1 of some 50,000 American troops (of a total force of more than 180,000) on the island's west coast. Japanese resistance was muted at first, belying the latent strength of General Mitsuru Ushijima's 100,000 troops waiting in caves and fortified bunkers. The Americans advanced, seizing two air bases that day, and pressed on toward the north of the island, suffering more than 1,000 casualties but gaining ground.

In the south, in a rugged area called Shuri, brutal fighting at close quarters amid torrential rains raged for more than 11 weeks. The Allied fleet also came under heavy fire; between April 6 and June 22, it suffered some 1,900 attacks from Japanese kamikaze planes that destroyed at least 30 warships, although the mighty Japanese *Yamato* battleship, on a final suicide mission, was intercepted and sunk.

By the battle's end on June 21, at least 12,000 Americans, over 100,000 Japanese troops, and as many Okinawan civilians had died. The Allies had won a bitter battle, but Japan remained defiant—as yet unaware of the atomic devastation the enemy would soon unleash. ■

The Battle of Okinawa—the largest amphibious assault of the war in the Pacific—was also one of the costliest in terms of human life, earning it the nickname "Typhoon of Steel."

Tadamichi Kuribayashi

Born in Nagano, Japan, in 1891, Tadamichi Kuribayashi, who commanded the Japanese troops on Iwo Jima, was a poet and writer as well as a gifted military leader. In 1928, he went to the US as a deputy military attaché and studied briefly at Harvard University. During the 1930s, he was promoted several times.

In 1944, as commander of the Imperial Japanese Army's 109th Division, Kuribayashi was sent to defend Iwo Jima. He ordered the fortifying of underground positions as an optimum defense against the superior numbers of American forces, who arrived in February 1945 expecting the battle to be won in five days. Kuribayashi's aim was to win time for Japan by inflicting casualties high enough to deter the US from invading the Japanese mainland. On March 17, as US forces closed in on his stronghold, Kuribayashi sent a message to the Japanese headquarters, together with three death poems. A final farewell radio message was received on March 23. How and when he died is unknown. His body was never found.

MY GOD, WHAT HAVE WE DONE?

THE BOMBING OF HIROSHIMA AND NAGASAKI (AUGUST 6–9, 1945)

IN CONTEXT

FOCUS
Nuclear weapons

BEFORE
March 9–10, 1945 A US firebomb raid destroys much of Tokyo, killing 100,000 people or more.

May 8, 1945 Nazi Germany surrenders unconditionally, ending the war in Europe.

July 26, 1945 The Potsdam Declaration demands that Japan surrenders immediately, but it is ignored.

AFTER
August 15, 1945 The United States accepts Japan's unconditional surrender.

January 1946 The United Nations (UN) calls for the elimination of nuclear weapons.

1949 The USSR conducts its first nuclear weapon test at Semipalatinsk, Kazakhstan.

The onset of World War II coincided with nuclear physicists discovering the theoretical possibility of splitting uranium atoms to release vast quantities of energy. In October 1939, Albert Einstein, the world's most revered scientist, wrote to President Roosevelt informing him that "extremely powerful bombs of a new type" might be built.

Once America entered the war, Roosevelt initiated the top-secret Manhattan Project to build an atom bomb. The project was spearheaded by a team of physicists under Robert Oppenheimer at Los Alamos in New Mexico. The scientific and

See also: The Japanese attack Pearl Harbor 138–145 ▪ Kamikaze pilots 277 ▪ The Japanese home front 278–279 ▪ Victory in Europe 298–303 ▪ Japan under siege 304–307 ▪ Japan surrenders 312–313

> … the Japanese were ready to surrender and it wasn't necessary to hit them with that awful thing.
> **Dwight D. Eisenhower**

technical challenges turned out to be formidable. Both Germany and Japan initiated atom bomb programs, but neither succeeded. Sourcing fissile uranium and plutonium and devoting large-scale industrial resources to the project (funded by some $2 billion of government money spent without the approval of Congress), the United States alone was capable of turning scientific theory into practical weaponry.

It was assumed by all involved that the new weapon was being built to be used. The overall head of the Manhattan Project, army engineer General Leslie Groves, had been tasked with both manufacturing an atom bomb and deploying the new weapon. In autumn 1944, he organized a special air group flying the Boeing B-29 Superfortress, a new long-range bomber. Led by Colonel Paul Tibbets, the airmen trained rigorously in preparation for dropping the bomb as soon as it became available. In spring 1945, Tibbets' B-29s were sent to Tinian island in the Marianas, within flying range of Japan. Groves drove his project forward, eager to have the new bomb ready before the war ended.

Moral questions

In May 1945, new US president Harry S. Truman—who had not been told about the Manhattan Project while vice-president—set up an interim committee under Secretary of War Henry Stimson to advise him on nuclear matters. The committee members were aware of moral and political issues regarding the bomb's use. America's official policy, despite many deviations in practice, was to avoid deliberately bombing civilians.

Targets selected

At around this time, a Chicago-based group of Manhattan Project physicists submitted a report suggesting alternatives to using the atom bomb against Japanese cities. Called the Franck Report, after physicist James Franck who headed the team, it proposed either dropping the bomb on a deserted place or giving the Japanese advance warning of where it would be used, so the population could be evacuated. The interim committee rejected the report.

A separate target committee, chaired by Groves, selected a list of cities for atom bombs to destroy. Its task was complicated by the fact that so many Japanese cities had already been reduced to rubble and ashes. Hiroshima was chosen because it was a relatively undamaged port city with military facilities, and because it was flat, which would maximize the spread of the explosion. Nagasaki only made it on to the tail end of the list, as its hilly terrain was considered less suitable. Cities on the target »

Young women, known as "Calutron Girls," monitor calutrons (machines that separated uranium isotopes) in the uranium enrichment facility at Oak Ridge National Laboratory in Tennessee.

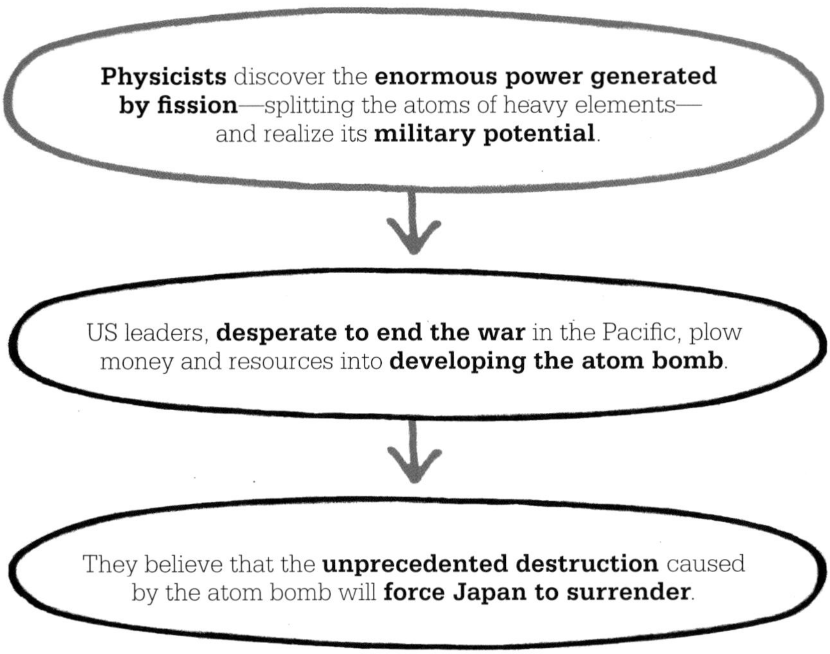

Physicists discover the enormous power generated by fission—splitting the atoms of heavy elements—and realize its military potential.
US leaders, desperate to end the war in the Pacific, plow money and resources into developing the atom bomb.
They believe that the unprecedented destruction caused by the atom bomb will force Japan to surrender.

shortlist were spared conventional bombing raids in order to preserve them for the atom bomb.

Invasion plans

On June 18, top US civilian and military chiefs met to discuss how the war could be brought to a successful conclusion. The atom bomb was not mentioned—most of those present had no idea the Manhattan Project existed—and the meeting resolved to attack Japan in every way possible, by sea, air, and land, to procure a Japanese surrender as rapidly as possible. In the event that naval blockade and firebombing of cities failed to persuade Japan to capitulate, a first seaborne invasion of the Japanese homeland was provisionally scheduled for November 1945, to be followed, if necessary, by a second wave of landings in March 1946. Military planners projected that 25,000 US soldiers might lose their lives in the first landings and 21,000 in the second operation. Despite these predictions, when US service chiefs, including Chief of Staff Admiral William D. Leahy and General Eisenhower, were privately informed of the intention to use the atom bomb they reacted negatively. The air commander in the Pacific region, General Carl Spaatz, demanded written authorization from the president, for fear of later being blamed for the consequences. However, none of the military chiefs' reservations about the bomb was pressed with any great urgency.

Tests and manufacture

On July 16, 1945, the world's first atomic test was carried out at Alamogordo in the New Mexico desert, producing an explosion equivalent to 25,000 tons of TNT and generating temperatures hotter than the core of the sun. The Manhattan Project had succeeded. The Potsdam summit conference of Allied leaders opened the following day. Facing difficult negotiations with Soviet leader Joseph Stalin amid steadily worsening US–Soviet relations, President Truman hoped his hand would be strengthened by possession of the new weapon. When Truman told Stalin of the bomb's existence, however, he did not achieve the effect he expected. Stalin already knew all about the bomb from Soviet spies inside the Manhattan Project.

While the Potsdam summit proceeded, the materials for the first atom bombs were shipped to Tinian for assembly. Groves informed Truman that the first bomb, a uranium-based device code named "Little Boy," would be ready for use in early August. A second plutonium-based bomb, called "Fat Man," would quickly follow, with a third in the pipeline.

On July 26, the Allies issued a statement calling on the Japanese to surrender unconditionally. Known as the Potsdam Declaration, the statement made vague apocalyptic threats regarding Japan's fate if it failed to surrender—but it did not specifically mention the atom bomb. The Japanese response

> We call upon the government of Japan to proclaim … unconditional surrender … The alternative for Japan is prompt and utter destruction.
>
> **The Potsdam Declaration**

Bombing targets	Estimated deaths caused
Warsaw, September 1939	25,800
Hamburg, July 24–August 3, 1943	43,000
Tokyo, March 9–10, 1945	At least 100,000
Dresden, April 13–15, 1945	18,000
Hiroshima, August 6, 1945	80,000, rising to 146,000 with later radiation deaths
Nagasaki, August 9, 1945	40,000, rising to 80,000 with later radiation deaths

The numbers killed in Hiroshima and Nagasaki exceeded those killed by conventional bombs in European cities. But the firebombing of Tokyo was the deadliest event.

was noncommittal, which the Allies interpreted as contemptuous rejection. Meanwhile, in the Pacific, Japanese forces were still attacking US warships.

Double shock

On the morning of August 6, 1945, Tibbets took off from Tinian at the controls of a B-29 he dubbed "Enola Gay," his mother's maiden name. On board were 11 other crew members and the "Little Boy" bomb. Accompanied by two other B-29s, the aircraft arrived over Hiroshima at 8:15 am. Dropped from high altitude, the bomb airburst over the city center, releasing an intense flash of light, heat, and radiation, followed by a blast wave that destroyed almost every building within 1 mile (1.6 km) of the detonation point. Firestorms ignited by the explosion devastated a much wider area of the city.

After the bombing, Truman made a radio broadcast announcing the existence of the atom bomb to the world and threatening the Japanese with "a rain of ruin from the air, the like of which has never been seen on this earth." In the absence of any immediate response by the Japanese government, the second atom bomb was dropped three days later. The original target was the city of Kokura, but bad weather forced the B-29s to divert to Nagasaki. The result was essentially the same as at Hiroshima, although the city's hills provided protection for some against the blast and radiation.

The death toll from the bombings of Hiroshima and Nagasaki can never be established with certainty. Estimates of deaths on the day and over following months—including those from radiation sickness—range from 80,000 to 146,000 at Hiroshima and 40,000 to 80,000 at Nagasaki. Most victims were elderly civilians, women, and children. On the day after the Nagasaki raid, Groves informed his superiors that a third atom bomb would be ready for use by around August 17, but he was told that no further bombs were to be dropped without the president's instruction. It was by then becoming clear that Japan intended to surrender. ■

The atom bomb is dropped on Hiroshima. The explosion ignites the surrounding air, causing a fireball to rise more than 60,000 ft (18,000 m) into the air, creating a "firestorm cloud."

THE SKIES NO LONGER RAIN DEATH

JAPAN SURRENDERS (AUGUST 15, 1945)

IN CONTEXT

FOCUS
Allied victory in the Pacific

BEFORE
June 21, 1945 The Allies overcome Japanese resistance on Okinawa.

August 6, 1945 The Japanese city of Hiroshima is destroyed by an atomic bomb.

August 9, 1945 A second atomic bomb is dropped on Nagasaki; Soviet troops invade Manchuria.

AFTER
September 1945 The Supreme Command of Allied Powers (SCAP) occupies Japan. It dismantles its army and begins to restructure its economy.

April 1946 A military tribunal in Tokyo begins the trial of Japanese leaders accused of war crimes.

By early June 1945, Japanese leaders knew they could not win the war but sought a way to avoid national humiliation. Japan's Supreme War Leadership Council, a six-man inner cabinet, was split between a "peace" party and a "war" party. Headed by Prime Minister Kantaro Suzuki, the former hoped for a deal with the Allies, but their search for a negotiated settlement ignored the reality of America's unwavering commitment to unconditional surrender. The "war" party favored a fight to the death as essential for the spiritual survival of the nation. Emperor Hirohito simultaneously backed the pursuit of negotiations and authorized military planning for Operation Ketsu-Go, the mass mobilization of Japanese civilians for a suicidal defense against invasion.

Political paralysis

Weeks passed while the divided Japanese leadership indulged fantasies of a peace deal brokered by the USSR or a sudden military victory that might persuade the

Japan was certain to **lose the war** but its leaders were determined to **avoid surrender**.

↓

When the **US dropped atomic bombs** on two Japanese cities and the USSR joined the war in the Pacific, **Japan's defeat looked certain**.

↓

Some Japanese leaders **wanted to continue fighting** to preserve Japanese honor, while others sought **surrender and peace** for the preservation of the nation.

See also: Japan on the march 44–45 ▪ The Japanese attack Pearl Harbor 138–145 ▪ The Japanese home front 278–279 ▪ Japan under siege 304–307

> If we did not act, the Japanese race would perish and I would be unable to protect my subjects.
> **Emperor Hirohito**

Allies to grant favorable terms. Suzuki did not respond to the Potsdam Declaration of July 26, which threatened Japan with "prompt and utter destruction" if it did not surrender. The war council remained deadlocked, with some members prepared to surrender if the emperor was allowed to remain on the throne, and others insisting Japan must be kept free from occupation. Only the double shock of the Hiroshima bombing on August 6 and the USSR's declaration of war on Japan two days later ended Japan's political paralysis.

On August 10, after the US had dropped the Nagasaki bomb, the emperor declared that Japan must "endure the unendurable" and surrender as long as his own position was respected. The Americans refused to commit themselves on Hirohito's future, simply stating that the Japanese would be free to choose their own government at some later date.

On August 14, Hirohito recorded a message of surrender to be broadcast on the radio. Extremist army officers attempted to stage a coup, hoping to seize the recording before its transmission. They failed, and on August 15 the Japanese people heard their emperor's voice for the first time—announcing their nation's surrender. ■

General Yoshijiro Umezo signs the unconditional surrender of Japan on board USS *Missouri* in the Bay of Tokyo on September 2, 1945.

Emperor Hirohito

Born in 1901, Japanese Emperor Hirohito succeeded to the throne on December 25, 1926. His regnal era was designated "showa," or "bright peace." Although in principle his imperial authority was absolute, in practice he refrained from involvement in politics. An exception was when he intervened to suppress an attempted coup by extreme nationalist army officers in 1936.

During World War II, Japan's enemies considered the emperor fully responsible for his country's aggression and war crimes. There is strong evidence of his commitment to Japanese expansion and his knowledge of criminal actions. The main act directly attributable to his authority, however, was the decision to surrender in 1945. After the war, the Americans found him ready to cooperate in setting up a Japanese constitutional monarchy. He renounced divine status in 1946, cultivating a modest, benign image at home and becoming an accepted symbol of peace-loving post-war Japan on the world stage. He died in Aoyama Palace in Tokyo in 1989.

FOR YOUR TOMORROW, WE GAVE OUR TODAY

THE COST OF WAR

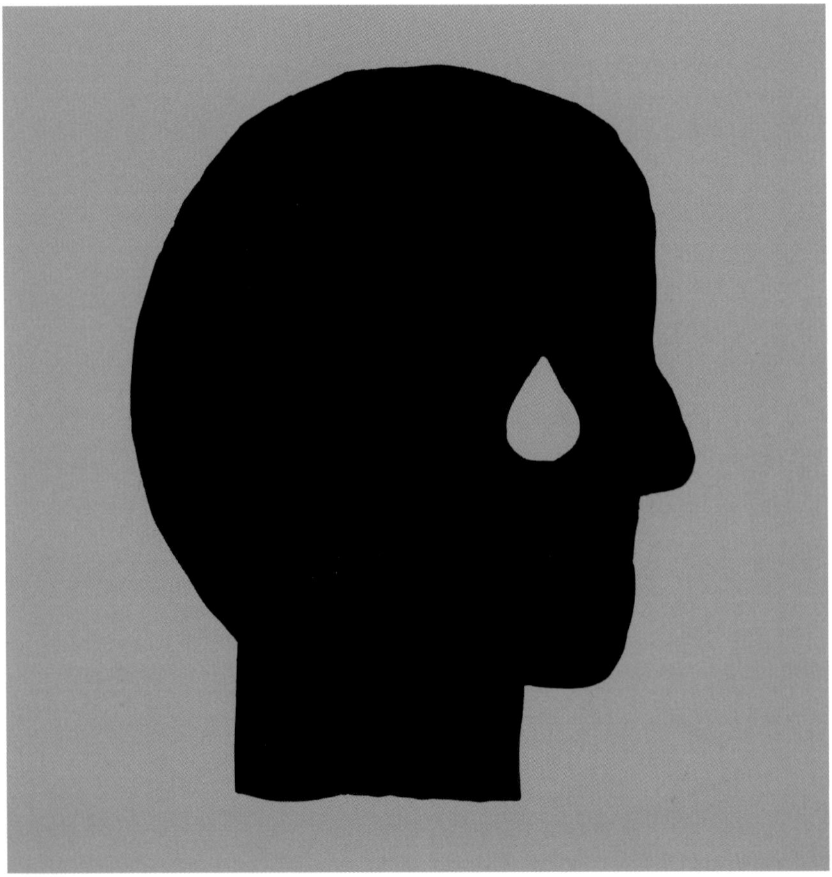

IN CONTEXT

FOCUS
Impact on humanity

BEFORE
1803–1815 The Napoleonic wars embroil Europe and cost up to 6 million lives.

1914–1918 World War I is the first modern global war, killing 18 million people, including 7 million civilians.

AFTER
1954–1975 At least 3.3 million civilians and soldiers perish in the Vietnam War.

1998–2003 In the Democratic Republic of the Congo, 5.4 million people die during the Second Congo War, mostly through disease and famine.

When World War II finally ended, people began to count the cost, and they have been counting it ever since. The simplest measure is in lives lost, but even this is not known with any degree of accuracy. The number of military deaths alone was huge, mostly young men with an average age of just 23. Nearly every nation had combatants—and at least some casualties.

The statistics are most reliable for the US and UK. The former lost more than 400,000 combatants, mostly in the last year of the war, after the D-Day landing took them into direct conflict with Germany; almost three-quarters of American casualties occurred there. The UK lost about the same number, and the Commonwealth also bore a heavy toll, with 87,000 Indians, 45,000 Canadians, and 40,000 Australians killed, for example.

See also: The destruction of Poland 58–63 ▪ Operation Barbarossa 124–131 ▪ The Holocaust 172–177 ▪ The Battle of Stalingrad 178–183 ▪ China and Japan at war 250–253 ▪ The bombing of Hiroshima and Nagasaki 308–311

The Lorraine American cemetery and memorial in St. Avold, France, contains 10,489 graves—the largest number of American World War II graves in Europe.

Germany lost more than half a million soldiers on the Western Front, but its biggest losses by far were on the Eastern Front, where about 2.3 million German soldiers died fighting the Red Army. It was there that the heaviest death toll of the war occurred in 1942–1943. In the Battle of Stalingrad, the German Sixth Army captured the city before being cut off by the encircling Red Army—up to 1 million Germans and their allies were killed, wounded, or captured. But despite being the victors, Soviet casualties were even higher in arguably the most deadly battle in history.

Soviet losses

The cost of winning the war in Europe bore very heavily on the USSR, which lost more soldiers than all the other combatants in Europe put together. The true number of Soviet losses is unknown—officially 8.7 million, the true figure is believed to be almost 11 million. The military death toll in eastern Europe doesn't end there. About 240,000 Polish soldiers died, including at least 22,000 murdered by the Soviet army in the Katyn massacre of 1940. Even more Yugoslav soldiers died.

Meanwhile in Asia, casualties were almost equally great. The heaviest death toll fell on China, which lost up to 4 million soldiers, and Japan, which lost more than 2 million. In the struggle for Okinawa in 1945, 100,000 Japanese and 50,000 American troops died.

In addition to those killed, there were also vast numbers wounded in combat. In the Allied armies, for every soldier who died on the battlefield, three were wounded badly enough to take no further part in combat. Japanese deaths were so much higher than the US because of the Japanese soldiers' refusal to surrender and because the American field hospitals were far superior. Many of the wounded were disabled for life. And those who recovered physically were often scarred mentally.

> Your name is unknown. Your deed is immortal.
> **Tomb of the Unknown Soldier, Moscow**

Civilian victims

More than any previous war, World War II dragged in huge numbers of civilians. Many were »

Casualty numbers for military personnel during World War II were highest for the USSR, but there were also heavy death tolls in Germany, China, and Japan.

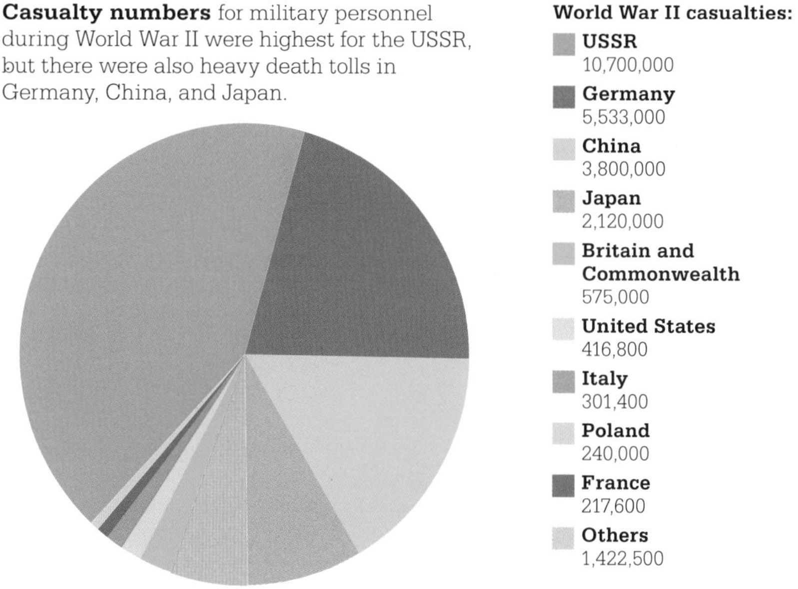

caught up directly in the combat when invading armies swept through their towns and villages, or were deliberately targeted in mass bombing raids on cities such as Tokyo and Dresden. Many more died in labor camps and death camps, from deliberate starvation, disease, cold, and worse. Civilian deaths are even harder to quantify than military casualties, but broad estimates suggest that while more than 20 million combatants died in World War II, perhaps twice that number of civilians died. This estimate includes a horrific number of civilians targeted for mass murder by the Nazis, who systematically killed more than 6 million Jews, Roma, and other groups in the Holocaust.

> The Savichevs are dead ... Everyone is dead ... Only Tanya is left.
>
> **Tanya Savicheva**
> **14-year-old survivor of the siege of Leningrad, in her diary, 1944**

National tolls

Numerically the worst-hit nation was the USSR, where the civilian death toll was almost equal to the total number of soldiers killed in the whole conflict. Some were deliberately killed or allowed to die by their own side; and many more were killed by the Germans during their occupation. In 2020, Russian military historian Mikhail Meltyukhov estimated that the Nazis killed 15.9–17.4 million civilians on Soviet territory, including at least 1.2 million during the prolonged siege of Leningrad (1941–1944). China lost at least 16 million of its citizens—mostly during the Japanese occupation.

Proportionately, Poland suffered the highest death toll, losing one in five of its population—almost 6 million people. Millions died in the Balkans, with Yugoslavia recording the highest number of casualties. Germany lost up to 3 million citizens, many as a result of bombing raids, which also claimed the lives of between 240,000 and 900,000 inhabitants of Japanese cities. By comparison, the UK lost about 60,000 civilians and France 173,000.

Famine and rape

Millions died as a result of famine: in the USSR, Java, and Vietnam; in Bengal province in India; and in Henan in China. And in Greece, 300,000—5 percent of the

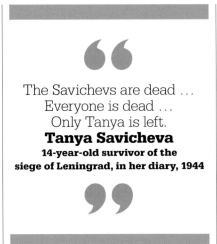

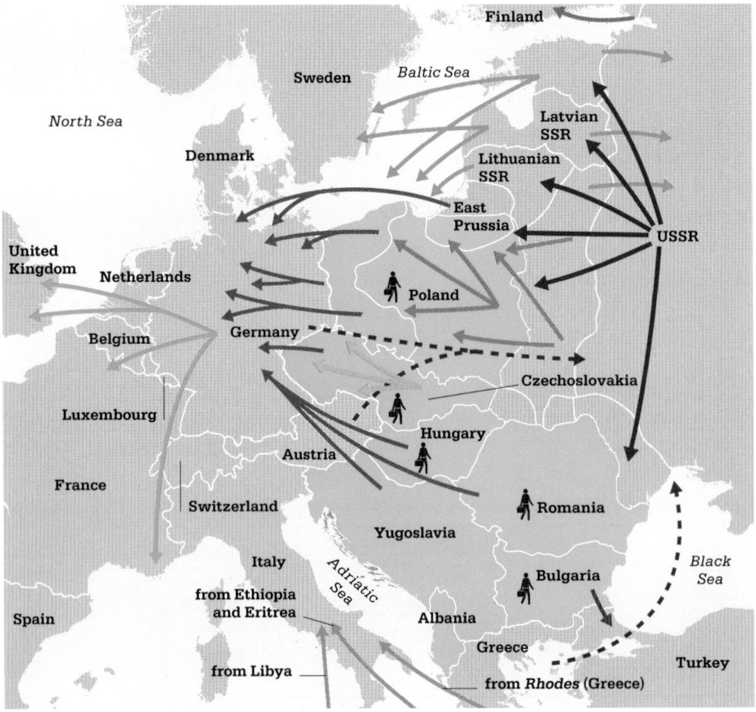

Between 1945 and 1952, more than 31 million people emigrated or were expelled, resettled, or evacuated. In the immediate aftermath of the war, many Jewish people tried to emigrate to Palestine, although the majority were detained by the British authorities prior to the creation of the State of Israel in 1948.

Key:

States that became communist 1945–1948

Peoples resettled, evacuated, expelled, or emigrated

- Russians forcibly repatriated (5.5 million)
- Russians (2.3 million)
- Germans (5.25 million)
- Poles (4.5 million)
- Czechs (1.95 million)
- Resettled by International Refugee Organization (1 million)
- Finns (410,000)
- Italians (230,000)
- Baltic peoples (200,000 to west, 22,000 to east)
- Turks (130,000)
- Jewish emigration to Israel 1945–1950 (286,000)

The British merchant ship *Mataroa* carries 1,204 Jewish refugees, many of them the survivors of concentration camps, to Haifa in Palestine/Israel in July 1945.

population—starved to death during the German occupation. Troops of several nations used rape as a weapon of subjugation or revenge. This was particularly true of the German army in Poland, the Japanese during the occupation of China and east Asia, the SS in the concentration camps, and the Red Army during the invasion of Poland and Germany. The true scale of this violence is unknown, but at least 1.4 million German women are thought to have been raped by Red Army soldiers in 1945–1946.

Emotional damage

A study of post-war mental health in Poland found that 30–40 percent of the population that had lived through the war suffered post-traumatic stress disorder. And Poland was by no means unique.

When the war ended, in Europe alone 20 million people were left displaced. Two years after the war, 850,000 people were still living in displaced-persons' camps in Europe, and between 1945 and 1952 more than 31 million people were resettled in an attempt to work with the continent's newly defined borders. Many displaced people did get home, but others returned to devastation—and many never returned home, including hundreds of thousands of European Jews. Tens of millions of children missed years of schooling.

Rebuilding cities

With industries and agriculture devastated, and with formerly prosperous cities such as Berlin, Dresden, and Tokyo reduced to rubble, rebuilding lives was a formidable task. France estimated the total cost of damage at about three times its annual national income. In Poland, 30 percent of buildings were destroyed, including 60 percent of its schools. In heavily bombed Germany, 49 of the biggest cities had lost 40 percent of their houses. Higher-than-usual rates of leukemia were recorded among the residents of the Japanese cities of Hiroshima and Nagasaki in the years following the end of the war, as a result of the atomic bomb attacks of 1945.

World War II was the most expensive war in history, costing an estimated $4 trillion or more. The biggest spenders were the Americans, but Germany, the USSR, China, and the UK also spent heavily. Remarkably, though, amid all the devastation, people began to pick up the pieces and rebuild shattered lives. ■

UNRRA

US president Franklin D. Roosevelt was aware of the massive refugee problem that was developing and, in 1943, he led 44 nations to create the United Nations Relief and Rehabilitation Administration (UNRRA)—preceding by two years the formation of the United Nations itself.

Initially, the intention had been that UNRRA would help only nationals from the Allied nations, but Jewish organizations pressed for it to cover any people who had been forced to flee their homes. When the war finished, UNRRA played a huge part in resettling displaced people, including helping 11 million non-Germans in Germany return home. It set up nearly 800 resettlement camps, housed more than 700,000 people, and delivered vital aid, food, and medicine in eastern and southern Europe. In 1947, its functions were taken over by the International Refugee Organization.

CIVILIZATION CANNOT SURVIVE THESE WRONGS BEING REPEATED

THE NUREMBERG TRIALS AND DENAZIFICATION (1945–1949)

IN CONTEXT

FOCUS
War crimes

BEFORE
1474 Burgundian knight Peter von Hagenbach is the first commanding officer to be convicted of war crimes.

1920 The League of Nations sets up the Permanent Court of International Justice (PCIJ).

1943 The Allies' Moscow declaration calls for Nazi leaders to be put on trial.

1944 The Allies agree to set up the United Nations, including an international court.

AFTER
1961 Adolf Eichmann, a chief organizer of the Holocaust, is kidnapped in Argentina, to be tried and executed in Israel.

1987 Klaus Barbie is tried and convicted of deporting Jews.

2017 The Yugoslav war crimes tribunal convicts Serbian president Slobodan Milošević.

When the surrender was finally signed, and the fighting was eventually over, the Allies were faced with the vexed question of what to do with the Nazis. There was a keen desire to bring to justice those who had initiated a war that brought so much pain and suffering to so many. And there was an even keener desire to punish those responsible for the horror of the Holocaust.

In 1943, Roosevelt, Churchill, and Stalin had met in Moscow to make the Declaration of Atrocities, promising retribution. Once the war ended, Churchill wanted to execute high-ranking officers immediately to avoid what he

New categories of crime created to charge the Nazi leaders at the Nuremberg Trials.

↓

Crimes against peace: planning, preparing for, and starting **wars of aggression**.

↓

War crimes: violating the international **laws and customs** of war in the **treatment of civilians and prisoners**.

↓

Crimes against humanity: deliberate, systematic, and widespread **attacks on a civilian population**.

See also: Nazi Europe 168–171 ▪ The Holocaust 172–177 ▪ Prisoners of war 184–187 ▪ The destruction of German cities 287 ▪ Victory in Europe 298–303 ▪ Aftermath 320–327

saw would be the pantomime of a show trial. But Stalin argued that they must be given a proper trial, and his view prevailed.

Tried for new crimes

In October 1945, 24 Nazi leaders, including Hermann Göring, went on trial in Nuremberg, accused of newly created categories of crime: crimes against peace, war crimes, and crimes against humanity. These hearings took place before the International Military Tribunal. The Nazis argued that they could not be tried for crimes that didn't exist when they were committed. But in the end, after listening to the horrors gradually revealed over many weeks, the tribunal found all but three guilty. Twelve were sentenced to death—Göring had already died by suicide—and the rest were given long prison sentences. Between December 1946 and April 1949, another 12 military tribunals (the Nuremberg Military Tribunals) tried lesser-known Nazi leaders.

> If we can cultivate … the idea that … war-making is the way to the prisoner's dock rather than the way to honors, we will have accomplished something toward making the peace more secure.
>
> **Robert H. Jackson**
> **Chief US prosecutor at the Nuremberg Trials, 1945**

The defendants at Nuremberg listen to their sentences being read out. Hitler, Himmler, and Goebbels had died by suicide in spring 1945 before they could be brought to trial.

Some argued that the trials achieved only "victor's justice," since the Allies had been guilty of their own atrocities, such as the bombing of Dresden. But most felt that the trials were crucial in establishing the rule of law as a means of settling disputes. Crucially, they set the precedent of legal punishment for war crimes and genocide.

The future of Germany

Meanwhile, the Allies sought to rid Nazis and Nazism from all public life across occupied Europe. Denazification was broad in its aims, and involved everything from removing Nazi publications from libraries to ensuring former Nazis were removed from key positions. In the newly formed Federal Republic of Germany, the swastika was banned, and advocating Nazi ideas was punishable by death—although capital punishment was abolished there in 1949.

It was very hard to establish just who had been a Nazi and who had not, so in 1949, when Konrad Adenauer became the first chancellor of the new German republic, he abandoned the policy, favoring the reintegration of Nazis into the new order so that the country could move forward. The Western Allies, now seeing the USSR as a bigger threat, were prepared to go along with this. The story in the West over the next few decades became one of Germany's redemption and success through the wise policies of the Americans, British, and French, culminating in the fall of the Berlin Wall in 1989. But not everyone agrees with this analysis. ■

PRESERVE IN PEACE WHAT WE WON IN WAR

AFTERMATH

IN CONTEXT

FOCUS
International relations

BEFORE
1815 The Final Act of the Congress of Vienna reorganizes Europe after the Napoleonic wars. It aims to achieve peace through a balance of power.

1919 After World War I, the Treaty of Versailles blames and punishes Germany for the war, with disastrous long-term consequences.

AFTER
1955 The USSR creates the Warsaw Pact, a defense treaty with Eastern Bloc nations.

1987 US president Ronald Reagan and Soviet leader Mikhail Gorbachev agree on a nuclear arms control treaty.

1989–1992 The USSR breaks up, Germany is reunified, and many countries in eastern Europe and central Asia become independent.

In August 1945, the guns of World War II fell silent. For many in the victorious countries, it was a time for celebration, and street parties were held in London, New York, and Moscow. But the excitement did not last long. When people stopped and looked around them, they saw a devastated world of death, destruction, and displaced people. Major German cities, such as Berlin and Dresden, were in ruins; in the USSR, 70,000 villages and 1,700 towns had been destroyed. The cities of Hiroshima and Nagasaki were polluted by lethal radiation caused by the atomic bombings, while in China, huge tracts of farmland had been wiped out by the deliberate flooding of the Yellow River to repel Japanese troops.

> Nearly every other people are prostrate and helpless. They look to [America] for help.
>
> **Lyndon B. Johnson**
> **36th US president (1963–1969), speaking in 1947**

Revenge and ruins

The end of the war did not bring an immediate end to suffering. Revenge killings occurred across many of the former war zones, and scores were settled, often with cruelty and violence. Soviet soldiers raped millions of Austrian and German women, regarding them as spoils of war. In France, tens of thousands of women vilified for consorting with Germans during the war had their heads publicly shaved. Even the persecution of Jews in Europe did not end with the fall of the Nazis. On July 2, 1946, 42 Jewish people were murdered in the Polish town of Kielce. Many Jews fled to Palestine, but the British, anxious not to alienate their Arab allies, intercepted 50,000 Jewish refugees and interned them on Cyprus.

Economies were also shattered, with the means of production in ruins and infrastructure badly damaged. Famine was widespread

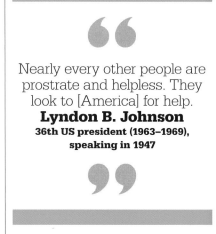

***Trümmerfrauen* clear away** rubble around the ruins of a hair salon in 1948 as part of the post-war restoration of Germany.

The *Trümmerfrauen*

One of the enduring German images of the post-war years is of armies of *Trümmerfrauen* ("rubble women"), hammers in hand, clearing away the rubble in ruined German cities.

They are often presented as the indomitable spirit of German womanhood—they were depicted as such in cheerful recruitment posters, and there are monuments to them in many German cities. This view of them, however, is only partly true. In East Germany, large numbers of women did willingly throw themselves into the work of rebuilding. Elsewhere, however, their numbers were quite small, as the work was often regarded as a punishment (former members of the Nazi Party were forced to do such labor), though some women were lured by the prospect of extra rations. Nonetheless, Germany's economic miracle ensured that the damage was swept away and the country rebuilt solidly in a remarkably short time.

See also: Failure of the League of Nations 50 ▪ Colonial ties 90–93 ▪ Victory in Europe 298–303 ▪ Japan surrenders 312–313 ▪ The cost of war 314–317 ▪ The Nuremberg Trials and denazification 318–319

The First General Assembly of the United Nations meets in London in 1946, attended by representatives of 51 states. Today, its 193 member nations gather at its headquarters in New York City.

in Europe and China, and rationing continued even in the victor countries. It was clear that the colonial era was also over. Japan's victories in Asia destroyed the power of the British and French in the region beyond recovery, and India's clamor for independence could not be ignored any longer. Demands for independence in Africa followed shortly after.

American dominance

As the European empires collapsed, the US, which had not suffered the same damage domestically as those nations situated in the main zones of conflict, emerged from the war with its economy and way of life intact. It quickly filled the power vacuum left by the largest European nations, establishing itself as the world's first superpower, boosted by its sole possession of atomic weapons. Consequently, it exerted enormous influence in shaping the post-war international order. In 1946, it was one of the driving forces behind the creation of UNICEF—the United Nations International Children's Emergency Fund—to provide aid to mothers and children in Europe and Asia.

The US also spearheaded the creation of the United Nations (UN) to replace the failed League of Nations, supported by Churchill and Stalin at the Yalta Conference, in February 1945. In San Francisco, in June 1945, with the war still raging, delegates from 50 nations agreed the UN charter, committed to two key ideas: that it would rid the world of "the scourge of war" and rebuild "faith in fundamental human rights."

The General Assembly was to be the UN's parliament, in which a representative from each member country could vote on proposals. However, the real power lay in the Security Council formed by the Big Four powers—the US, Britain, the USSR, and the Republic of China—later joined by France to make five. As permanent members of the Security Council, they would take the lead on all major decisions, though they were joined by six nonpermanent members, each serving for two years. An extra four nonpermanent members were added in 1965. However, some critics thought that, after the horrors of the war, only a federal world government would be able to maintain peace and that the UN would fail.

Stabilizing the economy

In addition to the UN, new financial organizations were formed in order to stabilize the global economy and promote economic cooperation. In the US, in July 1944, 730 delegates from all 44 allied nations gathered at the Mount Washington Hotel in Bretton Woods, New Hampshire, to establish the International Monetary Fund (IMF) and the International Bank for Reconstruction and Development (IBRD), which later became the World Bank, enabling countries experiencing short-term economic difficulty to borrow money. The USSR took part in »

> A world government must be created which is able to solve conflicts between nations by judicial decision.
>
> **Albert Einstein**
> **Physicist**

these discussions but refused to ratify them, arguing that these new institutions were simply organs of capitalism. The IMF began operating from Washington, D.C., in March 1947.

Allied divisions

In the end, an ideological battle between the US and the USSR split the Allies and shattered any hope that global harmony might emerge from the devastation of the war. Even as they forced the Germans into surrender in Berlin, Stalin's armies were brutally consolidating their control over eastern Europe. Despite promises made at Yalta of free and fair elections, Stalin was determined to use eastern Europe as a buffer zone to prevent an attack on the USSR by the West, even if it meant blocking democratic-socialist movements in these countries. Stalin's strategy was simple. Each eastern European state was to have a puppet government loyal first of all to the USSR, and each state's economy was tied to that of the USSR. If Soviet control was threatened, each state could use its own army or secret police to maintain power, or call on the Red Army for help. In February 1948, a coup sponsored by the USSR overthrew the government of Czechoslovakia and brought it into the Soviet sphere. Within three years, Bulgaria, Romania, Poland, and Hungary were also all under Soviet rule; Estonia, Latvia, Lithuania, Belarus, and Ukraine had already been subsumed as part of the USSR.

Western Allies were unsure of the extent of Stalin's ambitions. Would Greece and Turkey be next? In 1946, a civil war erupted in Greece between the Western-backed government and pro-communist forces. Britain was too financially exhausted to offer support, and US president Harry Truman was persuaded that his country should abandon its isolationist policy, and take a robust, interventionist attitude in foreign-policy matters. In March 1947, he outlined the Truman doctrine, which declared that the US would provide political, military, and economic assistance to all democratic nations under threat from external or internal authoritarian forces. It effectively committed the US to trying to contain the spread of communism.

Marshall Plan

With western Europe in ruins, the lure of communism was strong. US secretary of state George C. Marshall believed that the best way to prevent this was to provide aid to rebuild shattered economies quickly. Beginning in 1948, the Marshall Plan committed the US to spending 5 percent of its GDP on the recovery of the ruined continent and would see it provide $15 billion

> The United States should do whatever it is able to do to assist in the return of normal economic health in the world, without which there can be no political stability and no assured peace.
>
> **George C. Marshall**

The changing balance of power

After the war, there was a significant shift in the balance of global power. The USSR and the United States both emerged from the war as superpowers, while the major European nations experienced a decline in influence as a result of the impact of war and the loss of their colonies.

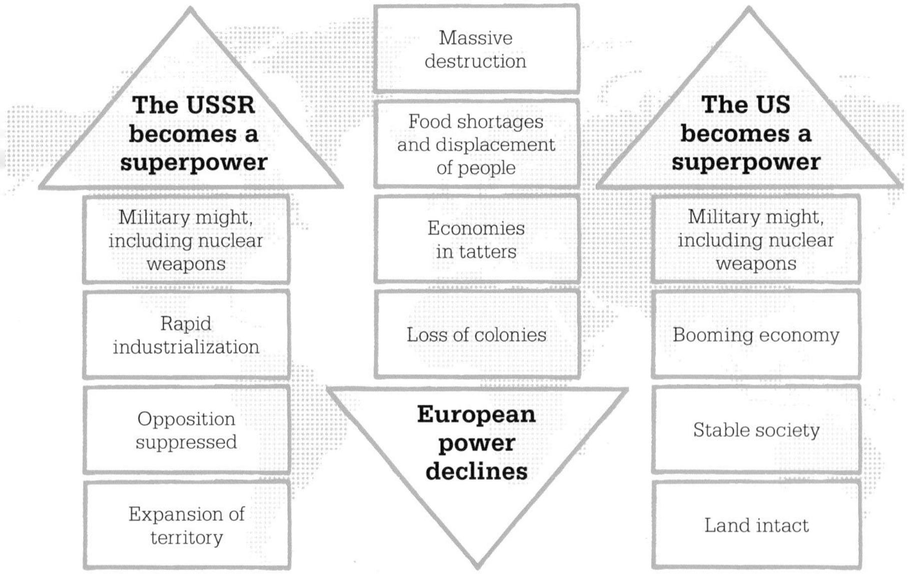

to rebuild cities, industry, and infrastructure. It would also remove trade barriers both within Europe and between Europe and the US. The idea was to give financial aid on a per capita basis, with larger amounts given to the main industrial powers of West Germany, France, and the UK, since they were deemed vital to recovery. Every European country was invited to participate, but there was a condition for receiving aid: the holding of free and fair elections. The intention of the message was clear, and Stalin forbade his eastern European satellites from taking part in the scheme.

The Cold War begins

Stalin was disturbed by the level of economic aid given to Germany and other countries. In June 1948, the tensions between the USSR and the Western Allies exploded into a full-blown crisis in Berlin when the Red Army blocked all access to the western sectors of the city by rail, road, and canal. Suddenly, 2.5 million people had no access to basic needs. For a year, the Western Allies conducted the largest air relief operation in history, transporting some 2.3 million tons of supplies into West Berlin over 11 months. By March 1949, the USSR had abandoned the blockade, but the Cold War between East and West—a long-running period of rivalry between the USSR, the US, and their corresponding allies—had begun.

In April 1949, Belgium, Britain, Canada, Denmark, France, Iceland, Italy, Luxembourg, the Netherlands, Norway, Portugal, and the United States joined in Washington to sign the North Atlantic Treaty. It was essentially a pact of mutual security, stating that a military attack against any of the signatories would be considered an attack against them all. The North Atlantic Treaty Organization (NATO) was to be the core of the West's military security against the USSR for the next 40 years, and when West Germany joined in 1955, the »

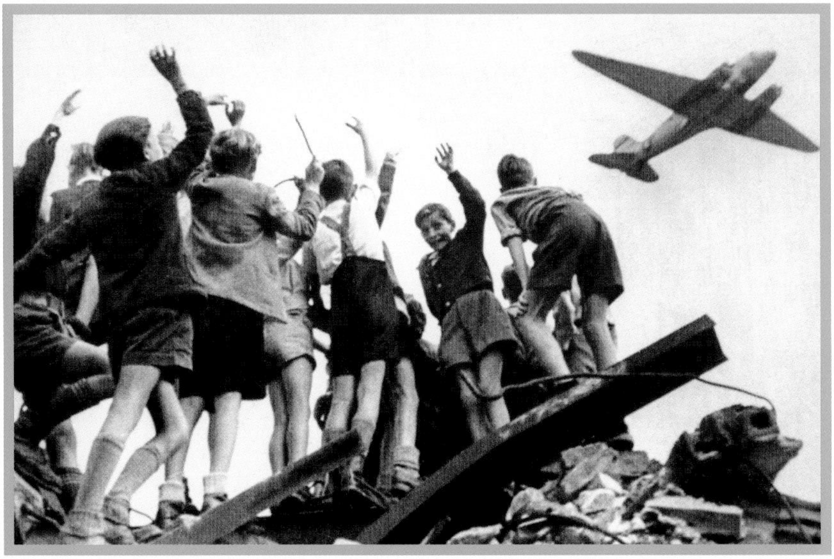

Children hail a plane delivering supplies during the blockade of Berlin. The Western Allies made 270,000 such flights over the course of the Berlin Airlift.

George C. Marshall

Born in Virginia in 1880, George C. Marshall entered the Virginia Military Institute at the age of 17 and remained an army man all his life. He served first in the Philippines in 1902, where he was quickly made a commander. Over the next 15 years he climbed through the ranks, overseeing the operations for the first US division to go into World War I in France in 1917. By the beginning of World War II, Marshall had risen to chief of staff, and oversaw the growth of the US military from a small army of 200,000 men to a well-equipped ground and air force of 8.3 million. Churchill described him as "the organizer of victory."

As secretary of state from 1947, Marshall devised and implemented the European Recovery Program, which came to be known as the Marshall Plan. The plan contributed to the post-war recovery of Europe, helped to establish NATO, and earned its creator the Nobel Peace Prize in 1953. Marshall left office in 1949 due to ill health, but remained on active service in the military until his death in 1959.

During the Cold War, Europe was broadly split between the communist Eastern Bloc, under the influence of the USSR, and NATO countries aligned with the US. The city of Berlin was split in two, separated by the Berlin Wall.

Key:
Warsaw Pact (up to 1968)
NATO states (1952)
Non-aligned nations

USSR responded by immediately forming its own security pact, the Warsaw Pact, joining the USSR with Albania, Bulgaria, Czechoslovakia, the German Democratic Republic (East Germany), Hungary, Poland, and Romania.

US policy in Asia

The Marshall Plan is regarded as one of the US's most effective foreign policy interventions. Similar thinking determined its policy in Asia: punishing Japan too severely could push it into the arms of communism. US General MacArthur made a point of exempting Emperor Hirohito from blame for the war to ensure continuity of rule, and even exonerated his secret 731 Unit, which had conducted germ warfare in China. Japan and West Germany quickly emerged as the most buoyant of all post-war economies. Like MacArthur, Chinese leader Chiang Kai-shek also feared communism—so much so that he even attempted to recruit surrendered Japanese soldiers to fight alongside his forces against Mao Zedong's communists. During the war, millions of Chinese people had joined the Chinese Red Army to drive out the Japanese. Most territories occupied by the Japanese were now under communist control, and the Red Army was almost a million strong. In 1948, the communist army, now renamed the People's Liberation Army (PLA) defeated Chiang's Kuomintang (KMT) in a huge battle during the Huaihai campaign of 1948–1949. Chiang fled to Taiwan, and the following year Mao declared the People's Republic of China, making China the most populous communist country by far.

A new order

Between 1945 and 1960, nearly 40 new countries in Asia and Africa achieved autonomy or even full independence. In a few places, such as Ceylon, renamed Sri Lanka, the process was swift and orderly. In many others, it was achieved with difficulty, often landing the newly independent countries in the hands of military juntas, or riven by tribal rivalries. In 1947, the British mishandling of the partition of

Chairman Mao Zedong applauding Red Guards at a military parade in Tiananmen Square, Beijing. Mao led the communist People's Republic of China until his death in 1976.

The Israeli flag features the blue and white colors of the Jewish prayer shawl and the Star of David as its central emblem.

Creating Israel

From the 1930s, rising numbers of Jewish people settled in British-administered Palestine to escape persecution in Europe. Known as Zionists, they saw Palestine as their ancestral homeland, as did the Arab Palestinians living there.

To secure Arab support in the war, the British tried to slow Jewish immigration—even sinking two shiploads of Jewish immigrants (the *Patria* in 1940 and *Struma* in 1942). After the war, Jewish immigration escalated, and a Zionist group called the Stern Gang launched a terrorist campaign against the British. When the Holocaust was revealed, support grew for the creation of a new Jewish state.

In 1948, the UN partitioned Palestine to create a Jewish state. On April 9, Zionist gangs killed over 100 Arab inhabitants of the village of Dayr Yasin, and two weeks later took control of Haifa and Jaffa. On May 14, the British left Palestine, and the State of Israel was declared. Arab armies invaded Palestine, but were quickly routed by Israeli forces.

India into two new countries—Pakistan, where the majority of the population was Muslim, and India, were the majority was Hindu—left around 20 million people in the "wrong" country. Up to two million were killed in the ensuing violence. The independence struggles of many French territories also led to bitter conflict and full-scale wars—in Algeria from 1954–1962, and in Indochina from 1946–1954.

Fairer societies

Free and fair elections did occur in most western European nations along with growing pressure for societies to provide greater social support. Even in the prosperous US, there was pressure for change. Marginalized groups, including Black Americans and women, had participated in the war effort as loyally and heroically as any, and were unwilling to go back to being second-class citizens. As a result, the post-war years saw the emergence of transformative movements such as the civil rights struggle and feminism.

Most countries in Europe moved toward social democracy, enhancing the role of the state in providing a social safety net, health care, education, and the provision and management of basic utilities and infrastructure. The UK's new Labour government created the National Health Service to provide free health care for all, and began a program for building social housing. Similar initiatives emerged in other countries.

Remarkably, the massive recovery programs and the widespread social support helped rebuild Europe with astonishing speed. Within three years, even devastated Germany was beginning its "economic miracle," and was soon the most prosperous country on the European continent. Shattered lives were pieced together. Ruined cities were cleared of rubble and rebuilt and, within 20 years, the most cataclysmic war in history was becoming a thing of the past as a post-war generation reached adulthood. But the Cold War and the threat of nuclear annihilation brought with it a new kind of fear. ■

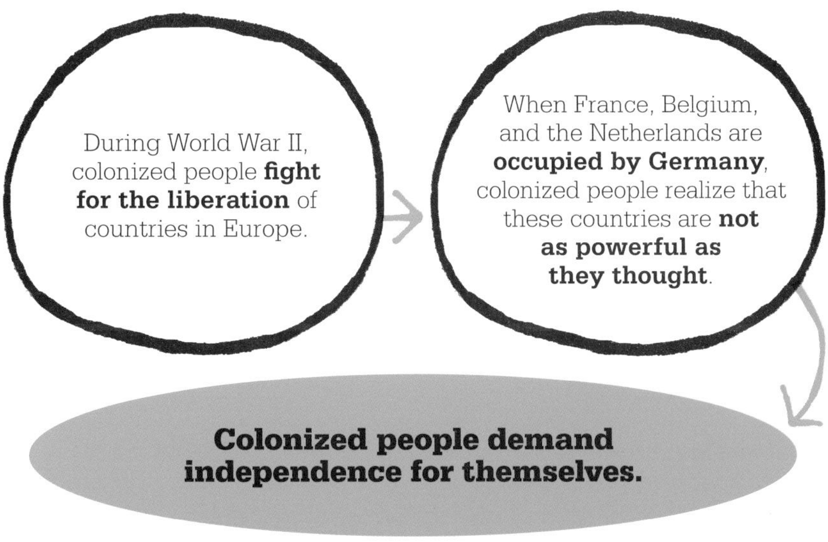

During World War II, colonized people **fight for the liberation** of countries in Europe.
When France, Belgium, and the Netherlands are **occupied by Germany**, colonized people realize that these countries are **not as powerful as they thought**.
Colonized people demand independence for themselves.

INDEX

Page numbers in **bold** refer to main entries.

D

E

F

G

H

I

J

K

L

M

N

O

P

Q

R

S

T

QUOTE ATTRIBUTIONS

THE SEEDS OF WAR

18 H. G. Wells, British author
20 Popular expression
22 Benito Mussolini, Italian dictator
24 Heinrich Himmler, leader of the SS
30 Nazi salute
34 Eric Fromm, German-born social philosopher
40 Francisco Franco, Spanish dictator
42 Sun Yat-sen, Chinese statesman
44 Hirozo Mori, Japanese nationalist financier
46 Adolf Hitler, German dictator
48 *Jewish Chronicle*, London 1938
50 Haile Selassie I, emperor of Ethiopia
51 Neville Chamberlain, British prime minister

EUROPE GOES TO WAR

56 Vyacheslav Molotov, Soviet politician
58 Hermann Göring, Nazi politician
64 Winston Churchill, British prime minister
66 British government Public Information Leaflet No. 3, 1939
67 Henry Harwood, British naval officer
68 Anonymous Finnish officer
69 John Hodgson of the 49th West Riding Division, British Army
70 Heinz Guderian, German Army general
76 Winston Churchill, British prime minister
80 Charles de Gaulle, French Army officer and statesman
88 Benito Mussolini, Italian dictator
90 Winston Churchill, British prime minister
94 Winston Churchill, British prime minister
98 Ernie Pyle, American journalist
100 Winston Churchill, British prime minister

THE WIDENING WAR

108 Franklin D. Roosevelt, US president
109 John Tovey, British admiral
110 Otto Kretschmer, U-boat captain
114 Kurt Student, Luftwaffe general
118 James Palmer, British tank soldier
122 Archibald Wavell, British general
124 Adolf Hitler, German dictator
132 Soviet slogan
136 Based on popular references to the massacre at Babi Yar
137 Nagano Osami, Japanese naval general staff chief
138 Franklin D. Roosevelt, US president
146 Franklin D. Roosevelt, US president
154 *Umi Yukaba*, Japanese military song
158 Mahatma Gandhi, leader of India's independence movement
159 John Curtin, Australian prime minister
160 Chester Nimitz, US admiral
166 Ivan Masiky, Soviet ambassador to Britain
167 Douglas Thompson, author
168 Adolf Hitler, German dictator
172 Nazi term first recorded at Wannsee Conference, January 1942
178 Vasily Chuikov, Soviet military commander
184 Alistair Urquhart, British soldier and prisoner of war in Japan
188 Albert Speer, Reich minister of armaments and war production
192 Winston Churchill, British prime minister
196 Franklin D. Roosevelt, US president
198 Winston Churchill, British prime minister

TURNING THE TIDE

208 Bernard Montgomery, British field marshal
210 Unnamed US infantry officer
212 Kiyotake Kawaguchi, Japanese Army commander
214 Karl Dönitz, German admiral
220 Heinrich Johannsen, eyewitness
224 Joseph Goebbels, Reich minister of propaganda
225 Declaration of the Three Powers
226 ŻOB, Jewish resistance movement in Warsaw
232 Unnamed German SS officer
236 US War Advertising Council poster
242 Mordecai Anielewicz, Jewish leader, Warsaw Uprising
244 Soemu Toyoda, Japanese admiral
250 Japanese slogan
254 Franklin D. Roosevelt, US president
255 Howard Whitman, *Daily News* correspondent
256 Dwight Eisenhower, supreme Allied commander, Europe
264 Winston Churchill, British prime minister
266 Vasily Grossman, Soviet soldier
270 Claus von Stauffenberg, German Army officer
271 Hans Thieme, German Army officer
272 History of the 146th Quartermaster Truck Company, describing the Red Ball Express
274 Roy Urquhart, British major general
275 Unnamed British army officer
276 Kimpei Teraoka, Japanese 1st Air Fleet commander
277 Heiichi Okabe, kamikaze pilot
278 Japanese propaganda slogan
280 Winston Churchill, British prime minister

ENDGAME

286 Joint statement by Churchill, Roosevelt, and Stalin
287 Arthur Harris, British Royal Air Force commander
288 Heinz Guderian, German chief of staff
290 Operation instruction issued to the Allied 14th Army
294 Alan Rose, British Army sergeant
296 Mark Clark, US Army general
298 Dwight Eisenhower, supreme Allied commander, Europe
304 Tomoyuki Yamashita, Japanese Army general
308 Robert Lewis, copilot, Enola Gay
312 Douglas MacArthur, US Army general
314 John Maxwell Edmonds, British poet
318 Robert H. Jackson, US supreme court justice and judge at the Nuremberg Trials
320 Douglas MacArthur, US Army general

ACKNOWLEDGMENTS

Dorling Kindersley would like to thank Mahua Sharma and Sanya Jain for design assistance; Ankita Gupta for editorial assistance; Shanker Prasad for DTP assistance; Assistant Picture Research Administrator Vagisha Pushp; Managing Jackets Editor Saloni Singh; Gwion Wyn Jones for additional research; Bonnie Macleod for additional editorial help; Alexandra Beeden for proofreading; and Helen Peters for indexing.

PICTURE CREDITS

The publisher would like to thank the following for their kind permission to reproduce their photographs:

(Key: a-above; b-below/bottom; c-center; f-far; l-left; r-right; t-top)

19 Alamy Stock Photo: Pictorial Press Ltd (br). Getty Images: API / Gamma-Rapho (tl). **20 Alamy Stock Photo:** PA Images. **23 Getty Images:** Albert Harlingue / Roger Viollet Collection. **27 Alamy Stock Photo:** Shawshots (tl). **Bridgeman Images:** © Look and Learn (br). **28 Alamy Stock Photo:** mccool. **29 Alamy Stock Photo:** World History Archive. **31 akg-images**. **32 Getty Images:** Keystone / Hulton Archive. **33 Alamy Stock Photo:** Sueddeutsche Zeitung Photo. **37 Alamy Stock Photo:** dpa picture alliance (br); Scherl / Süddeutsche Zeitung Photo (tl). **38 Alamy Stock Photo:** Scherl / Süddeutsche Zeitung Photo. **39 Alamy Stock Photo:** Alpha Historica (bl). **Getty Images:** Popperfoto (tr). **40 Getty Images:** Universal History Archive / Universal Images Group. **43 Alamy Stock Photo:** Photo12 / Ann Ronan Picture Library. **45 Alamy Stock Photo**: CPA Media Pte Ltd / Pictures From History (tr); World History Archive (bc). **46 Alamy Stock Photo:** Scherl / Süddeutsche Zeitung Photo. **49 Alamy Stock Photo:** History and Art Collection. **50 Alamy Stock Photo:** mccool. **57 Alamy Stock Photo:** Scherl / Süddeutsche Zeitung Photo (br). **Getty Images:** Bettmann (tl). **61 Getty Images:** Hulton-Deutsch Collection / Corbis. **62 Alamy Stock Photo:** Everett Collection Historical. **63 Alamy Stock Photo:** Niday Picture Library. **64 akg-images:** Sammlung Berliner Verlag / Archiv. **65 Alamy Stock Photo:** Everett Collection Historical. **66 Getty Images:** Popperfoto. **67 Alamy Stock Photo:** Trinity Mirror / Mirrorpix. **68 Getty Images:** Keystone-France / Gamma-Keystone. **69 Getty Images:** Hulton Deutsch / Corbis Historical. **72 Getty Images:** Mondadori Portfolio. **74 Alamy Stock Photo:** Everett Collection Inc. **77 Getty Images:** Fox Photos / Hulton Archive. **78 Alamy Stock Photo:** David Cole. **79 Alamy Stock Photo:** World History Archive. **82 Alamy Stock Photo**: mccool. **83 Getty Images:** Jean-Guillaume Goursat / Gamma-Rapho. **84 Alamy Stock Photo:** Prisma by Dukas Presseagentur GmbH / Schultz Reinhard. **85 Alamy Stock Photo:** Pictorial Press Ltd (tr). **Getty Images**: Heinrich Hoffmann / Galerie Bilderwelt (bc). **86 Alamy Stock Photo:** Everett Collection Inc. **87 Alamy Stock Photo:** Shawshots. **88 Alamy Stock Photo:** Scherl / Süddeutsche Zeitung Photo. **89 Getty Images:** SeM / Universal Images Group (tl); ullstein bild Dtl.. (br). **91 Getty Images:** Bettmann (tl); Keystone-France / Gamma-Keystone (br). **92 Alamy Stock Photo:** incamerastock / ICP. **95 Alamy Stock Photo:** Lordprice Collection. **97 Getty Images:** Hulton Deutsch / Corbis Historical (br); ullstein bild Dtl.. (tl). **98 Alamy Stock Photo:** FL Historical S. **99 Getty Images:** Keystone / Hulton Archive. **101 Alamy Stock Photo:** Scherl / Süddeutsche Zeitung Photo. **102 Alamy Stock Photo:** Trinity Mirror / Mirrorpix. **103 Alamy Stock Photo:** H. Armstrong Roberts / Classicstock (tl). Shutterstock.com: Glasshouse Images (br). **108 Alamy Stock Photo:** Everett Collection Inc. **111 Alamy Stock Photo:** Everett Collection Inc. **113 Alamy Stock Photo:** Albatross. **115 Alamy Stock Photo:** De Luan. **117 Alamy Stock Photo:** Colin Waters (tl). **Getty Images:** ullstein bild Dtl.. (br). **119 Alamy Stock Photo:** The Picture Art Collection (br). **Getty Images:** Albert Harlingue / Roger Viollet (tl). **120 Getty Images**: Heinrich Hoffmann / ullstein bild. **121 Alamy Stock Photo:** The Picture Art Collection. **123 Alamy Stock Photo:** Everett Collection Inc (br). **Imperial War Museum:** Cabinet Office Second World War Official Collection (tl). **127 Mary Evans Picture Library:** Sueddeutsche Zeitung Photo. **128 Getty Images:** ullstein bild Dtl.. **129 Alamy Stock Photo:** Everett Collection Historical (br); War Archive (tl). **130 Alamy Stock Photo:** Scherl / Süddeutsche Zeitung Photo (bl); Sueddeutsche Zeitung Photo (tc). **131 Alamy Stock Photo:** dpa picture alliance (bc). **Getty Images:** Culture Club / Hulton Archive (tr). **133 Alamy Stock Photo:** Everett Collection Historical. **134 Alamy Stock Photo:** ITAR-TASS News Agency. **135 Getty Images:** Hulton Archive. **137 Alamy Stock Photo:** CPA Media Pte Ltd / Pictures From History. **140 Alamy Stock Photo:** Granger Historical Picture Archive / Granger, NYC. **141 Alamy Stock Photo:** Granger Historical Picture Archive / Granger, NYC. **142 Alamy Stock Photo:** Niday Picture Library. **144 Alamy Stock Photo:** American Photo Archive (bc); Pictorial Press Ltd (tl). **148 Alamy Stock Photo:** PjrStudio. **149 Alamy Stock Photo:** incamerastock / ICP. **150 Alamy Stock Photo:** American Photo Archive. **151 Alamy Stock Photo:** Granger Historical Picture Archive / Granger, NYC. (bl); World History Archive (tr). **152 Getty Images:** Bettmann. **153 Alamy Stock Photo:** Everett Collection Historical. **155 Alamy Stock Photo:** Everett Collection Inc. **156 Alamy Stock Photo:** Matteo Omied. **157 Alamy Stock Photo:** World History Archive. **158 Getty Images:** Topical Press Agency / Hulton Archive. **163 Alamy Stock Photo:** Chronicle. **165 Alamy Stock Photo:** Scherl / Süddeutsche Zeitung Photo (bl). Shutterstock.com: Bob Landry / The LIFE Picture Collection (tr). **166 Getty Images:** IWM / Getty Images / Imperial War Museums. **170 Alamy Stock Photo:** Interfoto / Personalities (bl). **Getty Images:** De Agostini Picture Library (tc). **171 Alamy Stock Photo:** mccool (br); US Army Photo (tl). **174 Alamy Stock Photo:** World History Archive. **175 Alamy Stock Photo:** Shawshots. **176 Alamy Stock Photo:** Schultz Reinhard / Prisma by Dukas Presseagentur GmbH (bc); Alyssa Schu / ZUMA Press, Inc. (tl). **177 Alamy Stock Photo:** From the Jewish Chronicle Archive / Heritage Image Partnership Ltd (tr). Getty Images: API / Gamma-Rapho (bl). **181 Alamy Stock Photo:** Shawshots. **182 Alamy Stock Photo:** Pictorial Press Ltd (bc); Scherl / Süddeutsche Zeitung Photo (tl). **183 Getty Images:** Hulton Archive. **185 Getty Images / iStock:** Stefan_Alfonso. **186 Getty Images:** Popperfoto. **187 Alamy Stock Photo:** © Adam Eastland (br). Getty Images: AFP (tl). **190 Getty Images:** ullstein bild Dtl.. **191 Alamy Stock Photo:** Photo12 / Coll-DITE / USIS. **193 Alamy Stock Photo:** World of Triss. **195 Getty Images:** Bettmann (tr); Mondadori Portfolio (bl). **197 Alamy Stock Photo:** History and Art Collection (tl); Trinity Mirror / Mirrorpix (br). **201 Alamy Stock Photo:** Pictorial Press Ltd. **202 Alamy Stock Photo:** dpa picture alliance. **203 Alamy Stock Photo:** Gary Eason / Flight Artworks (bl); Interfoto / History (tr). **209 Getty Images:** Three Lions. **210 Alamy Stock Photo:** Shawshots. **211 Alamy Stock Photo:** Granger Historical Picture Archive / Granger, NYC. **213 Alamy Stock Photo:** Alpha Historica (tl). **Getty Images:** U.S. Navy (br). **216 Getty Images:** ullstein bild Dtl.. **217 Alamy Stock Photo:** Pictorial Press Ltd. **218 Getty Images:** Universal History Archive / Universal Images Group (tr). TopFoto.co.uk: (bl). **219 Getty Images:** Historical / Corbis Historical. **221 Getty Images:** Popperfoto. **222 Alamy Stock Photo:** Vernon Lewis Gallery / Stocktrek Images, Inc.. **223 Alamy Stock Photo:** Schultz Reinhard / Prisma by Dukas Presseagentur GmbH (bl). **Getty Images:** Keystone-France / Gamma-Keystone (tr). **224 Getty Images:** Roger Viollet. **228 Polish National Digital Archive**. **230 akg-images:** George (Jürgen) Wittenstein. **231 Alamy Stock Photo:** Pictorial Press Ltd (bl). Getty Images: Bettmann (tr). **234 Alamy Stock Photo:** Scherl / Süddeutsche Zeitung Photo. **235 Alamy Stock Photo:** Scherl / Süddeutsche Zeitung Photo (tl). **Science Photo Library:** Sputnik (br). **238 Alamy Stock Photo:** David Cole. **239 Alamy Stock Photo:** Shawshots. **241 Alamy Stock Photo:** Everett Collection Inc (tr); war posters (bc). **243 Alamy Stock Photo:** Photo12 / Ann Ronan Picture Library. **247 Alamy Stock Photo:** Zuri Swimmer. **248 Alamy Stock Photo:** Pictorial Press Ltd. **249 Alamy Stock Photo:** Everett Collection Inc. **251 Alamy Stock Photo:** CPA Media Pte Ltd / Pictures From History. **252 Getty Images:** Popperfoto. **253 Getty Images:** Keystone-France / Gamma-Keystone. **255 Getty Images:** Fred Ramage / Hulton Archive. **258 Alamy Stock Photo:** Trinity Mirror / Mirrorpix. **259 Bridgeman Images:** © Tallandier. **260 Alamy Stock Photo:** Interfoto / History. **261 Alamy Stock Photo:** Schultz Reinhard / Prisma by Dukas Presseagentur GmbH. **262 Getty Images:** Lt. Handford / Imperial War Museums (bl). **263 Alamy Stock Photo:** World History Archive. **265 Getty Images:** Bettmann (tl); Universal History Archive / Universal Images Group (br). **267 Getty Images:** Keystone / Hulton Archive. **268 Getty Images:** Sovfoto / Universal Images Group (t, bl). **269 Getty Images:** Sovfoto / Universal Images Group. **270 Getty Images:** ullstein bild. **273 Alamy Stock Photo:** Granger Historical Picture Archive / Granger, NYC. (tr); World History Archive (tl). **275 Getty Images:** Bettmann. **276 Getty Images:** Historical / Corbis Historical. **277 Getty Images:** Yasuo Tomishige / The Asahi Shimbun. **279 Alamy Stock Photo:** Shawshots. **281 Alamy Stock Photo:** Interfoto / History (tr); Shawshots (bl). **287 Alamy Stock Photo:** Shawshots. **289 Alamy Stock Photo:** Chronicle (tr). **Getty Images:** Serge Plantureux / Corbis (bc). **291 Alamy Stock Photo:** Everett Collection Inc (br). **Getty Images:** Hulton Deutsch / Corbis Historical (tl). **292 Alamy Stock Photo:** Scherl / Süddeutsche Zeitung Photo. **293 akg-images:** Pictures From History. **295 Alamy Stock Photo:** Vintage_Space (bl). **United States Holocaust Memorial Museum:** adapted from the Liberation of major Nazi camps, 1944-1945 map (tr). **297 Alamy Stock Photo:** marka. **300 Bridgeman Images:** Picture Alliance / DPA. **301 Library of Congress, Washington, D.C.:** LC-USZ62-13033. **302 Getty Images:** Photo12 / Universal Images Group. **303 Getty Images:** Photo12 / Universal Images Group. **305 Alamy Stock Photo:** Everett Collection Historical. **306 Alamy Stock Photo:** Shawshots. **307 Alamy Stock Photo:** Archive Image (tl); Vintage_Space (bl). **Getty Images:** PhotoQuest / Archive Photos (tr). **309 Alamy Stock Photo:** DOE Photo. **311 Alamy Stock Photo:** Granger Historical Picture Archive / Granger, NYC.. **313 akg-images:** (bl). **Alamy Stock Photo**: Everett Collection Historical (tr). **315 Alamy Stock Photo**: Immagia. **317 Alamy Stock Photo:** Matteo Omied. **319 Alamy Stock Photo:** Pictorial Press Ltd. **322 Getty Images:** Bettmann. **323 Alamy Stock Photo:** Interfoto / History. **324 Dreamstime.com:** Scorpion26. **325 Alamy Stock Photo:** Granger Historical Picture Archive / Granger, NYC. (tr); David Lichtneker (bl). **326 Bridgeman Images:** Sovfoto / UIG. **327 Getty Images:** Atlantide Phototravel